# LAST WORDS?

## How can journalism survive the decline of print?

EDITED BY

JOHN MAIR, TOR CLARK,
NEIL FOWLER, RAYMOND SNODDY
and
RICHARD TAIT

Published 2016 by Abramis academic publishing

www.abramis.co.uk

ISBN 978 1 84549 696 8

Printed and bound in the United Kingdom

Typeset in Garamond

Abramis is an imprint of arima publishing.

arima publishing
ASK House, Northgate Avenue
Bury St Edmunds, Suffolk IP32 6BB
t: (+44) 01284 700321

www.arimapublishing.com

# Contents

## Section 4: The UK regional press

## Section 5: An International perspective

## Section 7: The future

# Acknowledgements

These books are never heroic individual efforts, they depend on the efforts of scores of people, primarily the 50-plus authors who have given their services free of charge with very tight deadlines.

The commissioning editors (services also given pro bono) have been steadfast over a period of seven months, from an idle conversation to this tome, and never a cross word in half a year of very creative co-operation.

Tor Clark and Neil Fowler have been unflinching in the Herculean task of sub-editing more than 100,000 words. The great 'super sub', Professor Richard Keeble, added his muscle at crucial moments.

Finally, as ever, Richard and Pete Franklin at Abramis have done their jobs most professionally.

Now, it is down to you dear reader...

**John Mair, Oxford**
**Tor Clark, Leicester**
**Neil Fowler, Northumberland**
**Raymond Snoddy, London**
**Richard Tait, London**

# The editors

**John Mair** has taught journalism at the Universities of Coventry, Kent, Northampton, Brunel, Edinburgh Napier, Guyana and the Communication University of China. He has edited 18 'hackademic' volumes over the last seven years, on subjects ranging from trust in television, the health of investigative journalism, reporting the 'Arab Spring', to three volumes on the Leveson Inquiry. He and Richard Lance Keeble invented the sub-genre. John also created the Coventry Conversations, which attracted 350 media movers and shakers to Coventry University; the podcasts of those have been downloaded six million times worldwide. Since then, he has launched the Northampton Chronicles, Media Mondays at Napier and most recently the Harrow Conversations at Westminster University. In a previous life, he was an award-winning producer/director for the BBC, ITV and Channel 4, and a secondary school teacher.

**Tor Clark** is Principal Lecturer in Journalism at De Montfort University in Leicester. After studying Politics and History at Lancaster University, he worked for the Northamptonshire Evening Telegraph, before becoming editor, first of the Harborough Mail in Leicestershire, and then of Britain's oldest newspaper, the Rutland & Stamford Mercury, where he led a successful bid to the Heritage Lottery Fund to preserve its unique 300-year-old newspaper archive. At De Montfort University, he has launched two Journalism degrees, one accredited by the NCTJ. He holds an MA in Mass Communications from the University of Leicester and is now researching towards a PhD. He is reviews editor of the academic journal Journalism Education, a regular commentator on politics and media for BBC Leicester and a Senior Fellow of the Higher Education Academy.

**Neil Fowler** has been in journalism since graduation, starting life as trainee reporter on the Leicester Mercury. He went on to edit four regional dailies, including The Journal in the north east of England and The Western Mail in Wales. He was then publisher of The Toronto Sun in Canada before returning to the UK to edit Which? magazine. In 2010/11 he was the Guardian Research Fellow at Oxford University's Nuffield College where he investigated the decline and future of regional and local newspapers in the UK. From then until 2016 he helped organise the college's prestigious David Butler media and politics seminars. As well as being an occasional contributor to trade magazines he now acts as an adviser to organisations on their management and their external and internal communications and media policies and strategies.

**Raymond Snoddy OBE**, after studying at Queen's University in Belfast, worked on local and regional newspapers, before joining The Times in 1971. Five years later he moved to the Financial Times and reported on media issues before returning to The Times as media editor in 1995. At present, he is a freelance journalist writing for a range of publications. He presented NewsWatch on the BBC from its inception in 2004 until 2012. His other television work has included presenting Channel 4's award-winning series Hard News. In addition, Snoddy is the author of a biography of the media tycoon Michael Green, The Good, the Bad and the Ugly. He was awarded an OBE for his services to journalism in 2000.

**Richard Tait CBE** is Professor of Journalism at the School of Journalism, Media and Cultural Studies, at Cardiff University. From 2003 to 2012, he was director of the school's Centre for Journalism. He was editor of Newsnight from 1985 to 1987, editor of Channel 4 News from 1987 to 1995 and editor-in-chief of ITN from 1995 to 2002. Tait was a BBC governor and chair of the governors' programme complaints committee from 2004 to 2006, and a BBC Trustee and chair of the Trust's editorial standards committee from 2006 to 2010. He is a fellow of the Society of Editors and the Royal Television Society, treasurer of the International News Safety Institute and an independent trustee of the Disasters Emergency Committee.

# Introduction:
# The New York Times way: Every story should be worth paying for

By Mark Thompson

Winter is coming. How many times have we heard that on HBO's hit drama Game of Thrones? But though we have sat through five series so far, not to mention any amount of torture, murder and all round unpleasantness, the sun is still obstinately shining. The battle-weary inhabitants of Westeros must be beginning to wonder if those thermals were really such a good investment.

Here's my warning. Winter really is coming for many of the world's news publishers. Indeed, this year's Digital News Report suggests for some of them it is already here.

The economic challenge for any legacy newspaper company is simply stated, it is to grow digital revenue far and fast enough to offset the inevitable declines in print revenue, and at sufficient margins to defend – or increase – profitability. Many publishers have responded to this challenge by putting their faith in a model based on audience scale and digital display advertising. Surely advertisers would pay handsomely for the privilege of connecting with the vast audiences all that free digital distribution would unlock?

Most of the new digital news providers were launched with business models which were parasitic versions of the same idea. They aimed to rewrite and repackage other people's journalism for much less money than it cost to originate it, and then to use superior technology to out-compete the legacy companies in distribution and advertising monetisation. Again the result would be rapidly growing audience and revenue.

These models now look suspect. Digital display advertising is quite different from print advertising. Publishers enjoy far less pricing power, and even the largest of us are dwarfed by those who dominate the field, players like Facebook and Google whose immense scale allows them to undercut everybody else. The concept of adjacent display – carried over from print – makes little or no sense on smartphone, which is increasingly the platform on which people get their news. Consumption is also switching rapidly from the publishers' own environments to Facebook, Snapchat and other social media platforms; the Digital News Report suggests as much as 46 per cent of news is now seen on social and messaging platforms in the US, 35 per cent in the UK. This too puts direct and indirect pressure on pricing. Finally, the end-user's experience of digital display advertising is often grisly with sites overloaded with intrusive ads, and even some quality publishers giving over space to third party 'content discovery platforms', who sell space to God knows whom. No wonder so many users are opting to block ads altogether.

There is another way. At The New York Times, we believe there is a good business to be built around offering digital advertising experiences which users actually find useful and enjoyable. T Brand Studio, our branded content studio, didn't exist two-and-a-half years ago. Today its staff includes 70 journalists, videographers, designers and engineers. We recently opened a second centre of operations in London.

We expect T Brand to deliver more than $50m in revenue this year. Smartphone advertising revenue – driven by new flexible multimedia ad units which present inside the content stream – is currently doubling year over year. Video, sponsorship, audio, virtual reality and other innovations at the frontier of storytelling are all also part of our advertising growth strategy. Display still has a place, but we believe the digital advertising of the future will be dominated by stories conceived by advertisers, clearly labelled so they can be distinguished from newsroom journalism, but consumed alongside that journalism on their own merits.

This is a more compelling and creative vision of digital advertising than conventional digital display, and it requires new skills, talents and technologies, and substantial fresh investment. Audience scale and global reach will still count, but the audience which publishers will need to find will not be super-light users, the one-and-dones who spend a few seconds on many different sites, but truly engaged readers and viewers who are prepared to devote real time to content of real quality and relevance. If this is the right direction of travel, many of the coping strategies adopted by the majority of news publishers in recent years – clickbait and other forms of audience-gaming, an obsession with the top-line number of monthly uniques – will prove to be not just ineffective, but actively counter-productive because they damage brand and reputation, and point newsrooms at the wrong audience targets and user experiences.

In the developed world, adjacent display advertising in print and interruptive advertising in television and video have been the principal sources of funding of professional journalism. Both are now challenged and likely to come under increasing pressure in the years ahead. The plain truth is that advertising alone will not support quality journalism. News publishers with digital models, which rely solely, or even mainly on advertising, will either have to find other sources of digital revenue, eke out a marginal economic future with very low levels of content investment, or go bust.

At The New York Times, we are building a digital subscription business of scale. Far from plateauing, the rate at which we are adding net new subscribers quarter-by-quarter is faster today than it was three years ago. I expect digital subscription revenue to overtake digital advertising revenue this year. Combined with other digital revenue streams related to the Times brand and our core business, together we expect them to approach half a billion dollars of revenue in 2016.

The Digital News Report suggests few other news publishers are enjoying our success. It notes the number of people paying for news in the US has fallen, and some paywall strategies – like that of The Sun in the UK – have been abandoned. I've often heard the editors and CEOs of other newspaper groups say The New York Times, and the handful of other successful pay models, are special cases from which they have little or nothing to learn. Indeed, there is a real air of defeatism in the industry about even the possibility of getting readers to pay.

It's perfectly true we have natural advantages – a large domestic market with few other national rivals, a strong pre-existing tradition of home delivery subscription and a vast global opportunity. Most important of all is the fact we continued to invest strongly in quality journalism when most of our competitors were decimating their newsrooms. But this is also about a mindset: although we think there are powerful civic and commercial reasons for allowing very extensive free access to Times journalism – our pay model is far more porous than others – we believe every story we do should be worth paying for.

Digital advertising will not be enough. Membership, freemium models, e-commerce and events will be helpful, but again not enough. All news publishers need to ask themselves whether the journalism they produce is worth paying for. If not, they will suffer the same fate as a baker whose bread is not good enough to buy. Low quality journalism adds little to plurality and democratic debate and, though it is lèse majesté to say so in our industry, society will probably not miss it very much.

If you conclude instead that your journalism is worth paying for, or can be made so by increasing rather than cutting newsroom investment, the task then is to acquire the brand and direct marketing strategies and skills needed to shape the offer and take it to market. This is a mighty challenge on its own. Once print and TV news enjoyed such privileged distribution and prominence that it largely marketed itself. Now, we must go out and actively seek audiences like everyone else. That requires humility as well as considerable effort and expense, but there is no alternative if we are to build sufficiently large, deeply engaged audiences.

And there's something else. The separation of advertising sales from editorial decision-making, and the need for absolute clarity about what is newsroom content and what is commercial messaging, both remain essential. But, beyond these critical segregations of duty and of user experience, newsrooms and commercial divisions of news organisations must become far closer strategic partners than is generally the case today. An editorial strategy with no revenue

3

context is a forlorn hope. A strategy created solely by the 'business side', whatever that is, is a waste of good Powerpoint.

Editorial and commercial leaders need to work together on integrated strategies which combine editorial mission and standards, user experience, innovations in data, technology and creative design, and radically new approaches to monetisation. Not five different strategies, not even 'aligned' editorial and commercial strategies, but a single shared way forward. Until very recently, there was a sense the editorial leadership of news organisations should somehow be protected from the business model challenges which this industry faces. Carry on down that road for much longer and you will founder. Editors need to co-create and co-lead the necessary transformation of both news report and business. At The New York Times, we have one strategy and Dean Bacquet, our executive editor, and his senior newsroom and editorial colleagues, are just as responsible for devising and implementing it as I am as CEO.

In the coming storm, newsrooms and commercial departments who try to ignore reality, or each other, will catch their death from cold. Those who put quality and audience experience first, and figure out how to work effectively as a unified team will be well placed, not just to survive, but to grow stronger.

*This article was first produced by Mark Thompson for the Reuters Institute Digital News Report in June 2016*

## Note on the contributor
Mark Thompson is CEO and President of The New York Times. Previously he was Director General of the BBC 2004-2012 and Chief Executive of Channel 4 2002-2004.

# Print and Journalism – The Big Picture

\* \* \*

# Why print journalism can and should survive

**Raymond Snoddy**

Professor Roy Greenslade argues publishers and journalists must find a way to work together to find solutions to the crisis facing journalism across the developed world. Hardly a day passes without the announcement by a newspaper publisher that jobs must go, offices must be merged or closed. Cutbacks in the face of the march of the digital revolution have been the reality of the news trade for the past 20 years whether the publishers are seeking only profit or recognise a wider social purpose.

Journalists cost money so the last thing newspaper publishers want as they seek to protect profit margins or merely survive, is expensive journalists. They are often 'unproductive' in strict economic terms spending time and money on researching stories which have little if any positive effect on revenues.

But what happens when there is no-one left to produce original content? The newspaper industry has to reach a better accommodation with the powerful new media organisations which reap huge financial rewards by republishing newspaper content. Publishers and journalists also have to work together to find a solution to the threats facing the survival of the news trade.

Peter Preston, former editor of The Guardian, reflects on a 60-year career in print and acknowledges the decline in daily newspaper consumption in the UK– now down to six million a day and still dropping. Meanwhile digital consumption/addiction accelerates away with social media dominating reading time. "One habit falls, another takes over. An equation so basic you don't really have to think about it – nor try to set it in any historical context. But look back a while before you look forward," Preston argues.

Part of the problem for newspapers is there is too much free news out there – only 10 per cent of news on the net comes with any price tag attached. The trouble is the search for a successor business model to words on print pages, to ads around the side and a cover price on top of the masthead, has wandered into a cul-de-sac.

For Preston the bitter irony is that the reach and readership for newspaper news – for print plus digital reach has never been higher but the difficulty of making a profit from news has never been more mountainous. Despite everything, print offers the appearance of permanence and the reality of choice. And if you listen carefully you can hear the bricks of Facebook and Google crumbling as the next stage of media existence emerges from the mist.

Experienced City analyst Lorna Tilbian believes the death of print and newspapers has been much exaggerated and points to the uplift in sales during the referendum campaign. It was a sign people rely on newspapers to help them interpret complex events and how they will be affected personally. For Tilbian the referendum circulation rise demonstrated newspapers remain an important source of information at times of uncertainty and instability.

Adam Smith of WPP subsidiary GroupM notes how in 2016 the world will have spent around $530bn on advertising – about one per cent of global GDP. Within the total there have been winners and losers with over the past 20 years, TV, radio and outdoor retaining their share while the internet has dramatically taken share from print.

Once the fixed costs of selling advertising is absorbed, any additional revenue, goes straight to profits. Equally obviously, once a medium loses an advertiser it immediately hits profits and is difficult to replace.

How then to save newspapers? More marketing is part of the answer because digital print brands face a perpetual struggle to remain on advertisers 'preferred list'. If the print industry can make these choices for the ad world better-informed it will be to print's advantage. In the end a radical change in business strategy will be inevitable. The lorries, the newsagents and ultimately the analogue domain will have to be sacrificed in a ghastly dilemma giving up the bird in the hand of today's print profits for the two in the digital bush which has offered disappointing pickings so far.

According to Smith, the trajectory of circulation seems bound to deliver many publishers to this dilemma – this crisis within 10 years.

Richard Tait, former senior broadcasting executive, asks whether newspaper publishers have anything to learn from television – Channel 4 in particular – and comes to an emphatic 'Yes'. Channel 4 has weathered the storm of ever-increasing competition by getting closer to its audiences online, most recently through its website All4. ITV is doing something similar with its ITV Hub. Users have to register giving all-important demographic information and 13.5m people have indeed registered including no less than half of all 16 to 34 year-olds in the UK.

As a result Channel 4 has managed to turn TV pounds into online pounds. With newspapers £5 print has been turned into £1 digital and publishers have little detailed information on who their readers are, certainly compared with commercial television.

With print the arguments over the pros and cons of subscription have obscured the potential value of registration. The complexity caused by the Brexit vote, which could last for a decade, could be an opportunity for newspapers to re-establish in a digital form the link with its public which it once took for granted. Readers now want a two-way relationship with their sources of news, they want it on demand and on all devices as well as on paper.

Such an approach combined with registration, with or without subscription, might not ultimately be the answer for everyone but given the Channel 4 experience it would be difficult to imagine circumstances which would make matters worse.

First Raymond Snoddy takes a look across the horizon and suggests the death of print may not be as completely inevitable as some imagine and argues publishers must give greater emphasis on shoring up their print edition alongside digital, because print is the medium which still produces the lion's share of their revenue, which pays for original journalism. Journalism and ultimately society will suffer should they fail.

# Print has declined, but the evidence suggests it need not be fatal

**Print journalism is so important that ways must be found to sustainably finance it for the future, says longtime journalist and media commentator Raymond Snoddy**

By any standards March 26, 2016, was a symbolic date in the history of British journalism and the national newspaper industry which may speak volumes about the future. It was the day The Independent printed its last paper edition six months short of its 30th anniversary.

There was sadness at the loss even though The Independent continues to have an independent life on the internet with many fewer journalists – though still around 100 – and, some would argue, a diminished journalistic mission. At least it now enjoys a vastly extended international reach, dramatically reduced costs and a realistic prospect of profits after all this time. In Brexit month, June 2016, the online Independent had 319m page impressions and average daily unique visitors rose to a record 4.4m.

The closure was significant for many reasons, even though at the end the paper was selling a pitiful 55,000 copies a day, largely because of the decision to launch The i, a stripped down, low-cost version which would inevitably cannibalise sales of The Independent. It was emotional because it was effectively the end of a dream that post-Wapping, and with the undermining of restrictive print union practices, three journalists could go to the City, raise enough finance to launch a new national newspaper that was independent of the big newspaper barons such as Rupert Murdoch under the slogan: 'It is, are you?'

Circulation for a short time topped 400,000 a day putting it marginally ahead of The Times, later forcing Murdoch to unleash a price-cutting campaign against it. That was all before recessions, managerial mistakes, changes of ownership and above all the rise of the internet, which has threatened the viability of newspapers throughout the developed world, at least in print.

The enforced transformation of The Independent is important because many believe it predicts the likely fate of many, if not all, general newspapers which sceptics have already booked on the print equivalent of the lethal medical Liverpool pathway developed for the elderly. Surely it must be only a matter of time before more newspapers close or become internet only?

Some reach for metaphors of radioactive decay and talk of the 'half-life" of newspapers, usually putting it at around five years. However precise, or otherwise, such forecasts are, can there be doubt about the inevitable destiny even if it takes years to play out? In such a scenario The Independent is just the weakest and the first and will be followed into the ether by title after title, a process already under way in the US. In such a difficult world can The Guardian be far behind, or at least be forced to print on fewer days a week, again a phenomenon already seen in the US?

Pessimistic predictions about the future of newspapers have never been in short supply. Bill Gates said in 1997 there would be no newspapers by 2000, a forecast that soon had to be retracted. Even earlier Murdoch had suggested by the millennial year there would probably be only three national newspapers left in the UK, two conveniently owned by himself, The Sun and The Times, and then there would still be the Viscount Rothermere's Daily Mail.

That was before the impact of the internet and smart phones and the rise of new disruptive global giants such as Google and Facebook, which hoover up classified advertising on an industrial scale without, in the main, having the cost of producing their own original content.

In the current era the numbers on both newspaper circulation and advertising revenues are grim and the trends apparently implacable. UK newspapers have done badly against television and online in the battle for advertising revenue, although the situation is complicated because virtually all newspapers have an online presence and are part of the rise of digital.

According to media consultants Mediatique, using numbers from media buyers ZenithOptimedia and communications regulator Ofcom, in 1995 all newspapers, national, regional and local accounted for 65 per cent of total UK advertising. Television had a 27 per cent share and online zero. By the end of 2015 newspapers were on 16 per cent, TV had held on to its 27 per cent share of a larger cake and online accounted for 50 per cent.

The decline in sales has been almost as dramatic according to the official Audit Bureau of Circulation figures. In 1997 The Sun had newspaper sales of 3.87m, the Daily Mail 2.34m, the Daily Telegraph 1.12m, The Guardian 428,010 and The Times 821,000. The Daily Mirror came in at 2.44m, the once-mighty Daily Express 1.24m, the Financial Times 326,516 and The Independent 288,182 with the Daily Star on 729,991. The average circulation of the daily titles totalled 12.49 million.

Move on nearly two decades and by 2016 The Sun's paper sales had fallen to 1.78m, the Daily Mail to 1.58m, the Daily Telegraph to 472,033, while The Guardian was on 164,163 and The Times 404,700. The Daily Mirror was down to 809,147, the Daily Express sold just 408,700, the Financial Times 198,237 and the Daily Star, 470,369.

The total, 6.28m, had almost exactly halved since 1997.

But there are a number of paradoxes, problems and fallacies at play in such an out-dated, negative analysis of the future of print in general and newspapers in particular.

The first main fallacy is to extrapolate current trends to reach an oblivion point carrying the clear implication nothing can be done. This is possible but the death of newspapers is only inevitable if it is accepted as such by all those involved.

Consultants McKinsey & Company in their most recent analysis of global media trends argued many of the people likely to abandon newspapers and consumer magazines had already done so. Millions of households and individuals with broadband access had also retained subscriptions to both newspapers and magazines.

According to McKinsey, print markets will continue to decline but at a slower rate than in the immediate past. As print begins to approach its core audience then the decreases will be smaller.

"Over the next five years we expect combined spending on print newspapers and print consumer magazines to fall a cumulative $14bn, or 1.5 per cent compounded annually, less the half of the decline of the past three years," says McKinsey.

"Looking at just the last three years of the forecast period, we project the decline to be a relatively modest one per cent compound annually," the consultants add.

Another fallacy has been to see newspapers and their online versions as separate entities. This has been addressed by Newsworks, the renamed Newspaper Marketing Agency which has successfully promoted, at least in professional media circles, the concept of 'newsbrands' combining all newspaper platforms including online and mobile. As a result the industry in the UK can now boast official data demonstrates multi-platform newsbrands reach 47m people a month or 91 per cent of the population, a much greater reach than newspapers alone ever enjoyed even at their peak and even greater than Google in Britain.

'Effectiveness' and 'engagement' are two of the latest new buzz words in the advertising community and both play to the strengths of not just newsbrands, but newspapers in particular. A large independent study by econometrics consultancy Benchmarking for Newsworks found advertising with newspapers produced a return on investment of three times on average. Benchmarking also noted for advertisers to optimise their return on investment it would be in their financial interests to return their spending on newspapers to the much higher 2013 levels.

Similar results on the return on investment from newspaper advertising have been obtained by studies ranging from The Netherlands to New Zealand. RAM, the Swedish-based media research group, has studied issues such as consumer recall of newspaper advertising and propensity to buy or plan to buy after viewing newspaper ads. The analysis of impact was based on no less than 10,840 print ads across 15 European countries. Ad recall by industry goes from a low of between 43-45 per cent for sectors such as real estate, oil and banking services to between 56 and 59 per cent for sports and leisure to large retail and lotteries. Analysis of Have Bought/Will Buy by Industry ranges from a low of seven per cent for insurance and education to 26 per cent for food, drinks and lotteries.

Renewed arguments and research about the effectiveness of newspapers have certainly engaged the attention of Sir Martin Sorrell, the chief executive of WPP, the world's largest advertising and marketing services group, responsible for placing around $76bn a year of advertising. Until recently, Sir Martin was negative about newspapers and was much more excited by online, mobile and the new digital players such as Facebook and Google. A number of factors have led to his change of heart.

"Facebook can't really claim a three-second view when 50 per cent of the time the sound is off, is the same as a 15-second, a 30 second, a 60 second TV ad or someone reading The Times for 40 minutes," Sir Martin concludes.

Never mind the three-second views with the sound turned off, Sir Martin is also concerned about what amounts to fraud – that many of the supposed views of adverts were not made by human eyeballs at all but 'bots' or robots. And that is before you get to ad-blocking software which prevents online ads being seen at all.

Unsurprisingly the WPP CEO has called for much greater transparency and credibility on the measurement of online advertising in all its forms and indeed has attacked the increasing power of Google and Facebook. At the IBC conference in Amsterdam in September 2016 Sir Martin suggested regulatory authorities should look at the control exercised by the two companies over no less than 76 per cent of all online advertising revenue – a percentage that is growing – and argued they should be treated as media companies.

"They [Facebook and Google] are media owners not technology companies, they masquerade as technology companies. They are monetising inventory just like other media companies," Sir Martin said.

Will any of this help newspapers? For all of his self-proclaimed Damascene conversion Sir Martin's views are nuanced. He points to a chart in the annual study by legendary American media analyst Mary Meeker who logs time spent with a particular medium against percentage of advertising spend. For the US, at least, 24 per cent of time is spent with mobile but the sector attracts only eight per cent of advertising, suggesting an imbalance that will probably be corrected over time. For newspapers the gap goes in the opposite direction with four per cent of media time devoted to newspapers but 18 per cent of advertising, suggesting an imbalance of legacy spending that may not ultimately survive. Time spent is not, however, the same as effectiveness, trust or the level of engagement.

"There is engagement (with newspapers) that clearly shows and is a plus, and of course the supply and demand relationships may have shifted so much that the price of advertising in newspapers, even traditional newspapers, may have shifted so radically that they now represent a much better bargain," Sir Martin concedes.

But overall he believes the situation is serious for UK newspapers and a five per cent fall in circulation and a 15-20 per cent decline in advertising this year could be followed by something similar in 2017.

"What that means is the newspaper industry has to come together," says Sir Martin, who believes the necessary measures include setting aside traditional rivalries, co-operating more and saving money by moving towards a single advertising sales house for the industry.

Perhaps the most serious conundrum facing newspapers, despite the understandable trumpeting about the record reach of newsbrands, is it is newspapers – rather than the online millions of readers – which still brings in most of the revenue. It is therefore newspapers, rather than newsbrands, which fund the still significant teams of journalists who produce original information in the public interest, holding the rich and powerful to account. Unfortunately, it that very source of revenue which is ultimately at risk, unless the circulation decline of newspapers slows down, or even bottoms out. Hope that one day a crossover point will be reached, when online revenues will replace the yield from lost paper sales, seems forlorn in the face of the growth of Google and Facebook and the relatively low yield from online advertising.

Yet, when the country is faced with a crucial turning point, as with the EU referendum, when serious matters have to be discussed, there is a move towards newspapers. In the referendum month 92,000 more newspapers a day were sold on average – 2.7m more for the month. On the Saturday after the June referendum The Times sold an additional 100,000 copies, a rise of 18 per cent week-on-week while The Guardian has a record 17m unique browsers and 77m page views on the day after the referendum, combined with a significant boost to print sales of both The Guardian and The Observer. Regional newspapers enjoyed a similar boost with sales of The Scotsman up by 17 per cent on Brexit weekend.

Newspapers held on to two thirds of the sales the following month (July). Distinguished media analyst Lorna Tilbian argued the sales uplifts for newspapers "illustrate when fast-moving and complex events such as the referendum happen, people rely on newspapers to interpret what is happening, and to tell them how they will be affected."

She added: "The referendum circulation bounce unequivocally demonstrated print newspapers remain an important source of information and, at times of instability and uncertainty, they become even more valuable to their readers."

For good or ill, national newspapers may also have had a defining impact on the outcome of the referendum in a way that would never happen in a general election where voters rely more – at least for now – on traditional party and family loyalties.

The majority of national newspapers, including The Sun, Daily Mail and Daily Express, came out unequivocally for Brexit. The Mail and Express were little more than cheerleaders for Brexit, magnifying false claims made by the Leave campaign that the £350m a week which goes to Brussels, a gross figure, would instead go to the NHS after Brexit, or that Turkey would be able to join the EU by 2020.

But some of the Brexit supporting newspapers may also have helped to frame the longer-term narrative on one of the most explosive factors that led to a Leave majority – immigration and the EU's insistence on the free movement of people.

Liz Gerard, the retired former night editor of The Times, made a detailed study of migration coverage via the front pages of the nationals. She found that since 2010 the Daily Express had splashed on the issue on 179 occasions, almost all of them negative stories about migrants. The Daily Mail was not that far behind with 122 such splashes. Impact and influence indeed.

Luckily the national press, newspapers primarily rather than their online iterations, are also responsible for dramatic campaigns and investigations very much in the public interest. They include the work of Times journalist Andrew Norfolk who was vilified and denounced as a racist for his persistent coverage of sexual grooming in the Rochdale area and the team of more than 30 Daily Telegraph journalists who cracked the complex detail of the MPs' expenses scandal.

When Edward Snowden wanted to leak classified material from America's National Security Agency he could have gone straight to the internet. Instead he chose The Guardian and the New York Times to give his leaks maximum impact, credibility and trust. And those who leaked Trump's tax affairs went to theAnd those who leaked Trump's tax affairs went to the New York Times and the lewd video of his sexual boasts went to the Washington Post. In the UK it took the Daily Mail only a matter of days of campaigning to persuade the Government to promise a ban on the use of microbeads in cosmetics and personal care products, because of the damage they are doing to marine life. It took 10 months of undercover filming by the Daily Telegraph to expose current levels of greed, rule-breaking and possible corruption in English football, a campaign that led to the rapid departure of England manager Sam Allardyce after only one game in charge. Any of those stories, and others which appear on an almost daily basis, could have been researched and broken by digital online operators but with the possible exception of Buzzfeed it rarely happens.

Another common fallacy is to assume all print is the same and will ultimately be blown out of the water by digital, and even that all newspapers are the same, and will meet a common fate. In fact within the overarching world of print there are many different forms and a variety of funding models.

The arrival of ebooks was supposed to herald the death knell for the traditional book but in fact sales of ebooks have stalled and the traditional book has made a come-back. Tell Sir Ray Tindle (see chapter 24) newspapers are doomed and you will get a dusty answer, although he does concede classified advertising has come under increasing pressure from online.

Sir Ray, who has built a stable of more than 200 very local newspapers from scratch, starting out with only a post-war army demob payment, is still, at the age of 90, buying and launching new titles and happy to proclaim the local press will live forever.

It is also too easy to overlook the march of free newspapers and magazines, from Metro, (see Steve Auckland, chapter 25) to the Evening Standard and City AM to weekly free magazines such as ShortList and Time Out. At the beginning of this year Evening Standard editor Sarah Sands predicted distribution of the Standard would reach a million a day. It did during the Referendum campaign.

"There is a happy hour effect. People tend to do their emails in the morning and when they come out of work they just want to read something in an appealing and convenient package. It's usually the moment when papers can become more convenient than the internet," claims Sands who notes the average time spent with the Evening Standard is 25 minutes a day.

City AM, the specialist free daily aimed at the City of London and beyond, has a website and an app but co-founder and managing director Lawson Muncaster is committed to the primacy of print as well as being a true believer in free distribution.

"I am adamant you still need a paper product to demonstrate integrity. If you think of all the big things that have happened in the past few years, from MPs' expenses to doping in the Tour de France, it has all been led by indigenous newspapers, and although the online component can help, I still think you have to have that flag (print) to wave," says Muncaster.

The City AM executive argues too many publishers have rushed into digital too enthusiastically to the detriment of their main core print product. Specialist newspapers such as the Financial Times and the Wall Street Journal have successfully chartered their passage to the digital world while continuing to nurture their print editions.

William Lewis, chief executive of Dow Jones, reached for Dickens, in a recent interview to describe the present state of the US newspaper industry. "It is both the best of times and the worst of times," he said.

It was the best of times for the Journal (see Lewis's chapter 20) because print is stable at around 1.44m copies with digital subscriptions close to a million and the growing mobile potential to get excited about. It is the worst of times, Lewis believes, for the general American press because they are so much more reliant on advertising than the Journal.

Both the FT and the Wall Street Journal are aimed at business audiences and are able to charge sizeable sums for their journalism. For the FT the combination of digital subscriptions and newspaper sales – the FT publication is profitable on aggressively priced circulation revenues alone – means overall the FT has more paid-for readers than at any time in its 129-year history. But John Ridding, chief executive of the Financial Times Group (see his chapter 18) does not accept such strategies only work for specialist business publications aimed at the affluent.

"Yes, the FT is special and different. But differentiation is open to all publications – be it brand expertise, columnists or some other dimension. Private Eye, to make the point, is achieving circulation highs not seen since the target-rich days of Mrs Thatcher. And it (differentiation) is increasingly necessary for all publications. 'Commodity' publications which fail to distinguish themselves are probably doomed. A shake-out looms," Ridding warns.

The FT and the Journal are confident they can charge for their journalism as is The Times and Sunday Times, which first took its online coverage behind a paywall six years ago, sacrificing reach for revenue. Despite industry scepticism the Murdoch titles now have 182,000 paying digital-only subscribers and strong overall print and digital subscribers of 413,600. The business made a pre-tax profit of £10.9m in its latest financial results compared to annual losses of around £70m before the paywall went up.

At the other end of the scale the online Daily Mirror, The Sun, after pulling down its paywall, Daily Mail and The Guardian are all largely free and financed by advertising. After the Guardian Media Group announced The Guardian's annual loss had risen to £68.7m, up from £10.9m the previous year, there was growing speculation the paper would eventually have to charge for more of its journalism online. Seeking voluntary membership subscriptions at £49 a year may not ultimately bridge the gap, even though 50,000 have already registered.

Another hopeful sign for newspaper companies is, perhaps belatedly, there has been a renewed spirit of innovation, not just in coming fully to terms with the new digital world and looking towards the huge potential of mobile with new apps, but also in product extension and even new print launches. It may not transform its finances but beleaguered regional newspaper group Johnston Press (see section four) has linked up with Sky Television to provide local television advertising.

Trinity Mirror's New Day newspaper lasted only nine weeks and the plug was pulled on 24, a new 'national for the North' from the Carlisle-based CN newspaper group, after only five weeks. But Archant the Norwich-based regional newspaper group appears to have a success on its hands with the New European, a weekly newspaper for the 48 per cent who voted to Remain in the EU in the June referendum, in what was initially only planned as 'a pop-up paper' for a few weeks (see the last chapter) but is now a much more permanent publication.

Another new publishing model has come from Freddie Ossberg, a Swede who began life in financial services but who is in love with print. He is the founder of Raconteur, which publishes special supplements carried in newspapers such as The Times and The Sunday Times, which combine serious analysis and interviews with 'commercial features' or native advertising in the current jargon.

Dutch journalist Marten Blankesteijn has also come with another revenue-raising idea for newspapers. His start-up company Blendle, backed by the New York Times and Axel Springer of Germany, curates and offers readers access to individual articles, or even whole issues, from more than 100 publications for a small fee in return for 30 per cent of the proceeds.

There have also been a few examples of print rising again Lazarus-like from the dead after publications went online only. It seemed like another huge symbolic moment when in December 2012 Newsweek produced its last print edition after more than 80 years and went online only, with the new title of Newsweek Global, complete with dozens of redundancies. After a change of ownership IBT Media re-launched a print edition of Newsweek on March 7, 2014, and overall the business has also returned to profitability as a result. And although The Dandy comic in now only available online its stablemate, The Beano, still survives in print as well as online.

At least two other advantages can be identified for print, one positive, the other negative. The Scientific American has reported on a number of studies suggesting when we consume print rather than use a screen, a more permanent memory trace is created. Our brains seem to comprehend text better by correlating the message with the physical landscape of the tactile object. The texture, shape, folds, and even corners of print products, help to create that landscape map which aids long term remembering.

The other is a negative, which in a strange way could turn out to be a positive for print in the battle for survival. The availability and use of ad-blocking software is on the rise across the developed world for both online and mobile. As things stand more and more consumers are accessing content completely 'free' without having to view the advertisements which fund it. Some of the ad-blocking companies have even been trying to convince publishers to pay to have the blocks removed and allow their ads to be seen. It is not an easy phenomenon to combat, other than to appeal to the better nature of consumers, or perhaps more practically, actually withdraw access to editorial where ad-blockers are in place. Print obviously escapes the attention of the ad-blockers giving it an unexpected new relative advantage.

It would be hopelessly Panglossian to try to ignore the all-too obvious structural problems facing the newspaper industry. At stake is the proper funding of journalism and what former Guardian editor Alan Rusbridger calls the provision of 'independently verifiable information', unless solutions are found which go beyond cutting costs by sacking journalists and entering a downward spiral of declining quality and therefore revenues. The challenge is particularly acute because it is print rather than online which funds the lion's share of those journalists and journalism in the public interest. Journalism paid for by philanthropy, or cloud-funding teams of independent investigative journalists seems a fragile answer to the scale of the problem.

So what is to be done? There is no easy answer, although as Sir Martin Sorrell argues, deeper levels of co-operation between bitter rivals to reduce backroom costs is vital to maintain resources for original journalism. After all anyone can manufacture online lists. A list has even been created listing BuzzFeed's 27 best lists.

Former Daily Mirror editor and media academic Roy Greenslade (see next chapter) has appealed for publishers and journalists to work together to save journalism from the almost daily litany of job cuts, title mergers and office closures. Through Newsworks there has indeed been a growing degree of co-operation between newspaper owners although it has understandably until now focussed primarily on making the commercial case for newsbrand advertising.

Far more needs to be done to argue the positive case for newspapers and the important role they play both in Western democracies and society in general – and the gap which would be left if they were no longer economically viable.

The future is not inevitable – it has to be fought for. But at least there is a half way stage if all else fails, though hardly ideal. Andrew Neil, former editor of the Sunday Times, political journalist and publisher of The Spectator, has few worries for most magazines or specialist publications such as the FT. He fears for general newspapers, particularly the popular press, eventually the numbers sold will no longer justify the cumbersome process of printing newspapers and transporting them around the country. Neil believes he has a viable solution.

"Go online from Monday to Friday and then have a big lean-back weekend publication when people have the time to read. I can see that working," Neil believes.

It is a concept promoted in the US by David Boardman, former editor of the Seattle Times. He argues American newspaper publishers should stop fooling themselves and save what they are currently spending on newsprint, ink, lorries and drivers during the week and invest the money in top quality journalism to produce 'a superb, in-depth last-all-week Sunday, or better yet Saturday paper'. He advocates setting a date several years ahead to go from seven days publication to one in a fell swoop. That would be better than staggering on with four days, or three days a week publication, as some American newspaper now do. To the UK eye this seems like a counsel of despair, the consequence of losing the battle to protect print journalism but at least there would be a Plan B, if all else does in fact fail.

For an optimistic view of the longevity of print go to Tom Standage, deputy editor of the Economist. He forecasts (see his chapter 18 below) confidently there will still be a print edition of the Economist in 2050. Standage spoils the rosy image somewhat by adding it will be a super-premium product costing $500 a year for those who love print so much they will be willing to pay the price.

For the rest of the general press, local, regional and national, a way has to be found to finance adequately not just newsbrands but newspapers – journalism and ultimately society will be the poorer if it does not happen.

## Note on the contributor

Raymond Snoddy OBE, after studying at Queen's University in Belfast, worked on local and regional newspapers, before joining The Times in 1971. Five years later he moved to the Financial Times and reported on media issues before returning to The Times as media editor in 1995. At present, Snoddy is a freelance journalist writing for a range of publications. He presented NewsWatch on the BBC from its inception in 2004 until 2012. His other television work has included presenting Channel 4's award-winning series Hard News. In addition, Snoddy is the author of a biography of the media tycoon Michael Green, and of the acclaimed book on the British press, The Good, the Bad and the Ugly. He was awarded an OBE for his services to journalism in 2000. He is co-editor of this book.

# The last thing newspaper publishers want are journalists, but publishers and journalists must work together to save journalism

**From a commercial perspective, reporters are too expensive and are therefore taking the brunt of newspaper cutbacks. But they perform a vital public service, says Roy Greenslade, Professor of Journalism at City University and former editor of the Daily Mirror**

Hardly a day passes without an announcement by one newspaper publisher or another that jobs must go, titles must be merged and offices must be closed. Cutbacks have been the reality of the news trade in Britain for the best part of 20 years at national, regional and local level. And the same story has been unfolding in the USA, Canada, Australia and most European countries.

The cause, as we all know, is the onward march of the digital revolution. We who praise its advance cannot also help but lament its disruption. Everyone involved in the business registers concern because its fate is so uncertain. We need to disaggregate the 'everyone' because publishers and journalists are seeking very different outcomes. Nor should we regard all publishers as a single entity.

Publishers seeking only profit – such as the chains which control the bulk of the UK's regional papers – are different from those whose newspaper ownership is about prestige and political clout (and propaganda). And they are different again from the owner of the Guardian/Observer, the Scott Trust, which exists specifically to safeguard the papers' journalistic freedom and liberal values 'free from commercial or political interference'.

But no publisher, despite differing motivations, can escape the commercial effects of a technological revolution that is in the process of destroying the funding mechanism which has underpinned newspaper companies for more than 150 years.

Journalists are aware of this but tend to turn a blind eye to reality. They blame publishers for the cutbacks, or at least, the way those cutbacks are carried out. I know, because I have done so plenty of times in the past, belabouring, say, Trinity Mirror or Newsquest or the Telegraph Media Group for the imposition of cuts. Some have been more ruthless or cack-handed than others. Nor have journalists been too happy about executives enjoying handsome rewards for implementing redundancy programmes, a constant refrain by the National Union of Journalists.

It is irritating, probably intensely annoying, for those required to walk the plank. It does not, however, change matters. Whether chief executives are unpopular or over-paid or even incompetent is largely irrelevant. All are in the same boat and their task is clear: to ensure the survival of 'the product' for as long as possible. They must do so whether they work for public companies, where the appetites of investors must be satisfied, or private companies, where owners seek to make profits or, at worst, keep losses to a minimum.

Although journalists, even those without a smattering of economic knowledge, know this to be the case, they find it difficult to be dispassionate about it, not least because they are in the firing line. Leaving aside the grumbles of veteran hacks who have never come to terms with the post-Fleet Street era, journalists who have enthusiastically grasped the advances offered by digital transmission have also begun to be hugely critical of their employers. They have registered their anger about job insecurity, falling wages (including much-reduced payments to freelance contributors) and sometimes poor working conditions, such as the pressure to work longer hours, to move house to keep their jobs or to travel further to reach their offices. They also complain about apparent changes of direction by their managers who are struggling to cope with the fast-moving digital environment.

Then again, those of us who have been around for a long time know journalists have a long history of bellyaching. It goes with the territory. We always know better than those above us. Nor are journalists really appreciative of the fact the audiences for our journalism are far greater than we enjoyed in the pre-internet era. They dismiss the figures as the result of clickbait, and in some instances, but not all, they may be correct: maximising eyeballs is helpful in attracting advertisers (just as it was, and is, with newsprint sales).

Meanwhile, the overarching concern of all journalists is the gradual reduction in their overall numbers and the retreat from face-to-face, eye-witness reporting. At the international level, foreign postings have all but vanished. Nationally, regional offices have been closed. As for the headquarters' staffs, they spend decreasing amounts of time on the road.

Similarly, fewer and fewer reporters on regional and local papers are allowed to leave their offices. Conceding that much more can be accomplished on computers than was ever the case in shoe-leather days of yore (we now take online data journalism for granted, for instance), it remains the case journalism is undergoing severe retrenchment.

Many of the essays in this book detail what is largely regarded as 'a crisis'. If the authors (including me) are honest they will point to the distinction between the crisis facing publishers and the one facing journalists. In other words, they must differentiate between journalism as a business and journalism as a public service. This is the reasoning behind my earlier statement about publishers and journalists seeking different outcomes and it is the crucial split between the two.

The crisis we journalists face at the hands of publishers is the destruction of our trade and therefore the annihilation of a public service. This is not to criticise publishers, which is why I spent some time explaining the pressures they face and the way they are tackling them. It is simply to rationalise what is happening.

Here, in a nutshell, is the reality. Journalists cost money. So the last thing newspaper publishers want nowadays are journalists. By which I mean reporters, on-the-road reporters who spend time and effort to seek out stories. They are too expensive and, viewed in strictly economic terms, unproductive. They can spend many days, sometimes weeks and even months, on their research. And what do most of them have to show for it at the end?

Even if they land a story that provokes a political row, say, or brings down a high-ranking official, it is highly unlikely to attract new buyers. It might well add lustre to the newspaper, enhancing its status for holding power to account. But seen from a purely commercial perspective, reporters just aren't worth it. And they, rather than desk-bound journalists, are the ones being laid off. With them go skills and experience. With them go untold stories. With them goes the most potent and useful way of serving the public.

Publishers need to recognise the direction of travel. The public and the politicians who represent them need to campaign for the retention of reporters. And the funding, you ask? As I have written before, and more than once, we need to find an accommodation with the hugely profitable and powerful new media organisations which benefit from the journalism they recommend.

In fairness, publishers know that. As one senior News UK executive put it in an email to me a couple of days ago: "The republishing platforms reap financial rewards by distributing our content."

But what happens when there is no-one to supply that content? In recognising the crisis, publishers and journalists must work together to find a solution.

## Sources

The first version of this article was first published on Roy Greenslade's blog The Guardian website on September 23, 2016.
https://www.theguardian.com/media/greenslade/2016/sep/23/publishers-and-journalists-must-work-together-to-save-journalism

## Note on the contributor

Roy Greenslade is Professor of Journalism at City University in London. He writes a daily blog about all aspects of journalism at Guardian.co.uk. He was editor of the Daily Mirror 1990-91. Previously he worked in Fleet Street for national newspapers including The Sun and the Sunday Times. His seminal account of postwar UK national newspapers, Press Gang: How Newspapers Make Profits from Propaganda, was first published in 2003.

# I have seen the print future…
# Does it work?

**Peter Preston has spent six decades in and out of 'the print'. The former editor of The Guardian chronicles his personal journey from hot metal to Buzzfeed**

The trouble is simplicity, as in simple cause and effect. Fifteen years ago, Britain devoured around 15 million newspapers each morning. Now it's six million and falling. Meanwhile digital consumption/addiction accelerates away and social media dominate reading time and attention. One habit dies; another takes over. That's an obvious tale of cause and effect, a conclusion that broadcasters who don't much appreciate the printed press find easy recitation. One habit falls, another takes over. An equation so basic you don't really have to think about it - nor try to set it in any historical context. But look back a while before you look forward.

## My life in print

History has a way of answering questions - and my history in print began almost sixty years ago at the Witney Press twelve miles from Oxford. There, twice a week, academic ambitions pushed conveniently well to one side, some of us brought out the university paper Cherwell. And there, too, we registered the hard, creaky truths about newspaper production: an old, thumping flat bed press down below, a composing room that shook as the first copies emerged, and three men who knew the ropes. Bill sat at the Linotype keyboard and set every word; George was head printer and head of everything; and Trembly Charlie, who had a disconcerting habit of scattering lead slugs all over the floor as deadlines neared.

So I learned many things at the double. How to write stories that cut from the bottom. How to find extra space when tales wound up short. How to rummage in the big box of ancient wood type when you needed a headline bigger than 48 point. (We had a scoop about a planned highway through Magdalen meadows - but the only letters left that made any Countdown-style sense proclaimed nothing beyond "THE ROAD". OK, print it.). How not to panic or lose your temper. How to be very nice to Charlie when his hand started shaking again.

That was all good stuff, two years later, stoning in the woman's page at the Liverpool Daily Post. Even better stuff, seven years on, in the composing room at the Guardian in Gray's Inn Road where - one early miracle of new technology - teletype setting (aka TTS) delivered more sticks of lead bearing only a vague approximation of the copy pumped down the line from a threatened but still fully-staffed Manchester office.

## My Grand Tour of technology

Were there better ways of finding the future? Alastair Hetherington, my editor, perhaps more interested in Cabinet politics than printing systems, sent me on a tour of the US to report. I found a glorious newsroom at the Miami Herald, a faded pink paradise, huge picture windows overlooking a blue lagoon, which was pioneering optical character reading, OCR. But it worked slightly less well than our own TTS. Another one bit the dust. I sat in the newsroom of the Boston Globe, a computer on every desk - except in the editor's office, where new-fangled devices weren't welcome. I went to Massachusetts as Atex became a name to conjure with and saw computer keyboards begin to replace typewriters (except at the Guardian, where the National Graphical Association insisted on having their stalwarts retrained on qwerty boards so that their rights to double key stroking remained briefly inviolate).

Then I watched silently as, at last, the final remnants of hot metal were carried coffin fashion across the composing room floor, a way of life beaten out in traditional manner. I was there as journalists could at last set the paper themselves and lay it out on screen. I was around, and bailing desperately, when the IRA blew up our brand new Isle of Dogs print site. And all of this, one crisis after another, one false dawn after another, seemed to promise some publishing nirvana just around the corner. An era where the ancestral cry of the overseer as chapel meetings dragged on would be no more. "Oh Mr Preston, the pots have gone cold!" A world where communication - from editor to reader - was instantaneous rather than lugubrious. A world where editions flowed seamlessly, where pages could be changed in a trice: a world where putting the news out on paper was a pleasure, not an obstacle race.

## A new digital dawn in Fleet Street?

You could feel that print nirvana coming in the late 80s and through the 90s. New papers, new supplements, new thicker editions, the transforming wonders of colour - and the cost of the print union legions fading away as they left to find a new life for themselves. (Wapping had delivered moment of history as well as much bitterness). But, of course, progress has a way of tripping over its own shoelaces, so the full magic of profit and reduced costs never quite happened. More of everything on many more pages meant more competition, which meant more marketing budgets. And then there was the beginning of the internet, a true new frontier.

Was it a revolution or merely another string to a newsroom's bow? Core or peripheral? Small offices, and then much bigger offices, were needed to house a growing digital staff. Some newspapers - the Telegraph, the Guardian - thought they saw the point fast and developed theories of parallel, integrated production. Some - even the Daily Mail - watched and waited. Few quite predicted what would happen next.

But soon it wasn't - as mostly it remains - a question of either digital news or print news. Soon, ominously, the answer was clearly both: a daily paper produced on ever thinner resources, a digital posting in need of constant re-writing and re-editing. Could the staff who served online and print be truly integrated so that one team covered both? The Telegraph produced its giant wheel of a newsroom, one function lapping into another. Other papers invented even more complex copy and picture flows. Yet there was, and still isn't, any clear resolution.

Staffing increased inexorably in any case. Technical reinforcements were essential at every stage. More programmes needed more programmers. Tablets followed laptops as the device of choice - except that, as Rupert Murdoch discovered after he'd spent millions launching The Daily, tablets were merely one more excuse for devising digital editions and tweaking them hour after hour.

No. Obviously, it seemed, the basic answer would have to be different: smartphones in the wake of the iPhone, extra Apple and Android versions, material re-processed to fit different sized screens, and prospectively benefitting from the incontrovertible fact that users, especially young people, were used to paying to use their mobile phones. Here was the magic viability of feet firm on profitable ground - except that it didn't work out that way.

## News is free?

There was, as it transpired, too much free news material out there you didn't have to pay for. To this day, only about 10% of news on the net comes with a price tag. The central competition, therefore, had to be scrabbling for advertising riches to match the exponential growth figures as smartphones left tablets and laptops in the shade. Enter Netflix, Amazon and a host of streaming options. Enter an overwhelming demand for more video, together with ever more complex methods of measuring reader 'engagement'. Enter a fresh array of web-only contenders fuelled with start-up investment.

And, suddenly, there was no salvation in subscription formulas. The demand now is for more free - but more free in any every sense as ad blocking cuts revenues sharply and digital advertising to news-oriented sites stalls, leaving all those extra staff and all those investment hopes looking a trifle bereft. More, this is a general phenomenon on the new side of the fence. It isn't just newspaper sites that face a challenge. BuzzFeed and other wunderkind have to pause and ponder their profit forecasts. The Huffington Post runs out of Huff and puff. The Gawker has pulled the chain on its own legend.

## Digital, the new Concorde?

So those 60 years of personal history begin to weigh heavy again. It's natural to decide that life's shifts are permanent as one steady state supplants another. The future has arrived, and there's no need to ponder change any more. Think Concorde, the new, supersonic manifestation of air travel. Think manned space adventure. And, diminuendo, think newsprint perishing like the wrapping of fish and chips while digital communication inherits the earth. But who, pray, deemed history moribund, like the print it supposedly consigns to the waste bin? Who decided that a story which has altered course so many times in my lifetime was now dead and buried? One spectacular crash, one daunting energy crisis, and Concorde itself was history. We didn't need to go faster after all.

The difficulty with history's familiar progress schtick is that, to reach a simple, seemingly stable conclusion, you have to stop the clock and declare the entire race over, completely run. But we all ought to know by now that this is a marathon course without a finishing line. An article or, frankly, a book, which proclaims print closure is mere extrapolation, not conclusion: as that personal history tour of mine rams home. The future changed when they bought a rotary press in Witney. The future changed when the Liverpool Daily Post gave birth to Trinity Mirror - and changed again when the Guardian seemed to leave Manchester for good. Was it Eddie Shah and Today? Or the saintly Andreas and his Independent? Is the future free or nestling behind a paywall? For that matter, has any non-specialist news provider found a stable foundation that guarantees survival ten or twenty years down the road?

This chapter, quite deliberately, puts aside many of the facts, figures and calculations I use in my media day job at the Observer. If you're writing for a traditional book, hard copy between covers, then facts from the daily churn come as redundant delusion, potentially overtaken long before publishing deadlines loom. It's less than a decade since Steve Jobs gave us the first iPhone, barely seven years since the first Apple tablet. Our world has changed and changed again at a pell-mell pace - and, significantly, the oracles who forecast the death of print even a handful of years ago have had to cancel the small print of their last announcement. For - and this is a moment for brutal honesty - the search for a successor business model to words on print pages, to ads round the side and cover prices a'top the mastheads, has wandered into a cul de sac.

## Making money on reporting money

A few targeted (mostly financial) journals can make money still: though they, as we know, are vulnerable when non-boom turns to bust again. A few 'legacy' broadsheets from the Telegraph to the New York Times retain enough print clout to make money whilst they prod and price for digital salvation. An even smaller number of traditional quality papers - most notably the Times of London - have erected high paywalls and found a kind of hope behind them. But in the main and in the middle of the market, there is no sign of digital salvation. Facebook and the other giants of social media have hoovered up the advertising that goes with live news and begun to cut newspaper websites right out of the action.

Those sites have become like satellite franchised shops in a huge department store - except that they can be axed at the tweak of some Silicon Valley algorithm. Throw in ad blocking on top, adding more headaches to the core losses. Perhaps the great sea change you seem to feel can still, lazily, be awarded to the triumph of online over print: the old transition. But look a fraction deeper and the change is total. It isn't news on screen that's taking the palm: it is news as a pirated commodity, news as just another jar of goodies on the digital shelf. And no-one, if they're honest, knows where competitive services of news, in depth and breadth, will come from in a year or five. Print is vulnerable because it's expensive and slow and typecast as the loser of this drama. But there are no decisive winners in sight; there is no general theory of success and transition. The irony, the bitter irony, is that the reach and readership for newspaper news - for print plus digital reach - has never been higher, but the difficulty in making a profit from news has never been more mountainous.

## Back to my past?

So go back, if you will, to the start of this personal journey. Ask if, why and how print can be a part of the basic news mix. You might begin by looking at things that don't fit the simple template - things such as printed books, which once appeared doomed to death by Kindle, but have since found a much steadier state. Things such as magazines, where the rate of decline is far slower and far patchier than the one newspapers face. What's the appeal of a book on a library shelf or a table? Because it has the resonance of history, both broad and personal, of a statement about you, its owner, the person who chose it, that screen selections cannot reach. Many people, as a matter of fact, don't buy one way or the other: in print and online. They tend to buy both. There's a relationship.

Magazine subscriptions posit a relationship too. They offer a specific interest, they meet a specific need. And the magazines that, as a sector, have fallen less than any, if they've fallen at all, are the weeklies and monthlies rooted in print news and analysis: Private Eye, the New Statesman, the Economist, The Week, the Spectator. Of course some of them have flourishing online editions, but print and tradition are still king of these castles. And if you ask why, the answer reveals something crucial.

Deadlines imply choice. They necessarily involve editors making decisions about what's important, of deploying their judgments on a printed page to a fixed schedule. The Week, each week, lays one set of judgments on top of another. The Economist delivers a rounded commentary on world affairs so that even the busiest executive can keep in touch. Judgment confers understanding. OK: print schedules can traipse along behind the clock, victims of a clunking distribution system. But print also has the ability to make sense of events after the digital circus has left town.

For the moment, perhaps, such factors seem to count for something. Nobody expects the British Library to become a cyber coffee shop just down the road. Nobody expects some of the enduring mastheads of print commentary to disappear after centuries of dogged, argumentative existence. Nobody sees a future where expertise and experience don't count. These are all elements that, with luck, will find some place in the media scene of the day after tomorrow, elements that are integral rather than ephemeral.

## Journalism will survive?

But, just one more time, there are no certainties. Journalism is the art of story discovery and story communication, the art (and the science) of informing the world. That will always be there as long as the world turns. It is part of human nature as well as the binding of society. How such information is spread, though, varies from continent to continent and decade to decade. The rise of the mobile phone has connected Africa at last. The rise of Facebook has given the West new means of talking to itself.

Print is one part - a historic part - of this equation. It offers the appearance of permanency and the reality of choice. Now other tides sweep in. You can hear the death of television prophesied at media conferences. Listen hard and you can also hear the bricks of Facebook and Google crumbling as the next stage of media existence emerges from the mists. Is print dying? It's declining sure enough: but does that mean death? Who can tell? This is cancel-my-last-pronouncement territory in a land that eats experts for breakfast. But pose no such problems for journalism itself. That's a totally different thing.

## Note on the contributor

Peter Preston is the media commentator for The Observer. He was the editor of The Guardian for twenty years from 1975 to 1995 and is widely considered one of the most distinguished journalists in Europe.

# The next downturn – the launchpad for the new news

**We are at a critical point for news, says Jim Chisholm. Many of the traditional corporates are doomed. Google, Facebook and friends have taken over the asylum. But there is now a significant, brilliant energy of freelancers and anti-establishment wonks creating a whole new journalistic genre. Can this necessarily disparate bunch of renegades be turned into a sustainable machine?**

I'm two Jims. One is the 'seasoned veteran' 40 years steeped in the newspaper industry, still romanticising metal, whether hot or heavy. The other is the stats man in me, wedded to trends and research.

The romantic Jim thinks of nothing better than an hour with The Guardian, New York Times or maybe an occasional Telegraph or The Times. But then stats Jim kicks in and the figures say one thing…

### Print, as we know it, is on the way out

The closure of the printed London Independent may be the most visible of the relatively few closures of significant titles in the UK. Not only has the medium seen its online audience increase by 46% since it closed its print edition in March 2016[1], but the company is reporting a profit for the first time in 23 years[2]. This will come to mark the tipping point toward the tsunami of print closures that is coming[3].

Before I pile into the pessimism let me say that the value of the printed medium is considerable and sustainable; but let me repeat, 'not as we know it'. Today the reward for content remains as elusive as ever. In most cases cover price generates revenue, but only a small proportion of gross profit.

Print newspapers are probably the most effective advertising medium, but only if people read them, regularly and thoroughly. And print has some powerful advocates. Lorna Tilbian, the UK's most respected financial analyst of the media sector, put it recently[4]: 'Advertisers who are shifting their money away from print need to give this some serious thought. Newspaper readers are highly engaged with the content and, for advertisers, this engagement translates into hard revenue return on investment.'

You can read Lorna's own views about the future of print in chapter 6.

## The economics of news

Media survive by generating revenue from two sources:

- News consumers, who will pay for news, entertainment, or other gratification;
- Advertisers, who want to sell things to these consumers.

Print's problem is nothing to do with the medium's ability to embrace readers and entice them to advertisers. The problem is that the newspaper's reach of its target audience is no longer significant. For every one per cent decline in circulation, there is a 1.3 per cent decline in share of advertising. So a point is arising when, despite newspapers retaining some small circulation, their value to advertisers will be insignificant.

The following chart demonstrates how, over recent years as newspaper circulations across Western Europe have declined, so their share of advertising has declined precisely, and exponentially[5].

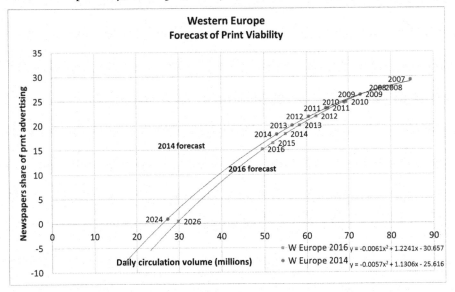

The chart compares my previous forecast from 2014, with that of 2016.

The curved lines project forward, assuming that circulation declines continue at their current rate[6] and that newspapers' share of advertising continues to reflect the declines in circulation, with the curve of the line confirming the relationship is exponential.

The most recent forecast suggests that across Western Europe, newspapers' share of advertising will hit a point zero in 2026. This is two years later than the previous forecast, largely because up-dated circulation figures show a slightly better performance than previously forecast. The UK pattern is fairly similar, but more brutal.

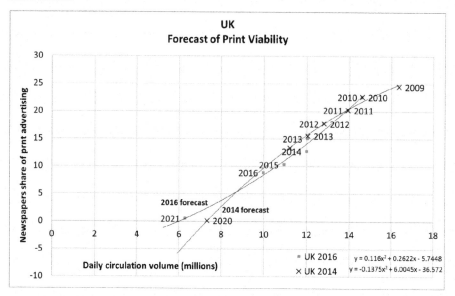

In the UK, the 2016 forecast of point zero is in 2021, one year later than previously forecast. The difference is that while circulations are performing marginally better than forecast, the relative fall in share of advertising has worsened.

The decline in the number of print titles across Europe has fallen by 4.4 per cent between 2011 and 2015[7]. In the UK, the most significant closure or, more accurately, transfer from print to digital has been The Independent. In the regions, closures have largely been among free weekly titles. But The Independent has a habit of catalysing an industry trend. Just watch this space[8].

As costs are cut, resources reduced, so product quality falls, and this only serves to accelerate the levels of print decline, particularly since resources have to be transferred to digital creation and production.

## The lessons of history

This is not the first time our industry has been through all this. In the late 1970s we were suddenly confronted by the new concept of free newspapers. Over time every urban home in the country was enjoying at least one free weekly newspaper, produced either by a new breed of publisher or, probably reluctantly, their traditional established paper. But free weeklies were to be a medium that would prove to have a life expectancy of just 20 years.

Meanwhile, over in Stockholm, Per Andersson, peddled his idea for a free daily newspaper around the traditional publishing houses. Having had no success, he approached the broadcaster Modern Times Group. Together they launched their idea in Stockholm, with inevitable effects on the traditional publishers. Today Metro is the world's largest printed newspaper with 15.6m readers, across 120 cities, in 23 countries. Online it has 35m visitors.

Also in the 1970s two sales people, John Madejksi and Paul Gibbons left the Reading Evening Post, and brought the idea of a classified motors magazine back from the United States. In time AutoTrader would decimate the motoring sections of every regional newspaper in the land. From motors the trend moved to property.

Today the vast majority of these free, or 'vertical', publications have seen their business move online. In the case of the free newspapers, many in the UK have closed. In the case of the verticals, some publishers have managed the transformation, while others have seen their business disappear to new entrants.

Newspaper advertising has been under threat for 35 years. For far too long we either ignored the threat, set up defences or, at best, we reluctantly imitated these impudent up-starts.

## Our real competitors are not our defined competitors

Perhaps the most misunderstood issue that we have faced over the last 40 years is how and why the consumption of news has changed. Newspapers competed with radio, then television, then the Internet, but meanwhile and more significantly they were competing with the garden, the golf course, the restaurant, the gym, and more recently the Play Station and now Facebook.

It's easy to believe that millennials are detached from the news for no other reasons than they are too busy getting on with their lives. However, a recent analysis from comScore[9] suggests that mobile is transforming the scale and means by which millennials are accessing news. To quote the report: '80 per cent of UK millennials access news/information content through mobile devices.'

The research reveals that their digital preferences show traditional leanings, with powerful implications for media owners. Indeed: 'Traditional media outlets such as the Telegraph, The Guardian and Daily Mail have a higher reach amongst millennials than amongst the total UK digital population.'

This should be very encouraging for publishers, but while market reach is high, engagement is thin. These 'new news' consumers have yet to be convinced to engage with us in the way previous generations did.

## But what is news?

Far bigger than the survival of print, are the future role and definition of what news is. From politics to tragedy, entertainment to business, the demands for news are changing.

In Western markets people are at best questioning if not abandoning the political process.

Our television screens are packed with experiential nonsense, which our most popular newspapers obsessively reflect in their coverage.

To illustrate this, firstly, let me put forward this supposition: newspaper brands no longer drive the political agenda. They are slaves to it. And this is shown in a tale of two referenda in which the social vs media experiences between the Scottish and UK leave votes are contrasted.

During the Scottish referendum campaign the level of social participation was palpable. As I commented at the time[10], it was the only time I could recall when the great population of Glasgow talked about anything except football. Yet the barometer of news interest was not reflected in newspaper circulation figures.

Only the Sunday Herald saw any increase in sale on the back of a partisan nationalist agenda, while the Daily Mail was the only daily paper to see any improvement in sales trend – from minus 8 per cent to minus 4 per cent.

While the indigenous Scottish titles flailed around before mostly supporting remain at the last hour, the social media, and micro sites had a field day. It was as if the indigenous news media were frightened to take a stance among the maelstrom of passionate social debate. Yet turnout to vote was a record 85%, compared with 72% in the UK referendum.

By contrast the UK European referendum was characterised by more apathetic social participation, while aspects of the media had a field day regurgitating the untruths and myths from a raft of allegedly responsible politicians and pundits.

## Opportunities in print

From the start, I have presented a view that print as a mass medium news provider is dying. The only question is at what rate, and what is the value of further investment.

Print still accounts for around 80 per cent of our industry's revenues, but reading the various publishers' annual reports you wouldn't believe it. Having under-resourced digital for too long, publishers have spent the last few years obsessing with digital at the expense of print.

While The Guardian has a coherent, well thought-through strategy of audience migration, through a combination of cross-promotion of content, plus a consistent print pricing policy (although it continues to lose millions of pounds each year) many publishers are simply seeing print as a distraction. Indeed, Politico[11], under the somewhat hyperbolic headline: 'What If the Newspaper Industry Made a Colossal Mistake?', highlighted research from the University of Texas, that points to continuing relative strength of print over digital in terms of overall consumption[12]. It should be noted however that this research was subsequently debunked in a compelling article in The Media Briefing[13] As the forecast above shows, any retention of print across time serves to protect the business until it achieves its point of inflection. For Trinity Mirror that point is in sight because they combine reasonable circulation decline with a strong digital performance. For other UK regional groups the picture is less optimistic.

So could print be the new New Media? Chava Gourarie certainly thought so in her article for the Columbia Journalism Review in December 2015[14]. Here she points to a range of iconic US digital news and magazine sites, such as Politico and Monocle that have subsequently launched print editions[15]

An old saying professes that 'in the past circulation was vanity, advertising was sanity.' But not any more. The forecast above assumes that some print circulation will remain, but not sufficient to engender sufficient advertising in itself.

So one hope for the printed newspaper is for it to survive on its cover price revenue, with other forms of revenue, niche advertising, sponsorship, targeted supplements or events, as a bonus

## Going weekly isn't weak

Publishers and editors see daily publication as a demonstration of their virility, but the fact is that the notion of readers even reading a majority of issues in a week disappeared years ago. Advertisers, no longer book more than one advertisement a week. And in truth only a third of a daily's monthly audience read on a typical day – that's two issues a week — and their daily digital audience is only seven per cent of their monthly reach[16].

Surely it would be far better to produce a fantastic weekly print product packed with great editorial, advertising and other benefits, rather than producing a daily, much of which is either regurgitated press releases, or wire stories that appear in any old place. Since 2009, 14 per cent of UK regional dailies had made the transfer[17].

One of print's great advantages over digital media is its visibility. Note how Microsoft, Google, Facebook all use analogue media – TV, print, outdoor – to promote their brands. The digital offering can continue to contain genuine daily stories, rather than pandering to a misbelief that readers need stacks of content every day.

Software services exist that enable a quasi-automated uploading of press-release material, which are much criticised but an essential element of local news curation.

All this content, and more can be celebrated, on the streets and coffee tables in a grand weekly offering which is promotable, visible, and distributable in a cost efficient and effective manner. Going weekly isn't a weak response to external factors, but a smart response to the changing demands and needs of news consumers and advertisers.

## Is news just another niche?

Walk into most cafes and bars and a cornucopia of new, hyper-local media are waiting to engage with you. All, are produced by locals who combine writing with selling with various levels of braggadocio, that generally reflect in the quality of their product.

Of course one has to be careful about the definition of news. In the past a newspaper's 'formatted set of surprises' included not just news and commentary, but arts, sport, features, business, classified and a range of other services. In many ways it was these services that brought in readers and revenue. So it is not surprising that as these items have spun off into their own print and digital verticals, that newspapers are finding that news is not enough in itself.

The Local Web List[18] catalogues 673 hyper-local websites in the UK, which is undoubtedly an underestimate. The problem for researchers and service providers is that to define, identify and quantify the depth and breadth of the local/hyper-local market, remains hard as many community news sites exist with a very low profile.

Many of these may be hyper-local publications are not new, and many could be described as 'lifestyle' businesses[19], *but* replicated across the country, they make a significant, disparate and undefinable platform. At this stage in their evolution, through their sheer numbers and voluminous distribution, it must be judged as a medium with considerable potential, be it in print or digital.

## The wonders of hindsight

Hindsight is a miserable pre-occupation that leads to bitterness, but only when one fails to learn from it. Perhaps our biggest tragedy has been our inability to project forward the lessons of one experience to another. I say this not as criticism, but as a fellow-traveller[20].

During the early 1990s I, and a group of similar digital adventurers, met with many pioneers in the new digital world, across Europe and North America. Today I confess to our sharing a common belief that the Internet was ours for the taking. This was a communications medium after all, we concluded. Partnership would be on our terms. Meanwhile we all sat back and non-invented.

## What next for news, print, journalism and for publishing?

Let's agree one thing. We all share the long-term goals of freedom of expression, holding the powerful to account while protecting and promoting the values that make society prosper. Against this backdrop what are or should be the outcomes, inevitable or desired? And what is commercially realistic?

Relative to the challenges in modern society, and the role of news and journalism, print is secondary. It's not many years ago that digital was regarded as the privilege of the rich, young and educated. I recently witnessed a beggar in Bangalore sitting on the pavement. One hand was held out soliciting money. The other held his phone to his ear. Today, thanks to mobile technology, digital is ubiquitous.

Now we see the opposite. Print is increasingly the pleasure of the rich and educated, if not the young. Books and magazines are increasingly niche, indeed boutique in value.

**Conclusion 1.**   Print will become a niche-only medium within five years.

**Action 1.**        Get over it.

From 1995 the industry moved to one of profits from principles, to the mosh pit of the stock-exchange. Only one principle would prevail. If you can't evolve, milk the cash cow. And the more it was milked the more the cow weakened, and the more the cow weakened, the more urgent the milking became. So if the current model of ownership and innovation continues, news as we knew it will disappear from large sections of our society.

**Conclusion 2**. The current, profit-motivated business model has failed, and the shareholders of these businesses deserve what is coming.

**Action 2**: News comes first. It will take a restructuring of the whole news value chain to resurrect the status and influence of news media but the ever increasing plethora of non-corporate players, community media, niche reporters, and investigative websites point to a route forward. However these guys need nurturing, support and a loose affiliation that can create gravitas and commercial viability with some form of central coordination, if they are going to truly exploit their potential.

### Who will survive?
Some of the national newspapers will likely survive the imminent tsunami. But for the local press there is a patchwork of print performance, digital adoption and strategic clarity. Sadly the performance in each local title is more likely to reflect the strategic influence and competence of its owner, than any local circumstance.

While it is all too easy to blame the Internet for everything that has gone wrong for newspapers, the fact is that digital is only part of a complex mix of different issues.

### Self-inflicted injuries
We have used pricing - both cover-pricing and advertising - as a tool of greed, not of growth. Oh how we used to gloat over the rates we could charge for recruitment advertising! Mostly gone.

The same with cover-pricing where the accountants would demand a cover price increase, in full knowledge that the sale would go down, but gross margins would go up. But they didn't want to hear any insight that indicated that the link between circulation and advertising, which was far more critical than any cover-price elasticity.

The known knowns and the unknown unknowns

To be sure many newspaper companies across Europe will fail. Some titles will continue, in some form. Some dailies will move from daily to weekly. Some, like The Independent, will become digital only, and many will disappear. Over time a few corporate news players will survive in some form or another, but most will find themselves irrelevant.

In the meantime, an energetic if dissembled new generation of news deliverers are emerging. The likes of Humans of Edinburgh, Bristol's B247 and the investigative journalism site, The Ferret, represent a massive movement, void of corporate culture and avarice.

If, and a big if, all these waifs and strays can find some cohesion, there seems to be sufficient market momentum to create a micro digital economy that can grow into a material medium. The key element to this is providing these well-intended, often highly talented players with the back of house capabilities, that any media business requires. This includes money management, national ad sales, common digital platforms, apps and add-ins.

We know that Google, Facebook and all the other intermediary players are costing us at least half of our potential revenue. If the news media had not become dependent on these revenue suckers, we would not be here talking about survival.

But the known unknown is what would be the effect of the news media disenfranchising itself from their destructive grip. No more Google Adsense, no more double-click revenue grab, no more Facebook revenue and data control, no more uncontrolled cookies And, as a consequence, no more ad blocking. We continue to do too little too late to counter these forces.

We publishers – along with the rest of society, by the way - have unwittingly drifted into a cabal in which we have little control.

On the one hand, the traditional news media industry need to work out how we are going to take on these behemoths, and regain control as the introducer of advertisers to buyers.

On the other the new news entrants have the opportunity to bypass all this intermediary interference, by being mobile, peer-to-peer, non-cookie based, and adopting alternative revenue streams such as Redfox Media's AdAppTive programme[21].

But beyond our control there is the economy. Since the beginning of the 20th century, the economic cycle has averaged around 11 years.

We know two things:

- During every cyclical downturn newspapers' share of revenue drops.
- We will likely see the next downturn between now and point zero. At this point, hundreds of newspapers across Europe will face extinction.

For the established players, caught up in corporate and shareholder demands, this is going to be very bad indeed. But for the new news entrants this will perhaps be the moment to make it. Their independent platforms may appeal to citizens reaching out for explanations for yet another intrusion of their prosperity. And their current low revenue needs will hold them strong relative to the money-hungry corporates.

## Notes

[1] Source: Press Gazette. http://www.pressgazette.co.uk/independent-readership-up-46-per-cent-while-mobile-offers-biggest-audience-for-some/. September 2016

[2] Source: Press Gazette. http://www.pressgazette.co.uk/the-independent-claims-profit-for-first-time-in-23-years-after-going-digital-only/. October, 2016

[3] Chisholm, April 2016. So the Circulation Tsunami begins. http://www.jimchisholm.net/694-2/

[4] Lorna Tilbian. July 2016. Advertisers Must Learn to Love Newspapers Once Morehttp://www.newsmediauk.org/Latest/tilbian-advertisers-must-learn-to-love-newspapers-once-more

[5] Source: Chisholm analysis, Circulation data from World Press Trends and advertising data from Zenith Optimedia.

[6] The model assumes that circulation declines are at current levels – a standard percentage decline each year. In fact rates of circulation decline have been accelerating though this may not continue as different types of newspaper will see different forms of decline.

[7] Title Numbers. Source. World Press Trends. http://www.wan-ifra.org/microsites/world-press-trends. September, 2016.

[89] Source: Jim Chisholm - Shaping the Future of the newspaper. The Independent's move from a broadsheet to tabloid format spearheaded a contamination of "tabloiditis" across the world. Within two years, hundreds if not thousands of newspapers across the world made the transformation. Very few of them had a strategic understanding of why they were doing it. WAN-IFRA

[9] comScore analysis: http://www.comscore.com/Insights/Data-Mine/Digital-native-Millennials-embrace-traditional-media-outlets?ns_campaign=EMEA_GB_SEP2016_DG_MILLENNIALS_AND_NEWS&ns_mchannel=email&ns_source=comscore_elq_EMEA_GB_SEP2016_DG_MILLENNIALS_AND_NEWS&ns_linkname=text_general&ns_fee=0&elqTrackId=9dcd43736da94d729e73474776be1321&elq=3742014cc44f4ecfbfc3d7c83dd98e3b&elqaid=3944&elqat=1&elqCampaignId=2538

[10] Source: Jim Chisholm, http://www.inma.org/blogs/ideas/post.cfm/news-media-fail-social-media-score-in-scottish-referendum. November 2016.

[11] Source: Politico. http://www.politico.com/magazine/story/2016/10/newspapers-digital-first-214363#ixzz4NWySvefs. October 2016

[12] Source: http://www.tandfonline.com/doi/pdf/10.1080/17512786.2016.1208056?needAccess=true. Hsiang Iris Chyi & Ori Tenenboim. July 2016

[13] Source: https://www.themediabriefing.com/article/print-vs-digital-the-media-meme-that-will-not-die . October 2016

[14] Source: Columbia Journalism Review, http://www.cjr.org/business_of_news/back_in_print.php. December 2015.

[15] New Print products, Tablet, Politico, The Pitchfork Review, Nautilus, Kinfolk, Monocle

[16] UK NRS/PADD : IPSOS/comScore MMX.

[17] Source: holdthefrontpage.co.uk

[18] Local Web List: http://localweblist.net/. September 2016

[19] A life style business, is one where it provides a single person or couple with a livable income but no more.

[20] As evidence of my own naivity look no further than my co-authored report: Opportunities in Electronic Publishing, August 1994.

[21] Source: www.RedfoxMedia.co

**Note on the contributor**

Based in Scotland, Jim Chisholm has worked in the newspaper industry for 40 years – 20 in management and 20 as a consultant advising media organisations in more than 50 countries on strategy and the future of media.

# In the public interest

**Print media advertising is in a self-reinforcing spiral of decline. Individual publishers have little defence as online competition burns and burgles their assets and profits. By acting together, publishers will buy more time to evolve into quite different businesses, says Adam Smith of GroupM**

The world will spend about $530bn a year on advertising in 2016. In the decades before the 2008 financial crisis, advertising often exaggerated the economic cycle thanks to advertisers' tendency to panic as a herd, alternately for the entrance and the exit. More hare than tortoise. Today's prolix economic recovery has encouraged tortoisism, the cautious subordination of enterprise to managerialism, shown by the rise of 'procurement' and worship of cash. This may pass. The appetite for risk may vary, but over the long term, advertising steadily accounts for about one percent of global GDP.

When there is no real growth, one must fight for market share. The internet became a measurable advertising medium in 1995, when it was reckoned to have attracted $100m in the USA. It overtook cinema's share in 1998, radio's and outdoor's in 2005 and print's (newspapers and magazines) in 2014. TV, radio and outdoor have preserved their share. The story of the last 20 years has been the internet taking share of advertising from print.

**Print and internet % share of global ad spend**

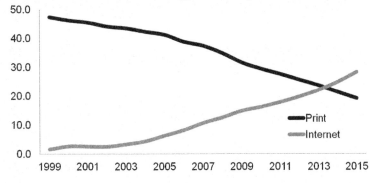

This pattern is repeated wherever print was a big ad medium. The UK is an extreme example because we started from the unusual position of having large national and regional newspaper penetration, a combination of education and a lot of railway stations, and having the ad-free BBC in TV and radio. Plus, the UK is the most-digitised western ad market. Reasons for this include London clustering and being Anglophone, but commerce explains more – having lots of credit cards, good infrastructure for delivery and returns, and high prices in the high street. Metro once told me it did well from e-commerce because commuters would see ads on the way to work and then buy online on the company's time. London Underground is now spoiling Metro's party by putting wi-fi in every station.

## Print and internet % share of UK ad spend

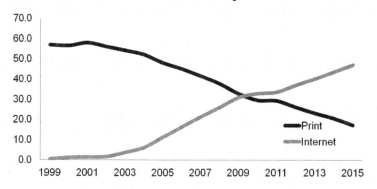

### It pays to advertise

Resident WPP sage Jeremy Bullmore says advertising comes in two types – that which looks for people, and that which people look for. The latter has little need of extravagant space, or artwork, or placement amid expensive 'content'. Its classic form was the classified ad, or the directory, and very profitable it was too. Google Search ate both these lunches. Google Search ad sales continue to grow at a furious rate. It discloses a bare minimum in published accounts, but our own 18 per cent increase in UK Google Search ad payments in 2015 gives you an idea.

The loss of advertising which people look for was print's first and worst ad problem. It affects newspapers and directories more than magazines. Losing any form of advertising is very damaging to media owners which rely on it. As long as a media owner covers its (largely fixed) costs of selling advertising, most of the incremental ad sales it generates drop straight through to profits. Correspondingly, once a medium loses an advertiser, or the advertiser chooses to appear less frequently, or to use cheaper spaces, it is profits which sustain nearly all the damage, and this is next to impossible to repair. Less profit means less investment and more economies. The title suffers, readers are deterred, copy sales fall, reach falls, and reach is how advertisers assess any medium.

## Our new American friends

Google and Facebook's market valuation depends on the amount of advertising they can sell. To keep this up, they need to gain share of display advertising. Both are keen to lure TV advertisers. They have a good case to make, given that the young are watching less TV, and watch a lot of video online. But neither Google nor Facebook invest anything in content, so the quality of online video is much worse than TV. I am not sure Google and Facebook properly understand how serious a problem this could become to advertisers. And that is before one considers click fraud and the ephemeral, distracted, small-screen attention span.

Google and Facebook are equally happy to take display ad share from newspapers and magazines. Circumspect print publishers will therefore imagine what the likes of Google and Facebook are whispering in advertisers' ears. It is safe to assume topics will include reach, and the ability to identify audience types in fine detail, and impressive methods of proving value for money.

Ad agencies have invested heavily in data and technology, mostly to manage ad investment in digital media. We practise 'econometrics', which is supposed to show how to optimise an ad budget. I am told print does not do well under such scrutiny.

I applaud Newsworks' retaliation in its 2016 'Newspapers triple ad campaign effectiveness' ad campaign. I wonder why I saw it only in newspapers? You may have noticed online brands are big TV advertisers. In the UK, this is the second-largest category after food. This is because TV still has rapid mass reach. If I had been Newsworks, I would have explored a contra deal with the commercial TV broadcasters. Other media too. The internet monopolies provide common cause.

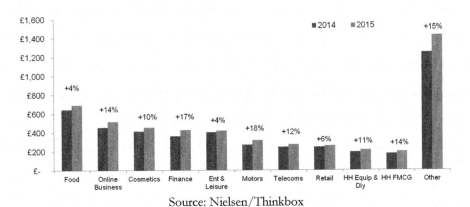

Source: Nielsen/Thinkbox

Print 'brands' have multiplied reach by going online, but have not managed to recover much lost advertising revenue this way. From 2011 to 2015 inclusive, for every £5 by which publishers' annual print advertising revenue fell, digital rose only £1.

## How then to keep print alive?
Against my own libertarian instincts, I think a deal more collectivism lies ahead.

**More marketing**. Good editorial environment is important to reputable brands, and newsbrands score well on engagement, safety and quality, but ad buyers simply have more choice online. Almost half of GroupM's digital ad placements by value are now automated (colloquially, 'programmatic'), which expands choice still further. Digital print brands face a perpetual struggle to remain on the 'preferred' list. If the print industry can make these choices better-informed, it will be to print's advantage.

**Reach**. The number-one priority for advertisers. Lorries and newsagents are an ever-more expensive way of maintaining this. Online and subscription seem to me the best way to preserve and indeed increase reach. Shedding lorries, newsagents and eventually the analogue domain is to say the least a radical change in business strategy, but I fear it is inevitable. It is a ghastly dilemma, sacrificing the bird in the hand of today's profits for the two in the digital bush which has borne such disappointing fruit so far. The trajectory of circulation does however seem bound to deliver many publishers to this crisis within 10 years.

**Ad sales**. Print ad sales are somewhat atomised. TV has three main sales points. Radio has two. Ad buyers do not have time to deal campaign-by-campaign with lots of ad sales houses. Our time has become much more valuable since we moved ourselves up the 'value chain' from processing orders to managing digital media and all its attendant data. We are tackling the campaign-by-campaign problem with the big blanket deals which have been the norm in TV for a generation. It is up to publishers to consolidate sales points to the extent competition authorities will allow.

**Data and technology**. The collaborative PAMCo (Publishers' Audience Measurement Company) cannot come soon enough, and the more titles it can cover, the better. It will give planners in ad agencies what they want more than anything, the means to calculate 'deduplicated' reach across many titles, digital and print. This is the ideal complement to automation, which provides the mechanism to 'ingest' multiple data sources (about consumer behaviour, mainly) and the optimise budget allocation against multiple objectives (picked from such as sales, awareness, click traffic, and reach and frequency).

**Trading**. Google and Facebook do not produce any content, preferring to remain distributors and agents, and to cultivate dependency upon them. This is anathema to media agencies, which are nothing without independence. For this reason we invest in our own data and technology and we set up our own marketplaces. These are designed to create advantage for all involved: advertisers, media owners, and ourselves. Put agencies to the test to see what they can do for you.

**Subsidy**. Print is a public good. We have no difficulty tolerating Channel 4, which had sales of £979m in 2015. National newspapers took a total of £1,025m in ad revenue in 2015. We predict the totality of print advertising to be £2,384m in 2017, and that is optimistic. In a bid for public subsidy, Paul Godfrey, president of Canada's Postmedia Newspaper Group, said the situation was 'ugly and will get uglier'. He pointed out to parliamentarians that government ad spend on print had halved in the past five years while doubling in online, most going to non-Canadian vendors. It can do no harm to sketch out a UK PR plan now.

## Note

All advertising data are from *This Year Next Year Worldwide* (GroupM, London, July 2016)

## Note on the contributor

Adam Smith spent seven years in steel trading before spending 16 years at Zenith Media. He joined WPP's GroupM in 2006 to publish titles including global and UK media investment forecasts, and GroupM's annual survey of digital media, Interaction. He has a law degree from Oxford, an MBA from Kingston and a CIM diploma. He is married with two children, a school governor and a councillor in his home town of Maidenhead, Berkshire. He has served on local MP (and since 2016, Prime Minister) Theresa May's campaign team since 2010.

# Variety may be the answer

**Over the last ten years the global newspaper industry has faced unprecedented turmoil. The increased prevalence of broadband has driven profound and ongoing changes in consumer behaviour, which have presented structural challenges and opportunities for publishers. Lorna Tilbian, Head of Media at London stockbrokers Numis, casts her eye over their prospects**

Any financial assessment of print's structural change has been overwhelmed by the severe downturn in advertising as corporate profitability and consumer confidence collapsed and balance sheets were overstretched after the collapse of Lehman Brothers in September 2008 and the ensuing global financial crisis. This downturn has been particularly felt in higher yielding classified advertising markets that have been changed forever, where the main categories of recruitment, property and motors have seen declines reflecting the initial weaknesses of their underlying markets in combination with the advent of powerful online players such as Rightmove, Auto Trader and Zoopla.

## Nationals

The business model for newspapers has not changed for decades. National newspapers generate their revenue from a combination of advertising and circulation (cover price) revenue. The typical advertising/circulation split for a national title is 55-45 per cent, in contrast to regional titles that operate with a higher dependency on advertising, in the 70-30 per cent range. As online, mobile and video becomes more and more important the bias towards advertising is likely to continue to creep up.

Display is the main source of national newspaper advertising, expected to account for £691m (-9 per cent) of revenue in 2016, according to Group M. Classified national newspaper advertising accounts for only £114m (-10 per cent) and is split between recruitment, property, motors and other classified advertising. The balance of £210m (+7.7 per cent) is represented by digital advertising.

Circulation revenue figures continue to decline, though the single digit falls in cash reflect the impact of cover price increases offsetting underlying higher copy sales losses. In the last few years underlying circulation falls have accelerated, caused by structural changes in readership habits. A range of websites, mobile and tablet apps, including versions of all key national titles, provide up to date news and satisfy the daily news requirements of a growing proportion of the newspaper readership.

Newsprint typically accounts for around 20 per cent of the cost base of a national newspaper, higher than regionals at around 12 per cent. Newsprint prices have fallen in recent years but this was reversed in 2016 and this upward pressure was expected to continue into 2017 on the back of a weak Sterling.

## Regionals

At the time of writing there were around 900 weekly local or regional publications and about 90 dailies in the UK. The regional market is dominated by a handful of large players, which own relatively contiguous regional portfolios.

Regional newspapers have become increasingly reliant on display advertising, as cyclical and structural pressures have hit classified revenues hard. Group M expect £349m (-9 per cent) of total advertising revenues in 2016 to come from display compared with £363m (-15 per cent) from classified and £200m (+14%) from digital.

As with nationals, the key classified categories of recruitment, property and motors are volatile revenue streams, dependent on the health of the underlying markets they serve. These classified advertising verticals have not only been hit hard by cyclical pressure, but also by the online players such as Rightmove and Zoopla in property and Auto Trader in the motors space, which are taking an increasing share of available marketing spend.

The circulation of regional newspapers has been in long-term decline for several decades, reflecting demographic change and increasing competition from other media. According to ABC data the average regional sales volume decline to the end of June 2016 was in the high single-digit/low double-digit range, with Trinity Mirror's Leicester Mercury outperforming at +2 per cent (winning the Premier League helps!) and the Johnston Press-owned Wigan Evening Post underperforming at -24 per cent. Cover price increases have been used successfully to manage circulation revenue decline to single digit percentages despite double-digit average volume decline.

There has been a divergence in the performance of paid weeklies and morning and evening daily titles. Paid weeklies tend to serve smaller communities where local ties are stronger. As a result, they have experienced more stable circulation. By contrast, declines in morning and evening daily titles have been more significant, as they tend to serve larger towns and cities where competition from other media is stronger and local community ties are weaker. The increasing trend of shutting smaller circulation daily titles and moving to higher-priced weekly titles has continued to increase.

The biggest expenses in running a newspaper business are employees who account for almost half of industry costs, followed by newsprint, which takes around 10 per cent. The remainder is accounted for by other activities such as distribution, production, retail costs and general administration costs.

## Revenue analysis

Historically, along with circulation, advertising has been the predominant newspaper revenue stream. News has rarely been profitable on a standalone basis and thus cover prices have effectively been subsidised by advertisers paying to reach audience.

The revenue split between advertising and circulation varies by country. The United States, at under 90 per cent, is the most reliant on advertising with Japan, at below 40 per cent, the least. Advertising overall is closely correlated with corporate profitability (which funds marketing budgets) and consumer spending (which pays for the goods which are advertised). Advertising is therefore a highly cyclical revenue stream. In addition to cyclical pressures newspaper advertising has come under structural pressure, particularly classified advertising, as spend has shifted to digital.

All things being equal, a rebound in corporate profitability and consumer spending should result in growth in national newspaper advertising. However, all advertising is not equal and the outlook for newspaper companies will depend on the type of advertising they are exposed to and able to capture. The prospect of cyclical revenue recovery in regionals is significantly impacted by the emergence of strong digital plays in the classified verticals.

There has been a significant difference between the performance of display and classified advertising, and between regional and national. Across the board classified advertising has been hit hard, with regional classifieds consistently hit hardest.

The continued significant declines in regional display advertising hammer home the structural pressures that the regional newspaper publishers continue to face in each of the classified sectors, a result of the transition to digital and the presence of large competing digital players in each of the key advertising verticals. There is some cause for optimism at national newspapers where both the Daily Mail and the Daily Mirror have reported hitting an inflection whereby the decline in physical advertising is being offset by growth in digital advertising.

## Newspaper advertising and circulation outlook

The outlook for UK advertising is volatile for 2017. Structural pressures will ensure national print display advertising continues to fall at around the high single digit level. For those players, such as DMGT, that have a strong online presence, there is significant scope for more efficient monetisation of the online property, meaning that combined print/digital advertising will at worst flat line, but at best grow in 2017.

Classified advertising remains under both cyclical and structural pressure. Given that current run rate remains around the -15 per cent mark for classified advertising, despite a more optimistic UK macro backdrop, it is hard not to predict that 2017 will see further declines in the high single digit percentages.

At face value, more people are reading newspapers than ever before, with more than half the world's adult population acknowledging reading a newspaper. This should help circulation revenues. But the key issue from a circulation perspective is that the reading audience, particularly in the developed world, is electing to access free content via newspaper websites, which have yet to find a circulation model that can replicate the circulation revenue stream that is made in print.

WAN/IFRA data suggests the global print audience remains at around 2.5bn with digital readership of over 600m, generating revenues of more than $200bn. While newspaper print circulations continue to grow in Asia and Australia and New Zealand, this is offsetting the declines that continue to be seen in Europe, North America, the Middle East and Africa, with Latin America flat. Scandinavian and Alpine countries continue to have the highest readership of newspapers per capita. Countries with a high level of readership tend to operate on a subscription and home delivery model.

A subscription model offers several advantages over newsstand copy sales with greater resilience to economic pressure and the ability to implement smaller, regular price rises. In addition, a direct billing relationship with the reader offers greater potential to sell additional goods and services while a better knowledge of the reader creates a more attractive advertising proposition. At face value, transition to an online paid model should be more straightforward.

## Digital

As with other areas of the media sector, the Internet has provided both opportunities and challenges for the newspaper industry. Broadly speaking, newspaper publishers have been slow to capitalise on the opportunities that digital presents and as such Group M estimates digital revenues currently to account for just over 20 per cent of national advertising revenues and 22 per cent of regional advertising revenues in 2016.

Historically, newspapers (especially regionals) have operated near monopolies defended by the high capital investment required to operate printing presses and distribution operations. The Internet removed both these barriers to entry and enabled the development of a range of online-only news sources that could operate in real-time. These included not only pure-play news organisations, but also search engine aggregators, Internet news portals with news feeds, and social networks. Most publishers responded by providing online versions of the print copy, which could be accessed for free online.

The next decade will see newspapers move away from a free ad-funded model towards a diverse range of online business models appropriate to the publisher's readership base.

## Online advertising

The predominant business model over the last decade for incumbent publishers has been free access funded by display advertising. The national publishers have all built significant audience, with Mailonline standing out with more than 13.6m daily average unique browsers, according to ABC data.

Given a shared cost base, particularly around core editorial, it is very difficult to split out specific profitability of the online offerings of each of the newspapers from the print titles. As with offline advertising, we think audience reach and demographics are key to determining online success. With more than 210m monthly average unique browsers, DMGT is best placed to monetise its online audience, which is younger and more affluent than its print readership. Momentum around digital advertising is continuing to build, though even at Mailonline it remains very low relative to the scale of the audience. Having said that, at Mailonline an inflection has been reached where digital advertising growth is offsetting physical advertising declines.

Display advertising is relatively structurally robust, and in some ways platform agnostic. Online display advertising is complementary to other types and it is unlikely to totally displace print or television. However, the same cannot be said for classified advertising. In 2006 classified advertising represented 68 per cent of total regional newspaper advertising and this is expected by Group M to have fallen to 40 per cent in 2016, the vast majority of this collapse being structural.

The Internet offers reach and functionality that is perfectly suited to classified advertising. Whilst historically regional newspapers have operated in local near-monopoly situations with respect to local advertisers and readers the Internet allowed the development of pure-play classified sites by vertical. Often the first-mover has been able to build a pre-eminent market share of 'eyeballs', which provides a powerful barrier to entry to regional publishers trying to create a local or hyper-local alternative.

However, the structural threat will vary by vertical. Although the post 2008 downturn in recruitment was overwhelmingly cyclical, the relative effectiveness and efficiency of online recruitment has meant that the impact of a cyclical recovery has been at best muted for regional newspaper classified advertising.

Meanwhile, as the combined revenues of Rightmove and Zoopla still represent more than 50 per cent of estate agent marketing spend, related print advertising will continue to face structural pressure, despite cyclical recovery, as an increased proportion of spend shifts to the two major online players. The post-2008 decline in print motors advertising has been structural reflecting both consolidation in dealerships and the success of online competition, with Auto Trader, the big digital winner. Since the recovery, its strong position has been bolstered by record new car sales from 2012 onwards as PPI refunds have been recycled into new family cars. By contrast, family announcements (births, deaths and marriages) should hold up reasonably well.

## Enterprise

Enterprise revenues are those derived from selling additional goods and services to a newspaper's readership base. Whilst still accounting for a small proportion of industry revenue, enterprise will become an increasingly important part of a diversified online model and is an area increasingly being investigated by a number of consumer publishers (both newspaper and magazines).

Four important factors will drive the development of enterprise revenues. Firstly, titles with affluent demographics have had the most success is generating enterprise revenues. Second, the larger the circulation, the larger the potential customer base. Third, a strong brand is trusted by potential consumers. Four, a direct billing relationship with readers, through a pre-paid subscription, provides a powerful advantage in driving Enterprise revenues.

## Paid content

The debate over charging for content continues to be at the forefront of the newspaper industry. Whilst a number of paid-content models have been introduced over the last few years, there is limited financial detail allowing an accurate assessment of the relative success of the varying models.

There are clearly a number of paid-content options ranging from a complete 'walled-garden' or models that work on a metered basis or pay per article. But there are several important factors that must be considered when assessing the paid-content debate.

Firstly, general national and international news has been commoditised and the market for it obscured by the BBC's significant online presence. Second, consumers will only pay for content they value. This can be for its journalistic enjoyment (favouring a particular columnist), its niche content (sports/financial/special interest) or its lack of substitutability. Third, the addictive popularity of smart phones and tablets may increase readers' propensity to pay for content that is delivered through an app. Consumers would therefore be paying for 'context' as well as content.

In summary, a true digital strategy will incorporate a range of revenue models suitable for the readership size and demographic.

## Note on the contributor

Lorna Tilbian is an executive director of Numis Corporation Plc and Head of its Media Sector. After a distinguished career as a top-ranked media analyst by Institutional Investor and Extel from 1987 to 2012, Lorna now heads the media banking franchise. Lorna acquired a stake in the newly launched Numis in 2001 after stints at Sheppards (1984-88), SG Warburg (Director, 1988-95) and WestLB Panmure (Executive Director, 1995-2001). Lorna appears in Campaign's A List 2017, currently sits on the Advisory Panel of Tech City UK's Future Fifty programme and has served as a Cabinet Ambassador (an Ambassador for Creative Britain) for the DCMS. Lorna is also a non-executive director of Jupiter UK Growth Investment Trust Plc and ProVen VCT Plc.

# 'Analogue pounds to digital pounds' – The digital alchemists of Horseferry Road

**Channel 4's overall income is growing fast on the back of new digital revenues. Does its success have any lessons for print, asks Richard Tait**

Does a case study about a successful commercial television company have any relevance in a book about the future of print journalism? It is a reasonable question and precisely the one the editors of this book asked themselves before including this chapter. You, the reader, will be the judge whether we have made the right decision, but the fact that it still seems a reasonable question to ask shows how far apart in some ways print and broadcast remain and how little they know (or understand) one another.

I say in some ways because in others convergence is already the reality of journalism in the UK and has been for some time. When a few years ago Cardiff Journalism School held a conference with the rather portentous title of 'Tomorrow's Journalists' we found that in the newsrooms the future had already arrived. Our recent alumni were using all the editorial and digital skills we had taught them to build careers which allowed them to move between roles and between media with an ease which made a mockery of the old, rigid demarcation lines which in the past had kept most journalists doing the same things for the same sorts of employers for much or even all of their working lives (Waldram 2010).

## If in doubt, blame the BBC

Those demarcation lines, however, still seem to exist at the top of media organisations. Mark Thompson, moving from Channel 4's Horseferry Road headquarters to the BBC and then on to the New York Times, is very much the exception – but the 'print' success story he describes elsewhere in this book owes much to his unique experience of leading two very different broadcasters with similar, though not identical, digital challenges to those now facing one of the world's great newspapers. In the UK, Ashley Highfield, going from running the BBC's Future Media and Technology operation to be chief executive of Johnston Press, is also still very much the exception rather than the rule.

Yet the more you look at those challenges – to both print and broadcast – the stranger the apparently mutual lack of interest in sharing solutions seems. Because the stories of the decline of print journalism and the tough times which commercial broadcast journalism have been through have so many similarities. When faced with the explosive growth of online, commercial television, like print, squandered its first mover advantage, investing too little and too late in online services and, again like print, has spent far too much time blaming the BBC's online operation for problems which were mainly of its own making (Tait 2013).

So if print and broadcast are facing the same problems, can they learn, even at this late stage, from one another's experience? Or put another way, given the scale of the crisis, why would they not want to learn *anything* which might help them? It is common ground that the central challenge is to turn, like a modern day alchemist, 'analogue' (or print) revenues into 'digital' revenues fast enough for the rise in the latter to compensate for any decline in the former and so avoid the cost-cutting which is hollowing out newspaper and broadcast journalism alike.

## Digital alchemy

One of the few organisations in the UK which has achieved this digital alchemy is Channel 4 Television. Channel 4 is publicly owned but commercially funded. It does not make its own programmes so it relies very heavily on advertising revenue. This should, in theory, make it even more vulnerable to digital competition than rival broadcasters which also have income from subscription and/or from their programme-making departments, or newspapers, which also have income from their cover price. And Channel 4's remit, laid down by Parliament, adds a further potential handicap – it has to appeal to precisely those hard-to-reach groups – particularly young people – who are shunning conventional media in alarming numbers. Its target audience is a potentially valuable one but notoriously tough to attract and retain (DCMS 2016: 86-87).

This apparent vulnerability was one of the reasons given by the government when it was revealed in September 2015 that it was examining whether Channel 4 would be better off privatised (Martinson 2015). However, when the Lords Select Committee on Communications (where, to declare an interest, I was the specialist adviser) investigated the case for privatisation in the spring and summer of 2016 a very different picture emerged. The committee concluded that Channel 4 was an under-reported media success story and it certainly did not need 'rescuing' by privatisation (House of Lords 2016). Channel 4 told the committee that on the central issue of revenues it was now 'broadly indifferent' whether viewers watched Channel 4 on their television sets or via its All4 digital service. Its growth of online revenues was 'dynamic and significant'. 'Put simply,' it told the committee, 'we are trading "analogue pounds" for "digital pounds"' (Channel 4 2016: 26).

**Surviving Brexit**

This claim was backed up by the forecasts of Enders Analysis who saw digital revenues doubling from £132m in 2014 to £269m in 2025. Even if Channel 4's traditional advertising revenues were to stay flat from 2016 (and Enders actually forecast a growth rate of 3.2 per cent a year), the increase in digital sales would boost Channel 4's revenues by at least £100m over the decade. Enders Analysis concluded that all the indicators pointed to a very sustainable current business model (Syfret 2015: 15). Claire Enders, the founder of Enders Analysis, underlined that point in her evidence to the committee – stressing that even if there was a Brexit-related drop in GDP and advertising income in the UK in 2017, the media business that would find it easiest to survive would be Channel 4 (Enders 2016: 119-120).

Certainly Channel 4 was showing no signs of vulnerability in September 2016 when it outbid the BBC for The Great British Bake Off. The secret of its financial success lies in getting closer to its audiences online. It was the first broadcaster to make all its commissioned content available online, launching its video on demand (VOD) service 4oD in 2006. In March 2015, it replaced 4oD with a more ambitious service – All4. This offers all its channels plus box sets, specially-tailored content and online services. To get the All4 service viewers have to register, giving Channel 4 really valuable data – demographic information as well as the ability to learn viewing preferences. Channel 4 has got more than 13.5m active registered users, including half of all 16 to 34-year-olds in the UK. Its enviable reach with valuable and hard-to-reach younger viewers is reflected in an average age for All4 users of 28 (Channel 4 2016: 26).

Channel 4 has been able to monetise this data in a number of ways to boost revenues on a scale many newspapers would envy. Its chief executive, David Abraham, started his career as a very successful advertising executive before going on to run first UKTV and now Channel 4. As a result of his experience, Channel 4 is in the forefront of new ways of tapping digital advertising revenues. Ernst & Young, who were commissioned by Channel 4 to report on market trends and their impact, found that registration was the foundation of its success:

> Channel 4 has also moved to obtain demographic data on on-demand registered users which significantly enhance ad premiums as advertisers can better target their audience. This development means that Channel 4 is able to monetise viewing to both linear television and to its VOD service (Ernst & Young 2016: 27).

Channel 4 was the first broadcaster in the UK to launch programmatic-buying on its digital services. This is an automated form of sales where advertisers use software and data to bid almost instantly for ad slots on the basis of what is the likely audience (Channel 4 2016: 26). Ernst & Young found that the speed of the automated process meant that adverts could be loaded in real time. The advantages of programmatic-buying included lower costs, improved ad effectiveness and more precise targeting. Although still at an early stage of development, it was already accounting for 15 per cent of Channel 4's digital advertising revenues and was forecast to double to 30 per cent by the end of 2016 (Ernst & Young 2016: 54-55).

## Channel 4 News for millenials

And the same focus on changing habits has resulted in big changes in the way Channel 4 News, produced by my old employer Independent Television News (ITN), approaches its digital audiences. ITN told the Lords committee that over the last two years the programme had revolutionised the way it approaches online content in order to reach the widest possible audience. 'The digital team has completely re-orientated its production approach to ensure that its material is accessible to millenials on all the platforms in which they are present, often consuming on mobile devices.'

Channel 4's editorial remit remained the same, but told in a different way. For example, stories were produced with captions and subtitles so they could be watched without sound on a mobile device. A very successful interactive project, Two Billion Miles, repurposed two years of Channel 4 News location reports on the migrant crisis to offer users a multiple-choice journey as a migrant across Europe. The overall result has been a spectacular increase in reach. In 2015, Channel 4 News videos had more than half a billion views on Facebook, with a trebling of Facebook likes to more than a million, with two thirds of the audience under 35 (ITN 2016: 173).

Channel 4 is not alone in successfully exploiting its knowledge of its registered users. Sky, with more than 12m digital subscribers, has long been a front-runner in knowing its audience and has now launched its own programmatic service AdSmart (Sky 2016). Just as at the launch of subscription television, when it bought into some of the key technology in areas such as conditional access, Sky has taken a stake in one of the leading US companies in the field of programmatic-marketing (Oakes 2016). And major print brands, like Time, are also now experimenting with programmatic-advertising in print as well as online (Sebastian 2015). Major newspaper brands like the Daily Mail are very aware of the potential of programmatic advertising, though as Guy Zitter, former managing director of the Mail, explains elsewhere in this book, there are still issues around how effective it can be in raising the maximum available revenue. Of course, television and print are different – though they are heading fast towards to the same digital space. The success of Channel 4 does not read directly across to the dilemmas facing the Guardian or the Western Mail. Nonetheless, Channel 4's experience does raise some interesting questions.

## Some lessons for the future?

First, has the passionate argument in the print media over the pros and cons of *subscription* obscured the potential value of *registration*, whether or not you decide to charge as well? As the Channel 4 case shows, knowing about your audience can be worth a lot of money if properly exploited. In the digital world, registration is the norm to access news and information on social media. Even the BBC, which has always been short-sightedly nervous of registration as a potential gateway to the dreaded (as it sees it) subscription, and is far behind its commercial rivals as a result, is moving to persuade licence fee payers to sign up for personalised services, announcing in September 2016 that access to iPlayer would be via registration and password from early 2017.

Channel 4's success in registering half the young people in Britain (and ITV are heading in the same direction with ITV Hub) seems potentially to put those print organisations that give their content away to anyone who uses a search engine, and consequently do not have as much detailed data about their readers and web users, at a disadvantage. They know less about their users' interests as well as less about what might attract advertisers, so they are also missing out on ways to use that data to fine tune and improve their editorial offering, whether in print or online. And their advertising revenues may be less well-targeted, more expensive to manage and probably smaller.

Second, as print brands move into the on demand digital space what they offer and they way they present it will have to change. Tailoring content, particularly video and graphics, for tablets and mobiles is not easy and no one can claim to have all the answers yet, but it is a fair bet that the more conventional newspaper online model (with video often hidden away at the bottom of the page) is not the one that will thrive in the long term. And getting it right means investment. Channel 4's success is also the reward for significant investment in its digital platform.

Third, the biggest reason Channel 4 is doing well is not its clever use of technology nor even being at the cutting-edge of the huge changes taking place in the digital advertising market, important though both of them are. Channel 4 is successful because it has something its audiences want – distinctive, high quality content. It has been fortunate that its not-for-profit model has partly protected it from the cost-cutting which has does such damage to many newspapers. But like many of the other case studies of success in this book – the New York Times, the Financial Times – it has invested to maintain editorial quality, despite facing some tough times.

## British journalism after Brexit

The next decade will be a huge challenge but might just also be an opportunity for British journalism. Whichever way you voted in the referendum, the realisation is sinking in that the UK is about to go through profound structural changes which could last a decade or more. The referendum campaign was a boom time for circulation and audiences as readers and viewers went back to the traditional media for information. The next few years could be the same – how will communities, industries, professions, institutions be affected by the challenges and opportunities Brexit will bring – at a local as well as national level?

There could be a real opportunity for print to re-establish in a digital form the link with its public which it once took for granted. But many of today's citizens expect a different, two-way relationship with their sources of news. They expect it on demand, and on all their devices as well as on paper. I do not know if a combination of investment in content and platforms, together with using registration (with or without subscription), programmatic-advertising and the other new commercial techniques will always have the desired effect. But, given Channel 4's experience, I cannot see too many circumstances in which they would make the current situation worse. This may be a real chance to secure a digital future for British journalism – but it could also, for some of the weaker players, be the last chance, given the unpredictable economic times ahead.

## Sources

Channel 4 (2016) Written evidence, House of Lords Select Committee on Communications, Inquiry: The Sustainability of Channel 4. Evidence Volume pp 21-43. Available online at http://www.parliament.uk/documents/lords-committees/communications/susainabilityofC4/SC4Evidence.pdf, accessed on 21 September 2016

DCMS (2016) Written evidence, House of Lords Select Committee on Communications, Inquiry: The Sustainability of Channel 4. Evidence Volume pp 86-90. Available online at http://www.parliament.uk/documents/lords-committees/communications/susainabilityofC4/SC4Evidence.pdf, accessed on 21 September 2016

Enders, Claire (2016) Enders Analysis – oral evidence, House of Lords Select Committee on Communications, Inquiry: the Sustainability of Channel 4. Evidence Volume pp 116-127. Available online at http://www.parliament.uk/documents/lords-committees/communications/susainabilityofC4/SC4Evidence.pdf, accessed on 21 September 2016

Ernst & Young (2016) The future of Channel 4 in a changing market environment, March. Available online at http://www.channel4.com/media/documents/press/news/Desktop/EY%20C4%20report%20FINAL%20160316.pdf, accessed on 19 September 2016

House of Lords (2016) A privatised future for Channel 4?, 11 July. Available online at http://www.publications.parliament.uk/pa/ld201617/ldselect/ldcomuni/17/1702.htm, accessed on 22 September 2016

ITN (2016) Written evidence, House of Lords Select Committee on Communications, Inquiry: the Sustainability of Channel 4. Evidence Volume pp 169-178. Available online at http://www.parliament.uk/documents/lords-committees/communications/susainabilityofC4/SC4Evidence.pdf, accessed on 20 September 2016

Martinson, Jane (2015) Government may privatise Channel 4, document reveals, Guardian, 24 September. Available online at https://www.theguardian.com/media/2015/sep/24/government-considering-channel-4-privatisation-document-slip-up-reveals, accessed on 19 September 2016

Oakes, Omar (2016) Sky invests $10m in programmatic ad tech specialist DataXu, Campaign, 25 January. Available online at http://www.campaignlive.co.uk/article/sky-invests-10m-programmatic-ad-tech-specialist-dataxu/1380656, accessed on 19 September 2016

Sebastian, Michael (2015) Well, this is different -- Time Inc. now selling print ads programmatically, Advertising Age, 10 February. Available online at http://adage.com/article/media/time-selling-print-ads-programmatically/297057/ accessed on 19 September 2016

Sky (2016) About Sky Adsmart. Available online at https://www.skyadsmart.co.uk, accessed on 18 September 2016

Syfret, Toby (2016) Channel 4: sustainability and privatisation, 18 December, London: Enders Analysis

Tait, Richard (2013) Self-inflicted wounds? The decline of local news in the UK, Mair, John, Keeble, Richard Lance and Fowler, Neil (eds) *What Do We Mean by Local?* Bury St Edmunds: Abramis pp 5-17

Waldram, Hannah (2010) Notes from Cardiff Tomorrow's Journalists Conference. Available online at https://hrwaldram.wordpress.com/2010/10/16/notes-from-cardiff-tomorrow's-journalists-conference-1-blogging-love-in-lobby-reform-local-gloom-and-blond-bombshells/#more-955, accessed on 22 September 2016

## Note on the contributor

Richard Tait is Professor of Journalism at the School of Journalism, Media and Cultural Studies, Cardiff University. From 2003 to 2012 he was Director of the school's Centre for Journalism. He worked on business magazines and then at the BBC where was editor of The Money Programme and Newsnight. He moved to Independent Television News (ITN) where he was editor of Channel 4 News from 1987 to 1995 and editor-in-chief from 1995 to 2002. He wrote a weekly column on media policy for the Creative Business section of the Financial Times from 2002 to 2004. He was a BBC governor and chair of the governors' programme complaints committee from 2004 to 2006, and a BBC trustee and chair of the trust's editorial standards committee from 2006 to 2010. He is a Fellow of the Society of Editors and the Royal Television Society and Treasurer of the International News Safety Institute.

# The UK national press

\* \* \*

# Self-inflicted wounds?

**Richard Tait**

Some years ago, my fellow editor Ray Snoddy came up with the brilliant image of the participants at the latest doom-laden media conference grimly tracking the predicted End-of-The-World-As-We-Know-It against their own planned retirement date to determine whether they cared or not. Britain's national newspapers – the most diverse and popular in any Western democracy – have faced so many near-death experiences over the last 20 years there is a danger of underestimating the scale of the current threat.

But this time could be different, unless the nationals learn from their mistakes – and those of others – and confront what could be a perfect storm of digital competition and economic slowdown. This section looks at how some of the best known titles in the UK are dealing with it as the competitive pressures mount and the time to find solutions is now.

Tor Clark has the distinction of having edited, among other papers, the country's oldest one – the Rutland and Stamford Mercury. These days he teaches journalism at De Montfort University and researches the history of the press. From his perspective, the 1980s were really 'the last of the good times' for the nationals. 'By the end of the 1990s the writing was on the wall, or rather the screen, and news consumption was shifting inexorably from paper to digital formats.' And now, the situation is as bad as it has ever been. He writes the end of The Independent as a printed newspaper in March 2016 'was the first major closure of a national newspaper for 20 years, but it was not thought by anyone to be the last.'

The problem is equally acute in all sections of the nationals. Paul Connew, after a career at some of the best selling newspapers in the UK – editor of the

Sunday Mirror, deputy editor of the News of the World – thinks 'Britain's printed press faces a fearful battle for survival' and he looks with trepidation to the US where 'the road map is already littered with the corpses of once powerful, highly profitable and seemingly impregnable titles.' His forecast is that within a decade four or five of the current nationals will no longer be around or online only.

One stable of papers he does predict will survive is the Mail group, with its strong editorial product and early and substantial investment in freely available online news. Guy Zitter spent 25 years at the top of the Daily Mail's commercial management as advertising director and then managing director. He believes newspapers that continue to adapt can have a good future. Despite the fall in sales, many titles are still making good profits. They will need new approaches to media buying and more direct contact with advertisers, and a business philosophy that starts from the proposition that 'newspapers need to run to where the ball is going not where the ball is.' But, he argues, there is plenty of life left in the often much-maligned older newspaper readers – they still have 79 per cent of the country's savings wealth and 70 per cent of its incomes.

Meanwhile, the other early heavy investor in free online news – The Guardian – seems to be facing something of an existential crisis. Peter Cole was deputy editor and news editor of The Guardian before becoming professor of journalism at Sheffield University. He unpicks the events of a truly terrible year for the newspaper. In May 2015 its much-respected editor Alan Rusbridger handed over control with, as he put it, 'a billion pounds in the bank' (in the hands of The Guardian's owner, the Scott Trust).

Within a year huge and unsustainable losses had forced big cuts in staffing and the plan for Rusbridger to become chair of the Scott Trust had been torpedoed by the new management. Cole makes clear The Guardian still has plenty to do to stabilise its position and he is nervous about the current strategy of appealing to readers to support The Guardian by paying for different levels of membership, in a hierarchy peaking at £599 a year for access to 'exclusive behind the scenes functions.' He concludes: 'It looks like the tough times ahead for news journalism will be testing for purists.'

The Guardian does not seem to have benefited much from the demise of its print rival the Independent, now online only. Paul Lashmar, a distinguished investigative journalist for print and broadcast, now leading the journalism team at Sussex University, worked on the Independent and chronicles its ups and downs from its idealistic launch in 1986 as a quality paper free from proprietorial interference. Idealism and commercial were always in tension, however, and he describes what he saw in its later years as a sad decline: 'Through the early 2000s the paper lost its way and lacked a soul. The Independent needed passion, flair, authority and vision if it was to grow but it felt tired'.

Donald Macintyre worked for the Independent for more than 25 years in many of the top jobs – political editor, labour editor, chief political commentator, and Jerusalem correspondent. He has more sympathy for the often-embattled editors who fought to retain the Independent's values through numerous changes of ownership. He accepts that mistakes were made, such as launching the Independent on Sunday, but retains respect for the many fine journalists who found a home on the Indy. And as a great newspaperman himself he still believes in the nationals, quoting Andrew Marr, one of his many editors, saying 'if you invented something light that could carry 150,000 words, slip into a rucksack, didn't need power and called it a newspaper, wouldn't everyone say "how brilliant"?'

Vanessa Clifford, too, believes that newspapers can be brilliant. As the interim chief executive of Newsworks, the industry's marketing arm, she thinks the tide is turning. In 2012, she writes, 'the popular narrative was that newspapers were dead'. In a multi-platform world she is now promoting newsbrands (digital and print) rather than print alone. And she is confident she has a good story to tell – newsbrands reach 47m people a month – that's 91 per cent of the population. And Newsworks research shows campaigns that use print have greater impact than those which rely on digital alone.

However, over the last three decades the newspapers have lost a huge amount of ground (and revenue) to the new digital platforms. Torin Douglas was for 24 years the BBC's media correspondent. He casts an expert eye over where the advertising has gone, believing that, although plenty of mistakes were made, 'there is little that publishers could have done to stop Google and Facebook, which are in a different business and, indeed, league.' If quality journalism, whether print or digital, is to survive, he argues, the advertisers must recognise that it is in their long-term commercial interests to support it as well as spending the bulk of their budgets on search engines and social media.

But there is support for the beleaguered nationals from their retailers – the 55,000 or so shops which sell papers across the country. Brian Murphy, head of news for the National Federation of Retail Newsagents (NFRN) sees every incentive for the newsagents to keep space on their shelves for the nationals – buying a paper remains 'a significant driver of footfall' for the retailers. And he thinks the nationals will prove more resilient than the pessimists predict – 'ownership of many news brands is not driven by profits – history has taught us that ego alone can be a very strategic supporter of newspapers.'

If he is right, Tim Crook, Professor of Media and Communications at Goldsmiths, will for one be delighted. He sees one of the unwelcome potential consequences of the disappearance of print the threat to liberty if newspaper records are replaced by digital ones. He quotes George Orwell's prescient vision in 1984 of a world where the state could destroy all inconvenient or embarrassing information: 'day by day and almost minute by minute the past was brought up to date.' Tracking and destroying every copy of a newspaper is a much more daunting challenge than wiping or altering the digital record.

Some of the nationals' problems may well be self-inflicted wounds – managerial or editorial misjudgements or a combination of both. But what comes across strongly from all these chapters is a passionate belief that newspapers still matter and the commitment of editors, journalists, managers, marketers and retailers to keep the show on the road despite the problems and challenges.

The nationals may not all win their fight for survival (though I would not rule it out), but if so it won't be for lack of effort. Whatever your own choice of paper and, indeed, whatever your reservations about the ones you can't stand, British journalism, public life and democracy are all the stronger for having the biggest possible range of voices in print. Long may they all survive.

# The ups and downs of British national newspapers over 300 years

**The UK population has a long and proud history consuming print journalism, especially newspapers, which extends back 300 years. If print journalism is dying, as many chapters in this book contend, the decline is rapid in the context of its history. But an historical perspective is necessary to try to understand the significance and rapidity of this decline, argues Tor Clark**

More than seven million copies of the Daily Mirror covering the Queen's coronation in 1953 are thought to have been sold, a weekday record for a UK national newspaper set by what was then Britain's biggest-selling daily newspaper (Hagerty 2003; Engel 1996; Williams 1998). At the same time, every Sunday the News of the World sold more than eight million copies, when many families were in the habit of buying and reading more than one paper that day. These were astonishingly high newspaper sales in a country with a population of around 50 million.

Huge sales were not confined to these two titles. Lord Beaverbrook encouraged journalism which pushed the sales of his Daily Express to more than four million a day as it became the voice of the British middle class in the middle of the 20th century. Many other papers shifted more than a million copies every weekday (Daily Herald, Daily Mail etc) and even more on Sundays (Sunday Express, Sunday People etc).

The consumption of printed national newspapers by such a relatively small population was almost a national obsession in those heady days and looking back on them now they can be seen as a high water mark of the impact and influence of UK journalism.

## In the beginning
Before railways, of course, all newspapers were local. Many actually carried national and international news, rather than local news, though their advertising columns were local. Annual consumption of newspapers rose from 7.3m in 1750 to 12.6m in 1775. The first Sunday paper appeared in 1780 (Williams 1998: 49).

The earliest papers which could claim to be 'national' were in London, where they circulated among the informed or influential, allowing for relatively swift communication at a time of generally very slow communication between the capital and the provinces. The Times, the long-established paper of the Establishment, launched as the Daily Universal Register, in 1785, building a London base from which it was soon to grow.

## Development in the 19th century

The coming of the railways and the growth in interest in newspapers, particularly fuelled among the working classes by the radical press which emerged to challenge social iniquities in the early 19th century, transformed UK newspaper consumption and laid the foundations for the huge growth which would begin at the end of that century.

At the same time social reforms, especially Forster's 1870 Education Act, sparked a surge in literacy, from very low levels at the start of the 1800s, to virtually full literacy by 1900. All these factors combined to create a population which was used to newspapers, which wanted newspapers and which was able to read newspapers.

It has been estimated by 1850 daily newspaper sales were around 60,000, while Sunday papers achieved 275,000 (Williams 1998: 49). Press taxation, especially the Stamp Act, held back rapid expansion until its removal in 1855, after which the Daily Telegraph became the first paper to really expand, achieving sales of 300,000 per day by 1890. Indeed, the second half of the 19th century was the period during which the firm foundations were laid on which the huge growth of the industry would be built in the 20th century.

## The Northcliffe Revolution

The arrival of Alfred Harmsworth, Lord Northcliffe after 1905, can be seen as the catalyst of newspaper expansion. Technological changes had played their part in making it easier to design, produce and print newspapers, but Northcliffe was a newspaper genius, getting readers hooked, and many of his innovations became vital in the UK national press achieving huge audiences in the following century.

1896 was an important year in the rapid development of the UK press. In that year Sunday newspaper Lloyd's Weekly is thought to have become the first newspaper to sell a million copies. Also in 1896, after establishing his winning formula for growing readership in magazines, Harmsworth launched the Daily Mail, incorporating styles and techniques from American journalism, especially a short, snappy writing style. Within four years that paper had notched up a circulation of almost a million.

In 1903, Harmsworth's Daily Mirror first appeared, initially pitched unsuccessfully at women. But not being put off by early failure, he relaunched it as an illustrated paper and it became the first daily paper to achieve sales of a million by 1911. Into this mix was thrown the initially unsuccessful Daily

Express in 1900 and the left-leaning Daily Herald in 1912, both of which would become multi-million sellers within a few years.

Many successful papers were run by men who became known as the Press Barons after receiving peerages. Northcliffe and his brother Harold, later Lord Rothermere, ran The Times, Daily Mail and Daly Mirror. Max Aitken, Lord Beaverbrook, bought up the struggling Daily Express and turned it into a multi-million-selling middle class bible between the wars. Julius Elias, Lord Southwood, ran the Daily Herald and Sunday People. The Berry brothers from South Wales, later Lords Camrose and Kemsley, began as magazine owners but expanded into local and national newspapers, later owning the Daily Telegraph and Sunday Times.

Northcliffe led the way and sowed the seeds of a mass national press before the First World War, but the competition intensified in the 1920s and 30s, leaving the sector damaged but dominant.

## Press Barons battle it out between the wars

Between 1921 and 1936, 30 national newspapers closed, but the leading handful of those which survived established huge mass circulations during this time, and reading habits which would not start to break down until the 1980s (Williams 1998: 61).

Though Northcliffe died in 1922, his brother Rothermere remained in control of much of the family's empire. Beaverbrook established himself as a hugely important media mogul. Lord Southwood, chairman of Odhams Press and owner of the sensationalist People, which achieved sales of 2m per week, acquired a half-interest in the Daily Herald and during the 1930s used circulation-building gimmicks to boost sales, selling door-to-door and offering readers crockery sets, the Encylopaedia Britannica, preferential subscription rates and other such incentives. Other publishers were forced to use similar tactics and so by the mid-1930s sales had reached huge levels.

Sales of newspapers doubled in the inter-war years with the Mail, Express and Herald accounting for just under half the total. The Herald and Express circulations rose to over two million per day and the Mail's high point was 1.85m in 1930.

## Post-war success

The rationing of newsprint during the Second World War might, at first glance be seen as bad for the national press, but it actually increased their circulations and their advertising revenue. If only a finite space was available for advertising, that advertising space could be sold at a premium to the advertisers which wanted it, especially as they had nowhere else to go when all the news providers were affected by the same paper rationing.

If newspapers were only a limited size, but packed with the serious and important news of global warfare, many readers regularly consumed multiple newspapers daily. The Mirror and Express emerged from the conflict as the dominant papers for the working and middle classes respectively, their successes driven by ambitious and talented owners (particularly in the Express's case), executives and journalists, including many of the now-legendary figures of Fleet Street.

The Mirror's normal sales reached towards five million daily, not reaching their high point until 1967, while the Express's sales once established at four million per day remained at that point until after Beaverbrook's death in 1964. Indeed, both papers retained huge mass circulations until the 1980s. On Sundays, the News of the World became the biggest-selling newspaper in the country, but had serious mass-selling rivals, especially the Sunday People and Sunday Express.

## The last of the press barons

In 1960, the Mirror Group bought the multi-million selling Herald and decided, despite its large circulation, to change it into the Sun, a paper for the middle classes, as it did not want another daily paper in its own stable challenging its flagship title. That noble experiment, led by the Mirror's innovative and influential guiding hand Hugh Cudlipp, did not succeed, but foretold later innovations. But its failure let in the most influential press baron of the later 20th century into the market, whose influence kept newspapers and interesting, influential and commercially successful for the rest of the century.

Australian newspaper tycoon Rupert Murdoch entered the UK newspaper market in 1968, buying the country's biggest-selling paper, the News of the World, but it was with his next purchase, the Sun, for £1m from the Mirror Group the next year that he was to make his biggest and lasting impact on UK newspapers.

Murdoch, interestingly, had huge UK newspaper heritage in his background, through his father's friendship with Northcliffe and, though Northcliffe died a decade before Murdoch was born, the two of them will probably go down as the two most important press barons in British history, sharing many similarities.

Like Northcliffe a century earlier, Murdoch set about changing the style of newspapers, by adapting the short, snappy style of the Daily Mirror into a sexually-laden tone which proved irresistible to UK readers. Within eight years of taking over the paper, in 1977 it had outstripped the sales of the formerly dominant Mirror, and risen to regular daily sales of four million, under the editorship of Kelvin Mackenzie in the 1980s, not uncontroversially at times.

Indeed, such was the impact of the Sun that in the late 70s the Express group even launched into the crowded red-top sector with its own downmarket tabloid Daily Star, which though never as successful at the Sun or the Daily Mail, captured a small but loyal audience and remained in publication.

The 1970s also saw Vere, third Viscount Rothermere, and his editor David English, cleverly reposition the Daily Mail to challenge effectively the domination of the mid-market by the Daily Express, which went through several ownership changes as its readership declined from the glory days under Beaverbrook.

To some extent this period is about the upstart Sun and Mail replacing the more tired Mirror and Express as market leaders in the red-top and mid-market sectors, and in so doing, giving the whole industry a shot in the arm.

## 1980s as end of an era
It did not necessarily seem it at the time, but the 1980s can now be viewed at the last of the good times for the national press. Numerous newspaper launches in that decade suggested the industry was strong. The revolution in printing processes and technologies inspired by Eddy Shah at Warrington and Rupert Murdoch at Wapping cut costs and allowed innovation, especially more colour and greater pagination.

Even more importantly, this breaking of the power of the print unions allowed exciting, good-looking entrants into the sector. Shah launched the Today newspaper and former Telegraph journalists launched the Independent and Independent on Sunday, all of which lasted a reasonable period. Shorter-lived launches following the relaxation of printing processes included the Sunday Correspondent and later, the leftist News on Sunday.

And so it was that during the 1980s, readers could choose between five quality broadsheet newspapers, three mid-market tabloids and three red-top tabloids. It seemed the sector was in rude health and, with the power of the print unions broken, all titles moved away from Fleet Street, opened new printing plants and expanded and improved their publications.

## Decline since the 1990s
Going into the 1990s, national newspapers were confident and dominant. The Sun infamously even claimed its influence had swayed the result of the 1992 general election with its headline 'It was The Sun wot won it!'

But the 80s had also seen a huge change in other news sectors, with an expansion in television especially. Whereas going into the 80s, there had effectively been two channels with three small news broadcasts each, by the end of the decade there was a host of terrestrial channels as well as the arrival of satellite and cable television, all offering regular and accessible news. Radio had beaten papers for immediacy as far back as the Second World War, but papers had survived and thrived, still driving the news agenda. But TV had come on in leaps and bounds through the 80s and was a much easier way of accessing news than reading newsprint.

Circulation was sliding before the arrival of free news on internet platforms, but this development hastened the decline of hard copy sales of national newspapers. At the same time younger readers got into the habit of accessing news free-of-charge on digital devices. By the end of the 1990s the writing was on the wall, or rather the screen, and news consumption was shifting inexorably from paper to digital formats.

## Will UK national newspapers survive?

In the 21st century, the decline of national newspaper circulations has mostly gathered pace because of direct competition of free, easily accessible digital news, often provided by the same organisations, especially The Guardian and MailOnline, both of which have become huge globally-significant news brands.

In March 2016, six months before its 30th anniversary, one of the UK's most acclaimed newspapers, The Independent, closed its printed product. The paper had been born in the heady post-Wapping days of the 1980s but could not survive on circulations reportedly around 50,000 per day. It was the first major closure of a national newspaper for 20 years, but it was not thought by anyone to be the last.

Generalist national newspapers, which sold multi-millions of copies only 20 years earlier, were in a steep, and most would argue, terminal decline (excluding the Financial Times, which as a specialist publication, quickly understood the value of its specialist content and harnessed the web to market it). They were still widely read. They were still influential. They still had some of the best journalists and newsrooms. They still broke most of the national news stories. But they were just not being bought in as large a quantity as they had been.

## National newspaper circulation decline since 1950

A fascinating report by Communications Management Inc in 2010 presents a stark picture of the decline of national newspaper consumption in the UK, USA and Canada. Referring to the UK, the report states:

> In 1950, the average daily total paid circulation for British national daily newspapers was about 21m (equivalent to almost 150 per cent of households); the total paid circulation for British Sunday newspapers was about 31m (equivalent to more than 200 per cent of households). By 2010, the average daily total paid circulation for British national daily newspapers was about 10.1 million (equivalent to 39.9 per cent of households); the total paid circulation for British national Sunday newspapers was about 9.9 million (equivalent to 39.0 per cent of households).

These statistics show a loss of half the daily and two-thirds of national Sunday newspaper circulations in 60 years, a very rapid decline, which has not slowed since. In July 2016, though some national newspapers were actually experiencing small gains in circulation, the overall trends, especially over a significant historical period, were dramatically down.

The Sun had declined to a circulation of 1.7m, from a high of 4m in the 1980s. The Daily Mail, regularly exceeding 2m as recently as a decade ago, had shrunk to 1.5m sales per day. The two post-war giants have hit particularly hard times. The Daily Mirror has declined to 773,000 per day and the Daily Express to 422,000, a tenth of its regular Beaverbrook era sale. Express red top stablemate the Daily Star, only launched in 1978, has overtaken its more prestigious rival, now selling 516,000 per day.

In the quality market, the Daily Telegraph, the last broadsheet daily to sell a million copies, is down to 488,000, The Times sells a respectable 450,000 and the Independent's upstart former stablemate the tabloid-sized The i is doing quite well since its sale to regional publisher Johnston Press, selling 297,000. International internet journalism pioneer the Guardian has seen its daily hard copy sale decline to just 166,000, even without competition from the Independent. Finally, the Financial Times, which has made more of a success out of the digital world, still sells 194,000 pink papers every day.

Sunday newspapers tell a similar story with the Sun on Sunday, the replacement for the News of the World, which closed in 2011, selling 1.5m per week and another recent arrival, the Mail on Sunday, which only launched in the early 1980s, selling 1.4m. These are respectable circulation figures, but cannot compare with the eight million the News of the World sold every Sunday, 60 years previously.

UK daily and Sunday newspapers were remarkably successful after a slow start, but that success has now become a rapid decline, a decline the industry has been trying for a decade to understand and address. The future is uncertain. However easy it might be for the head to acknowledge this decline, the heart can't help but mourn its consequences, the loss of a vital component of the nation's culture, lifestyle, entertainment, politics and even self-perception if it becomes terminal.

## Sources

Engel, M. (1996) Tickle the Public: One Hundred Years of the Popular Press, London: Gollanz & Prentice-Hall.

Greenslade, R. (2003) Press Gang: How Newspapers Make Profits from Propaganda, London: Macmillan.

Hagerty, B. (2003) Read All About It! 100 Sensational Years of the Daily Mirror, Lydney: First Star.

Williams, K. (1998) Get Me a Murder a Day! London: Arnold.

## Note on the contributor

Tor Clark is Principal Lecturer in Journalism at De Montfort University, Leicester, UK, where, among other areas, he lectures on the history of journalism. He was a journalist in the UK regional press from 1988 until 2004, including editing Britain's oldest newspaper, the Rutland & Stamford Mercury. He is a regular commentator on politics and media issues on BBC radio and has written about various aspects of politics and history for Total Politics magazine. He is co-editor of this book.

# Don't switch off the life support... yet

As a columnist for **The Drum**, the international media and marketing industry website, and a regular broadcaster on media issues, Paul Connew has long argued the future of news is digital. But, as a former editor of the Sunday Mirror, deputy editor of the Daily Mirror and a US Bureau Chief, Connew confesses he's also still 'addicted' to reading newspapers in print as well as online, an addiction, or nostalgic passion, which has led to some revealing generation gap breakfast table debates with a teenage son that feeds into his vision of things to come

Is print dying? A no-brainer question... Ultimately, the answer is YES. But print newspapers, like most living, breathing entities are fighting to survive and the moment of death is unpredictable. Maybe a better analogy is to view Britain's national and local newspaper industry as a patient in intensive care, on life support, but with earnest commercial research technicians locked in the search for a cure while uber-enthusiastic high priests of the digital church hover outside the door, preparing to pronounce the last rites.

Their day will come, but how soon is another question, one that has already proved the more prematurely damning prophets of the digital age wrong. Optimists argue the death of newspapers was also predicted with the emergence of the mass TV age. Earlier still, some forecast the first crackles of radio waves heralded their demise.

But this time the pessimists have a stronger case in arguing the impact of Google, Facebook, Twitter, YouTube, BuzzFeed, Vice, BBC Online, Apple's phone and ipad, Quartz, Snapchat, Instagram et al, pose a vastly greater existential threat to the future of print newspapers as UK readers have devoured, loved (or loathed) them for generations.

**Lessons from America?**
If Britain's printed press faces a fearful fight for survival, the US road map is already littered with the corpses of once powerful, highly profitable and seemingly impregnable titles. Big metro titles like the Rocky Mountain News and

the multi-award winning Seattle Post Intelligencer have vanished. The once mighty Tribune company went into bankruptcy and even the great Washington Post of Watergate fame had to be 'rescued' by Amazon's Jeff Bezos. Apart from the $250m small change Bezos paid to acquire the Post, he's pumped tens of millions more into the search for a sustainable business model, invested heavily in digital expansion and last year overtook arch-rival the New York Times in unique website visitor traffic.

Others, such as the Philadelphia Inquirer, survived only by converting to tax-exempt, non-profit status (a model advocated by some UK and European media academics).

Just 20 years ago the New York Times entered the Internet Age with a website, declaring: 'The Times is hoping to become a primary information provider in the computer age and to cut costs for newsprint, delivery and labor.' It turned out to be a rocky road. But some consolation emerged in 2015 when the Times' paywall policy saw revenue from its paywall surpass revenue from digital advertising for the first time.

It's still hard to argue with US media academic Clay Shirky's words of a few years ago: 'There is no general model for newspapers to replace the one the internet just broke... Even the revolutionaries can't predict what will happen.'

The paywall experiment in the US is proving a mixed bag and no guarantee against going to the wall. US research suggests 90 per cent of print journalism revenue still stems from display advertising. Even without the growing challenge of ad-blockers, news outlets can't jack up the rate for online ads because a large majority of online readers ignore them anyway. It's also hard to escape the stark statistic from the renowned Pew Center in Washington DC and the Newspaper Association of America, that US print ad revenues crashed from $44.9bn in 2003 to just $16.4bn in 2014, with little sign of revival. Indeed, the Pew Center branded 2015 'the worst year for newspapers since The Great Depression', along with the revelation 65 per cent of America's $60bn annual digital advertising spend now goes to just five techno giants - Google, Facebook, Yahoo, Microsoft and Twitter, with 'legacy news' receiving a paltry slice of this digital bonanza. Distinguished media academic Jeffrey Cole, director of USC's Digital Future Center, predicts only four major dailies, the New York Times, USA Today, the Washington Post and Murdoch's Wall Street Journal, will survive in print.

## UK and US: Mirror images or not?

It's often said where America leads Britain is bound to follow. In newspaper industry culture, there are many similarities, but also crucial differences. For starters, the cut-throat, competitive world immortalised in Hecht and MacArthur's classic newspaper comedy The Front Page survived far longer in Fleet Street. Our appetite for robust newspapers, broadsheet or tabloid, national or local, has proved stronger, both before and since the internet revolution. But undeniably, the pattern of decline is the same, albeit at a slower pace this side of the Atlantic.

The Reuters Institute's 2016 Digital News Report strikes a similar ominous tone to The Pew Center. Few of Britain's publishing execs would argue with the opening sentence of the Reuters Report's UK section: 'Over the last year the newspaper sector has been hit hard by a sharp fall in print advertising, by the growth of ad-blockers and by problems of monetising content on mobile devices.'

Reuters reports The Guardian's losses mounting to almost £50m a year with plans to cut 20 per cent of its cost base, and the sobering statistic that while Mail Online might be the world's most visited English language website, it missed revenue targets by £7m and remains loss-making.

Mail Online's digital advertising growth has reached an impressive £44m, but has to be set against the Mail's print advertising figure of £80m. Predictions Mail Online (with 800 journalists on board) would soon produce ad revenues to match those of the print 'mothership' now more resemble a distant digital star. In May, DMGT even had to issue a warning to investors after its newspaper division reported a 29 per cent fall in profits, triggering a 13 per cent nosedive in the share price. The profit slump was largely the result of a six-month 13 per cent decline in print ad revenues at the Daily Mail, Mail on Sunday and Metro. With circulation figures inevitably declining too, good reason to fear worse is on the horizon.

On September 29, 2016, DMGT announced they were increasing cost cutting plans from £15m to £50m with 400 jobs to be cut across the group. The next day Trinity Mirror confirmed it is targeting a further £20m in cuts. It spectacularly symbolised the scale of the crisis confronting the industry.

Print advertising in the UK fell by £112m in 2015 alone, according to Enders Analysis. That's the equivalent of half Fleet Street's profits, or the total wage bills of the Times, Sunday Times and Daily Telegraph combined. Cue even more swingeing job cuts.

Enders Analysis chief executive Douglas McCabe told Media Guardian in May 2016: 'Print advertising is going through a structural shift, a hugely significant shift… and there doesn't seem to be an awful lot sales teams can do about it.' Likewise John Gapper's observation in the Financial Times that 'Fleet Street is following Britain's regional papers and US metropolitan ones in being hollowed out.'

Even the FT has warned staff of 'daunting trading conditions in 2016', reports Gapper, despite its £844m sale last year to Japan's largest media company Nikkei. However, Reuters cites the FT as an example of one title where 'fortunes are looking up' via the 'paid content route', with its new access model based on paid online trials producing an eight per cent growth to 780,000 paying subscribers, of whom 566,000 subscribe to a digital platform. Reuters also focuses on The Times' considerable achievement in returning to profit for the first time since 2002 (£21m in the year to June 2015), and the paper's paywall is also proving a relative success with around 150,000 digital subscribers.

## Rupert and the paywall

Set against The Times' success, Rupert Murdoch's oft-declared pledge that the paywall represented the future at both ends of the market place proved wrong. The Sun's paywall strategy had to be abandoned after fewer than 200,000 people signed up. In principle I agree with Murdoch's belief news isn't a giveaway commodity. In practice, popular paper readers clearly expect their online news for free and loyalty is an old habit that now dies all too easily.

How much Rebekah Brooks' restoration as CEO and ex-Sun editor David Dinsmore's appointment as COO served to change Murdoch's mind is a source of much speculation beyond the new Little Shard HQ of News UK. Sun editor-in-chief Tony Gallagher gave a taste of the future when he told a March 2016 London media conference the title would become a 'holiday operator and betting company as well as a newspaper.' And Rebekah Brooks has been particularly vocal in talking up the new 'Sun Bets' partnership with Australian bookmaker Tabcorp, a strategy based on statistics suggesting the UK has 14m punters, 55 per cent of whom frequently read the paper.

But one of the greatest challenges facing tabloid papers moving online is so much of social media, including Facebook, is quintessentially tabloid already. Another is the inevitable future increase in 'sponsored content' raises the issue of how to effectively ring-fence editorial independence. Even Sky, in which Murdoch's 21st Century Fox is the dominant shareholder, has switched millions of pounds worth of its advertising budget from print (including Murdoch titles) to websites like Facebook. In the words of Enders Analysis' McCabe, it represents 'a seismic shift away from print media'.

## Births, deaths and mergers

'The industry needs to make a clear admission the historic model for newspapers is bust. But many in the industry are in denial.' So, another of my old bosses David Montgomery told the Financial Times in February. Reviled by many journos as a 'costcutter general' when he headed the Mirror Group, 'Monty' was also an early reader of the internet's economic impact and in October 2015 he succeeded in selling his Local World group of provincial titles to Trinity Mirror for £220million. The deal cemented Trinity Mirror's position as the UK's biggest regional newspaper publisher, despite a continuing programme of closures and cutbacks.

On the positive side, at least in the short-term, it helped TM report a 42 per cent rise in pre-tax profits for the first half of 2016, to £66.9m, up from £47m. It also helped jack up revenues across Trinity by 30 per cent year-on-year to £374.7m. But analysts were quick to flag up the Local World acquisition merely masked the continuing decline in its core business, exemplified by plans to make further savings of £15m this year, with yet another round of journalistic job culling on the agenda.

Little wonder, perhaps, Trinity Mirror's ill-fated decision to launch a new national daily, the New Day, in the climate provoked scepticism among many journalists and media commentators. It gave me no pleasure to predict in my column in The Drum that New Day was 'a bold gamble doomed to failure', a failure made all the more inevitable by a curious magazine formula with no website, a gender-specific promotional strategy which almost 'disowned' a male audience, an inadequate launch budget and a cack-handed cover price hike policy, plus, a mission statement billing itself as 'the paper for people who don't read newspapers'. And so it proved!

If things are tricky at Trinity, they are decidedly worse at arch regional rival Johnston Press, where closing titles, axing journalists and a share-price crash saw its capitalisation sink to little more than £11m, with persistent City rumours chief executive Ashley Highfield, an ex-BBC digital big cheese, is planning to buy back some of the company's hefty debt pile at a steep discount ahead of a £220m bond repayment due in 2019.

One bright spot came with JP's £24m purchase of the i, the Independent's successful spin-off which outgrew its parent and proved there can still be a market for a modern, bite-sized, paid-for print title appealing to a largely youthful, well-educated audience. I wasn't alone in fearing for the i's future under Johnston, but the title hasn't just survived but thrived with circulation hitting record levels (320,000).

Elsewhere the CN Group took a high-risk gamble with in June 2016, with the new newspaper entitled 24, billed as 'the North's National' with a 40p cover price and an ambitious circulation area ranging from Preston to Lockerbie and Hexham to Workington. The north's national went south in less than six weeks, three weeks less than the New Day.

Bucking the trend was the New European, regional publisher Archant's pop-up newspaper experiment in the wake of the EU Referendum and aimed at the 48 per cent of Remain voters. Originally given a four-week lifespan, the niche weekly sold better than anticipated, even at £2 and has been given a life extension, makes a modest profit and has doubtless given other publishers food for thought on the potential of the pop-up concept.

## Who can survive the cliff fall?

'It's time to recognise the whole UK newspaper industry is heading for a cliff fall, that tipping point when there is no hope of a reversal of fortune.' The words of City University professor and former Mirror editor, Roy Greenslade in his Media Guardian blog in May 2016. Like Roy, I've long been resigned to the future being digital, although we've begged to differ on how soon that day will come, and I've been the more optimistic. A media student recently asked me how many national titles I expected to still be around in ten years' time. Tough question. My best guess response: The Mail titles, yes; The Times and The Sun too (but that could depend on Rupert still being around); the Mirror, hopefully; the Telegraph, only possibly (but probably not under the Barclays' stewardship).

I doubt the Express stable will be around, and The Guardian will have joined The Independent in an online-only form.

The regional and local paper landscape will continue to contract heavily and I tend to agree with another Greenslade contention, that cutbacks in this sector all too often produce 'an end result that looks like a paper, but the content lacks any real value. It's not journalism. It's pointless material without any public benefit'. Maybe less a tipping point more a 'perfect storm' when falling circulation and advertising figures and unsustainable print, transport and marketing costs collide. But can countless job cuts and remote subbing hubs prove anything but self-destructive?

Wearing my PR consultant hat, I've ceased to be amazed how these days you can send out a press release, complete with headline, and it appears verbatim, headline and all, across a string of local papers. In a slightly anarchic, experimental moment, I once even included a couple of spelling errors in a headline and the opening paragraph. Yes, you've guessed, at least five titles failed to spot the deliberate mistake! Proof, perhaps, of Nick Davies's scenario a few years ago in his book Flat Earth News where he warned of 'churnalism' and 'PR-generated oven-ready copy'.

## The Generation Game

'Dad, you've already read the news online, so why are you sitting there reading out-of-date, dead tree newspapers?' A breakfast table question from my 16 year-old son, who's genuinely interested in news as well as ecology, but never picks up a newspaper and consumes his newsfeed via a variety of hand-held, cyber sources. The answer, Son, is there is still something special, sentimental and tactile about flicking through those pages over the muesli and coffee, taking it, rather than the smartphone, to the loo to read, and even on the commuter train into London, if I do admittedly update constantly on my phone. The look of bemusement and plain 'sad dad' pity on his face spoke for a generation.

Even before the digital revolution, the arrival of the mobile phone and the Twittersphere, newspapers were struggling to pin down the elusive butterfly of young readers. A snapshot of the Reuters UK study exposes how much bigger the challenge now is as the digital revolution unfolds at a breathtaking pace. Just one example: 28 per cent of 18-24 year olds now list social media as their main source of news, outreaching TV for the first time and far outstripping newspapers. But only around ten per cent in the English-speaking world support the notion of paying for online news, according to Reuters and other research studies. Whether or not that is reversible constitutes a huge challenge for news publishers in search of a digital future.

Then there are figures suggesting 50 per cent of 18-24 year olds are quite content to have their 'tailored' newsfeed to their apps decided by an algorithm rather than a human editor - even a digital convert like me struggles to get his head round that one. First the robot news editor/copytaster, then the robot reporter? Cue mirth over August's story of how Facebook fired its human trending team in favour of algorithm-only and promptly pumped out one bogus, libellous celebrity story and a porn video stunt about a man masturbating with a McDonald's chicken sandwich!

But September 9th 2016 marked a far more serious and sinister show of Facebook's power, with its run-in with Norway's biggest newspaper and that nation's prime minister over the censoring, whether by alogorithm or diktat, of the world-famous, iconic Vietnam war napalm girl photo. It's a view of Zuckerberg's power chillingly illustrated by the algorithm-driven 'fake story' furore surrounding Facebook and the US presidential election and how much that was a factor in Donald Trump's victory. Although, amid a global firestorm of protest and derision, Facebook eventually backed down, it underscored the digital behemoth's dominant position in the 21st century media landscape. It also, for me, finally put paid to Mark Zuckerberg's claim he isn't effectively the world's most powerful editor and publisher but merely a 'platform' provider.

Meanwhile ad-blocking figures are steadily rising, particularly among the young, adding to publishers' elusive quest for the Holy Grail of an effective, ad-funded online business model. Trinity Mirror, for example, is adding just 13p of digital advertising for every £1 of print ad revenue it loses.

## All is not lost, buckle up for the ride!

But all isn't total doom and gloom. Nearly 7m people still regularly buy UK daily and Sunday papers, albeit down from 13m a decade ago. The bulk are much older than the coveted 18-24 bracket, but that's still enough to ensure some print titles will survive the next decade or so. What their sales figures, business models and journalistic head counts will be by then, is the make-or-break issue.

Vice founder Shane Smith, who began in print publishing, ruffled TV industry figures in August 2016 with an aggressive, expletive-laden MacTaggart Lecture at the Edinburgh International TV Festival. On one point I believe he was right: Debunking the notion young people aren't interested in news, Smith argued in effect it was really all about 'how you deliver it, stupid. Duh!'

Let's not forget either UK newspapers still tend to set the agenda for mainstream TV and radio as well as triggering the social media debate, whether of the intelligent and thought-provoking variety or the barking mad troll tendency. Cliché or not, content is increasingly king in the global digisphere. Reality dictates newspapers are going to have to forge closer relationships with the likes of Facebook and Google with their voracious appetite for content. With the right financial deals and with shared platforms to provide news creators with great advertising opportunities, it could yet toss a digital lifebelt to a drowning industry.

It's undoubtedly true the newspaper business was historically complacent and slow to wake up to the internet age and lacked visionaries to match the Zuckerbergs, Jobs and Gates of this brave new world. If we had, he, or she, would now be as revered as Gutenberg, Caxton and Wynkyn de Worde.

I began this chapter comparing the newspaper business to a patient on life support. Maybe an analogy for the future would be that of a space traveller – or, rather, a cyberspace traveller - buckling into his seat, preparing for a journey into the great unknown, aware it will be one helluva of a bumpy ride but fascinating all the same. Above all, whatever the final destiny of newspapers in the evolving digital galaxy, I'm convinced of one thing: Real journalism WILL survive the trip.

## References

Pew Research Center (2016) State of the Media

Reuters (2016) Reuters Digital News Report

Jarvis, Jeff. (2016) Death to the Mass, (Essay for annual report of Scandinavia's Tinius Trust)

Mance, Henry (February 2016) UK Newspapers: rewriting the story,(Financial Times article)

Gapper, John (May 2016) Fleet Street is being sunk by the internet (Financial Times article)

Jackson, Jasper (August 2016) Mirror publisher's profits leap after Local World takeover (Media Guardian)

Greenslade, Roy (May 2016) Suddenly, national newspapers are heading for that print cliff fall (Media Guardian)

Greenslade, Roy (August 2016) Johnston Press may buy back debt to ease its financial headache (Media Guardian)

Sweney, Mark (May 2016) Silicon Valley's hoover leaves newspapers hunting for profit (Media Guardian)

Thielman, Sam (August 2016) Facebook fires trending team and algorithm without humans goes crazy (Media Guardian)

## Note on the contributor

Paul Connew is a media commentator, broadcaster, former editor of the Sunday Mirror, deputy editor of the Daily Mirror and News of the World, former US Bureau Chief for the Mirror Group, and currently a media columnist for international media website The Drum. He is also a PR/Media consultant to corporate, celebrity and charity clients, and a longstanding judge of the British Press Awards and the Royal Television Society Awards. He was a contributing co-author of the book After Leveson.

# Near death and the defibrillator: Problems and solutions for national newspapers – can advertising still be the saviour?

**Guy Zitter spent 25 years leading the Daily Mail's commercial operation and learned a few lessons about national advertising in the process. But all is not lost for the nationals, he believes, especially where their audience and innovation are concerned**

For national newspapers the last couple of years certainly seemed to be a near-death experience. Bear in mind, though, the national press has had a see-saw flirtation with forecast death for many decades.

If you go back to 1972, 75 per cent of the UK population were readers of UK national dailies. The Sun was selling 4.25m per day, the Daily Express 3.4m, the Daily Mirror 2.6m and the Daily Mail 1.7m. Figures are not available for the profitability of the national newspapers in 1972 but the Mail was certainly running at a loss and its activities had to be funded by other interests of the Rothermere family.

By 2002 total UK national daily newspaper readership had dropped to 53 per cent. Every title but the Mail was down in circulation.

The other interesting difference in 2002 was all newspaper profitability was massively greater by then. A combination of money from floating Reuters, revolution in the industrial climate (Margaret Thatcher) enabling printing cost reduction and the introduction of colour had laid the foundation for a complete change in newspaper economics. Ad revenue on the Daily Mail was at near record levels, having risen 280 per cent during the 90s, and profitability was 330 per cent up over the same period.

Jump forward to today and the picture is very different. Circulations down but circulation revenues remain relatively stable in the stronger titles. Paid for circulation is in decline, hardly surprising with Metro and the Standard giving away 2.2m copies, but cover prices have frequently risen to mitigate the revenue loss. Where the money has been haemorrhaging is advertising.

## Classified advertising

National newspaper advertising revenues have a range of identifiable problems. Taking the traditional classified sector first; it became clear in the 90s the internet was going to be massively disruptive. Search for a job, house, holiday, car on the internet and in moments you can see what is available without having to buy a newspaper. The only way to counterbalance this was by investing in or starting your own businesses which enabled the company to be in the up-lift as well as the down.

The Guardian and AutoTrader are prime examples. Without that investment the Scott Trust would have been unable to continue funding The Guardian. The Mail tried PeopleBank as a CV search platform in 1996, which was the right concept but too early. DMGT then bought Jobsite which ran on a less disruptive model and clambered into the property market with Find A Property and Prime Location. All of these traded profitably but their income could not replace the money which had been coming into the print classified revenues in regional Northcliffe Newspapers, the Standard and the Mail.

The capital value of these new businesses, however, attracted far higher price to earnings ratios than those available from the more traditional business so sale or flotation did in fact generate huge returns rather than trading income. One way or another, therefore, the classified revenue damage has been counterbalanced, at least by the Mail and The Guardian.

## Display advertising

The category which traditionally held up especially well was retail. It is still the largest category today. The reason was simple. It worked to the extent it was measureable, that is if Sainsbury's normally sold five tonnes of sausages on Saturday and they sold 50 tonnes after they put an offer in the Daily Mail. This model is under pressure because of the growth of databases which are being built up by almost every advertiser and enable them to email the offer directly to their own audience. It is cheaper and can be targeted. The problem for the advertiser though is all of their competitors are doing the same and they are only marketing to their existent database.

On the face of it national newspapers' advertising revenue problems should not be as severe as recent figures suggest. National dailies, if Metro and the Standard are included, still sell or distribute more than nine million copies per day. The Sundays come in at 6.2m. National titles in combination with their internet sites are actually reaching a higher proportion of the UK market than ever before. Total readership across print and digital news brands is 35 per cent of the total UK population daily, 63 per cent weekly and 90 per cent monthly with the highest monthly reach among the youngest groups (18-34) who tend to access via mobile devices. Arguably national newspapers should be able to take a large, or nearly as large, slice of the cake as before. They are reaching a higher proportion of the UK population. That is not happening. Why?

All of the national newspapers' digital audiences can also largely be found via re-targeting, so unique access has gone and with it control of pricing. The internet provides almost infinite advertising opportunity and clearly marketing budgets are not infinite so price pressure is downwards. Nevertheless, on the surface it would appear a model which produces an audience in a trusted environment should be able to be monetised.

## Media buying

This is more difficult than it looks. The vast majority of advertising revenue comes via media intermediaries. They, in theory, the guardians of their client's marketing/media budgets, guide the money into a relatively small proportion of the large opportunities the internet provides. A great deal of discussion has taken place around how this is done and the transparency (or lack of) in these deals.

Used properly the internet can provide excellent returns and very cost effective marketing but in many instances there is insufficient understanding of exactly what is going on and scrutiny of it. According to Ebiquity (the largest UK media auditor) 75 per cent of the money in the marketing pot does not actually reach the publisher from an advertiser using 'programmatic' or automated bid-based advertising on the internet. If this huge percentage is being lost in the pipe between the client budget and the media owner there two very obvious questions, firstly, where has the money gone and secondly, how can the money possibly be effective when most of it is not reaching the target audience?

To answer the first question one has to look at the media buyers as this money is placed in their hands by the client company's marketing department. The transparency in this process resembles wet cement. Some media buyers offer their clients a guarantee of cheaper space/time if no transparency is required. This kind of contract protects the media buyer from accusations of sharp practice or fraud.

The Association of National Advertisers in the US published a report in mid-2016[1] which found: 'Non transparent business practices were pervasive across the media agency spectrum.' It also acknowledged the existence of cash rebates and rebates in the form of 'service agreements' in which suppliers paid for low value consulting/research or provided free inventory. The 'potentially problematic agency conduct' included the agency or its holding company acting as principal to purchase media on its own behalf and reselling it to its client at mark-ups of up to 90 per cent. In some cases the answer to where the money has gone has to be in large part to the agency itself.

To answer the second question we can take a quote originally attributed to Lord Leverhulme: "I know 50 per cent of my advertising doesn't work, I just don't know which 50 per cent."

The 50 per cent of the advertising budget which does not work is almost certainly the 50 per cent which does not even reach the publisher or target audience. Agencies which feel unfairly accused of this practice can or should resolve the issue by simply providing full transparency to their clients and/or the media owners.

## The new competition

These are not the only problems as newspaper websites are competing with huge opposition. The Guardian's web traffic grew in the first quarter of 2016 but its digital revenue declined. In the same quarter Facebook's net income increased 300 per cent and its margins jumped from 26 per cent to 37 per cent. In effect 90 per cent of the increase in mobile revenue is going to Facebook and Google. They are omnipresent. Combine this with agencies' own income influencing advertising decisions, and the internet begins to resemble a monopoly based around algorithms and not a supposedly neutral distribution platform.

So, actual print is in decline but the audience accessing news content from the print parent is at an all-time high.

## Will newspapers survive and if so how?

They cannot make expensive mistakes. Why The Guardian thought it was feasible to print in Berliner proportions is bewildering. Broadsheet or tabloid printing capacity was freely available and could have been done under contract. If the desire to own the presses was a priority then at least buy some that would be able to contract print for other clients in the UK and amortise the capital cost of press over capacity across a broader business base. Get the printing done as economically as possible.

## Hang on to existing circulation

Do not lose any of your existing print customers. They are older, in the habit of buying a newspaper, and probably very loyal. They are gold dust, and must be treated as such. No sudden changes in editorial direction, format or large price movements. Any change has to be gradual evolution not revolution. There may be opportunities to increase circulation and to find these the obvious route is to examine what has worked historically.

Magazines are under less pressure than national newspapers at the time of writing. Some, for example The Spectator, are putting on sales. There were two instances where the Mail managed to capitalise by adding a magazine to its newspaper offering. The first was six months after the launch of The Mail on Sunday. Circulation had gone past the million mark at launch but fell back to just above 600,000. The company gambled, with Vere Rothermere's money, and launched You magazine. Circulation doubled overnight to 1.2m and continued to climb.

The second was with the launch of Weekend magazine. There was a large and heated debate about the viability of Weekend. Saturday went from being the worst circulation day of the week at circa 1.5m to 3m at peak. TV listings had been deregulated and the monopoly of the Radio Times and TV Times was broken. Weekend is still the largest and most comprehensive TV listings product in the market and Saturday still way outsells every other day of the week.

Those bold moves were right for the time in terms of scale and scope but there are always opportunities to stretch into another stream of content. The trick is to find content that, when added to what is already in the existent newspaper, increases the appeal to the extent people will pay more for it or pay for it separately. As part of a digital package this could be video.

## Creating more commercial revenue

Part of the problem is internet over-supply and the very large media buying middlemen putting pressure on price or not using national newspapers at all for a variety of reasons. Strategies to counterbalance this must include developing and maintaining direct advertiser contact. If the client is convinced of the value of the newspaper to his business the agency will have to work very hard to knock the newspaper off the schedule.

Google and Facebook have teams selling direct to clients and one way or another the national newspapers must do the same. Why would newspapers expect to be part of the expensive marketing process unless they have demonstrated their worth to the people writing the cheque? The audience newspapers have to offer in print is older but they have 79 per cent of the savings wealth of the country at their disposal and 70 per cent of the income. They own their houses and have substantial pension schemes. This is the first time the generation following them is unlikely to be as wealthy. They are also living longer and longer as healthcare has improved. This is an incredibly valuable audience and this will need to be explained and proven to clients and their agencies time and again.

The media buying practices outlined earlier have to become unsustainable. National newspapers have a very powerful voice and in the end they will have to confront the shortcomings and abuse of the system by writing about it. The fear this may damage their short term revenues may be giving them pause for thought but publicising the problems will engender a reaction which eventually must change the practice or produce legislation which forces that change. To do nothing to resolve this is not an option as no model based around any advertising revenue on the internet can survive otherwise.

Thinking beyond the traditional model, all the national newspapers are now running with significant advertising inventory unsold. This either shrinks the pagination to the point where consumer value is called into question or is handed over to journalism which otherwise would not have made the cut. This inventory is not only huge, it is hugely valuable in both print and digital. The newspapers have the opportunity to trade this inventory for equity. A huge number of start-ups come to the market each year all of which need marketing to get off the ground. The newspapers could become incubators for these businesses taking the return for the inventory in capital value rather than income. Run properly this may prove more profitable than normal advertising space sales.

This different approach to the use of print and digital inventory has to be mirrored by an open minded management with a strong entrepreneurial bent. Identifying what may or may not work is akin to an investment banking process rather than normal commercial sales.

All of these measures and the success/survival of Britain's national newspaper industry in the end depend upon one single factor which is having a highly motivated team of people across all of the different disciplines who believe in their publications. The pace of change is increasing and the decisions made today which seem to be correct may have to changed in a matter of months as technology evolves and people's behaviour changes with it.

National newspapers need to run to where the ball is going not where the ball is, as does every other business. The problem is the ball may change direction and so the business must as well. This is not a comfortable experience but adaptability is vital. The newspaper companies with the right management will survive. They may end up putting animated cartoon figures into their interactive digital news content in order to get the under 30s to read it.

Profits are still pretty robust. The Telegraph made £48.3m in 2015 with a circulation of under 500,000. The Mail still is at around £100m in print alone. Done properly there will still be print editions in 15 years' time and their digital offshoots could be large and very profitable.

### Note
[1] An Independent Study of Media Transparency in the US Advertising Industry by K2 Intelligence

### Sources
Newsworks, NRS, ABC, Mediatel, US ANA Report, Financial Times, Numis.

### Note on the contributor
Guy Zitter is director of Boiling Oil Ltd. Previously he was advertising director of the Daily Mail 1989-1994, managing director of the Daily Mail 1994-2014. He is non-executive director at Easy Property and board adviser at Student High Street. Boiling Oil consults to several businesses in the media, retail, and fin tech sectors. His career in media spanned 34 years but he has also owned a run a night club, restaurant, and travel business. He loves his wife and two children. He likes fine wine, cigars, and skiing.

# Guardian of 'open' online news?

**Peter Cole examines the financial pressures on newspapers in the digital age – using the Guardian, of which he was once deputy editor, as a case study**

All the emphasis over the last decade has been on the death of print, the subject of this book. The future is digital, goes the mantra, but how do we pay for the content, the reporting, the journalism? Particularly when the customer, the reader, has shown little inclination to pay for news online. The presumption (hope?) has been that once digital dominance is established (and it almost is) the advertising will move online and thus fund the journalism.

But what happens if the beneficiary of this revenue is not the publisher of the news website or the employer of the news gatherers, the journalists? This is the latest problem facing the online news providers, particularly those that do not charge for their content. The big two UK newspapers in terms of size of online audience are the Mail and Guardian. Neither charges for using its site; both during 2016 announced cost-cutting and redundancies. These are very different organisations – the Mail a listed public company, the Guardian owned by a trust. The Guardian's problems are the greater just now.

This chapter provides a case study through the Guardian of pressures in the digital age that go further than the death of print, and affect the life of digital.

## Crisis

How different it all looked at the end of May 2015. Alan Rusbridger's 20-year editorship of the Guardian had just come to an end. After a series of farewell events, where management and editorial colleagues effusively praised him for his leadership, vision, inspiration, wisdom and foresight, he was 'banged out' of Guardian HQ, near King's Cross station in London, to head for the less frenetic atmosphere of Lady Margaret Hall, the Oxford college where he was becoming Principal. It was au revoir, not goodbye, for, as he reminded the guests at his many exit parties, he would be back in little over a year to take over the chair of the Scott Trust, owners of the Guardian Media Group (GMG), publishers of the

Guardian and Observer newspapers and digital platforms in the UK, United States and Australia. He shared stages at his leaving parties with his successor as editor-in-chief Katharine Viner and Dame Liz Forgan, chair of the Scott Trust. The smiles and tributes gave no hint of what was to come.

Rusbridger's legacy seemed secure, editorially and commercially. He had an international reputation as one of the great editors, who had grasped and understood the digital future while his rivals were still concentrating on print decline. His career had recently been crowned with a prestigious Pulitzer Prize for the Edward Snowden revelations, following numerous awards for the WikiLeaks, phone-hacking, cash-for-questions and other investigations. He had built the Guardian's website into one of the world's leading news platforms. And, he said, he left GMG in good financial shape. When I interviewed him shortly before his departure from the newspaper he drew attention to digital revenues 'rising strongly', to the cash and investment fund (reserves) standing at £842m with more to come from the future sale of the stake in Ascential, the magazine and events group. 'I think,' he said, 'for a new editor to come in with a billion pounds in the bank is quite a nice position' (Cole 2015: 27).

The joy of her 'inheritance', if she had time to see it that way, did not last long for Viner. Andrew Miller, chief executive of GMG, left soon after Rusbridger and was replaced by David Pemsel. This quickly became the new controlling axis at the Guardian, and it became evident to them very soon that the financial situation was well removed from Rusbridger's 'quite a nice position'. The figures looked considerably worse than the previous financial year. A combination of falling advertising revenues (print and online) and mounting costs (particularly staffing) meant that unless action was taken quickly a crisis was not far away. Viner and Pemsel addressed the staff in January 2016 to outline a three-year strategy to cut costs by £54m a year, the equivalent of 20 per cent (Martinson 2016a)

When GMG's annual report was published in July 2016, it confirmed the seriousness of the situation and the need for the Viner/Pemsel rescue plan. The total pre-tax loss was £173m. The operating loss (earnings before interest, tax and other deductibles) was £69m. And the cash and investment endowment fund had dropped by £74m to £765m over the financial year. The maths were not difficult: losses at this level, and an endowment fund reducing at this rate, meant the future was finite. Rusbridger told Media Briefing in March 2016 that when he had left the Guardian at the end of May 2015 'we were one month into a new financial year and everything looked fine. We were going to make £100m out of digital compared with £80m, and it all looked completely sustainable. The last Scott Trust meeting I was at they were saying everything's changed in the last six months, and it's all going to Facebook' (Rusbridger 2016a).

## Causes

So what brought about this sudden deterioration in the Guardian's fortunes? Put simply, lack of expected growth in online advertising revenues and rapidly increasing costs, particularly in the area of staffing.

On the BBC Radio 4 Media Show (27 July 2016), Douglas McCabe, of Enders Analysis, said that losses of roughly £1m a week were not sustainable. There would be extensive redundancies and a variety of cost cutting. The Guardian had overestimated how much advertising revenue they would get from print. But digital revenue was also going down. This was unexpected. Online advertising was not growing, but the key issue was that it was moving away from news sites to social media, increasingly to Facebook and Google. The Guardian's cash pile was depleted, and might last 10 years at this rate. Losses at current level were not sustainable in the short term.

Viner described the situation in March 2016 at the London (British Library) conference of Newsworks: 'Journalistically it is an absolutely brilliant time. It's thrilling but at the same time the commercial model is undermined at all points. Fewer people are buying newspapers; advertisers are leaving print; digital advertising is going to Facebook and Google – quite dramatically so last year – instead of news organisations' (Viner 2016a). She developed her theme in a long and wide-ranging piece in the Guardian (print and online) entitled 'How technology disrupted the truth'.

> Facebook, which launched only in 2004, now has 1.6bn users worldwide. It has become the dominant way for people to find news on the internet – and, in fact, it is dominant in ways that would have been impossible to imagine in the newspaper era. ... This means that social media companies have become overwhelmingly powerful in determining what we read – and enormously profitable from the monetisation of other people's work.

> Publications curated by editors have in many cases been replaced by a stream of information chosen by friends, contacts and family, processed by secret algorithms. The old idea of a wide-open web has been largely supplanted by platforms designed to maximise your time within their walls, some of which (such as Instagram and Snapchat) do not allow outward links at all.

But the trouble is that the business model of most digital news organisations is based around clicks. News media around the world has reached a fever pitch of frenzied binge-publishing in order to scrape up digital advertising's pennies and cents. (And there's not much advertising to be got: in the first quarter of 2016; 85 cents of every new dollar spent in the US on online advertising went to Google and Facebook. That used to go to news publishers.) (Viner 2016b).

## Strategy

By the time the full detail of the Guardian's financial position was revealed in July 2016, some of the strategy to deal with it was already being implemented.

Kath Viner and David Pemsel had outlined 'Project 2021' to staff six months earlier – with cuts of £54m a year being sought, (Martinson 2016a). Pemsel told them the new management team needed to safeguard the Guardian in perpetuity as it bridged the transition from print to digital. 'Growing the cost base more than revenue is simply not sustainable' (ibid).

The detailed report in July showed that GMG had budgeted for an increase in online advertising revenue of more than £20m; in fact, it declined by £2m. Total staff numbers increased from 1.650 to 1,813 over the year; of these 1,050 were in editorial and production (up from 925). By September 2016, the voluntary redundancy scheme had resulted in staff reductions in the UK of more than 260 (about 80 in editorial) saving about £17m a year, and a further 40 (out of 140) were being sought in the US (Martinson 2016b).

Other elements of the recovery strategy included enhancing the Guardian's membership offering (see below), growth in the US and Australian websites, and seeking or developing other revenue streams. GMG also looked to other sources of funding, stating on its website: 'News organisations around the world can no longer rely solely on advertising and sales revenues. As Guardian Media Group looks beyond traditional sources of funding, the backing of third parties who are willing to support journalism while respecting its editorial independence and freedom to enable the coverage of important subjects that may too easily be neglected elsewhere' (Guardian Media Group 2016). Such funders have included the Bill and Melinda Gates Foundation, Joseph Rowntree, Humanity United and the European Climate Foundation (theguardian.com 2015).

## Politics

In the early part of 2016, backchat emerging from the Guardian suggested that the 'Rusbridger legacy' was under attack, that he was being scapegoated for the emerging financial crisis. A Financial Times report (27 April 2016), clearly 'informed' if not sourced, claimed that

> … his record is now in doubt. His journalism is still admired but his evangelism for a business approach of being 'open and free' – spurning any online paywall and instead relying on growth in the digital readership to gain advertising – is in question. The Guardian's expensive expansion, with 480 of its 1,950 employees added in his last three years, has left it bleeding cash. The Guardian has long suffered from over-optimism about revenues and an ingrained inability to control costs. Many people put the primary blame for the profligacy on Mr Rusbridger.

The FT article quoted Claire Enders, of the well-regarded Enders Analysis, saying: 'Alan took the lead all the way along on its digital transition, and made predictions with blithe insouciance and naivety. His revenue forecasting record is abysmal.'

Suddenly the revered former editor was being put in the frame for the problems the company was now facing. There seemed to be no questioning of any responsibility attaching to commercial management. Non-editorial staffing had increased just as rapidly as editorial. It soon emerged that another major issue was in play. Was it still appropriate for Rusbridger to take over as chair of the Scott Trust, despite the support and public enthusiasm for the appointment from the person he would succeed, Liz Forgan? It became clear that Viner and Pemsel were of the view that it was not. When I asked Rusbridger shortly before he stood down as editor-in-chief, and before the concerted efforts to reverse his appointment as chair of the Trust, whether he foresaw any problems for his successor in having him in this powerful role he said: 'I am constitutionally not allowed to discuss the direction of the paper with Kath, or anything like that. Wise heads, defenders of the journalistic order, and protectors of the independence of the editor: I think Kath would welcome having me in that role. I'm not going to be breathing down her neck' (Cole 2015: 28). That was Forgan's view too. It turned out not to be Viner's.

There were protracted meetings of the Scott Trust in May 2016, for some of which Rusbridger, still a member of the Trust, was asked to sit outside the room while the matter was discussed. He decided to resign from the job he had yet to take up, and on 13 May emailed the editorial staff to tell them. (Rusbridger 2016b). He quoted the words of the chair of GMG. Neil Berkett, at the time he stood down from the editorship:

> Alan has set the standard for journalistic leadership in the digital age, His appointment to lead the Scott Trust coincides with rapidly rising readership, continued innovation and secure finances at the Guardian. His successor will inherit a global media organisation in very strong health and with clear prospects for future growth.

Rusbridger's email added tersely: 'Kath (Viner) and David (Pemsel) clearly believe they would like to plan a route into the future with a new chair and I understand their reasoning.' It was later announced that Alex Graham, the former chief executive of Wall to Wall Media and member of the Scott Trust since 2012, would become the new chair of the Trust (Jackson 2016).

**Membership**

Much is pinned on membership, currently standing at more than 50,000 paying members. Rusbridger was driving it when he was editor-in-chief. He said in interview with this writer that it was a 'serious, commercial and heavily researched' brand extension. He was convinced it was part of the future (Cole 2015: 27). He even inspired the acquisition of an old goods shed near King's Cross and Guardian HQ to be developed as a location for Guardian members to meet and events to take place. The project, managed by Pemsel, was cancelled in January 2016 by Viner/Pemsel as part of the assault on losses. But membership remained firmly in the strategy. Pemsel told the Digital Media Strategies 2016 seminar that GMG aimed to make its membership scheme account for a third of overall revenues within three years. He said:

In this new strategy we've said membership will involve content we expect members to pay for. One size does not fit all. When you have something that has been dedicated to the sort of journalism we have been.., the trust we have with our readers suggests there's an opportunity to create communities around the philosophy of membership and ask our readers to contribute more (Pemsel 2016).

While rivals such as The Times associate membership with bolt-ons to subscriptions – events, film screenings, competitions and gifts – the Guardian separates the two. Psychologically the distinction is important. Subscribers pay, whereas members belong, are 'part of' – actually in most cases they pay too (they are part of the revenue-raising strategy). The emphasis is on the website – where 'open' journalism means the freedom to consume journalistic content online without paying for it – with regular appeals appearing all over the site. However, paying print readers (through subscription or on an issue-by-issue basis at cover price) are not excluded from the appeals to 'support our journalism for less than the price of a cup of coffee a week' (Membership 2016).

Editor-in-chief Kath Viner, together with star writers like Polly Toynbee and Owen Jones, make impassioned appeals for readers to contribute to the costs of reporting. Viner: 'I want to ask you, our readers, to help fund [our] journalism through a monthly payment, so that we can continue interrogating what has happened, and why, and what needs to happen next.'

Membership comes in different forms at different costs. First there is the 'supporter', the 'cup of coffee a week' member referred to by Viner. You pay £49-a-year to 'support the independence of the Guardian' and get access to tickets for Guardian events. For £149-a-year you can become a 'partner' which brings six tickets a year to Guardian events (or four Guardian books) and 20 per cent discounts on further events and Masterclasses. The highest status of membership is 'patron', which, for £599-a-year demonstrates 'deep support for keeping the Guardian open and independent' and provides invitations to 'exclusive behind-the-scenes functions'.

And lastly, in the hierarchy of members, you are invited to 'Alternatively, join for free' or 'become a friend.' What the Guardian might, but doesn't in this case, call 'open membership'. Friends receive 'regular updates from the membership community' and may book tickets to some Guardian events. Of course, if you are already buying the print versions of the Guardian or Observer, both the most expensive in the non-specialist national newspaper market, you must add to your membership fee the £2-a-day (cover-price, Monday to Friday; Times £1.40), and £2.90 (Saturday; Times £1.50) for the Guardian and on Sunday £3 for the Observer (Sunday Times £2.50). Which might beg the question: what's the difference between 'open' online journalism paid for in part by a necessarily large number of paying members, and paywall protected online content free to subscribers?

It looks like the tough times ahead for news journalism will be testing for purists.

## Sources

Cole, Peter (2015) A changing of the Guardian, British Journalism Review, Vol. 26, No. 2 pp 19-28

Guardian Media Group (2016) Funding and investment. Available online at https://www.theguardian.com/gmg/2015/jul/23/funding , accessed on 30 September 2016

Jackson, Jasper (2016) Alex Graham appointed seventh chair of Scott Trust, Guardian, 22 September. Available online at https://www.theguardian.com/media/2016/sep/22/alex-graham-appointed-chair-scott-trust-guardian-media-group accessed on 30 September 2016

Martinson, Jane (2016a) Guardian News & Media to cut costs by 20 per cent, Guardian, 25 January 2016. Available online at https://www.theguardian.com/media/2016/jan/25/guardian-news-media-to-cut-running-costs, accessed on 30 September 2016

Martinson, Jane (2016b) Guardian Media Group to cut nearly a third of US jobs, Guardian, 16 September 2016. Available online at https://www.theguardian.com/gmg/2016/sep/15/guardian-media-group-to-cut-nearly-a-third-of-us-jobs, accessed on 30 September 2016

Membership (2016) Details available online at theguardian.com, accessed on 30 September 2016

Pemsel, David (2016) Quoted in Press Gazette, 10 March. Available online at http://www.pressgazette.co.uk/guardian-chief-exec-aim-is-for-membership-fees-to-make-up-a-third-of-revenue, accessed on 30 September 2016

Rusbridger, Alan (2016a) Quoted in Media Briefing, 1 March. Available online at https://www.themediabriefing.com/article/article-article-alan-rusbridger-on-the-skill-value-and-necessity-of-journalism-to-facebook-and-google, accessed on 30 September 2016

Rusbridger, Alan (2016b) Quoted in Press Gazette, 13 May. Available online at http://www.pressgazette.co.uk/alan-rusbridger-falls-on-his-sword-rather-than-chair-scott-trust-opposed-by-editor-and-chief-executive/, accessed on 30 September 2016

Viner, Katharine (2016a) Quoted in Press Gazette, 1 March. Available online at http://www.pressgazette.co.uk/guardian-editor-katharine-viner-says-plan-get-readers-paying-it-rules-out-online-paywall, accessed on 30 September 2016

Viner, Katharine (2016b) How technology disrupted the truth, Guardian 12 July pp 25-27. Available online at https://www.theguardian.com/media/2016/jul/12/how-technology-disrupted-the-truth , accessed on 30 September 2016

## Note on the contributor

Peter Cole is Emeritus Professor of Journalism at the University of Sheffield, former news editor and deputy editor of the Guardian, editor of the Sunday Correspondent and News Review editor of The Sunday Times.

# The Independent is dead, long live The Independent

**Paul Lashmar argues the very paradigm shift that allowed The Independent to exist is what killed off the print edition in 2016 but might just allow the online only version to flourish in the future**

Suddenly, some 30 years ago, the cost of the means of production of newspapers dropped dramatically mostly due to Rupert Murdoch taking on the print unions over Wapping and Eddy Shah launching the Today newspaper. Prior to 1986 you had to be a millionaire ready to squander your fortune for political influence or have the support by a large commercial organisation to be able print a national newspaper in Fleet Street. At the beginning of 1986 three senior journalists at the Daily Telegraph, Andreas Whittam Smith, Matthew Symonds and Stephen Glover, recognised the game had changed and grabbed the opportunity to produce what they anticipated would be an exemplar of the art of the serious broadsheet newspaper. Launched on Monday, October 6, 1986, The Independent was Britain's first new quality national newspaper for 131 years. Computers – which had just arrived in newspaper offices – meant the whole printing process could be outsourced at the best price and without the print unions being able to use their once great muscle.

The new kid on the block reached its all-time circulation high of over 400,000 by 1989. In the second twist in the Independent story, it was Rupert Murdoch and a fickle audience that disrupted the triumvirate's vision in the early 1990s. More targeting the Daily Telegraph, Murdoch launched a predatory price war by The Times stable of papers that was to hamstring The Independent's still shaky finances. Still without a viable readership, The Times price drop was a kidney punch for The Independent which lost rather than built circulation and revenue. 'The Indie' would stagger along wounded for another 20-plus years. Finally the most recent owner (since 2010), Russian billionaire Evgeny Lebedev, fed up with the financial drain, flogged off the economically successful little sister paper The i, put the print version out of its misery, but has kept on the online-only version. Again the now dominant means of production for distributing modern news – the internet – succeeded so effectively that Lebedev could not see any point maintaining a printed newspaper with a small and ever declining paying readership. On page three of the beautifully produced final printed edition in March 2016, founding editor Andreas Whittam Smith, summed up pithily The Independent print edition's fatal problem: "The technology that enabled us to establish ourselves has, 30 years later, rendered the printed edition unviable."

But now comes twist three. In April 2016 denuded of the original staff except for a handful of top names, the internet version looked set for gradual decline. What chance did it have against the internet worldwide news behemoths like Mail Online, Guardian and the BBC? Yet, by August The Independent had grown its audience by 46 per cent year-on-year after moving to a digital. The title had added 6.6m readers to its total daily audience across online and mobile over the last year, up to 21.2m, according to Published Audience Measurement Company (PAMco) data. (Mayhew 2016). This may not be quite up there with the Mail Online which had a total audience readership of 30.6m in the same period, but it shows the importance of successfully targeting the UK mobile users audience. Whether this will drive enough revenue to The Independent site to make it viable if still an open question.

There are certainly lessons to be learnt from the three decades of the The Independent. It was always a curious newspaper riddled with paradoxes and sudden swerves in editorial direction. Could it have been run better? The Independent arrived blinking in a Fleet Street of Murdoch, still strong unions, Mrs Thatcher and a press encapsulated in a sketch in the satirical sitcom Yes, Prime Minister which Sir Jim Hacker turns on his Cabinet Secretary, Sir Humphrey saying: "Don't tell me about the Press. I know exactly who reads the papers. The Daily Mirror is read by the people who think they run the country. The Guardian is read by people who think they ought to run the country. The Times is read by the people who actually do run the country. The Daily Mail is read by the wives of the people who run the country. The Financial Times is read by people who own the country. The Morning Star is read by people who think the country ought to be run by another country. The Daily Telegraph is read by the people who think it is." The Independent's target readership was for people who thought for themselves.

I recall reading the first edition of The Independent and felt it had sense of aspiration and purity for its journalism. It was a bit of relief from the rather soft left predictability of the The Guardian. I was on The Observer at the time and wasn't too concerned. (The Independent on Sunday did not come along until 1990 and was planned to be an European orientated newspaper). The new Independent was a delight to behold, crisp, beautifully produced and the use of quality photographs shot be great photographers was a delight. The paper excluded high production and news values and felt liberal but with a slight sense of 'noblesse oblige'.

In its original form The Independent was very much the vision of its then editor (now Sir) Andreas Whittam Smith, an aesthete born to look like a central casting university professor, but with a touch of the buccaneer. He had a strong sense of what the ideal newspaper should be and said he would run the paper like conducting an orchestra by drawing out the best in everyone. It benefited from being able to hire many of the quality journalists who had walked away from The Times, sick of Murdoch's underhand ways. This reinforced the sense that the paper held lofty ideals. As the academic Patrick Champagne notes, the good journalist is one who conforms to the principles taught in journalism school of ethical and quality journalism: "He or she is a news professional, who tries to ward off the two major threats that constantly weigh on the intellectual autonomy of journalist production: on the one hand, political partisanship; on the other, the quest for circulation at any price one sees in the scandal sheets, (Benson and Neveu 2005, 58)." For many of its original journalists this was what The Independent was all about: a newspaper that was not a tool for individual or commercial power. Unlike many of its rivals, it should not be corruptible and Whittam Smith decided the paper should stay out of the parliamentary lobby, the system whereby political reporters receive unattributable Downing Street briefings. Whittam Smith also decided the paper should largely ignore royal stories. (These lofty positions were later rescinded).

It was funded by diverse sources and did not seem beholden to controlling proprietors then rampant in Fleet Street like Maxwell, Murdoch and increasingly invasive at The Observer, Tiny Rowland as well as the Rothermere family over at the Mail. The Independent prided itself on its title. The paper described itself as 'free from party political bias, free from proprietorial influence' – a banner it carried on the front page of its daily edition. (By now owned by Lebedev this banner was dropped in September 2011). Launched with the advertising slogan 'It is. Are you?', and challenging The Guardian for centre-left readers, and The Times for the centre-right. The message was reading The Independent enhanced your cultural capital.

Placing The Independent experience in an academic framework is a useful exercise. Champagne, a collaborator with the French philosopher Pierre Bourdieu has noted: "The media field's immanent power of consecration – the power to say who and what is important, and what we should think about important things and people – is based on its own legitimacy, which journalists have collectively accumulated in the course of history (ibid). Of the various concepts perhaps Bourdieu's 'journalism field' theory neatly identified the place of The Independent in British journalism. Through field theory Bourdieu characterises the way the journalist connects with their profession, how their field interacts with the political and economic fields. He identifies a 'habitas' – a structure that organises practice and the perception of practices and how they assert agency. This defines the environment news journalists create and the 'doxa' the shared presuppositions which exists in journalism. Most journalists have common shared presuppositions of what is good journalism, what are professional news values and the damage caused by commercialisation (Benson and Neveu, 2005, 3). And the new Independent embodied those normative journalistic values, a doxa so powerful which perhaps explains, however vestigial at points, high journalism values have remained as a common and distinguishing thread for The Independent through all its trials and tribulations. Independent journalists shared a habitus journalists on many more commercial papers envied but had to supress.

Bourdieu noted the real world has a nasty way of imposing itself on any idealism in the French press. He observed in the wake of the Second World War world intellectuals had set up a number of print ventures. The most famous of course was Sartre's involvement with setting up Libération in 1973. Sooner or later the political economy model interrupted the higher values. These two poles, journalism idealism versus the commercial are always in tension. The Independent mostly sought to inform but we can now see that paper's flaw was it didn't really have a naturally large catchment. It had a core of dedicated readers who remained loyal but they were too small in numbers to sustain the newspaper. Private Eye nicknamed it woundingly as The IndescribablyBoring and sometimes, as much as it tried to have a light touch, sometimes it was all bit too pompous. There is not enough of the public, whatever the citizens may say, who are wildly keen on paying for aesthetic, high-minded detailed journalism, as much as they might admire it.

Champagne observed: "Caught between the competing imperatives of 'freedom of the press' and the 'laws of the market', few professions are represented in such starkly opposing ways" (Benson & Nevue 2006, 48). And so for The Independent. By 1994 the paper was financially limping along with circulation dropping when Tony O'Reilly took an interest in the paper and then gradually took it over to make it the flagship of his stable of newspapers. In May 1998 he poached Simon Kelner from the Mail on Sunday as editor. My own relationship with The Independent began with a phone call from Kelner in the July of 1998 inviting me to join the paper as an investigative journalist. For three years I produced investigations and more. It was a tough relentless gig with little in the way of resources but there were outstanding colleagues and it certainly had its moments.

Kelner was an oblique choice for The Independent. I have known him since I was 23 doing investigations for The Observer and he was 21 and a sports sub. Although he was to maintain some of The Independent's doxa he could not have been more different from the aesthete Whittam Smith or the polymath Andrew Marr (another predecessor). At the time, he was editing Night & Day magazine for the Mail on Sunday, although he had been at The Independent at launch (as deputy sports editor) and had another spell at the paper in the mid-1990s as night editor and features editor.

Whenever I start to wax lyrical these days about working on The Independent my wife reminds me I would call it a 'sausage factory' at the time. The handful of journalists' prodigious productivity rate in terms of stories published per day, if not quality, was an indication of what was soon to happen across news journalism. Editing the paper's more robust journalism was left to deputy editor Ian Birrell. The paper retained a number of key figures who embodied Whittam

Smith's vision for a higher forms of journalism like Patrick Cockburn, Robert Fisk and Kim Sengupta. They have all survived to this day.

There were false dawns. I remember The Independent's initial response to the internet. Some papers thought it could be ignored. The Daily Telegraph was early in the game. At The Independent the senior management were earlier adopters who thought it was going to big earner and advertising would just expand online at the same rates as the paper. The internet editors thought they were going to make a personal fortune. It did not work out like that. The circulation fluctuated around the 200,000 mark. Simon Kelner's strength was as a populist and the weekly guide had an innovative '50 Best' feature most weeks which was a real boon for time-poor readers trying to work out what to do with their kids over the bank holiday or what gadget to buy. These days we are used to these as listicles as powerful clickbait on the internet. In that respect Kelner was ahead of his time but circulation continued to fluctuate, up when there was a redesign but then a slow decline. The paper was resized to tabloid in 2004 and a temporary increase in circulation followed. The 20p i was invented in his reign and its simplicity was attractive to readers who did not want a large paper to read.

In 2001, I resigned from the daily to move out of London. But several months later, I was called in to help The Independent on Sunday by the then deputy editor Michael Williams in the wake of 9/11. My arrangement with the cash-strapped Sunday edition flourished journalistically until 2007 when, after cut back after cutback I concluded I would probably earn more delivering the paper than writing for it. I wrote hundreds of stories in my time working for both papers. I am still particularly proud of the work we did on the Sunday paper over the Weapons of Mass Destruction and the Iraq War and which was highly sceptical of Blair and his intelligence chiefs' claims. All paradoxes, contradictions and wrong turns aside I still have a soft spot for the paper and wrote my last piece – on the Hatton Garden robbers – for the daily print edition in January 2016. The circulation was just 55,000.

Through the early 2000s the paper lost its way and lacked a soul. The Independent needed passion, flair, authority and vision if it was to grow but it felt tired. It did not have the visionary leadership, intellectual or public profile Alan Rusbridger brought to The Guardian. After 1997 you rarely heard an Independent editor on the broadcast news or anywhere really until quite recently. Its news was not distinct. Columnists ruled the roost. I'm one of those journalists who believes everyone has opinions but journalists are there to dig out the facts that count. Of course, I recognise some columnist are perceptive and are fine writers. But few write with conviction on more than four issues a year leaving a lot of space filled by guff. And there was a lot of guff. In 2007, Alan Rusbridger astutely said of The Independent: "The emphasis on views, not news, means the reporting is rather thin, and it loses impact on the front page the more you do that."

It was the product of too many compromises and cutbacks. A newspaper has to stand for something an audience finds unique even if it reflects their own bigotry. As Sir Humphrey remarked in that famous 1987 exchange: "The only way to understand the press is to remember they pander to their readers' prejudices." The Independent always tried to be objective and avoid pandering to prejudices. Unfortunately not enough readers wanted to pay for The Independent's brand of objective reporting and a non-partisan centrist view.

The cessation of the print edition prompted a wave of nostalgia and mourning by staff members past and present. Reunions were held to celebrate the highlights of three decades of The Independent. For all its problems The Independent had maintained a thread of quality over the years and its former journalists still share a doxa and camaraderie.

But I can end with some good news. Amol Rajan was appointed as editor in 2013 and proved to be a thoughtful, accessible and engaged choice with an instinctive fee for the mobile generation. He departed for the BBC as media editor in December 2016. The current team have a real feel for what is needed to survive online. Whether its growing readership will translate into enough revenue is yet unproven. And remarkably the online Independent news does retain a hint of the aspirational journalism Whittam Smith cultivated some 30 years ago. But perhaps, like vinyl, the newspaper will one day make its reappearance as a tactile and uplifting experience that the digital cannot replicate.

## References

Benson, R and Nevue, E. (2005) Bourdieu and the Journalistic Field, Cambridge: Polity Press.

Mayhew, F. (2016) Independent readership up 46 per cent while mobile offers biggest audience for some. Press Gazette. 24 August. Last accessed 7 September and can be seen at: http://www.pressgazette.co.uk/independent-readership-up-46-per-cent-while-mobile-offers-biggest-audience-for-some/

## Note on the contributor

Dr Paul Lashmar is a Senior Lecturer and leads the Journalism team at the University of Sussex. His Doctorate investigates the links between the intelligence services and the media which is also his core research interest. He is also an investigative journalist and has worked in television, radio and print. He is a former Reporter of the Year in UK Press Awards. He has been on the staff of The Observer, Granada Television's World in Action current affairs series and The Independent. He has also produced a number of TV programmes for BBC's Timewatch, Channel 4's Dispatches series and he reported for Newsnight. Paul covered the 'War on Terror' at The Independent on Sunday from 2001-2007. He has authored or co-authored four books. His textbook on multimedia journalism Online Journalism: The Essential Guide was co-authored with Steve Hill (Sage 2014).

# It was, oh yes it was

**We shall miss the printed Independent, says Donald Macintyre who worked for the paper when it launched – as well as when it died**

My last long Independent piece, a 30th anniversary reflection on Wapping, included an unfortunate error. It made the hardly original point that the newly launched Independent had gained from the rival Times being produced in an East London fortress besieged by pickets, but it 'gained even more because Murdoch's coup, however brutal, made it easier for a new newspaper to launch at all with new technology'. It also said the Independent would celebrate its own 'happier' 30th anniversary later this year. Did anyone who read this before publication know how wrong it would soon look? The announcement the printed Independent was ceasing publication came three weeks later.

The title lives on of course, in the hope of achieving what its owner Evgeny Lebedev predicted will be a 'sustainable future' for 'the world's most free-thinking newsbrand'. Its journalistic big names, some with already large internet audiences in their own right, mainly stayed online. But a newspaper is more than the sum of its parts. Perhaps the only bonus of its relentless job cutting over the years was an absence of factional strife. The team, and it was a team, was too busy producing the papers. Now 100 of those 175 journalists, many young and talented, the equivalent generation to those who helped to launch the Independent in the 80s have gone. They too were part of the Independent's character. So, were long-standing now vanished niches of the paper, like gardening from the distinguished Anna Pavord, or chess from grandmaster Jon Speelman (full disclosure: he's my cousin). This prompted media commentator Raymond Snoddy's assertion: "It is cynical to talk about a new wondrous era in journalism when so many experienced journalists have been sacked."[1] Having risen above and then fallen slightly below its print-era level of just over 3m, the website saw the biggest surge, an impressive 44 percent, among its rivals during the Brexit referendum, to an average 4.4m unique browsers per day. During July it also had the biggest fall, to just under a still healthy 4m.[2] But this is not just a matter of numbers Preserving the Independent spirit as well as its title will be a challenge for a website which was already more noisily different from its deceased parent than most newspaper-spawned online versions.

Besides the category-transcending Patrick Cockburn and Robert Fisk, many of those big names were commentators: Grace Dent, John Rentoul, Steve Richards (who has now left) Mary Dejevsky, Matthew Noman, Yasmin Alibhai-Brown, and, after an outstanding 18 years as political editor, Andy Grice. Yet when Andreas Whittam Smith realised his unique vision in 1986, there wasn't even a political columnist in the conventional sense. Along with the arts sport and business coverage, it was news which drove the paper. Not just home editor Jonathan Fenby, arguing for the Independent's first big scoop, MI5 agent Peter Wright's revelation in Spycatcher of the plot against Harold Wilson, but his iconoclastic deputy and successor John Price, an unfailing motivator of the men and women, who were among the best journalists of the era. Other talents included the late Tony Bevins in Westminster, David McKittrick in Northern Ireland, photographers like Brian Harris, not to mention some of the finest foreign correspondents ever assembled. All helped to ensure a circulation of 327,000 by June 1987, and make the paper attractive enough for those like the pre-eminent commentator Peter Jenkins to join. The paper was animated by a spiky integrity, symbolised by Whittam Smith's comprehensively enforced 'no freebies' rule, including revolutionarily, on the travel pages, and secondly by a restless curiosity and scepticism about conventional wisdom embodied by Price, who patiently explained to more than one reporter recruited from Fleet Street that he wouldn't actually know what the 'line' was until they had been out on the job.

Whittam Smith was an inclusive editor, regularly pausing on his newsroom visits to speak to a young reporter or sub-editor. Nor could he have been more forgiving, when, soon after becoming political editor in 1994, I made my worst mistake in more than 25 years' continuous work for the paper, buying into a Labour official's over-optimistic inference from a John Major local paper interview that the Prime Minister had supported electoral reform. We rightly, and swiftly, published a prominent apology.

The title and the slogan 'It is, are you?' had a double meaning: No proprietor and no party allegiance. The first flowed from Whittam Smith's initial limitation of investor holdings to ten percent. But both meanings appealed to its new staff (average age 31) despite a straw poll finding 90 per cent supported Labour. I had probably felt closer to The Guardian, which my father had read since the News Chronicle died in 1960. Yet there would have been something irresistible about a new non-party paper even if Whittam Smith had not cheerfully recruited Wapping refuseniks like Isabel Hilton and the entire Times Labour staff, David Felton, Barrie Clement and myself. The approach fitted the mid-80s zeitgeist, an increasingly overbearing Thatcher government, and a Labour Party under Neil Kinnock only just beginning its long march back to electability And although the first pre-election leader in 1987 written by Matthew Symonds, undoubtedly reflecting the views of the author's fellow-founders and his own somewhat SDPish leanings, strongly criticised Labour's still unilateralist defence policy, it set a benchmark by not endorsing any party.

## Disappearing Sparrows

All this survived Whittam Smith's editorship. In Westminster the almost daily list of questions I got from his astute successor, Ian Hargreaves, were invariably the right ones. And in those heady days of an increasingly likely Labour victory I'm not sure how many other editors would have published a piece 'with apologies to' Bertrand Russell's Nightmares imagining a fictional Labour chief whip waking up in a cold sweat after dreaming a newly-elected Tony Blair had decided to appoint Tories, including John Major, to his Cabinet. 'That was very odd' Blair's lieutenant Anji Hunter told me, all hurt innocence. Hargreaves was also calmness itself when I received the full 30-minute 'hair dryer' treatment from Gordon Brown after writing a passing, but accurate, reference to the concern of Scottish MPs about his promotion of proteges for shadow cabinet posts. Brown, it should be said, much later made a sparklingly funny speech as Chancellor at the paper's 20th anniversary celebrations, apocryphally describing the frustration of toiling on a Budget only to find the Independent's splash the following day was about the 'disappearing sparrow'.

Hargreaves rarely showed he didn't have it easy. But one night during a party conference in Glasgow I walked with him along the Clyde as he discussed the difficulties of dealing with David Montgomery, the downsizing-obsessed CEO of Mirror Group , which by now part-owned the paper, its first harsh taste of proprietorship.

The common, though not quite universal view of commentators, reinforced by Lebedev's bullish claim the 'future is digital', was the paper had been killed off by the internet. No-one can question that web readership has had a devastating impact on print circulations. But is the story quite so simple? In the early phase, the Independent had seemed the platonic ideal of a profitable newspaper. But there were problems. The Sunday paper, for one. I'm glad the Independent on Sunday survived until this spring, not least because it rescued me and others, including its last editor Lisa Markwell, after the Sunday Correspondent's closure, to which the IOS had greatly contributed. I remember our gloom after its launch, so damned 'handsome' to use a favourite word of its first editor Stephen Glover. The front page picture was of an ecstatic mum Dawn Griffiths clutching her baby, with the characteristic Ian Jack headline 'Enter young mother with a smile saying what words can't'. The Review, for which Jack, later the paper's editor, was responsible, was, as Neal Ascherson said, 'beautiful'. The Correspondent was dead by November.

But the Sunday paper depleted the daily's resources in a faltering economy. Not that we cared much at the time. The IOS felt so, well, classy. In his riveting Paper Dreams Glover dates his own eventually terminal break with Andreas to the IOS-only lunch he hosted at City Road for the new PM John Major. Major initially called it off, furious, as Glover relates, at a front page story the previous Sunday, 'written by Don Macintyre, had reported when the Prime Minister arrived in Bermuda for an Anglo American summit he looked tired enough to draw concerned enquiries from President Bush'. Glover neglects to mention that while my original story was every bit as unexciting as this description suggests, it had been colourfully embroidered on his orders by then news editor Peter Wilby to suggest Major lacked Margaret Thatcher's staying power. This rather un-Independent-ish rewrite made me as angry as Major when I saw the paper at Heathrow the following morning, disproportionately so, I realise in hindsight, but the lunch went ahead and, perhaps hubristically, our colleagues on the daily paper were not invited.[3]

As with the daily paper, the classiness survived the change of editor. Jack picked three ideal candidates to ride the party leaders' buses in the 1992 election, all uncontaminated by the incestuous relationship between lobby journalists and politicians: Blake Morrison (Kinnock), Isabel Hilton (Major) and Zoe Heller with Paddy Ashdown. As a Fife man, Jack could also be fastidious. When he understandably questioned my plan to lunch with Jeffrey Archer, an engagement favoured by Westminster journalists because of the novelist's supposed closeness to the Tory high command, I wholly failed to cheer him up him up by quoting Lloyd George's remark to an appalled King George V about the likelihood that he, Lloyd George, would meet Trotsky on a trip to Moscow: "Sire, I cannot choose whom I meet in your service."

**Gambles too far?**

Smartly and sometimes brilliantly edited though it was throughout its life, the IOS was surely a gamble too far. The chairman (Lord) Marcus Sieff, who as the former head of Marks and Spencer knew how to run a successful business, had opposed its launch, but was outvoted by the board, including Whittam Smith. Yet as Glover would honestly write 'The Independent was no longer making anything like enough money to cover the Independent on Sunday losses'. But the IOS was only one factor. Murdoch's predatory pricing through most of the 90s could easily have killed the paper. The Independent also came late to establishing its own web presence. And Alan Rusbridger's strategic, if noble, gamble in not charging for Guardian journalism online also inhibited its non-Murdoch rivals, especially the Independent, from doing so. For a man who has now publicly admitted, proclaimed even, he knew from his appointment he would be the Independent's last editor,[4] Amol Rajan, backed by the creative flair of his indispensable deputy Dan Gledhill, and a resourceful young news editor Matt Moore, presided over an often excellent paper, outstanding given the meagre resources, and a fine redesign. Both Gledhill and Moore have now left. John Rentoul loyally disputed Spectator Fraser Nelson's suggestion it was less the internet than the hugely successful i that 'did for' the Independent.[5] But even if the striking graphic published by Nelson exaggerated the symmetry between the rise of the i and the Independent's decline, the i had become an asset which the Lebedevs have now cashed in for £26m, in the process paradoxically challenging the conventional wisdom that print is necessarily dead. And it would have helped if a fraction of the millions spent on the launch of the still struggling TV channel London Live had gone towards promoting the mother paper.

Yet does the printed Independent's fall also reflect something less tangible? When Tony O'Reilly eased out MGN in 1995 his benevolent ownership prolonged the Independent's claim to be worthy of its title. Simon Kelner, the longest serving editor, was a notably strong personality, of course, if also occasionally more stubborn in his brief second term than in the first. In Cairo in 2011, four days before Mubarak's fall, I paced the terrace of the city's Marriot Hotel vainly imploring the editor not to run a front page headline 'Will the Egyptian Revolution run out of steam?' But Kelner's editorship from 1998 did not make the downmarket plunge some had patronisingly predicted. And with the dubious distinction of having worked on three papers when they went from broadsheet to tabloid, I'm certain the Independent's transformation to 'compact' which Kelner drove, was easily the most successful. The idiosyncratic front pages were often superb. I was deputed by the political staff to question the huge blank space and the single word 'Whitewash' on the day of the Hutton report, only to realise the following morning how stunning it was. I also knew as Jerusalem correspondent how robustly as the paper's first Jewish editor, he resisted pressure to modify the paper's often highly critical line towards Israel's government. Equally for a single proprietor, O'Reilly was as good as it got. I was at the Independent lunch for Alastair Campbell at which all the journalists present opposed the Iraq war; it wasn't just that Kelner so rightly positioned the paper on Iraq, O'Reilly seemed almost to relish his editor's taking a sharply different view from his own.

When O'Reilly was forced to part with the papers, the Lebedevs certainly reprieved them, and without serious interference, 'notwithstanding,' as Kelner put it in The Guardian, 'Evgeny Lebedev's frequent appearances in [the Independent's] pages,'[6] at least until it endorsed the coalition before 2015 election. Rajan insisted this was not ordered by Lebedev; yet it's hard to believe it did not reflect the owner's choice. Either way, it magisterially defied the allegiance of the paper's still loyal readers, 47 per cent of whom by now supported Labour compared with 16 per cent for the Liberal Democrats and four for the Tories. The masthead mantra 'Free from Party Political bias, Free from Proprietorial interference' had been removed earlier, perhaps far-sightedly, under Chris Blackhurst's editorship. Rightly or wrongly, it now felt as if these two founding principles had both been abandoned.

Yet 2016 could surely have been an Independent moment. In the year of an EU referendum, a momentous US election, and convulsions within the main UK political parties, it's still hard to believe there was no space for the enquiring liberal non-aligned paper it was founded to be. Leading journalists, Cockburn, Fisk, Rupert Cornwell, David Usborne, John Lichfield, Kim Sengupta on the foreign side alone, remained as serious assets. Maybe, of course, it really was ahead of the curve again. And maybe it's too romantic to recall Andrew Marr's elegiac remark, when he edited the paper in the 90s, to the effect of: "If you invented something light that could carry 150,000 words, slip into a rucksack, didn't need power and called it a newspaper, wouldn't everyone say 'how brilliant'?" But Marr was on to something. The internet has done some great things for journalism, including, paradoxically, by giving it a much longer shelf-life than the one that used to be confined to dusty libraries. But newspapers derive part of their special character by being trusted by its readers to make choices about what is important, giving them the pleasurable challenge of moving outside their immediate field of interest. Whether a web-only version can rise above the tendency of social media, which drives much of its readership, to keep its users within their comfort zone, is an open question. As is that of whether the Independent and its sister app, can emerge from what Lebedev called this 'historic transition', as, like the newspaper, more than the sum of its still formidable parts. Either way its 30th birthday in October was hardly what it might have been.

## Notes

[1] Snoddy, Raymond (2016) 'A spotlight on the *Indy* and the *Boston Globe*' *Mediatel Newsline* 16 March. Available online at
http://mediatel.co.uk/newsline/2016/03/30/the-indys-call-to-arms-and-the-future-of-the-boston-globe/ Accessed on 15 September 2016

[2] Jackson, Jasper (2016) 'National newspaper sites' traffic slides after Brexit bounce' *Guardian* 18 August. Available online at
https://www.theguardian.com/media/2016/aug/18/national-newspaper-traffic-brexit-telegraph-facebook Accessed on 15 September 2016

[3] Glover, S. (1993) Paper Dreams; The story of The Independent and The Independent on Sunday by one of its three founders, London: Jonathan Cape.

[4] Rajan, Amol(2016) 'From the start, I knew I'd be the Independent's last print editor' *Spectator* 20 February. Available online at http://www.spectator.co.uk/2016/02/diary-686/ Accessed on 15 September 2016

[5] Nelson, Fraser (2016) 'The *Independent* hasn't died, it has merely changed its form' *Spectator Coffee House Daily* (Blog) 16 February Available online at
http://blogs.spectator.co.uk/2016/02/the-independent-hasnt-died-it-has-just-changed-its-form Accessed 15 September 2016

[6] Kelner, Simon (2016) 'The paper had a real soul' *Guardian* 26 March Available online at https://www.theguardian.com/media/2016/mar/26/former-independent-editor-simon-kelner-the-paper-had-a-real-soul Accessed 15 September 2016

## Note on the contributor

Donald Macintyre was labour editor of the Independent, political editor of the Independent on Sunday, and successively political editor, chief political commentator, Jerusalem correspondent and parliamentary sketchwriter of The Independent. This chapter is an updated and slightly expanded version of an article which appeared in the June issue of the British Journalism Review.

# From newspapers of influence to newsbrands...of influence

**Newspapers can still be an integral ingredient of the advertising mix in the 21st century, and huge amounts of research supports that argument, says Vanessa Clifford, CEO of Newsworks, the trade body that markets the UK's national newspapers**

I joined the trade body for UK national newspapers Newsworks from the media agency Mindshare at the end of 2012, coming on board in the same year that the organisation rebranded from the Newspaper Marketing Agency, in order to reflect the multi-platform nature of newspapers (a term swiftly replaced by the more digital-friendly newsbrands).

What followed has been a period of change for both Newsworks and the titles that we represent. From an industry perspective, the past four years have seen newsbrands' reach surge, up to 47m readers a month at the last count[1], driven by a boom in digital devices and ever-more accessible online formats; unprecedented industry collaboration, demonstrated by initiatives such as PATS and PAMCo (more on these later); and new and diverse challenges emerge, from Facebook to ad-blocking. What remains unchanged is the population's demand for verified, trusted journalism, whether that's on paper or online, and newsbrands' ability to evolve and innovate.

Over the same period here at Newsworks, we've implemented a robust research programme to provide quantifiable proof of newsbrands' influence and effectiveness; launched popular annual events in the form of our Shift conferences and Planning Awards; and undergone an overhaul of our communications strategy to ensure our messages are reaching more people than ever.

None of us know exactly what the next four years will bring, but one thing is for sure: newsbrands will continue to influence, inform and investigate, while Newsworks continues to prove and promote their value to media agencies and advertisers.

There are undoubtedly challenges to be met, but I believe there is also much to be positive about.

## What does Newsworks stand for?

In 2012 the popular narrative was that newspapers were dead. Stories about their ageing profile and the decline of print readership dominated coverage and the Leveson Inquiry brought bad publicity and the threat of further regulation. Lacking a modern, united voice, the industry was being eclipsed by other media.

In this climate, the Newspaper Marketing Agency rebranded as Newsworks in May 2012, driven by the need to reflect the multi-platform nature of today's titles. The change was instigated by the then CEO Rufus Olins and accompanied by a change of terminology, from newspapers to newsbrands. As Olins put it at the time: 'The media landscape is evolving fast, and this is affecting the national press as much as any other medium. We need to start thinking differently – it's not just about printed newspapers, it's about newsbrands in all their forms.'[2]

With this in mind, Newsworks set about adopting a strategy to successfully change the climate around the industry among media agencies and advertisers, and increase consideration of newspapers as an advertising medium. In short, to prove that newspapers worked. A new brand identity accompanied the change of direction, emphasising Newsworks' role as representative of an innovative and effective industry.

Our aims were to highlight growing audiences, levels of reader engagement, brand values, the trusted context newsbrands provide and the agenda-setting role of national titles. To promote these themes, a communications strategy was designed to engage target audiences throughout the year. It introduced ongoing 'drumbeats' of small-scale activity, complemented by big newsworthy 'crescendo' initiatives.

These themes have continued to inform our strategy over the past four years, with newsbrands' influence, innovation and advertising effectiveness taking centre stage and fuelling a robust insight programme. The term 'newsbrands' has since become an accepted and widely used word in industry dialogue, while awareness of newsbrands' multi-platform presence has been reflected in methodology changes, such as the Advertising Association and media best practice agency Warc amending their Advertising Expenditure Report to encompass newspapers' digital ad spend.

While the newspaper industry, and as a result Newsworks, continues to be faced with new challenges – from the rise of Facebook as a news distributor to the growth of ad blocking – these are issues that the industry will navigate, together more than ever. Collaboration has, and continues to be, a key part of Newsworks' agenda going forward.

## What has Newsworks achieved?

Since Newsworks' advent, providing quantifiable proof of newsbrands' role and strengths has been at the core of the organisation. Key pieces of research are informed by the over-arching themes of influence, context and effectiveness seeking to change the industry's focus to content, brands and audiences, rather than simply platforms.

From 'Day of influence' to 'Generation News' to its largest and most recent study on effectiveness, Newsworks has sought to provide media agencies with robust evidence on what newsbrands have to offer and how they work with other media. New research projects are launched at industry events, bringing together stakeholders, media agencies and advertisers to hear the findings. The client services team also regularly visit media agencies and clients to present the findings in a more interactive environment.

Promoting and landing core industry statistics, such as newsbrands' reach, is also a central part of Newsworks' role. National Readership Survey (NRS) Print and Digital Data (PADD) and ABC data are published on the website and regularly promoted on Twitter and Newsworks' weekly email bulletin, while larger initiatives such as our ad campaigns have helped establish informative and sometimes surprising facts. WPP's CEO Sir Martin Sorrell has even quoted the fact that newsbrands reach more people in the UK than Google.[3]

**Shift conferences**

Newsworks' key themes also inform the programmes for its events. Shift, Newsworks' annual conference, first took place at the British Library in April 2013. Named to reflect the shift from print newspapers to multi-platform newsbrands, the inaugural annual event provided insight on the latest thinking and trends for the national newspaper industry, with keynotes delivered by the Daily Mail's chairman Lord Rothermere and Trinity Mirror's newly-appointed (at the time) CEO Simon Fox, who managed to woo the audience with a live magic trick. The morning, which saw the launch of GuardianWitness and Tony Gallagher (then at the Daily Telegraph) give an insight into the role of an editor in the digital era, was described by Campaign as a sign that 'a reinvigorated Newsworks appears to be helping newsbrands find a collective voice.'

In 2014, the conference focused on newsbrands' influence and included live 'Day of influence' pitches from media agencies to a Dragons Den client panel. Six leading newspaper groups collaborated for the initiative, creating a unique advertising package across all of their platforms and offering agency planners the chance to influence 20m people on a single day. A live audience vote decided the winner, PHD's Emma Callaghan for Expedia, who proposed activity to drive tourism to the Philippines in the wake of Typhoon Haiyan. The campaign, which was designed by Ogilvy, ran across newsbrands' platforms on 29 August 2014 and motivated 62 per cent of those who saw it to find out more about the Philippines, a true illustration of the influence of newsbrands.

In the same year, Newsworks launched Shift North in Manchester. Speakers have included The Sunday Times' David Walsh discussing his 13-year investigation into Lance Armstrong's doping (a session which has since been viewed 57,000 times on YouTube) and The Times' Andrew Norfolk, who delivered a harrowing and moving account of how he eventually broke down the wall of silence surrounding years of child abuse in Rotherham.

## Newsworks Planning Awards

Another annual industry event comes in the form of the Newsworks Planning Awards. Created in 2013 to celebrate the UK's outstanding planning talent in media agencies and beyond, the awards feature a range of categories including best content partnership and best topical campaign, as well as new categories for 2016 – best use of insight and an effectiveness award.

Past chairs have included Unilever's Marc Mathieu, HSBC's Amanda Rendle and Aviva's Jan Gooding, with the most recent jury of leading marketers and agency experts headed up by RBS's David Wheldon.

Since the awards were launched, we have seen a record number of entries from media planners each year, with the entries providing a wealth of case studies on Newsworks' website.

## PATS

Announced in 2014 and successfully rolled out in 2016, the Publishers Advertising Transaction System (PATS) is a non-profit industry initiative designed to make transactions between publishers and media agencies simpler and more efficient.

Created by Newsworks' stakeholders and developed by Mediaocean, the system enables both agencies and publishers to deliver audiences across brands regardless of platform. It acts as a technology bridge between agency buying systems and publisher platforms, providing a single and shared point of reference across the transaction process.

All of Newsworks' stakeholder publishers now use PATS and have been receiving a steady stream of orders from media agencies through the system since it launched. This number is increasing as new partner agencies are added via the Adazzle and Prisma buy-side systems.

The next stage of the plan is to widen PATS' use beyond Newsworks' national newspaper titles to other publishers such as regional titles and magazines.

## PAMCo

Launched in 2015 as a replacement for the NRS, the Publishers Audience Measurement Company (PAMCo) oversees the audience figures for newspapers and magazines.

The change was instigated by UK newspaper publishers who wanted measurement to cover all major routes to market (print, mobile, tablets, PCs and laptops). Led by Simon Redican, PAMCo is preparing to replace NRS information with Audience Measurement for Publishers (AMP) data.

Commercially, the launch of AMP will mean that for the first time both buyer and seller will be able to calculate the total reach and frequency of newsbrands' campaigns across all platforms, critical for a sector which has invested huge amounts in distributing its content far and wide and has bigger reach than at any time in their history. AMP will help publishers to monetise this as truly multi-platform digital players.

The above examples are just some of the initiatives Newsworks has created or, in the case of PATS and PAMCo, helped to launch. All of them are rooted in industry collaboration and have helped create a united front for an industry that has historically been notorious for in-fighting.

It's true that competitiveness is part of the culture of newsbrands; in some ways that is what makes the British press so vibrant, but there is also a spirit of collaboration among newsbrands now, particularly commercially, as they evolve to meet the challenges of our digital age.

## The importance of research

Providing agency planners with insights and proof of newsbrand effectiveness is a central task for Newsworks and research projects underpin the events we hold. Since rebranding, Newsworks has undertaken 12 large-scale studies in conjunction with expert partners. Here's a run-down of some of the most pivotal:

## Effectiveness

The most recent addition to Newsworks' body of research, a trio of effectiveness studies, provide robust evidence of the impact that newsbrands have on:

- ROI: Many individual case studies over the years have proven the effectiveness of newsbrands as part of the media mix. Yet there had been no large-scale study to conclusively demonstrate and quantify the return on investment that newsbrands deliver to advertisers.

  Newsworks commissioned the highly respected econometrics consultancy Benchmarketing, led by managing director Sally Dickerson, to carry out a detailed analysis to provide this evidence. Benchmarketing conducted a meta-analysis of more than 500 econometric models from 2011-2016. Results revealed that advertising with newspapers increases overall revenue return on investment by three times on average, while showing that current investment in print has fallen below effective levels and advertisers should return to 2013 spend levels.

  The project also saw the creation of an ROI optimiser to help media planners find the optimum level of investment in print newspapers as a proportion of the total budget, for a range of different budget levels and sectors.

- Business effectiveness: Effectiveness expert Peter Field focused on the most recently published case studies from the IPA Effectiveness Awards to demonstrate that both print and online newsbrands have a measurable, widespread and long-term impact on campaign business effectiveness.

Findings show that campaigns using print newsbrands deliver a 36 per cent uplift in business effects compared with campaigns that don't use print newsbrands, while the biggest business effects across the whole sample (+5 per cent) are seen when both print and digital newsbrands are used in campaigns.

• Brand health: Newsworks collaborated with media agencies to measure five client campaigns across newsbrand print and digital platforms. BDRC Continental conducted matched controlled exposure tests. The analysis provided the net uplift in brand metrics, taking into account competitor shifts, across all newsbrand platforms, both solus and in different combinations.

The study found that print is the most effective single newsbrand platform for brand building, driving an average 5 per cent uplift in brand health measures, while print plus digital newsbrands is the most efficient combination, leading to a 17 per cent uplift in brand health measures.

## The battle for attention
For this project, Newsworks teamed up with PwC to explore the importance of attention in a world saturated with infinite content. The study challenges the time-spent argument as too simplistic and introduces an attention score, ranking 15 media types and suggesting that quality time drives advertising impact far more than dwell time.

Results found that regular consumers who are fully immersed in a media are more likely to respond positively to advertising than those who are using multiple devices simultaneously. Based on an attention equation, national print newspapers achieved the highest media attention score – 80 per cent among their regular consumers.

Commenting on the findings, Douglas McCabe, CEO and head of publishing and tech at Enders Analysis, said: "Advertising is increasingly being traded on an audience basis, taking too little into account of the respective qualitative strengths of different media experiences. Consumer immersion in trusted content has a massive impact on awareness, trust and effectiveness of its associated advertising. Attention feels an important step in the right direction."[4]

## How people buy
Conducted by research companies Flamingo and Tapestry along with behavioural economics expert Dr Nick Southgate, this study examined the consumer decision journey, with a focus on the roles of different media channels along the path to purchase.

It found that a high proportion of shoppers worry about making a mistake when buying a product, particularly with bigger purchases, despite the endless opportunities to compare and contrast online. If anything, shoppers now have access to too much information and are bombarded with messages, which makes their buying choices more unclear. In this context, the study found that newsbrands play an important role in the path to purchase, helping people filter information and guiding them on what to focus on.

The findings were developed into an interactive planning tool, to help media planners choose the right channels to move people along the purchase journey and drive sales.

## Generation News

In a connected age, the role of newsbrands as a trusted lens on the world is more important than ever, according to the findings of Generation News. Conducted in partnership with the University of Bath and Flamingo and Tapestry, the study explored newsbrand habits, providing evidence that they are stronger and greater in number than ever before.

The study particularly addressed the myth that young people are no longer consuming news, showing that 74 per cent of 18-34 year olds turn to newsbrands to get a balanced point of view and 78 per cent agree their newsbrand introduces them to stories they wouldn't otherwise read.

## Tech Nation

One of Newsworks' earliest research studies, Tech Nation was conducted in partnership with Kantar Media to explore how technology has both reflected and shaped how people think and behave. It found that we have become a nation of tech lovers irrespective of age, with only about one in five people saying they have little interest in new technology and devices.

By using TGI Clickstream analysis, the research also established five new groups based on tech habits, each amounting roughly to 20 per cent of the UK's population, and followed that up with ethnographic and quantitative research. These groups formed the basis of a Geek Calculator, allowing users to input their tech habits and be appointed a relevant group. It had more than 200,000 users and made it onto the homepage of MailOnline!

## Industry overview

According to latest NRS PADD data, newsbrands reach 47m people a month across all platforms, that's 91 per cent of the population.[5] Not only do they have huge reach, but newsbrands also engage people – it's pretty hard to multi-task while reading. TouchPoints 2016 data shows that on the days they read them, people spend 70 minutes reading newspapers in print and 50 minutes on tablet[6].

It's this sort of insight that has changed the mind of Sir Martin Sorrell, once a newspaper sceptic, who in recent years has hailed the strength of newspapers: 'I think with traditional media, particularly newspapers, [the market] will realise they are more powerful than people give them credit for,' he said[7].

More recently, newsbrands' print circulation and online traffic boost in the wake of the EU referendum has underlined the important role they play, particularly in turbulent times. ABC data reported that 90,000 extra newspapers were sold each day in June 2016, the month of the vote, meaning more than 2.7m extra papers were sold in June compared with May. Online there was also a huge swell in unique browsers with the UK newspaper market up 11 per cent month on month and 31 per cent year on year, as readers sought reliable up-to-date news content[8].

Simeon Adams, partner at Goodstuff, explained the uplift perfectly when he said: "In uncertain times people are clearly still turning to trusted news sources and brands for clarity and understanding. Like it or not, the referendum has demonstrated the enduring importance and influence of a free press."[9]

Within the industry there is often talk of how and when the pendulum will swing back to newsbrands. The Brexit boost is encouraging in that it proves people's appetite for trusted and informed journalism is undiminished, showing that in the short term the pendulum can very easily swing back. The challenge lies in how newsbrands can adapt and evolve to instigate longer-term change.

This is something that Newsworks and its stakeholder titles are continually working towards. Whether it's joint, structural changes to how the industry operates, as with PAMCo and PATS, or individual innovations such as titles diversifying (e.g. Sun Bets), launching creative branded content solutions  or experimenting with new technologies such as AR and VR, newsbrands are continuing to move with the times. However, as Newsworks' effectiveness research quantifiably proves, there is still huge value for advertisers in print, which not only supercharges the ROI of other newspaper platforms when it's included in the mix, but also of other media.

Having robust research to remind agencies and advertisers of the value of newsbrands remains key in times of such uncertainly and constant change in the industry. There are currently many question marks over digital media measurement and standards. Facebook has been called out for 'marking their own homework'[10] after admitting to a miscalculation that resulted in an overstatement of its video metrics. In light of this and other issues around online fraud, we're proud to be supporting and publishing independent data and in-depth research.

From an editorial perspective, we'll continue to praise and promote great journalism. From important investigations such as the Panama Papers, Rotherham child abuse revelations, exposé of charity fundraising methods and sporting doping scandals, to catchy headlines, breaking news and front page splashes, newspapers play a vital role in our society, one which we'll carry on championing.

We are incredibly proud of what we've achieved so far, both as an as an industry and as an organisation, while being acutely aware of what more needs to be done. The next few years are guaranteed to bring much change, and with it innovation, as newspapers continue to evolve, develop and harness the opportunities of our digital world.

## Notes

[1] NRS PADD Jul 15 – Jun 16 + comScore Jun 2016

[2] Rufus Olins, quoted by Campaign, 21 May 2012

[3] Sir Martin Sorrell quoted by News Media Works, 18 September 2015

[4] Douglas McCabe quoted in Newsworks' press release, Attention paid is critical factor in assessing advertising impact finds PwC & Newsworks report, 28 April 2016

[5] NRS PADD Jul 15 – Jun 16 + comScore Jun 2016

[6] IPA TouchPoints 2016

[7] Sir Martin Sorrell, quoted by the Guardian, Monday 29 June 2015

[8] ABC, July 2016

[9] Ibid

[10] Sir Martin Sorrell quoted by Bloomberg, 22 September 2016

## Note on the contributor

Vanessa Clifford is CEO of Newsworks, the marketing agency for newspapers. She joined the company in 2012 as client services and strategy director, before becoming deputy CEO in 2014. Prior to this, Vanessa worked at Mindshare for 12 years as a managing partner and head of publishing.

# Where did the advertising go?

More than 30 years ago, in 1986, Fleet Street underwent a technological revolution, belatedly joining the computer age. It sparked a renaissance of newspapers and a boom in press advertising. But the digital seeds sown then would ultimately lead to an exodus of ad revenue from print, initially to specialist websites for property, travel and recruitment, later, overwhelmingly, to Google and Facebook, whose new targeting systems enabled advertisers to sidestep the traditional media, says media commentator and advertising industry expert, Torin Douglas

## The first computer revolution

In January 1986, Rupert Murdoch moved his four national newspapers to a new computerised printworks in Wapping, bypassing the print unions which had resisted the new technology. In March, Eddy Shah launched Today. In September, hot-metal printing ended at the huge Daily Telegraph presses in Fleet Street, to be replaced by a high-tech plant in London's Docklands. In October, The Independent was launched, followed by a wave of new papers embracing the lower-cost production methods.

Computer screens and keyboards replaced typewriters for journalists and advertising teams. Freed from union restrictions, publishers unleashed a wave of specialist supplements, offering more choice for readers and better audience segmentation for advertisers.

But in due course it became clear computers, algorithms and the internet could deliver segmentation and targeting far more efficiently than printed newspapers, which is why so much of the press advertising has been gobbled up by Google and Facebook.

To understand how and why the change happened, we need to look back to that earlier revolution, to see the benefits it brought to advertisers, readers and society (not least in the delivery of high-quality, independent journalism) which are now at risk, if not already lost.

It took two years for the full impact of post-Wapping creative innovation to emerge. On September 16, 1988, I wrote in Marketing Week:

"The truly astonishing mass of new sections that arrived on my doorstep at the weekend represents the final stage in the liberation of our national newspapers from the tyranny of the trade unions that held back pagination and editorial development for so long.

"The first wave was Wapping, where Rupert Murdoch was heralded, aided and abetted by Eddy Shah. For the first time, a national newspaper publisher was able to produce papers on the management's terms, rather than the unions.

"The second wave, post-Wapping, saw the rest of Fleet Street capitalise on Murdoch's breakthrough, signing dramatically different agreements with their unions and moving to new computerised typesetting and printing facilities, gradually adapting their papers to the new technology.

"The third wave sees the journalists, backed by their management, for the first time taking control of the new opportunities and starting to produce new types of newspaper sections. Last weekend, more newspapers started producing more editorially-led innovation than at any time since the Sunday Times introduced the two-section newspaper and colour magazine in the 1960s." (Douglas, 1988, Marketing Week)

That weekend in 1988, The Independent launched a two-section Saturday paper and a ground-breaking colour magazine. The Telegraph switched its colour magazine from Sunday to Saturday, launching a new magazine called Seven Days in its stead. The Times moved to a four-section Saturday paper. The Sunday Times produced its eighth section, called New Society, a partwork about Italian food and a second colour magazine previewing the Olympics. The Mail on Sunday also carried an Olympic magazine – funded entirely by 3M. The Observer launched Section 5, a London leisure, arts, property and listings section, the Sunday Mirror a colour magazine and the Sunday Telegraph a total redesign.

Amid today's cornucopia of creativity, and the constant global stream of new apps, websites, social media, memes and video, this may not seem much. At the time, it was a giant leap.

## There was a separation between 'church and state' that everyone understood

Crucially in those days, the twin revenue streams of cover price and advertising (display and classified) provided a robust funding model for high quality, independent journalism – and a much purer one than the blurry lines of today's 'native' advertising.

There was a separation between 'church and state' that everyone understood – journalists, sales departments, advertisers and readers. It was plain to see what was editorial and what was an advertisement. The occasional 'advertorials' – pages of editorial paid for by advertisers – had to be clearly labelled as such, under the Code of Advertising Practice. And if advertisers threatened to remove their advertising because they didn't like what was being written about them, the best newspapers resisted the threat and waved them goodbye.

The most famous example concerned the Sunday Times expose of the Thalidomide scandal. In his book Good Times, Bad Times, the distinguished editor Sir Harold Evans recalled the start of the paper's campaign in 1972 to persuade Distillers, which owned the drug company involved and had always denied negligence, to accept responsibility:

"I told Denis Hamilton (the paper's managing director). He was very relaxed about it. I also told the advertising manager, Donald Barrett. 'Distillers are our largest single advertiser. As a group they spend £600,000 a year' he told me. 'I know that won't stop you and it shouldn't,' he added. (Distillers withdrew all their advertising after the beginning of the campaign.)" (Evans, 1984)

Commenting in The Journalist in British Fiction and Film, Sarah Lonsdale wrote: "If we compare this incident to the famous Telegraph repression of criticism of the banking giant HSBC in 2015, it is clear we are operating in very different worlds."

For many publishers in the 1980s, particularly the quality broadsheets and local newspapers, classified advertising for jobs, cars, and houses was a crucial element of the business model. The Guardian carved out a highly profitable niche in public sector job advertising, for which it created weekly editorial supplements on education, health and social and charity work.

Its Media Page, created in 1984, soon became a Media Section, carrying several pages of editorial designed to keep the ads apart and attract readers in the media, whether or not they were looking for a job. When I wrote a weekly column about the media, for The Times from 1982-84 and later for the Independent, I was under no illusions: I knew it was in the hope media advertisers would place their ads there. But, in those days at least, media sections were allowed to be independent and to write frankly and fairly about the publication itself and its rivals.

The Guardian, under the protective mantle of the Scott Trust, also benefited from the classified ads in its highly profitable sister publications, the Manchester Evening News and Auto Trader. In those days, the best regional newspapers and trade papers were cash cows for their owners – but they were ripe for milking by others when the digital revolution took hold. Some publishers saw the writing on the screen and moved smartly to launch or buy websites of their own. Others were slower to respond.

As Guy Zitter points out in another chapter, the Guardian and the Daily Mail group were among the smart ones, gaining a lucrative foothold in the digital world. But the gains there still did not make up for the loss of classified print revenue.

## Where there were newsprint pounds, there are now only digital pennies
One reason for the discrepancy was advertising space on the internet was infinite, whereas space in a printed newspaper was relatively scarce, and could be

made scarcer by publishers cutting paging at times when the price of newsprint was going up. In traditional advertising terms, when demand for space exceeds the supply, the price goes up, but on the internet the supply is limitless. Where there were newsprint pounds, there are now only digital pennies (at least for traditional publishers: Google and Facebook, using a different model, have precipitated a digital gold rush).

Nowhere did this become clearer than at The Guardian. Despite becoming one of the largest and most influential English-language newspaper websites in the world, with 155m monthly browsers in April 2016, it posted a £69m loss for the year (and a total loss of £173m, after exceptional items and write downs) as, like other newspapers, its print circulation and advertising revenue sharply declined. And though its global audience continued to rise, its digital revenues fell by almost £2m to £81.9m as – the paper itself reported online – 'Facebook and Google ate up the bulk of the money made from mobile advertising.' (Jackson, Guardian, 2016).

"Facebook's quarterly profit and revenue blew past Wall Street estimates on Wednesday as the company's hugely popular mobile app and a push into video attracted new advertisers and encouraged existing ones to spend more. Total revenue rose 59.2 per cent to $6.44bn, compared with the estimate of $6.02bn." (Tynan, Guardian, July 27, 2016)

The same week, Adweek reported: "Google is still the primary moneymaker for parent company Alphabet. During the second quarter of 2016, Alphabet's revenue hit $21.5bn, a 21 per cent year-over-year increase. Of that revenue, $19.1bn came from Google's advertising business, up from $16bn a year ago." (Johnson, Adweek, July 28, 2016)

So dominant have Google and Facebook become in the digital advertising world that the News Media Association, the UK's trade body for publishers, has called on the Government to intervene. It estimates the two giant US companies now take 90 pence of every pound spent of publishers' digital revenue. (Hammett, MediaTel Newsline, September 22, 2016)

**So how have Facebook and Google built such a huge share of the market?**
"Facebook is winning because it has amazing advertising products that work incredibly well," said Will Haywood, former VP for Europe at Buzzfeed, at a recent Newsbrands debate. (Pidgeon, MediaTel Newsline, September 19, 2016)

Many would say the same holds true for Google, which revolutionised the advertising process in 2000, when it launched AdWords, linked to its world-beating search engine.

"The bulk of Google's $75bn revenue in 2015 came from its proprietary advertising service, Google AdWords," reported Eric Rosenberg, in Investopaedia.

"When you use Google to search for anything from financial information to local weather, you're given a list of search results generated by Google's algorithm. The algorithm attempts to provide the most relevant results for your query, and, along with these results, you may find related suggested pages from an AdWords advertiser. Any recommended websites you see when logged into Gmail, YouTube, Google Maps, and other Google sites are generated through the AdWords platform.

**I know half of my advertising works, I just don't know which half.**
"To gain the top spot in Google advertisements, advertisers have to outbid each other. Advertisers pay Google each time a visitor clicks on an advertisement. A click may be worth anywhere from a few cents to over $50 for highly competitive search terms, including insurance, loans and other financial services." (Rosenberg, Eric, 2016, Investopaedia)

Through a second advertising programme, AdSense, "Google served as a matchmaker, marrying advertisers with Web destinations," wrote Ken Auletta, in Googled: The End of the World As We Know It. "If Intel wanted to advertise on technology blogs or a hotel in London wanted to promote itself on travel sites, Google put them together via a similar automated auction system."

Revenue from AdSense advertising made up 23 per cent – or $15 bn – of Google's total 2015 ad revenue. (Investopedia, 2016)

Auletta wrote: "It was Google's ambition, its founders liked to say, to provide an answer to the adman's legendary line: 'I know half of my advertising works, I just don't know which half'. Unlike the ads traditional media had sold for more than a century, based on the estimated number of people reading a newspaper or watching a programme, Google's system ensured advertisers were charged only when the user clicked on an ad.

"And unlike traditional analog media companies, which can't measure the effectiveness of their advertising, Google offered each advertiser a free tool: Google Analytics, which allowed the advertiser to track hour by hour, the number of clicks and sales, the traffic produced by the keywords, the conversion rate from click to sale." (Auletta, Googled.)

Further innovations enhanced Google's offering to advertisers. And the scale of Google and, increasingly, Facebook make their algorithms even more effective and attractive to advertisers. "These two global behemoths are forcefields so magnetic that they suck every penny towards them." (Alps, 2016, MediaTel Newsline)

They were also helped in the early days by the complacency of publishers and advertisers.

"In 1995, Craig Newmarket launched craigslist.org, a website where people could post apartments for rent, job openings, services for hire, products for sale, dating invitations. It seems clear this posed a threat to newspaper classified sections, which produced about a third of their ad revenue. But newspapers usually saw craigslist as a quaint web bulletin board." (Auletta, Googled)

In 1996, nine of the ten major US newspaper groups were invited to save their classified business by joining a network to sell advertising on the web. The advice was rejected. "Newspaper classified advertising plummeted from nearly 18bn dollars in 2005 to about nine billion dollars in 2008." (Auletta, Googled)

## The end of the world as we know it

UK local newspaper publishers were almost equally slow to respond, according to Matthew Engel, writing in the 20th anniversary edition of the British Journalism Review (June, 2009):

"By the millennium, the future of ink on paper as a means of communication was already starting to be questioned, but the new Big Four powers of the regional press pushed on regardless. They did invest in the internet but without any clear idea how this would pay for itself. There was an assumption their traditional small-ad revenue would migrate to the web with the readership. It didn't." (Engel, 2009)

But what more could newspapers have done? In the early days, they should have responded to the challenge of the specialist websites, which were the first to eat their lunch. Local newspapers had 'owned' their classified advertising markets and could have held onto more of their revenue if they had recognised the threat earlier and acted smartly, though digital pennies would still not have added up to the print pounds.

But I believe there is little publishers could have done to stop Google and Facebook, which are in a different business and, indeed, league. The arrival of internet search and algorithm-based targeting really did mean 'the end of the world as we know it' for traditional media.

Most newspapers have now 'gone digital' and are trying to generate new forms of income: paywalls to replace cover price revenue; schemes to share editorial material with Google and Facebook (which, to the frustration of publishers, distribute – but don't directly invest in – their editorial content); and, in the case of The Guardian, 'membership' to help fund its journalism.

But should advertisers now do more to help? Responding to news of The Guardian's losses and Facebook's gains, Tess Alps, chairman of Thinkbox, the TV research and marketing body, urged advertisers and agencies to consider the longer-term effect of where they spent their media money. "Do they really want a world where there is no national, quality journalism or culturally specific entertainment to place their ads in?" (Alps, MediaTel Newsline, August 1)

## Sources

Douglas, Torin (1988) Changing power of the third wave, Marketing Week, 16 September.

Evans, Sir Harold (1984) Good Times, Bad Times. Bedford Square Books

Lonsdale, Sarah (2016) The Journalist in British Fiction and Film: Guarding The Guardians from 1900 to the Present London: Bloomsbury

Rosenberg, Eric (2016) How Google Makes Money, Investopaedia. Available online at http://www.investopedia.com/articles/investing/020515/business-google.asp

Auletta, Ken (2009) Googled: The End of the World As We Know It, Virgin Books

Engel, Matthew (2009) Local Papers: An Obituary, British Journalism Review, Vol 20, No. 2.

Tynan, Dan (2016) Facebook's journey 'only 1% done' after surge in revenue, Zuckerberg says, Guardian 27 July. Available online at https://www.theguardian.com/technology/2016/jul/27/facebook-ad-sales-growth-quarterly-results

Pidgeon, David (2016) Newsbrands debate strategies as they square up to Facebook and Google, MediaTel Newsline, 19 September 2016. Available online at http://mediatel.co.uk/newsline/2016/09/19/newsbrands-debate-strategies-as-they-square-up-to-facebook-and-google/

Jackson, Jasper (2016) Guardian's losses hit £69m but it gains more than 50,000 paying members Guardian 27 July. Available online at https://www.theguardian.com/media/2016/jul/27/guardian-losses-members

Johnson, Lauren (2016) Google Ad Revenue Hits $19 Billion, Even as Mobile Continues to Pose Challenges, Adweek 28 July. Available online at http://www.adweek.com/news/technology/googles-ad-revenue-hits-19-billion-even-mobile-continues-pose-challenges-172722

Hammett, Ellen (2016) Publishers lobby Government to clamp down on Facebook and Google, MediaTel Newsline, 22 September. Available online at http://mediatel.co.uk/newsline/2016/09/22/publishers-lobby-government-to-clamp-down-on-facebook-and-google/

Alps, Tess (2016) This is for everyone, MediaTel Newsline, 1 August. Available online at http://mediatel.co.uk/newsline/2016/08/01/this-is-for-everyone/

## Note on the contributor

Torin Douglas has been writing about advertising and the media for more than 40 years. He worked for Campaign and the Independent Broadcasting Authority before joining the team that launched Marketing Week in 1978. From 1982, he wrote a weekly column about advertising and the media, first for The Times and then for the Independent. He presented Advertising World for LBC Radio from 1984-89 and was then media correspondent for BBC News for 24 years. He is the author of The Complete Guide to Advertising (1985). He is a visiting professor in media at the University of Bedfordshire and holds an honorary doctorate from the University of West London.

# Don't forget the reality of why consumers are still buying the printed word...

**Members of the National Federation of Retail Newsagents (NFRN) actually see print readers every day. Brian Murphy, the NFRN's Head of News, spells out why he believes print still has plenty of life left yet**

Several million newspapers and magazines are sold every day across the UK. That's a fact. So they remain an important product for independent newsagents and convenience store owners, despite overall numbers of sales declining.

With both new front covers and content every day, newspapers remain fresh and appealing to all types of consumer. We believe online cannot benefit in the same way from this face-to-face interaction, the passing customer, nor the impulse sale.

Newspapers remain a significant driver of footfall, too, with shoppers often purchasing other lines when they come in to buy a newspaper or magazine; their attractiveness to retailers therefore is maintained. The desire to stock them is strong and the space they take up not onerous.

Independent retailers can boost sales and reach customers online can't by offering services such as home news delivery. In return for going that extra mile and delivering to those who want or need it, such as the elderly, ill or infirm, retailers can be assured of long-term revenue and security whilst developing customer loyalty at the same time.

There are also very other strong factual arguments to support this argument:

- Ownership of many news brands is not driven by profits – history has taught us ego alone can be a very strategic supporter of newspapers. None of the major news groups seem to be planning to sell and to cut off the product that feeds them. These same owners are generally shrewd business people too and will not to be in the habit of putting all of their eggs in unprofitable online baskets ongoing for the sake of it.

- The political gain for owning and maintaining a physical product can speak volumes. Ask current MPs and advertisers.

- The current cost price of newspapers is far lower compared to the perceived value. Yet each brand has created a daily habitual, and often zero-risk purchase, that other FMCG commodities would die for.
- Consumer demographics indicate those likely to buy a newspaper will live longer and are often those who can afford it either as a habit or a treat.
- Newspapers are currently sold through 55,000 shops, with another possible 5,000 below-the-radar outlets involved, mostly through undefined selling space or without strict retail agreements. This is another factor other products envy.
- While many of the profits generated sit at the top of the business tree in the hands of the owners, there is nothing to prevent this model changing whereby retailers earn more and in turn do more to support the overall sector.
- Local news and events drive content and readership, as do fads and niches. No other market has the flexibility to test and explore changes and developments both locally and nationally yet still build or maintain trust.
- Despite being free, online readership is already slowing and is not widely considered profitable in the way that traditional print has been.

**Note on the contributor**

Brian Murphy has extensive knowledge of the news supply chain. Before joining the NFRN in 2005, he worked for WH Smith (Retail) and then Smith's News (wholesaler), directly managing the world's largest news accounts at London railway stations and airports.

# If print dies so does freedom

**Whilst we embrace the multimedia excitement of online digital media that replaces print editions with 24-hour publication by the second and in all dimensions, we may also have sleep-walked into Orwell's dystopian Nineteen Eighty Four world of memory holes and totalitarian surveillance says Tim Crook**

### Eating the news

You can eat a newspaper, but not an online publication. Why does this seemingly useless piece of information have any significance? The answer is very simple. The tangible printed form is a real object that can be concealed. The digital form has no connection with the existential human body apart from the fading memory of something having been seen.

Put another way something censored in written printed form can always be found. Its equivalent digital jumble of 01 coding once deleted leaves no visible and attainable trace record. Print is permanent. To remove it requires burning or some other method of destruction. Digital online communication disappears when the electricity is turned off, or the broadband cable of data cut.

### The Catastrophe

Many people of my generation are increasingly distressed about the exponential implosion of newspaper circulation, loss of journalism employment and the abject failure to replace this loss with proportionate increases in journalists working online with a sustainable economic model.

My local shop and newsagent proprietor before retiring last year explained why the newspaper and magazine stand had been reduced by three quarters with an expanded display of vodka and other hard liquor. Paper sales had not just been decimated, but reduced by nine tenths in ten years. There was a similar reduction, inevitably, in the number of paper boys and girls. Several villages no longer had any paper delivery.

Of course, it was possible to cite examples of the trend being bucked and news media publishers successfully combining a digital and print relationship. Private Eye continues to significantly eschew the digital dimension, the Tindle newspaper group continues to buy up failing newspaper titles, open new ones, survive and make a profit. The Economist and the Times/Sunday Times, and Spectator sustain a digital and print partnership which is profit-led and expansionist. But the fact remains the vital social habit of buying and reading a newspaper is in catastrophic decline and I personally cannot resist. I have tried subscribing to The Times for a year or two, but found redeeming the vouchers for the papers could not be maintained as a daily habit. I piled up my copies of the papers and magazines in the university newsroom, but the students were rarely moved to pick up and read them.

I tried to be seen to be at least the only lecturer prepared to visibly carry around a newspaper in a department with multiple journalism undergraduate and postgraduate programmes in the hope I became a role model, encouraging my colleagues and the younger generation to retrieve the habit. I even invaded the corrupt and perverted space of online conversation to evangelise the beauty of print and mock the superficiality and superfluous vapidity of the digital cyber usurper. (Crook nd 2013)

I have pointedly bought copies of the printed edition of Le Figaro, and Country Life, two beautifully designed and produced newspaper and magazine forms in the hope I could be re-charged with the loyalty and need to be a committed and consistent consumer in the future.

## Book v Newspaper

This has been to no avail. Whereas I will always prefer to buy and read a book over its Kindle, digital downloaded version, and my expenditure on the book form remains dangerously high and reckless, the book folders on my smartphone and tablet have been neglected for two years. Several hundred downloads never swiped open.

There is a cultural value and significance to the book which has not transferred to the newspaper, or magazine. The former has constitutional literacy; the latter is a throwaway redundancy. I will gladly spend £30 to £40 on AbeBooks, or Ebay to acquire a first edition of George Orwell's Left Book Club edition of The Road to Wigan Pier (1936), despite having several paperback versions published more than 70 years' later, but nothing can persuade me to spend the same amount of money on a subscription to New Statesman or The London Review of Books.

## Demonstrating the problem in Academia

There are journalism programmes in universities now which do not teach print design and publication. The great Harold Evans' five volume manual on editing, design, typography and layout from 1972 is an historical anachronism. We might as well be reading about calligraphy and illumination from the Middle Ages.

This state of affairs makes me feel like a falling man of history, unable to do anything to resist an unendurable destiny of social disempowerment and political vulnerability. I have had nightmares about desperately trying to locate articles and features I had been so sure about, but no longer exist in virtual space and for which there is no longer any refuge or recourse in public libraries, which used to have the architecture of huge chapels lined with hundreds of thousands of books on shelves floor to ceiling.

I have punished myself with the indictment of hypocrisy when distributing pamphlet sheets containing ten statements and facts banned and censored in the UK over the last 50 years to 150 students in a lecture theatre. I then projected the same text onto the huge presentation screen from an externally published website.

I then asked ten of the students to do their best to destroy their sheets of paper and compared this inconvenience and difficulty with the speed and effortless deletion operation in the online software embedded on the lecture hall computer. Two clicks, one username and password, and whoosh. In a split second the ten resonant maxims were gone as though they were never here nor there.

Meanwhile the students were still tearing into the paper, scrunching it up into a ball, some were wondering what would have happened if they ate the paper; others whether the smoke alarm and sprinklers would have been activated by a little conflagration.

I then asked the remaining 140 students to imagine there had been an executive government order backed by judicial injunction ordering them to surrender their sheets/pamphlets, and making it a criminal offence to possess or distribute them. What would they have done with their manifesto of subversion, resistance and liberty? If they wanted to keep it, how would they hide and conceal?

Most realised the state was faced with complex and myriad difficulties in search and retrieval. How could it be so sure all of the students would give up their hot property? How could it be so sure of identifying and confirming who had received the paper? Was there a reliable data trail in credit and swipe card transactions? If free how could it have been receipted? The paper so offensive to state authoritarian approbation became a fugitive and victim of oppression, but it was easy to protect and harbour. It had no digital signature.

Once it had escaped from the originating printing source it would be well-nigh impossible to track and destroy. When the 140 students with their own individual copies of the pamphlet dispersed into their own complex social and physical human networks the challenge facing the authoritarian tendency was the same as trying to contain a virulent and contagious disease. I am sure the United Nations had wished Ebola had been an internet virus.

It quickly dawned on the students the digital version erased before their eyes, had, while available online, been connected with every downloader. The originator's dangerous creation while ostensibly wiped was always stored somewhere on the computer's hard disc, and had been mirrored by some digital back-up facility.

Even somebody seeking to evade GCHQ and NSA style surveillance by encrypting and sheltering behind onion style proxy servers, was still traceable through surveillance, intervention and infiltration.

## Orwell's memory holes

George Orwell in Nineteen Eighty-Four fully predicted and realised the dangers of combining totalitarian control with manipulative technology in social communication. He conjured the implication of the memory hole down which truth and the public record can be annihilated in a blast furnace or bonfire of human identity and history. What was being destroyed was also cultural dignity and independence.

> This last was for the disposal of waste paper. Similar slits existed in thousands or tens of thousands throughout the building, not only in every room but at short intervals in every corridor. For some reason they were nicknamed memory holes. When one knew that any document was due for destruction, or even when one saw a scrap of waste paper lying about, it was an automatic action to lift the flap of the nearest memory hole and drop it in, whereupon it would be whirled away on a current of warm air to the enormous furnaces which were hidden somewhere in the recesses of the building. (Orwell 1975:33-4)

When communication and information is centralised by technology onto one electronic platform Orwell's vision of control is realised. This is what the internet has achieved. It means Winston Smith's dystopian world of destroying the past is materialising into reality:

> This process of continuous alteration was applied not only to newspapers, but to books, periodicals, pamphlets, posters, leaflets, films, sound-tracks, cartoons, photographs – to every kind of literature or documentation which might conceivably hold any political or ideological significance. Day by day and almost minute by minute the past was brought up to date. (Ibid 35)

## Loss of family identity

The material newspaper form of local public record was essential in constructing my own family identity. My mother died having erased anything connecting her with her parents. A breakdown in the relationship with her father meant he had never seen either of his grandsons. It was several days concentrating on the brown newsprint of the Wigan Observer which enabled me to discover a report of my grandmother's funeral, the mourners and family friends attending, and the valedictory meeting of Up Holland Urban District Council, where my grandfather celebrated the end of a 40-year career in local government and the esteem in which he was held by the local community.

This record of the 1950s does not exist in the early 21st century. The local newspaper industry has neither the manpower nor media institutions on the ground to achieve such micro-reporting and writing of the first draft of history. The online equivalents are unlikely to archive in the same way. And business failure and digital indebtedness to hosting servers could so easily result in the wiping of whole swathes of online journalism. This is condemning future generations to a rootlessness of origin and historical reference. Without family history in the social context you will be without family identity.

## The secret deletions

I have no doubt the Orwellian liquidation and alteration of information is carrying on without challenge or social and political discomfiture. The European Court of Justice ruling in 2014 on the right to be forgotten through Google browser data processing means hundreds of thousands of articles and online records are being disconnected to the searching process. This, in the old days, would have been the equivalent of a reference library without any catalogue or index. Courts in England and Wales regularly issue secret injunctions suppressing links to archives, and directly removing entire postings.

I have seen the Metropolitan Police change the detail of an important online media release which had huge significance in determining the public interest debate at the centre of the story. This was the case of the three Bethnal Green Academy schoolgirls who had travelled to join ISIS in Syria. What was in the letter given to the girls by the deputy head teacher to be passed onto their parents after it was suspected that their friend had gone to Syria a few months earlier? Did the letter say their friend was missing, or specifically state they believed she was with ISIS in Syria? Did the girls hide the letter from their parents? As an online editor I blinked with disorientation and confusion as a key line in the police bulletin was now different. Had I read the original release wrongly? Fortunately, I could rely on the Press Association to explain that the Met Police had indicated initially that the deputy head teacher had said the schoolgirls' friend was believed to be in Syria. Then they had clarified this was not the case. She had only been described as missing. In the online digital age, without verifying correlatives, and the permanence of a printed artefact, everything becomes malleable, illusory, ephemeral and without boundaries. It is as though the human body loses its skeleton, skyscraper concrete its steel mesh, the uniform and suit their essential stitching.

## Conclusion

I feel responsible for having let down the current younger generations who look at newspaper buying and reading as something quaint and bad for health – a bit like smoking a pipe or wearing a bowler hat to work. Flapping the Daily Telegraph newspaper over grilled kippers at breakfast was something my father did and I imagine I should be doing now. This is nostalgic fantasy. I often forget he was born in 1915 and died in 1986, and I am now 57. We have plunged helter-skelter into blindly and thoughtlessly abandoning the art of quotidian reading by newspaper. The aspirant authoritarian and totalitarian can certainly wise up to the prospects for control, manipulation and disrupting the art of verification. This will always be something that can be avoided so much more reliably by exploring volumes of newspapers rather than forlornly search-engine surfing with the prevailing moniker: 'Some results may have been removed under data protection law in Europe.'

This is something I experienced when writing the name of a famous and global celebrity in the Google search-box. There were 39,200,000 results in .66 of a second. Speed and scale were astonishingly impressive. But I could not help worrying about those results which 'may have been removed' secretly. Print may be dying, but democracy and liberty may be also passing away with it.

## Bibliography

Crook, Tim (2014) Lily-livered defeatism must be challenged to save print editions of newspapers, Conversation, 2 January. Available online at
https://theconversation.com/lily-livered-defeatism-must-be-challenged-to-save-print-editions-of-newspapers-21716, accessed on 10 September 2016

Orwell, George (1975) Nineteen Eighty Four, England, Harmondsworth: Penguin Books

## Note on the contributor

Tim Crook is a professor in the department of media and communications at Goldsmiths, University of London, visiting professor in Broadcast Journalism at Birmingham City University and a longstanding journalist and author. He is also chair of the professional practices board of the Chartered Institute of Journalists.

# Success stories

\* \* \*

# Survival of the fittest

**Richard Tait**

The greatest fear of those who doubt the future of print is that the first casualty of the crisis facing newspapers will be good journalism – that the process of cost cutting will hollow out those titles that survive as businesses to the point at which they will not be worth reading – full of sponsored content, 'churnalism' (barely disguised press releases) and click-bait.

There is depressing evidence that that process is already well underway, particularly in the regional and local press. There are once great newspapers in the United States, which are a shadow of their former selves. But the case studies in this section should be an antidote to the more apocalyptic predictions. In all of them, good journalism is not seen as the inevitable victim of economic survival but the essential ingredient in keeping newspapers and magazines strong. It is a case that Mark Thompson, chief executive of the *New York Times*, makes powerfully in his foreword to this book. The encouraging news is that he is not alone in seeing a future for quality journalism.

The Financial Times has moved in my professional lifetime from a comparatively small, respected, but specialised British newspaper to a global media brand. It is also one of the industry's great success stories of digital transformation. It now has more paid-for readers than at any time in its history and its print circulation is profitable before advertising. John Ridding, the chief executive officer who has overseen this transition, has little time for those who argue there are no lessons for other newspapers. And he points out that his business strategy – subscription for digital readers and a realistic cover price for print – only works because of the quality of the editorial product: 'The fact that the FT editorial team has become so invested in relevance and return, engagement and real connections with our readers is a primary factor in our multi-channel growth and the resilience of print.' Why the FT's long standing owner, Pearson, thought it was a good idea to sell such a powerful and successful brand to Nikkei in the summer of 2015 is anyone's guess.

And you could ask the same question of our next British success story – the Economist, where Pearson at about the same time sold its 50 per cent stake to the Agnelli family. Tom Standage, deputy editor and head of digital strategy at the Economist is already planning for a world where there will be no display advertising and the print version will be a luxury product. He believes paywalls will work so long as the content justifies the subscription: 'It can only work for publishers who have the sort of premium content that readers regard as too valuable to do without.'

The key is editorial quality and the Economist is already profitable just on its print and digital circulation revenues. But he has bad news for any newspaper hoping to replace print advertising revenue with digital advertising: 'This is a fantasy and print publishers who try to move to a digital-ad model are doomed to failure.'

William Lewis, after many years in senior jobs in the UK newspaper industry, is now chief executive officer of Dow Jones and publisher of the Wall Street Journal, the biggest selling print newspaper in the US. He believes 'the lesson from America – a country whose titles have taken the biggest digital battering of all – is simple: there is a newspaper model that works.' The priority is editorial quality – 'quality will out – whatever the platform or mode of distribution.' The experience of the Wall Street Journal is that there is clear evidence people will pay for good journalism – digital subscriptions are overtaking print sales and circulation revenues have now overtaken advertising.

The London Evening Standard, on the other hand, has a very different model – it stopped charging a cover price in 2009 and has seen its circulation grow from less than 200,000 to more than 900,000. Doug Wills, the Standard's managing editor, says this has turned the paper round: 'Advertising at a higher yield has matched the circulation growth and Evening Standard Ltd has gone into the black in recent years after more than a decade of losses'. The rise in circulation has been accompanied by website growth of up to 55 per cent year-on-year to almost 15m unique browsers a month. The success reflects the quality of the editorial product – with campaigning journalism on London's social issues.

In the rather different world of magazines, the quality challenge extends to advertising and promotion as well as editorial. Dylan Jones, Editor-in-Chief of the UK lifestyle magazine GQ, casts his expert eye over the expectations of the new generation of readers, starting with his teenage daughters, 'Moneypit 1 and Moneypit 2'. They do not care much who produces the content they're reading, or whether it is advertising or editorial 'as long as the Content is VERY VERY good'. The same quality threshold which is essential for the journalism also applies to advertising and promotions – all the more so as ad-blocking technology threatens to disrupt the business models of the industry: 'All they care about is its quality, and its ability to engage with them immediately. Which is one hell of an opportunity'.

So, if the survival of the fittest means that those who invest in quality prosper, it may be a bit early to write good journalism's obituary. In David Hare and Howard Brenton's savage satire *Pravda*, set in the 1980s, the fictional press baron Lambert La Roux boasted that bad newspapers sell much better than good ones – on the evidence of these case studies, that is no longer true, if it ever was. What an irony it would be if the digital revolution, which is so often seen as good journalism's nemesis, turns out to be a white knight after all.

# Who wants today's papers? The Buggles, Donald Rumsfeld and other reasons to be positive about print

**It is easy, tempting and often wrong to predict new technologies will kill the old. If they have unique strengths and are ready to adapt – including their business model – existing formats can survive and succeed, says John Ridding, CEO of the Financial Times Group**

Ten years ago at a media investment conference in New York I was asked if print newspapers would still be around in ten years as a significant format. Digital delivery was developing fast, with the disruptors, led by Google and Facebook, seizing share of audience at an accelerating pace. White flags were being readied to hoist above many traditional print mastheads. I replied: "Yes, for sure," and was greeted with scepticism by the analysts who had studied the downward charts in print circulation and advertising, extended the trends to zero and placed me in the camp of the 'flat earthers' who didn't 'get' the world of change and pain being visited on established titles.

Ten years on, I'd still say yes to the same question. And I'd point to the FT's transformation as part of the evidence. The FT did 'get' the world of change, and now has more paid-for readers than at any other period of its 129 year-history. It is true that most of those subscribers are now digital, that the FT has become a majority digital business, and that we expect future growth to be driven by mobile and new features from video to interactive graphics. But an equally important truth is the FT's print circulation is now profitable, before advertising, with engaged and loyal readers.

The FT is in many ways different to other titles, and specialist in its focus on global business. But it needn't be a special case. Broader trends, along with some eclectic and surprising pundits – including the 1979 one-hit wonders The Buggles and Donald Rumsfeld (stay with me) – support the case for broader resilience and a rational transition to a mixed model of news delivery.

First, as with the New York analysts, it is easy, tempting, and generally wrong simply to extend trends to the end of the line and to assume new technologies herald the end of the old. In 1922, for instance, *Radio News* magazine said radio would kill the newspaper industry. "Seated comfortably in the club car of the 21st Century Flyer… the president of the Ultra National Bank removes a small rubber disk from his vest pocket and places it over his ear", imagined the leading radio journal of its day. "A moment hence, he will receive by radiophone the financial news of the world", read the confident forecast of print decline (Farrell 1922: 823). I'm on a plane as I write this – there is plenty of print being read, but not so many small rubber disks relaying the world's financial news.

Radio itself was then sentenced to decline and demise with the advent of TV. But, as the Buggles sang in Video Killed The Radio Star, radio had and retains attributes which have ensured its survival. "In my mind, and in my car" goes the first verse, referencing the intimacy of the radio experience. Indeed, as Nielsen reports, radio still reaches more Americans each week than any other channel (Nielsen 2016).

For those interested in an expert and entertaining analysis of The Buggles' lyrics as they relate, with surprising insight, to video, Netflix, IP, and other media matters, I recommend Smead Capital Management (Smead 2015). But the main point is simple. If a technology or platform has unique attributes and the right business model they have the means to survive and succeed, and to re-position themselves profitably on the ever-expanding spectrum of formats and channels.

Newspapers do have unique attributes. At a time of limitless information and limited time, they provide the valuable service of selection and judgment for readers and an informed hierarchy of importance. They also enable the satisfaction of completion, a contrast with the wormholes of the web. They are an attractive format for advertisements, with tactile and visual appeal, part of the reason why luxury advertising in print has held up so well. And while personalisation is an obviously powerful driver of engagement with audiences, serendipity should not be understated. As Donald Rumsfeld said famously, albeit on another topic, "There are things we know that we know… There are known unknowns… But there are also unknown unknowns" (Rumsfeld 2002). Those things you don't know that you don't know, what expert editors believe is important, or what appears by coincidence alongside the article you are reading, can be a pleasing surprise and an important stimulus.

These factors help explain the relative resilience of print circulation. Decline is real, but it isn't as drastic as is often portrayed. As the Pew Research Center wrote in its 2016 report, US newspaper circulation declined for the second consecutive year in 2015 but was relatively stable over the decade – "a 1.1 per cent drop in 10 years: hardly disastrous" (Barthel 2016). Likewise, national readership data from Nielsen Scarborough showed 51 per cent of those who consume a newspaper read it exclusively in print (Nielsen Scarborough 2015).

What is drastic, and damaging, is the decline in print advertising. In the US, newspaper advertising spend fell $8.6bn in five years, from $25bn in 2009 to $16.4bn dollars in 2014 (Barthel 2016: 27). In the UK, the decline was from £2.9bn in 2011 to £1.9bn in 2015 (Warc 2014, 15, 16). In continental Europe, the trend is similarly unfriendly (European Audiovisual Observatory 2015). These are big falls. And they go straight to the bottom line. Unsurprisingly, they have caused casualties, alarm and predictions of the endgame at the hands of disruption and the new digital giants who have combined scale with audience and data smarts to awesome effect.

But hold the obituaries page. The challenge posed by print advertising decline and the excessive dependence on advertising it reflects is a problem, to a large extent, of publishers' own making. And it has been exacerbated by their own response to the structural decline in this revenue stream. Simply blaming Google and Facebook is easy, but simplistic. For too long, newspaper publishers emphasised reach at the expense of return, and treated circulation as a loss-leader for advertising. This wasn't just a business model – albeit deeply flawed – it also played to the egos of proprietors and newsrooms, seeking to reach and influence as many as possible. ABCs, a flawed measure for a flawed model were the currency of success, ignoring the quality, yield or profitability of circulation.

That was bad enough. Worse still, when advertising started to decline in the face of structural and cyclical challenges, the response was often to double down on volumes, through price wars and loss-making bulk to fight the ebbing tide. And for bad measure, a parallel line of defence was to cut newsroom costs – reducing quality and circulation. So the death spiral spins.

Implicit in this narrative and crucial to reversing the downward spiral, the format can and must be separated from the revenue model. Just because advertising has been a disproportionately dominant element in the revenue model of newspapers doesn't mean a decline spells doom. If publishers pivot and re-think the business approach they can find a more secure and sustainable path. That has been the experience of the FT. We took two big and critical decisions in 2007 – to develop a paid-for metered model online, and, most relevant for this book, to raise steadily and significantly the price of the newspaper. It had been stuck at £1 for five years. In January 2008 the price increases started, rising to £1.50 for the weekday edition and now standing at £2.70. The Weekend FT has just risen to £3.80. Alongside the price rises we took out bulk and low-yielding circulation and closed marginal print sites. The result was £30m of net costs (aka loss) in print and distribution was transformed by 2012 into a profit – albeit small. Crucially, though, it showed the newspaper could stand on its own two feet.

Importantly, our path to print profitability reflected a pragmatic as opposed to doctrinaire commitment to newspapers. We are very much channel agnostic. Having started as a print journalist, I do have an emotional attachment to newspapers. Some ink will always linger in the veins of print people. But ultimately the FT strategy is led by its readers. If they don't want print, we won't deliver it. The fact is, they do. And they do so as part of a portfolio of formats – perhaps a digital summary when they wake, the newspaper over coffee or at the weekend, desktop on arrival at work, e-mail alerts through the day, video when on a mobile device.

Not losing money on print is obviously good for business. But there are additional benefits. It re-establishes the rightful order for an independent media. To summarise the late, great Henry Luce, the primary relationship of a newspaper should be with its readers, not its advertisers. Hard-headed Mad Men and Women get this, too. Proof of quality circulation, through successful price rises and robust readership has enabled the FT to take advertising share in most markets and in most sectors. Confident pricing and quality circulation – even with the consequence of reduced volumes – are not an alternative to advertising. They are a support. After all, if the publisher doesn't value their content and price accordingly, why should the reader?

At this point, the objection is often raised: "OK. That's fine for the FT. It's a specialist business publication for the affluent." Up to a point, Lord Copper. Yes, the FT is special, and different. But differentiation is open to all publications – be it brand, expertise, columnists or some other dimension. Private Eye, to make the point, is achieving circulation highs not seen since the target-rich days of Mrs Thatcher (Bond, 2016). And it is increasingly necessary for all publications. 'Commodity' publications which fail to distinguish themselves are probably doomed. A shake-out looms.

Quite often, it seems, the strongest resistance to increased newspaper pricing is internal. The lure of 'reach' runs deep through traditional news organisations. On announcing the aforementioned FT price rise back in 2007, and justifying it on the excellence of FT journalism, I immediately received an email from one of our economics writers. "I hope you know what you are doing," it read. Decoded, it meant, "I sincerely doubt you know what you are doing." By contrast, I received only half a dozen reader complaints. All of whom stayed loyal when given the price comparison with a cappuccino from Starbucks and the obvious lack of comparison with the cost, complexity and value of the product. The fact the FT editorial team has become so invested in relevance and return, engagement and real connections with our readers is a primary factor in our multi-channel growth and the resilience of print.

Just as print publishers must change their business model to build content revenues, though, so they must also adapt that product and content to the format. Certain forms of journalism are simply better suited to print than online or video – and vice versa. Successful publications will understand that and respond accordingly. At the FT, for instance, the days when the quarterly results of a top blue-chip would make the front page by default are long gone. Rather, value added reporting and analysis, either through exclusivity or judgment, are the preserve of print. Those breaking blue chip earnings can and should go online, immediately.

More fundamentally, the editorial mindset needs to change to 'digital first' – in line with the speed and user experience required by readers. Lionel Barber, editor of the FT, has successfully embedded that transformation at the FT, along with a multi-media operation which builds stories and deploys them with maximum effect across our respective formats and channels. The Weekend FT with its 'lean back' reads of culture, life and arts remains, perhaps, a print first publication. Unsurprisingly, its circulation has been especially resilient.

So, who wants today's papers? (with apologies to Mick and Keith). As long as the content retains its quality, and is right for the format, the readers do. And loyal readers secure advertising. As long as publishers understand advertising is not a sufficient condition of survival, and value their print content through pricing, the presses can still roll..

# References

Barthel, Michael (2016) Newspapers: Fact Sheet, State of the News Media 2016, *Pew Research Center*, 15 June. Available online at http://www.journalism.org/2016/06/15/newspapers-fact-sheet/, accessed 1 September 2016.

Barthel, Michael (2015) State of the News Media 2015, *Pew Research Center*, 29 April, pp 27. Available online at: http://www.journalism.org/files/2015/04/FINAL-STATE-OF-THE-NEWS-MEDIA1.pdf, accessed 1 September 2016.

Bond, David (2016) Print-only Private Eye bucks online trend, *Financial Times*, 11 August. Available online at: http://www.ft.com/cms/s/0/5d3e70f2-5fcd-11e6-b38c-7b39cbb1138a.html?siteedition=intl#axzz4JU3DO6ga, accessed 1 September 2016.

European Audiovisual Observatory (2015) Yearbook of the European Audiovisual Observatory 2015, *European Audiovisual Observatory*. Available online at: http://www.statista.com/statistics/434708/newspaper-advertising-expenditure-in-the-eu/, accessed 1 September 2016.

Farrell, J (1922) The Newspaper of Tomorrow, H. Gernsback (ed) *Radio News*, March, New York: Experimenter Publishing Co, Inc. pp 823. Available online at http://www.americanradiohistory.com/Archive-Radio-News/20s/Radio-News-1922-03-R.pdf, accessed 1 September 2016.

Nielsen (2016) Audio Today: Radio 2016 – Appealing Far and Wide, *Nielsen*, 25 February. Available online at http://www.nielsen.com/us/en/insights/reports/2016/audio-today-radio-2016-appealing-far-and-wide.html, accessed 1 September 2016.

Rumsfeld, Donald (2002) Press Conference, NATO Speeches, 6 June. Available online at http://www.nato.int/docu/speech/2002/s020606g.htm, accessed 1 September 2016.

Nielsen Scarborough data (2015) USA + Current Six Months, R2 2014 – R2 2015, Scarborough.

Smead Captial Management (2015) Video Didn't Kill the Radio Star, Smead Strategies, 11 August. Available online at http://smeadcap.com/smead-strategies/smead-blog/entries/2015/08/11/video-didnt-kill-the-radio-star/, accessed 1 September 2016.

Warc (2016) Newsbrand advertising revenue in the United Kingdom (UK) from 2012 to 2017, by platform (in million GBP), *AA/Warc Global Advertising Expenditure Report Quarter 2 2015*. Available online at http://www.statista.com/statistics/301155/newsbrand-advertising-revenue-by-platform-uk/, accessed 1 September 2016.

Warc (2015) Newsbrand advertising revenue in the United Kingdom from 2011 to 2017 (in billion GBP), *AA/Warc Global Advertising Expenditure Report, Quarter 4 2015*, pp 87. Available online at http://www.statista.com/statistics/262733/newspaper-advertising-revenue-in-the-uk/, accessed 1 September 2016.

Warc (2014) Newspaper advertising expenditure in the United Kingdom (UK) from 2010 to 2015 (in million GBP), *AA/Warc Global Advertising Expenditure Report November 2014*. Available online at http://www.statista.com/statistics/293926/newspaper-advertising-expenditure-in-the-united-kingdom/, accessed 1 September 2016.

## Note on the contributor

John Ridding is the chief executive officer of the Financial Times Group, a role he has held since 2006. Prior to that he held a series of editorial positions at the FT, including Paris correspondent, Hong Kong bureau chief, Asia editor and deputy editor, before moving to launch the FT's Asia operations and then moving into management.

As CEO, John has led the FT's transformation to a digital and content business model, expanded its global operations and acquired a number of companies that support its multi-channel strategy. Last year, John led the FT in its acquisition by Nikkei of Japan to form a global media alliance. John now sits on the Nikkei board. John also sits on the board of Room to Read, a global charity that supports literacy in developing economies.

# Navigating the print-to-internet shift

**Most publishers who try to move to a free, high-volume, advertising-supported internet model from a traditional print base will fail, according to Tom Standage. "They will fail because they still have the high costs associated with the old model, everything from a huge staff and their pensions to the cost of print and distribution."**

There is no doubt that print will survive, although its survival will be patchy and mostly confined to premium niches such as architectural and fashion magazines—the kinds of beautiful, glossy publications you want on your coffee table. Among news publications I think The Economist will be one of the "last men standing" with a print edition—not because we are not serious about digital (we are) but because we have enough devoted and wealthy readers that even a $500 super-premium print edition would probably be viable in 2050.

Few publications attract such devotion, however, and for this model to work you need to provide something distinctive and essential that people are willing to pay for. This is the basis of our approach: the deal we have with our readers is essentially that they pay us to save them time every week, by filtering the news down to its essentials and telling them what it all means. We produce a "finishable" bundle of content that they can actually get to the end of (you can, by contrast, never finish the internet), and we are agnostic about whether they consume that bundle in print or digital form. Our aim is not to move subscribers from print to digital but to give them as much choice as possible about how to consume our journalism. As it happens, about half our subscribers take print and digital, about a quarter take print only, and a quarter take digital only. We sell print-only and digital-only subscriptions at the same price, and the print+digital bundle at a 25 per cent premium. We are profitable on circulation alone, so this model works regardless of whether people want print in the long term or not.

The majority of our revenue (65 per cent and rising) comes from circulation, with much of the rest coming from specialist business-to-business enterprises such as the Economist Intelligence Unit, conferences and events. The remainder, the advertising-driven revenue, is split roughly evenly between traditional display advertising in both print and digital and new forms of advertising such as sponsorship and "thought leadership" (our version of content marketing – we don't do "native" ads). We expect display advertising to have pretty much vanished by 2025. We are sorry to see it go – print advertising had very high margins in the past, and extra print pages were almost pure profit for publishers. But those days are never coming back.

## The fantasy of online advertising

Many publishers seem unwilling to accept this, though. They hope to find a way to replace declining print revenues with online advertising. This is a fantasy, and incumbent print publishers who try to move to a digital-ad model are mostly doomed to failure. Some digital-publishing startups have managed to sustain themselves from digital advertising revenue – Gawker managed it for a while, for example – but it's difficult. When Verizon bought AOL it emerged that the Huffington Post was not profitable, for example, and it's a pure-digital news operation that doesn't even have to pay for a lot of its content. So if it can't support itself from digital advertising alone, that bodes ill for others trying to do the same thing. And the situation is even worse for incumbent publishers (e.g., the Guardian) trying to switch to this model, because they have far higher costs as a result of their print legacies: larger newsrooms, pension liabilities, physical assets such as printing presses, and so on.

That does not mean that all incumbents are doomed: just those that try to switch to a free, ad-supported model. It doesn't work now, and the chance of it working in the future will only get smaller, as ad-blocking becomes more widespread and the shift to mobile consumption pushes down advertising rates. Publishers live in hope that some new kind of advertising will be invented that will somehow pay the bills: people at the Guardian have argued for years that it is still "early days" for the web and that something will turn up eventually. Perhaps, but it seems unlikely. Video advertising, native advertising and other forms of advertising provide only small incremental revenue streams for publishers, and the majority of online ad spending in the West now goes to Google and Facebook, not to publishers.

That means publishers will have to look for other sources of revenue. Conferences? Travel? Financial services? Philanthropic supporters? Diet clubs? All these have been tried, but again the resulting revenues are merely incremental. The obvious answer is to ask readers to contribute, as they used to in the past. And yes, that means having some kind of paywall, because asking people to pay up voluntarily for something they can easily get for nothing doesn't really work (though the Guardian, in its determination to remain free, hopes to prove otherwise). That, in turn, means having content that people cannot get elsewhere. Like what? There is no single answer. It could be analysis of current affairs; columnists people can't do without; local sports news;

business information that gives traders an edge. There are subscription-based publishers who differentiate themselves in each of these ways. When readers consider it so valuable that they cannot do without it, they will pay.

Many publishers (including the Economist and the New York Times) operate metered paywalls that allow readers to sample a few articles each week without paying; but to get access to everything they must pay up. The metered model also allows publishers to take full advantage of social media to promote their journalism to new readers in a way that a watertight paywall doesn't. (This is why the Times has recently relaxed its paywall slightly.)

Another form of funding, which currently sustains many digital-news startups, is outside investment from VCs or other backers. They are betting that the startups (such as Vox) will eventually find a way to make money. That's quite a risky bet, and already we are seeing signs of a shakeout. The most likely scenario is that telecoms and cable giants will buy the best of these firms at knock-down prices, and subsidise them from broadband and cable-TV rents. Verizon bought AOL, for example, to bolster its ad-tech business (it dreams of being number three in online advertising the US, behind Google and Facebook); it and other firms may also buy digital publishers who can provide content to fill their digital pipes, and keep subscribers paying.

So much for the question of how to fund a news organisation in an era when advertising revenue is shifting away from publishers and towards Google and Facebook. That is the biggest challenge facing publishers. The second biggest is working out how to structure their relationships with those big technology platforms. Are they friend or foe?

## Resolving the relationship with technology giants

The short answer is: they are not your enemies, but they do not have a duty to be your friends, either. That said, they have a great deal to offer publishers. Google sends a lot of traffic to the Economist, helps people discover our journalism, and provides a widely used mobile platform. Publishers in Spain and Germany who demanded that Google stop linking to them quickly realised it was a mistake when their traffic collapsed. And although Facebook and Google take the lion's share of digital advertising revenue, the idea that this revenue would go to publishers instead if they didn't exist is mistaken. It would just go to other digital platforms because the ads that publishers sell are no longer − for the most part − the kinds that advertisers want to buy.

Facebook can also be a great source of referral traffic for publishers. But might it also provide a new revenue model? Facebook's Instant Articles feature encourages publishers to upload content directly to Facebook's servers, so that articles appear instantly when Facebook users tap on them. This allows publishers to reach a potentially huge audience, but at the cost of losing control over their distribution. Publishers can also sell ads inside Instant Articles. Might this be a viable publishing model? Probably not, but even if it were, Facebook could change its terms at any time. It is not Facebook's responsibility to provide a new business model for news organisations. If they don't like the terms, they don't have to use the platform.

The Economist uses Facebook as part of its sampling strategy, placing a handful of pieces in Instant Articles each week, and posting links to the rest of our content, pointing back to our website where readers are invited to subscribe. From our point of view Facebook is a great way to reach potential new readers: 60 per cent of Americans have never heard of The Economist, and Facebook is a very good way to reach them. Similarly, we also use Twitter, LinkedIn and Snapchat Discover to put our journalism in front of readers. We don't expect them to subscribe straight away, and most of them will never subscribe at all. But as we search for new readers and continue to build our circulation, the first step is to introduce ourselves, and social platforms are an amazingly efficient way to do it. If it stops being a good deal, we will stop doing it.

A final question is whether all news platforms – broadcast, print and online – will converge and start chasing the same sources of revenue. This is already happening, but there will still be a range of business models and revenue sources and we are already seeing a split. BuzzFeed gets its revenue from native advertising, for example, so which platform the content is viewed on doesn't matter. VICE gets an increasing chunk of its revenue from television commissioning. Others (including the Economist) will get most of their revenues from readers, with advertising and other activities providing extra profits. Some news outlets will no doubt benefit from philanthropic support. Old-fashioned display advertising will be a much smaller piece of the puzzle. But there is no right answer. As someone said of the music industry ten years ago: the new model is that there is no single model.

## Note on the contributor
Tom Standage is deputy editor and head of digital strategy at The Economist.

# Lessons from America

**Paid-for journalism will hold the powerful to account, says William Lewis, CEO of Dow Jones and Publisher of The Wall Street Journal**

In essence, the newspaper trade is a simple one. It is the business of storytelling – and, fortunately for those of us who are passionate about newspapers, the world is full of stories to tell. Be it the impact of Brexit or a new US President, the battle against ISIS or the trials and tribulations of the Chinese economy. We are not short of copy.

But a lack of stories is not the newspaper industry's problem. It never has been and it never will be – not in a world packed full of politicians, plutocrats and poltroons who need taking down a peg or two on behalf of the citizenry. Making the pursuit and publication of those stories pay its way has, however, become a crisis for most publishers – particularly those who have built businesses on the back of newsprint.

Ironically, that is in itself a great story. How great journalism survives and thrives in the Digital Age is probably one of the most important stories of our time. Mature media markets like the United States are at the pencil-sharp end of this tale. American newspapers have suffered from tumbling print circulations; commensurate dips in advertising revenues have followed. These trends – if not exclusively triggered by the digital revolution – have certainly been accelerated by digital developments.

America is also home, of course, to many – if not most – of the companies that help define the Digital Age. From the Silicon Valley start-ups which claim to be the future of news, to giants like Facebook and Google which have gobbled up so much of the online advertising cake, thanks in no small measure to newspaper content created by others. Indeed, to add another ironic twist to the story, the algorithmically automated hands which now help distribute much of today's journalism (great or otherwise) are the very same hands around the throat of our industry.

Digital platforms and social networks are the behemoths of the modern media landscape. What was already a challenging market for journalists and their commercial colleagues working in 'traditional' media has become a brutally tough one – and nowhere more so than in the US. Put simply, America's own newspaper industry has been among the biggest casualties of the disruption that US-led digital innovation has wreaked.

But before the digital defeatists write the obituary for the Great American Newspaper, consider this: the appetite for quality journalism is as keen as ever. Perhaps even keener, as audiences find the fare slopped out to them by new entrants and aggregators – pumped up on steroid-like venture capital – is not quite to their taste. People remain highly engaged with news brands they trust for their quality, for their reach and for their honesty.

Why is that important? Because, ultimately, engagement will trump the digital traffic numbers which have so obsessed – and depressed – many in the newspaper business. Because when it comes to consuming the content that matters, people will choose healthy eating over digital junk food. The lesson from America – a country's whose titles have taken the biggest digital battering of all – is simple: there is a newspaper model that works, a model based on paid-for journalism delivered through digital memberships and a much-cherished print product - not giving up on print and scavenging for online advertising scraps. It is a mobile-focused, multi-platform approach supported by smart advertising, not enfeebled by low yield digital ads or ads not even viewable.

It is a model which champions a rational, rather than a purely romantic, attachment to print - carving out a key role for beautifully crafted papers, appropriately paginated and sensibly targeted at core markets. It is a model which recognises the marketing power of printed newspapers and the physical connection they make with readers and communities, one that celebrates the aesthetics of newspapers, the very best delivering a glorious mix of the familiar and the serendipitous.

It is the newspaper model we have developed and invested in at Dow Jones and our flagship, The Wall Street Journal. Other publishers – established players and new entrants - are beginning to reach similar conclusions. The fact is more than half of Dow Jones revenues are now digital, while The Wall Street Journal remains the biggest selling print newspaper in the US. Quality will out – whatever the platform or mode of distribution.

Of course, there are some who contend mainstream newsrooms have been terminally disintermediated. There are even some radical souls who argue a story not shared on social media cannot be news at all. The notion that a story's mode of distribution might be valued more highly than the story itself is a little concerning. The danger is the price of the new distribution of news is the hollowing out of journalism - being able to share something will trump whether an item is objectively accurate.

Algorithms like the one which powers Facebook's news feed are engineered to give us more of what they think we want. This is the so-called echo chamber problem with social media, an environment which reverberates with news and opinions that tally with the occupant's existing views. The polarising effect on the big issues of the day can be quite startling, triggering mini-cyber wars in which truth is often the first casualty. But threats like these – that somehow truth itself can be disintermediated – are the very issues which give journalism and great storytelling its purpose.

Great stories are hard work. They often have to be dug out of the dark corners the bad guys have hidden them in. They take effort, skill and sometimes courage. These are qualities the public respect, value and trust - enabling a free press to play its vital civic role. This role comes with responsibilities: the freedom of the press and some swivel-eyed conspiracy theorist's freedom of expression on social media are two very different things.

The good news for publishers with the courage to back the quality of their content is there is clear evidence people are willing to pay for it. At the time of writing (September 2016), there are 948,000 digital-only subscribers to WSJ worldwide, out of a total Dow Jones subscriber base of over 2.5 million. This digital total is set to break through one million before the end of 2016 and surpass print subscriptions in the near future. Indeed, circulation revenues at the Journal beat total advertising revenues in the fiscal year to 30 June 2016 – a fact which speaks volumes about the value of premium content.

As a digitally led subscriptions business, Dow Jones has happily discovered readers want to read, and advertisers want to be associated with, facts and stimulating opinion - not made up lists masquerading as journalism. For those publishers who dismissed paywalls in the mistaken belief eyeballs alone would make a business model, harsh commercial reality is biting hard. Complacently, they waited for the digital ad dollars to roll in. They didn't. Journalistic freedom rather than journalism for free is what we should be about.

Dow Jones is rapidly becoming a membership organisation – growing subscriptions, but also getting closer to customers and rewarding their loyalty, with exclusive access to premier events and top writers. Rather like prevention is better than cure, reader retention is better than costly reacquisition.

However acquired and retained, providing a global audience with top class journalism now involves dealing with major technology companies. These relationships are, to say the least, interesting. A few of these companies have grown into the big beasts of our age. Having exchanged brilliant free services for hugely valuable customer data, these firms are now woven into the social, political and economic fabric of our lives.

Such power demands the hawk-like attention of proper newspapers committed to holding the powerful to account. But not everyone in the technology game always appreciates such attention. It is fair to say there is a tendency for some tech entrepreneurs to view themselves as intrinsically virtuous - even heroic – especially when compared with old world industries. While their pioneering spirit is to be applauded, Silicon Valley stars can be prickly and precious – seemingly unable to compute why anyone would want to question or criticise them.

That is all the more reason for tech coverage to be as tenacious as anything faced by politicians or traditional big business. (Not least because of the influence some titans of tech have over the media market!) Holding the technologists to account journalistically, covering the digital sector without fear or favour, is one level of relationship. Holding them to account commercially and partnering with them from a position of strength is another.

Dealing with them can be difficult. Newspapers are increasingly dependent on these platforms for content distribution - platforms which also munch up most of the advertising pie and have been slow to offer clear subscription pathways for content creators. Put bluntly, they have milked profits from content created by others. In fairness, there are some signs smart tech companies are beginning to listen to the needs of the news business. They are becoming better partners commercially by understanding our quest for new members and the pathways to membership we want to map out.

But quality content originators deserve concrete improvements elsewhere. Stopping the theft of journalism would be a good place to start and it is good to see regulators around the world now taking the plight of the news industry seriously. The free ride the tech companies have enjoyed on the back of brilliant content created by others needs to hit the buffers. Mutually beneficial partnerships with the titans of tech are, of course, possible and desirable. The best of these partnerships have blossomed because they are rooted in confidence – confidence in the quality of our content and the brand strength that generates.

In the case of Dow Jones, that confidence is reinforced by revenue diversity, rather than an over reliance on advertising. A suite of high value, data driven information products, coupled with a compelling newspaper membership proposition, means Dow Jones operates in a genuinely mixed media economy - not one that has the competitive life sucked out of it by just a few powerful platforms.

Such diversity is important: anyone who thinks digital advertising will be enough to pay for top quality journalism needs to book a bed at the ostrich farm and join the others with their heads stuck in the sand. That is not to say advertising is dead. But a new era of realism has dawned, one that requires advertising sales teams willing to do more than wait for the phone to ring. It involves a harder sell, but better direct relationships with clients and a more exciting portfolio of advertising opportunities to promote.

Major advertisers are driven by results – which means they are far more interested in engagement than platforms. These advertisers are smart enough to see straight through efforts to bump up junk traffic by publishing a made-up list. They also have some serious questions about digital advertising. While much-maligned print has 100 per cent viewability, digital numbers are, to be polite, a little more opaque. Ad blocking software has only heightened advertiser unease.

In common with other publishers, programmatic advertising is an important part of the Dow Jones portfolio – and it is growing rapidly. But clients are also advised to consider much deeper engagement and content creation opportunities. Advertisers love the ability to talk to their customers in exciting new ways – often including print, as well as elements such as video. Despite being written off, the power of print remains strong – especially in terms of engagement rates. A multi-media approach is difficult to manage for many publishers, but it is vital to maintain a print presence in key markets.

The closure of the printed edition of The Independent in the UK, particularly in its metropolitan heartlands, was a mistake. It may have been struggling to make the sales of yesteryear, but its owners axed an iconic, classy paper with real newsstand presence and a great brand – leaving themselves with a pitiful graveyard of a website.

Conversely, Politico – the influential Washington-born political news site branched into printed products from its online origins. It distributes papers from newsstands across the DC area and even provides home delivery for subscribers. Politico would not claim its printed service is a major revenue spinner – its focus is subscriber based content verticals – but it is noteworthy it associates print with visibility and authority in a key market.

So being passionate about print is not to be confused with Luddism. Publishers may not wish to print the same copy volumes, paginations and editions of old, but to desert the newsstand in core locations is to cut a very special cord with the public. However, pride in a print heritage must not cloud a vision for future growth – growth led by mobile. Moving faster to mobile is a priority for Dow Jones – and for all of the continued success of our printed products, the current poor visibility in the print advertising market only heightens the need for speed. Mobile-first or even mobile-only is where many audiences are going or have already arrived. We need to get ahead of them.

The newspaper industry must embrace mobile and place a proper value on the content it creates, ditching hopeless business models doomed to failure. In short, we need to:

- Invest in innovation – remaining proud of our print heritage while gearing up for mobile-led growth

- Harness technology to drive us towards our creative and commercial goals, rather than let tech lead us by the nose

- Get closer to our customers, understanding them better, making them members and rewarding their loyalty

- Diversify revenue streams to meet the challenges of a radically altered advertising market

- Attract and retain talented people drawn from diverse backgrounds to keep us fresh and relevant

And above all we need to:

- Reinforce journalism's civic role – holding the powerful to account through the power of great storytelling.

Remember, we are not short of copy.

(This chapter is based on a speech delivered by William Lewis at the NewsMediaWorks Future Forum conference in Sydney, Australia on 2 September 2016)

### Sources
2016 Dow Jones Sales and Subscriptions Report, audited by PricewaterhouseCoopers LLP (www.dowjones.com/about)

### Note on the contributor
William Lewis was appointed CEO of Dow Jones and Publisher of The Wall Street Journal in January 2014, following more than two decades as a journalist and a media executive.

Before moving to News Corp, he was previously Editor-in-Chief of Telegraph Media Group and it was under his editorship that the Telegraph published the MPs' expenses scoop in 2009. He was named UK Journalist of the Year as a result. Having begun his career on the Mail on Sunday, Lewis worked for the Financial Times for several years before becoming Business Editor of The Sunday Times in 2002.

# The right time, the right place, and a changed business model

**Print does have a future, says Doug Wills of London's
Evening Standard, but there needs to be radical thought and action.
His newspaper's recent history shows how it can be achieved, he argues**

When I was chief sub-editor of an evening newspaper in the 1980s I knew that I had to change my job. After all, the writing was on the wall. Everybody was telling me that newspapers were dead and the future was computers. I had a baby boy and a mortgage to support. I had to act.

Journalist friends were going into radio, television or the dreaded PR. I'd already been turned down by the Today programme; I didn't fancy television; so I applied for a press officer position with a computing company. I spotted a job offering a salary I could only aspire to in newspapers and was offered the position. I only then asked what I would actually be doing. I should have known: my role would be to get nice things said about the company in newspapers! Not for the first or last time during my 40 years in the publishing game, I realised that editorial is King, and that newspapers are the Kingdom. So, I stayed in that land and honed my skills for the circulation wars and battles for the public's attention that lay ahead.

OK, the battlefield has dramatically altered and newspaper folk have learned, albeit slowly, a few tricks on how to fight clever and sometimes change sides. Even those with ink in their blood couldn't ignore the advance of technology and red balance sheets.

One thing that has not altered though is that the holy grail for PR agencies is to get the positive attention of newspapers for their clients. If they can't get a journalist to write favourably about their products or profile, they will pay enormous sums to get the prime advertising spot in print to get their message to the public.

Why? Surely it is madness to pay multiples of the cost of an online campaign to appear in dead-tree media. Not so. Despite prophecies to the contrary over the decades, those who make the ultimate choice (the public) continue to turn to print for crucial aspects of their lives. And large and influential numbers continue to choose newspapers and magazines as their information platform of choice.

This past year has reinforced this fact. When big decisions need to be made and one needs an inside track (as during the referendum debate), when you want to trust somebody who knows what is really going on (like when the Prime Minister resigns followed by most of the cabinet), when you want to share the celebrations of an amazing run of triumphs (such as the UK team sweeping the board at the Rio Olympics), people turn to their trusted publisher. For many it will be a newspaper although, numerically, for more it will be a digital platform but still with a well-known and respected brand.

## Trusted brands

Whether it is in print, on mobile, web or tablet, the important factor for most is to turn to a brand that they can trust.

The big publishing groups took a while to learn it, but all are now wise to the fact that they have to publish everywhere on every platform to stay in the game. You have to think on your feet. You have to respond to the public's needs.

## It's news they want

Readers have shown through the years what they want above all else: that's news. It might be the latest on entertainment, sport, business or travel...but it's news that is the driver.

It is argued that ever-smarter phones and 4G speeds are today satisfying that appetite, and that newspapers are in a death spin. Really? If this was so surely it would be in London with a youthful multi-cultural, celebrity-focused, technically-obsessed, business-orientated society. Not so. There are now more newspapers read in London than ever before.

Let's take the case of the Evening Standard which has proven that if a publisher adapts to today's world then the soothsayers have got it all so wrong when they proclaim the end of the print world is nigh.

It always helps to put things in an historic context. In November 1990 when the Tory party was facing a previous leadership crisis, the Evening Standard was publishing an average of just over 500,000 copies a day. On the day in November 1990 Margaret Thatcher resigned it shot up to 821,000 copies.

Let's roll on 26 years to the referendum on June 23, 2016. The average daily pick up of the Evening Standard for the week following the vote was 965,000 copies. The highest ever figure for the Evening Standard was the edition carrying the 2005 General Election result: 996,000 copies. A flash in the pan? No. The average pick up of the Evening Standard for normal working days during the year to the end of September 2016 was 900,000 copies. It is heartening to see that people still turn to their newspapers as well as their smart phones. This, they certainly do. The Evening Standard is now read across all platforms (phone, web and apps) by 11,959,000 a month (source NRS PADD July 15).

## The lessons of history

So how did the Evening Standard prove wrong the talk of the death of newspapers being inevitable? For this it is worth going back to the Standard's roots.

The Standard was first published in 1827 when even then there were circulations wars and newspaper closures. The Morning Journal closed in 1830 but by the 1850s the Standard found it more difficult to compete with a strong rival called The Morning Herald. So the Standard halved its cover price from two pennies to one! Sales soared and the circulation of the three-penny The Morning Herald fell away. The Standard held its price at one penny for almost 100 years.

From the outset, Londoners like all readers have shown that they are hungry to read the big stories.

As shown by the readership boost from the European referendum result to Margaret Thatcher's resignation, big political stories have always seen readers turn to their newspaper. A canter through the circulation figures of recent history does though at the same time reflect the decline of sales of the traditional paid-for newspaper.

From the heady days of regular sales between 500,000 and 600,000, by the late 1990s it was down to the 400,000s. In 1997, Tony Blair's Labour landslide victory had 679,000 Londoners buying their Evening Standard, 240,000 more than the normal daily sale. But during the following decade the Standard faced more and more competition with the Metro in the morning and the rise of the Internet and the growth of smart phones.

There were, though, still the huge stories - and none bigger than that on September 11, 2001. On 9/11, the TV news film of the planes crashing into the Twin Towers shocked the most hardened of journalists in the Standard's newsroom. It was early afternoon and the Standard had already printed large numbers of its papers. The presses were changed up with the awful and dramatic pictures and story and kept rolling, and a total of 532,000 copies were sold. The following day, when the Standard could print earlier, the sale was 708,000, some 300,000 copies greater than the average sale of the previous week.

As the decade went by competition for the Standard became tougher. Rupert Murdoch came on the scene in 2006 with the launch of the free TheLondonpaper, pumping out 500,000 copies a day.

Associated Newspapers, then owner of the Evening Standard, launched the free newspaper LondonLite. This was another 400,000 copies given free to Londoners. The Standard's circulation was under pressure.

## The toughest of markets

Even when there were huge London stories that broke during the day, the Standard's sale couldn't get to its old heights. In July 2005, London Wins The Olympics managed 434,000 copies and London Bombings sold 416,000. The average sale for that month was 350,000. The trend continued. In February 2009, the ABC figure was 278,000 copies, just 149,000 of these fully paid.

Now, let's remind ourselves, today the pick-up figure is 900,000. That's a readership of more than 1.7m. How has the Standard achieved this when nearly all other newspapers have seen dramatic falls in their circulation?

The continuing success of the Metro demonstrated that there was a market for a free newspaper in the morning. However, the expensive failed venture of News Corporation with TheLondonpaper had shown that the afternoon market was tough; at that time the Evening Standard was losing tens of millions of pounds a year.

In what has become newspaper folklore, the Evening Standard was in 2009 bought from Lord Rothermere's Associated Newspapers by Alexander Lebedev, a former KGB officer. So what did the new company do to bring about such a transformation? Was it a Russian revolution? No. As all of London now knows, it was something far more shocking: the Standard went free, but the real revolution was that it broke all the old rules and did what nobody expected – it remained a quality newspaper.

Overnight, Londoners were given copies of exactly the same type of newspaper for which they had previously paid 50p a copy. The Standard retained its pagination; its news and picture desks with exclusives and expert reporting on breaking news; its columnists; its city section with highly-acclaimed writers and analysts; its sports coverage with international dispatches from correspondents; its revered arts critics. All given to readers for free. Not just to the readers who were buying less than 200,000 copies a day but, initially, three times as many readers.

The business model was fundamentally redrawn. A year earlier, the Standard had been distributed through 8,000 outlets from Bournemouth to Cambridge, from Milton Keynes to Southend. The new operation distributed three times as many papers through one-tenth of the original number of outlets. The distribution was contained within the North and South Circular Roads, with the focus on hand distribution by franchisers in the central zones served by the busiest tube stations.

## Proving the doubters wrong

The new editor in 2009, Geordie Greig, with the backing of publishers Alexander and Evgeny Lebedev proved the doubters wrong. The editorial team continued to set the agenda, including major campaigns that highlighted and brought about change over serious social issues including the Dispossessed, those who were falling out of society losing out in housing, employment and education.

A growing loyal readership followed and within a year the print run was increased to 700,000 copies a day. Under the new editor Sarah Sands, who was promoted from deputy editor, the growth continued. At the beginning of 2015, the print figure was increased to more than 900,000.

Where 7,000 copies were in September 2009 sold at Liverpool Street and nearby stations, 68,000 copies are now picked up by readers. In Victoria and Westerminster it was 5,000 copies, it is now 32,000. In Waterloo and Southwark, it has risen from 7,000 to 38,000.

Advertising at a higher yield has matched the circulation growth and Evening Standard Ltd has gone into the black in recent years after more than a decade of losses.

Under the new owner, the group was innovative in different ways. ESI Media defied the pundits in 2010 by launching a new newspaper, The i. The model was that there was a demand for a serious newspaper that gives readers an at-a-glance briefing as well as considered comment and analysis from acclaimed writers. This was achieved by working with material from The Independent's editorial team. Five years later the pundits were proved wrong when The i celebrated its 5th birthday with a circulation of more than 300,000 copies and a strong advertising revenue income.

The i's sale to Johnston Press in March 2016 for £24m underlined again that with innovation newspapers continue to be significant players in the publishing world.

Yes, there will always be casualties among the titles, as there was when the Evening Standard launched in the 1800s. The Independent in print was the latest casualty in 2016.

From this, though, the ESI Media Group has shown that it is possible to build on the spirit of the title. The group has invested in a range of digital platforms across web, mobiles and tablet apps. The launch of the subscription tablet app demonstrated that a substantial number of readers was delighted to be offered a digital version of their daily newspaper presented in a page-by-page format, and happy to pay for this

## The spirit remains

The spirit of The Independent with quality journalism, columnists and foreign correspondents such as Patrick Cockburn and Robert Fisk has seen the digital traffic rise to 75m unique visitors. The appetite from readers for informed journalism saw this figure rise even higher during the political turmoil in the summer of 2016.

At the same time it was not only the Evening Standard's print copy that had seen demand soar from a public hungry for informed news and opinion. Investment in the Standard's digital platforms resulted in traffic on its website grow by 55 per cent year-on-year to almost 15m unique browsers a month. As with The Independent, the digital audience has little respect for particular digital platforms, the mission of the editorial team is to make the latest content available across all social media.

Talk of newspapers being at the end of their era is missing the very thing that attracts journalists into the business: an excitement and desire to tell the story to everybody.

The world of publishing has never been easy, journalism has never been comfortable. The scoops go to the journalists who can read the signs of a developing story, think on their feet and react quickly.

It was a battle for the Evening Standard when it launched in 1827. It is the same for today's industry leaders now whether they are publishing on paper or digitally. The brave and the brilliant will survive – whatever the platform.

### Note on the contributor

Doug Wills is Managing Editor of the London Evening Standard and The Independent. He began his career as a trainee reporter with Thomson Regional Newspapers and held a number of positions in the provincial press, including deputy editor. He moved to London in 1986 at the time Robert Maxwell was launching the short-lived London Daily News and the London newspaper market was as competitive as it is today.

# King Content

**Journalism has undergone revolutionary changes in the last 30 years, says acclaimed magazine editor Dylan Jones, but the old adage still holds true**

It was 30 years ago, almost to the day. I had been hired by one of those advertising agencies that are meant to know better, to sprinkle some fairy dust over a project they were creating for a big US beer brand who were having a push in the UK. The first meeting went fairly well, as they appeared to be in thrall to the part of the creative sector I was representing, by which I mean they seemed as though they were taking me seriously.

I was editing a not uninfluential style magazine at the time and I had already lost count of the number of chancers from the advertising industry who had turned up at my door wanting what they perceived to be a short cut into the hearts and minds, and, more importantly, wallets of the 18-30 year-olds who consumed our brand. This mob were different, though, as they didn't expect their request to be a fait acompli. The money they were offering was fairly substantial and they looked as though they were being respectful of my apparent ability to conjure up some consumers for them. So we sat around a gigantic oval office in their offices in Covent Garden, a postcode which almost guaranteed cache at the time, and started discussing the project.

It was actually quite simple, and largely went like this:

"So, it's like this," said the rather blousy account director from the agency. "The client is coming into the UK for the first time and has asked us to come up with something that sparks the interest of opinion formers, something that might filter down to your man on the street, you know, your basic civilians."

So far, so good.

"And they like the idea of some guide of guide to what's going on, something that tells you what's trendy about London."

Their idea, which must have taken as much time to formulate as it did to pick up the phone from the client, was to produce a 48-page 'style guide' to our fashionable city, an A5 brochure of cool which good be distribution in style magazines, including mine, and various bars and gyms around London. The agency bod carried on for another 20 minutes, trying to make the idea sound a bit more complicated than it actually was, before looking me straight in the eyes, dropping her chin a little, and then dropping her voice an octave or two before saying, "And we'd like to give it some fairy dust."

These days, that fairy dust is called content. For the past five years or so, all anyone in our related industries can talk about is content. Actually I should probably dignify it by capping it up: Content. Doesn't matter what business you're in, at some point in the not too distant future you're going to be wanting some Content. If you've got a website, you'll be needing some Content; if you've got any kind of social network presence, you'll be in the market for some Content; if you've got a video platform then you'll be in the business for some Content. Yada yada yada.

Content has become such a buzzword that, like my fairy dust experience 30 years ago, people don't really know what it is they're asking for, they just know they need some. Why? Because people keep telling they do, that's why. Instead of PR companies offering 'bespoke solutions' (PR) they'll be offering 'bespoke Content' (notice how respectful I'm being?); instead of advertising agencies offering 'tailored product' (ads) they'll be suggesting 'personalised Content' (see, I've got the hang of it); and if you speak to any digital agency (who will try and sell you anything they can get away with, as though the internet was just some huge secondhand car market) and they'll lean over their desk (sorry, 'communal work station') and tell you what you need is a 'fully integrated, 360, digital Content-rich experience that fully engages the customer as well as appealing to those free spirits who don't wish to knowingly engage with anyone'. Like I said, fairy dust.

The thing is, while none of their suggested solutions are wrong, the two fundamental problems are a) the wrong people are producing the Content, and b) the Content tends not to be very good (because the wrong people are producing it), which makes clients very suspicious about the whole notion of Content, because so much of it is so poor.

In a way, I suppose this is not is surprising. Traditionally, ad agencies have employed as many people to sell product as they have employed to come up with ideas, although these days it appears to be the salespeople who are doing the talking and promising the Content (Content they have no idea about generating). And if you do end up with one of the advertising creatives, it's a good bet their idea of 'Content' is simply making a REALLY EXPENSIVE FILM. Wave a cheque in front of an advertising creative and they'll start jumping up and down about this film idea they've had for ages and interestingly the idea is perfect for your product.

In the newspaper, print and website world, the situation might even be worse. Why? Well, Content is old-fashioned layman's terms could be classified simply under advertorial, sponsored editorial or promotions. For a while it's been called native advertising, but it's fundamentally the same thing. And the problem in the print business (or the print+ business, which is old school print companies with a digital component) is the people who have traditionally been charged with looking after the promotions or advertorial departments are those people who haven't been quite good enough to work in editorial or advertising. Whereas these days they need to be better than both, or at least have the capability to straddle the divide, which is why the Content world is still a bit like the Wild West. On the one hand you have a world of clients with all of these editorial opportunities they don't know what to do with, and on the other you have a bunch of so-called creatives who don't have any ideas, or who have no affinity with this new medium. In this respect it's a perfect storm.

This should be the easiest play in the world. Not only is there a huge growth industry out there, which is a godsend for all of those in our industry who are bellyaching about the decline in ad spend, but there is an ever-expanding generation of consumers who are perfectly willing to accept Content. Actually, they're not perfectly willing at all (too passive, sorry), they're actually desperate for content. And they're not that bothered who produces it, as long as it is – deep breath – VERY VERY GOOD.

Take my 15 and 17 year-old daughters, who for the purpose of this exercise I shall call Money Pit 1 and Money Pit 2. Like every person their age, they spend every available waking second glued to their phones. When they're somewhere where they can't get Wi-Fi – 'nightmare!' – then they'll idly flick through a magazine or newspaper, but the rest of the time they'll be checking their phones, surfing texts, emails, Snapchat, Instagram. News feeds, YouTube and all the other stuff these days is just OUT THERE. And, again like every other teenage consumer, they are actively looking to be entertained, and sold to. And because of the nature of the devices they consume this information on, and because the old co-dependent church and state relationships of editorial and advertising no longer apply in the same way, they are not especially bothered by who is responsible for the Content. It doesn't really matter to them if the Content they are watching/reading is produced by a magazine company, a newspaper company or a car company. It could be LVMH, it could be Asos, could be Renault, Elle or Marmite, could be the Daily Telegraph, Mini Cheddars or Harper Collins, could be Apple, Swatch or Kellogg's. They don't really care who produces it as long as the Content is VERY VERY good. They don't really care about provenance, don't really care if it's editorial or advertising, don't really care if it's produced in London or Belgium, all they care about is its quality, and its ability to engage with them immediately, which is one hell of an opportunity.

On top of this, because they have been brought up in a world where they expect to be buying everything at the touch of a button, not only do they expect this material (sorry, Content) to be very very good, in an ideal world they'd like to be able to buy whatever it is, too. So if they are watching a film containing a great piece of music, a great pair of shoes and possibly a great destination, they'd ideally like to be able to buy into all three immediately (hey, their father can afford it!), which for clients, for advertisers, for people with money looking to engage with new and existing customers, is an even bigger opportunity, possibly the biggest opportunity there's ever been.

But the industry needs to hurry up and get engaged, as the consumer is running out the door. A recent report produced jointly by the Dublin-based internet-ad researcher PageFair and the software company Adobe, shows almost 200m people in the world are using software to remove the ads from their web pages. Even more worrying is the fact this number has grown by over 40 per cent during the last 12 months. According to some sums repeated by the Sunday Times, this will have cost internet publishers some $22bn in 2015 alone.

"The genie is out of the bottle," said Johnny Ryan, the head of ecosystem at PageFair. "You are going to get adblocking everywhere, it is just a matter of time."

As if this wasn't enough to scare both advertisers and online publishers alike, 2015 was also the year in which Apple announced its new operating system I iOS9 would offer adblocking, meaning when you open your Safari browser on your Apple device - iPhone, iPad, iWhatever - you can now choose whether or not to block ads in your settings. Obviously this doesn't preclude Apple from sending you their own messages, but then if you control the means of distribution, and you've convinced old-school Content service providers to give you their Content for free, for 'sampling', 'data capture' and 'free advertising', why should they worry?

A journalist discussing this problem a while ago said the biggest problem with all of this adblocking activity was nobody has yet managed to find a way to produce effective ads on the small screens of mobile devices. Well, this is obviously not true, as most people who own mobile still engage with advertising, most do so willingly. The bigger problem is advertisers haven't looked at the problem from the point of view of the consumer. Because if they did they would see all the consumer wants to do is be entertained, which is what we have always expected from our advertising. Yes, we'd like to be watching something that has some bearing on our consumer habits, and no, we don't want to be lied to. But we're here, ready, willing and able to engage with whatever it is you're about to show us. Could be advertising, could be Content, but we're here. We won't be here forever, as frankly we've got better things to do (we're busy people), but we're here.

Some people have already given up. "For digital publishers it is an existential threat," says Sarah Wood, the co-founder of Unruly, a company which advises other companies on video ads, "and digital publications are experimenting with new monetisation strategies as a matter of urgency."

But then this again ignores the issue. Consumers are perfectly prepared to engage with advertising, and indeed Content, as long as you make it interesting, relevant and entertaining. People - consumers, us, 'we' – don't hate advertising, far from it, when advertising is good and relevant and informative and smart and funny and entertaining and cool and and and... we like it. Love it. The display ads in a magazine have always been as important as the editorial, as they are part and parcel of the same experience, they are part of the same world.

Some have advocated legislation, which to me seems farcical: seriously, you want to force people to watch advertising, as though they were being brainwashed in A Clockwork Orange? No, adblocking is just another challenge thrown at the ad industry, in the same way the internet initially proved to be a challenge. But every challenge is also an opportunity, and as we all know, most of us are perfectly happy to consume advertising as long as it's on our terms.

Many years ago, I became the editor of one of the first British men's magazine, a title long since turned to dust. My first issue happened to coincide with Christmas, and so I took a copy home with me when our family had its annual celebration. On Christmas Eve, as I was washing up with my brother in my mother's kitchen, he asked me what I was up to. So I showed him the first issue of the magazine I was responsible for. No word of a lie, he then proceeded to flick through the magazine, saying things like 'Oh, that looks like a good car'... 'I've heard of that record'... 'I've seen that film'... 'Are Lloyds any good? I've been having problems with my bank for ages'... etc etc. That's right, he was looking at the ads. I was a bit miffed as for him the editorial was on a par with the commercial segments of the magazine. And it's a story I've been telling advertisers (and potential advertisers – after all, everyone's a potential advertiser) ever since.

These days, exactly the same thing applies to Content. If it's good, if it's relevant, and if it's entertaining and sold in the right way, it works. Seriously, what could be simpler? So, who's got some fairy dust?

**Note on the contributor**
Dylan Jones is the Editor of GQ and a Trustee of the Hay Festival. He is a board member of the Norman Mailer colony.

# The UK regional press

\* \* \*

# Hope and despair fight it out for the future of local journalism

**Raymond Snoddy**

After serving local communities for nearly 300 years, are local newspapers in danger of finally running out of road as the loss of the 'rivers of gold' – classified advertising for jobs, cars and homes to the internet – continues to bite? With circulation declines leading to further revenue losses, which in turn lead to more local journalists losing their jobs, what is to be done? Are there any solutions to what appears to be an intractable problem?

In a comprehensive look at the past, present and future of an industry that helps bind local communities together in a troubled world, ten editors and former editors, academics and senior executives reveal the sometimes troubling truth, combined with more than a dash of hope.

Tor Clark, former editor of the Rutland & Stamford Mercury, now Principal Lecturer in Journalism at De Montfort University in Leicester, reviews that 300-year history and concludes sadly and reluctantly that unless a sustainable way can be found for people to pay for their local news, the local press won't survive in print format.

Without such a model it is possible, likely even, he believes, "that the slow death of local newspapers, after a distinguished history of up to 300 years, could now be in sight."

Former regional editor Keith Perch, now of the University of Derby, comes up with an equally pessimistic view after a detailed study of the performance and finances of the Leicester Mercury, which he used to edit. From a peak of 150,000 copies six days a week the circulation of the paper was down to 29,317 in the first half of this year. Revenues have dropped by 82 per cent, a figure matched almost exactly by the fall in staff. Perch details how and why such a decline occurred and emphasises the closure of district editions to cut costs has led to hundreds of towns throughout the UK losing their daily newspaper coverage with the number of stories falling by more than 85 per cent.

At the age of 90 Sir Ray Tindle, founder of Tindle Newspapers – described recently by Prince Charles as 'a legend' – is an unashamed optimist about the future of the local press, and is still buying and launching local papers. Sir Ray has also had to cut costs but it is his proudest boast that so far he has not made any compulsory redundancies. Sir Ray's secret is to back the most local of weekly papers and concentrate exclusively on local news and he believes overall the local press is fighting back and will prevail.

Steve Auckland, former chief executive of regional media companies Northcliffe and Local World, argues print is currently undervalued and part of the fight-back incudes championing the need for more regulation of the internet giants. "Newsbrands need to lead the fight to create a more appropriate legislative framework to ensure Facebook and Google behave responsibly – and pay taxes. They also need to have more confidence in their ability to influence and create an emotional response," argues Auckland.

Roger Parry, former chairman of Johnston Press, writes of 'the educational and at times traumatic experience' of chairing for nine years one of the UK's largest regional newspaper groups. On his office wall to this day Parry has a 2003 graphic from investment bank Merrill Lynch showing Johnston Press as one of the best performing media stocks in Europe for the second year in a row. That was before the double deluge – the 2007/8 crash and the migration of classified advertising to the internet.

Parry believes local news, features and advertising still matter but the role of print in delivering them has to change. "The future of local media is a subscription-based relationship offering a multi-media solution. Work out what people will pay for, in terms of both content and format, and offer it to them. Easy to say, hard to do," argues the former JP chairman, who hopes print will survive as part of a multi-media offering.

Michael Gilson, editor of The Argus in Brighton has a very different take – one based on the socially important stories his young reporters have broken and brought to public attention. They range from failings in the NHS to the plight of the homeless and suicides in a supposedly secure mental health home. The stories all happened within a 12 –month period. He asks: If not The Argus who? "We know journalism is in crisis but very little has been said about the profound democratic deficit that would follow any meltdown," notes Gilson.

Since 2008 more than 8000 journalists in the UK have lost their jobs, newspapers have folded, commercial television news has been decimated and it's almost as if no one has noticed – at the same time as government press officers and PR's have multiplied.

There are two approaches on the much criticised debate around 'clickbait' – the slightly artificial manufacture of material specially designed to achieve online clicks, often involving lists, usually trivial material masquerading as news. Alan Geere, who has edited newspapers in many countries, assessed a number of regional newspapers in the UK to weigh their clickbait quotient and concluded the pervasive influence of clickbait has been exaggerated.

His analysis, which looked at papers including The Northern Echo, the Norwich Evening News and the Northamptonshire Telegraph, showed a lot of local news, sport, information, comment and entertainment of a high standard. "Perhaps it's time," Geere suggests, "for the regional press to get off its high horse and start to realise the full potential of the 'new media' at its disposal."

A rather more critical view of 'listicles' – a portmanteau of 'list' and 'article' – comes from Sean Dodson a journalism lecturer at Leeds Beckett University. Dodson also highlights the new phenomenon of splashes such as 'out-of-date pasty sold to young mum'.

For Dodson the local newspaper landscape looks like fewer journalists, fewer scoops, fewer hard questions, less topicality and weaker attribution. "It all contributes to the drip-drip-dripping away of seriousness and credibility in the regional newspapers of Great Britain," he argues.

And finally in the local section, hope of sorts from David Hayward, formerly of the BBC College of Journalism now Senior Lecturer in Journalism at De Montfort University in Leicester. The future – or at least one aspect of the future – could be online news videos distributed on social platforms and using native advertising. All newspaper staff, Hayward believes, need to be able to create and share compelling video but it needs to become part of the core business.

"Let's be clear, print is not dead yet. It is sustainable in the short term but for how long?" asks Hayward. "The regional press is certainly in need of radical change. That needs to happen now and creative online distributed video needs to be right at the heart of it," he says.

# Three hundred years in the growth and decline of the UK regional press

**The UK regional press – local newspapers – have been the backbone of their communities for up to 300 years, but as the 21st century takes shape are we seeing the final chapters of these once great local institutions? Tor Clark, a former editor of Britain's oldest newspaper, takes a historical overview of the rise and decline of the sector**

Local newspapers in the UK for about 150 years, from the mid-19th century to the early 21st century, were a bastion of local life – wherever you lived. The press may have been referred to as the Fourth Estate in a national context, but the connection was even more important locally, with local newspapers serving a core civic function in their communities.

Local newspapers came to define the 'natural' boundary of an area, beyond the often artificial historical, ecclesiastical or political boundaries imposed on geography. They were produced in a central town or city and served the area radiating out from it, often defining a community better than the other boundaries ever could.

They chronicled and legitimised local life. If it was in the newspaper it had to be true. They offered a shared sense of community to all who read them and interacted with them – because even before the internet and UGC, there were always many ways of interacting with the local press when all you had to do was write a letter or call into a High Street office.

The local press was a pillar of the community, a beacon of trust and reliability. Its staff were respected, sometimes local celebrities, its publication eagerly anticipated, its photographs scanned in the paper itself and gazed at in the High Street office window display.

Local people could not imagine a time when the 'local rag' would not be an integral part of local life. But in 2017 we find all that has changed. Local newspaper circulations have fallen off cliffs. Many proud daily papers have become weekly, only selling as many in one weekly edition as they used to on just one night in a week. Local paper staffs have been cut and so many offices closed that many papers which have proudly borne their town's names for more than a century no longer have an office or staff in that town; in some cases the staff are not even in the same county.

What is the big story of the local press? When and why was it so popular? Why has it declined and is local print journalism destined to die forever?

## A golden age

Metropolitan evening newspapers once looked insurmountable in their domination of their markets and their communities. They were home-delivered in their thousands, sold in newsagents' shops in every town and village and if you didn't have time to call into a shop, you could collect one from a vendor on your local high street.

In an era when workers used public transport rather than private cars, the local paper was a perfect companion for that bus, tram or train journey home from the factory, office, shop or other urban workplace.

Evening papers were clever. Once the national dailies had been published, in an era before 24-hour television news, they knew they had a near monopoly on breaking news throughout the rest of the day. This remained the case until the end of the 20th century.

But now papers which sold a quarter of a million copies a night 25 years ago struggle to shift 50,000. Papers which sold 100,000 are down to fewer than 30,000, and some which sold 40,000 a night in the early 1990s now sell half of that once a week.[1]

Most of them still exist. They still have the best local news-gathering networks. They still produce huge amounts of original local news, but fewer and fewer local people actually go out and purchase the print product. As a Midlands managing director warned in the early 1990s, if we look carefully at circulation decline over the years, we can now statistically predict when the last copy will be sold.[2]

Of course, journalists are still out there working really hard for their local communities, posting their stories online, tweeting the latest breaking news or updates, posting on Facebook and using other digital outlets to get their stories noticed. But none of these digital outlets generates enough direct income for their proprietors. In the internet era, no-one in the regional press seems yet to have found a way to make sustainable money out of local journalism.

## In the beginning

For about 150 years before the arrival of the railways all papers were local. At the beginning of the 18th century there were 35 papers being produced in London.[3] But while many of these early papers were local in name, their content was often national and international.

The Rutland & Stamford Mercury, which claims to be Britain's longest established paper in continuous print under one title, achieved early success and retained its position because of its geography, its location 100 miles north of

London on the Great North Road. News could be brought from London on the stagecoaches of the 18th century and set onto paper by local printers, before being distributed across the region.[4]

But these papers were few and far between. Two major national developments, one fiscal, the other socio-economic, created a surge in the launching of the local papers which were then to dominate their communities for the next 150 years.

## Growth in the 19th century

It's a long story, told very well elsewhere[5], but from the early 18th to the mid-19th centuries, successive governments had sought to control newspapers by imposing excessive taxes on them. By the mid-19th century, thanks in part to the efforts of the radical press in the UK, those efforts had failed and taxes were removed from newspapers, never (so far) to be re-imposed. The mid-1850s marked the final repeal of the newspaper stamp tax (the 'tax on knowledge' as it came to be known) and several local papers date their foundation from around that time; for example, the Harborough Mail and the Grantham Journal in the Midlands. Nationally, the Daily Telegraph launched as soon as the major taxes were removed and went on to lead the way for the national press in the later part of the 19th century.

Economically, the industrial revolution caused huge developments in the way we lived, the populations of towns and cities grew as they attracted workers to the new thriving industries and entrepreneurs saw large and growing audiences for news.

Add in the final, educational, piece of the jigsaw and the UK had created a perfect storm for newspaper consumption. Just as urban living expanded, so did literacy. The ability to read had been on the rise dramatically throughout the 19th century, but the widespread provision of primary education after Forster's Education Act of 1870 meant that by the turn of the century, literacy was practically universal.

Large cities launched newspapers, such as the Leicester Mercury in 1874. Elsewhere industrial towns found they had the populations to sustain six-nights a week news. In Northamptonshire, the Winfrey family realised that, if they linked up small industrial towns and villages in the north of that county, with Kettering at its centre, they could develop a network of daily and weekly newspapers, crowning their empire with the launch of the Northamptonshire Evening Telegraph in 1898.

The period from the end of the 19th century to the First World War was boomtime for the UK regional press. Even in an era before universal suffrage, one area would frequently have several different papers proposing different political views. In Leeds, the Yorkshire Conservative Newspaper Company published the Yorkshire Post, while its rival Leeds Mercury was of a far more progressive character. Many communities had morning and evening local newspapers. Many had multiple, competing evening titles. Williams notes 1900 as the peak of provincial daily newspapers, with an estimated 171 being published at that time.[6]

## Inter-war consolidation

After the First World War, the economic hard times saw a contraction in the regional press and the beginnings of trends which would accelerate much later on and hasten the sector's decline. Hard times forced many titles to close or merge. This was the national on the national stage. In the regions the Leeds Mercury was acquired by its rival, the Yorkshire Post in 1923, and though it published separately until 1939, it was eventually merged with the larger daily title. Small towns which had happily supported two papers often saw them merge in the interwar years. Also in 1923, in the Leicestershire market town of Market Harborough, the Midland Mail merged with the Market Harborough Advertiser to create the Harborough Mail. These were not isolated examples.

National publishers began at this time to buy up and string together local papers to create regional chains alongside the small regionally-based groups which had grown organically through launch and acquisition. In this way, the Berry brothers from South Wales not only took over the Daily Telegraph but also created a chain of regional papers. The regional arm of the Daily Mail group, Northcliffe Newspapers, was launched in 1928, and remained a major player in the sector for more than 80 years.

Also at this time the national press in the UK began to dominate and eclipse the regional press in economic terms. The circulation wars during the inter-war period drove up sales of the mass circulation national dailies, especially titles such as the Daily Express, Daily Mirror and Daily Herald. Before radio could cement its dominance of immediate news during the Second World War, the national press was the leading news medium.

## The post-war provincial press

The regional press was equally affected by the rationing of newsprint during and after the Second World War and the removal of those restrictions in 1955 led to the last of the golden eras for local newspapers, as described above, in the 1950s and 60s. Before the domination of television and in an era of greater local identity and less social mobility, the provincial press was hugely important to its local area.

From the 1950s to the 1990s several factors help provincial newspapers stay on top of their markets. Firstly, the chains which had started to emerge in the inter-war years continued to expand with new operators entering these markets. Companies expanded and merged. Old family-owned firms, once the backbone of the sector, were snapped up by the growing conglomerates. By the 1990s, after huge amounts of 'consolidation', four big companies had emerged: Newsquest, Trinity Mirror, Johnston Press and Northcliffe Newspapers. These 'Big Four' were not the only players in this market, but they were bigger than all the rest.

They cut costs and made 'synergies' between their localised publishing operations to maximise profit margins and, until the turn of the century, they still controlled the biggest local advertising categories, from which they made their money: property, cars, jobs, other classifieds and display advertising,

## The impact of frees

Cheeky upstart entrepreneurs had recognised the regional press was a good place to be and often launched free newspapers into markets served by long-established titles. These papers made an impact and were often then bought up by the big players. Interestingly, many frees had a major impact on new towns and some even established market dominance; for example the Milton Keynes Citizen, the Yellow Advertiser in Essex new towns and the plethora of frees which operated around Solihull in the West Midlands.

The frees took readers and advertising from the established paid-for titles, which often launched their own frees in direct competition, making many local markets crowded and confusing. Most frees eventually ended up in the hands of the Big Four and many suffered badly in economic downturns because, with a few notable exceptions, they were rarely viewed by their audiences as having the prestige of their longer-established paid-for rivals.

## Conglomeration – The role of the Big Four

Though evening newspaper circulations began to slide in the 1990s, many paid-for weeklies enjoyed their last rich pickings in the era immediately before the use of the internet for news and shopping became established and widespread in the early 2000s. Domination of local advertising markets in the pre-internet era guaranteed big income, especially in jobs markets. It's easy to forget if you wanted a job in the 20th century, you either had to buy specialised trade magazines, such as Press Gazette, Nursing Times, or The Times Educational Supplement, or buy your local papers on the night it had the local jobs section.

As an example, in the mid-1990s, as the economy took off again after the recession, the Corby edition of the Northamptonshire Evening Telegraph sold 8,000 copies every night except Thursday, jobs night in the ET, when it sold 9,000, a huge increase caused by local people seeking to take advantage of the economic upsurge.[7] Most local papers had a monopoly in jobs advertising which became a huge earner for the sector.

The Big Four owners increased their profit expectations in this period, from single figure margins to above 20 per cent and extracted maximum value from its existing titles while continually buying up smaller groups as they became available. Social changes, such as more women going to work, the growth of television and the loosening of many people's historical ties with the areas in which they lived, had already affected local newspaper-buying habits, but that slow decline would be exacerbated by the widespread adoption of internet use in the 21st century.

## Post-internet 21st century decline

As is documented exceptionally well elsewhere in this book, internet-based business took the advertising which had previously been almost the sole preserve of printed media. That pulled the economic foundations out from under an industry which only a couple of years before had been booming. The speed of that transformation is hard to imagine looking back on it. Those in the industry at the time could be forgiven for not comprehending the full horror of what was happening to their ad volumes.

At the same time as their economic life was being sucked from them, newspaper groups had a big debate about online news and its leaders decided to put most of its paid-for print content online with free access in the hope it would attract audiences and advertising, in a similar way to the thinking behind free newspapers 20 or 30 years earlier.[8] Many editors wondered why their readers would want to continue paying out hard cash for a hard copy newspaper when they could get it free online. Few publications stood firm against 'giving away the shop' online for nothing.

Meanwhile, the big corporate owners, still used to big profit margins and often with sizeable debts to pay back after borrowing to make acquisitions of other papers, were initially reluctant to reduce profit expectations. But the cash was not flowing as readily from advertising and newspaper sales so profits could only be maintained by cutting costs, chiefly people and property. Journalists were restructured, not replaced and made redundant. Offices were closed and production and print operations centralised in regional hubs.

With fewer, or no, people on the ground to report local news, other operators moved in. Public relations companies, often staffed by former local paper reporters, produced oven-ready copy for their clients and sent it to the grateful local papers, to fill their pages.

Rival independent local websites and small community magazines also sprung up to distract attention and investment. The local newspaper started to be known as 'legacy' media. Back in Market Harborough, the Harborough Mail celebrated 150 years serving its community in 2004. But just over a decade later its former staff enjoyed a reunion dinner in a Thai restaurant operating out of the paper's former town centre offices, as its editorial staff worked from the regional centre they had been relocated to when the office closed. This scene of a once-dominant local paper ceasing even to have a presence in the area it serves is now common.

## Can the local paper survive?

Elsewhere in this book, local newspaper group entrepreneur extraordinaire Sir Ray Tindle makes an eloquent case for the survival of the local press, but his analysis is not rose-tinted. He argues the local press is facing its toughest times and must remain resolutely local, focused on and connected to local communities. He is right these localised news operations are still the best and he is right they can survive, but his recipe for continuation will not work for all

163

local papers. The bigger the paper, it seems, the harder it will be to survive, though the relative failure of credible alternative news providers to emerge online does offer some hope to the remaining established providers.

It is a depressing story for all who have been involved in and cherish the UK regional press because local communities still need their local news providers. But the simple truth is this: unless a sustainable way can be found for people to pay for their local news, it won't survive in print format. The local press is immensely important and valuable to its local communities, but without a definite model for creating a sustainable economic future, it is possible, likely even, that the slow death of local newspapers, after a distinguished history of up to 300 years, could now be in sight.

## Notes

[1] See for example, Birmingham Mail, Leicester Mercury, Northamptonshire Evening Telegraph circulations since 1990 in ABC (Audit Bureau of Circulations) data.

[2] Staff address by MD of Northamptonshire Newspapers around 1992.

[3] Williams, 2009.

[4] Newton and Smith, 2000.

[5] See various specialised accounts of the rise and fall of the radical press in the UK, or authoritative general histories such as Williams (1998) or Curran & Seaton (2010) Power Without Responsibility, Abingdon: Routledge.

[6] Williams, 2010: 136.

[7] The author was deputy news editor of this title in the early 1990s.

[8] It was a major topic of conversation at the Johnston Press editors' conference in 2001, with the Newspaper Association of America sending a speaker whose message was that good website content could boost hard copy sales. There were many sceptics in the audience but the policy was decided.

## Sources

Clark, T. (2013) 'Can Local Newspapers Survive in the Digital Age?' in Mair, J. Keeble, RL. and Fowler, N. (2013) What Do We Mean By Local? The Rise Fall, and Possible Rise Again, of Local Journalism, Suffolk: Abramis

Newton, D. and Smith, M. (1999) History of the Stamford Mercury, Stamford: Shaun Tyas

Riley, E. (2006) Life is Local – The History of Johnston Press plc, Edinburgh: Johnston Press

Williams, K. (1998) Get Me a Murder A Day! Arnold: London

Williams, K. (2010) Read All About It! A History of the British Newspaper, Abingdon, Oxon: Routledge

## Note on the contributor

Tor Clark was a journalist on UK regional newspapers from the 1980s to the first decade of this century, including editing Britain's oldest newspaper, the Rutland & Stamford Mercury for three years. He is now Principal Lecturer in Journalism at De Montfort University, Leicester, UK. He witnessed at first-hand the end of the golden era of local newspapers and the beginning of their decline. As a Journalism academic he has continued to monitor and chronicle that sector in books, articles and broadcasts. He is co-editor of this book.

# Newspapers – the fightback

**Sir Ray Tindle, founder of UK regional media group Tindle Newspapers, has been in newspapers longer than most. He acknowledges the current problems but says there is still plenty of life left in the local press**

The press has had a rough time these last few years. Everyone knows about the recession and the new competition and there's little new or remarkable to be said about the serious downturn in revenue almost every paper has had to overcome.

What is remarkable is the scarcity of publicity given to the fightback being conducted every day. Little has been heard about the great efforts made by all newspaper staffs to continue to bring out good papers in the current circumstances. The determination to succeed is clear in every newspaper house, and so we are grateful to the owners and editors of this book and its predecessors for covering this subject.

There have been some closures, though these have been partly offset by launches. All or almost all newspapers have been considerably affected by the fall in revenue and the subsequent reduction or elimination of profit.

Several of our own TNL newspapers, mainly the bigger ones, have gone into loss at times during the recession but the group as a whole has remained in profit – a reduced profit, of course. Reduced staffs have had to overcome all today's problems and bring out their papers in good order and in good time every day or every week for months and years on end despite the shortages. That they have done so is in the highest tradition of the Press and is greatly to the credit of all involved.

## Local papers are needed

Communities need an independent local newspaper. There are always problems cropping up in most towns and villages. To function properly, local democracy needs an independent local paper. Local councils need a local paper to explain their decisions and plans to the residents. Minorities and individuals need the paper to air their views or objections. Churches, schools, clubs, charities and local sports all need the detailed publicity a local paper gives them. Local businesses know their customers do not normally travel from other towns to use their shops. The local paper, which is read by the very people who should be their customers, is ideal for them.

Hundreds of local papers have continued to appear despite a major diminution of the income which makes their existence possible. Lessons have been learned from this difficult situation and better newspapers are emerging as the result.

A more viable, more effective Press is already arising and, as has been the case with all previous recessions, revenue will rise again. In the past it has always returned to exceed its own previous high levels. At the moment, the national economy is not helping a lot but that, too, will improve when the Brexit issue has settled down and confidence returns.

Of course, in the meantime no newspaper can continue for long to spend more each week than the income it receives. Reduced staffs are 'holding the fort' and bringing out excellent papers despite the problems. Thanks at least partly to them, a better, more efficient newspaper industry may well appear following the difficulties we are currently facing.

## Keeping the staff in the picture

At the start of the recession I turned the usual Christmas Eve staff gathering at our Farnham office into an occasion when I also told everyone just how things were going for the company. I told them from the beginning I would not solve any problem facing us in this recession by compulsory redundancy while any other solution existed. All managements will have done the same. We would not, of course, during the downturn, automatically replace people who left voluntarily.

This worked reasonably well for seven years. But on Christmas Eve 2015 I had to tell the staff at Farnham, for the first time in the recession, the fall in revenue, which had been an annual feature, looked greater than ever. I warned the year had been particularly bad and 2016 looked even worse. I asked the whole staff to consider, along with management, the alternative courses of action we might have before us, together with their problems. Obvious examples were (i) adding to the cover price could further affect circulation, and (ii) adding to advertisement rates might further reduce the volume of advertisements offered to us.

The 'fightback' in the newspaper industry has taken many different forms but all or almost all are being successfully conducted not only by the big groups but also by the independent family-owned local newspapers. Our own TNL 'fightback' as originally planned has worked well so far at Farnham and also at almost everywhere else in our family group.

## 1000 local newspapers in the UK

Paul Sinker of the News Media Association tells me there are today 1,000 local papers in the UK reaching 40,000,000 people every week. (JICREG 2015). Each will have found its own path through the recession years of reduced revenue. A few have succumbed along the way but the fact to emphasise is 1,000 local papers are published every week or every day plus 1,700 associated websites. The local media are there in great strength because they are doing a necessary, positive, effective job. Many have been doing that job for years. 71 of my own titles are over 100 years old.

Life is local. Nine out of 10 people spend the majority of their time and money within five miles of home and they're proud of the area they live in. (Consumer Catalyst, Think Media 2014). Readers are more than twice as likely to act on the ads in local media than those on TV and social media. (Consumer Catalyst, Think Media 2014). I am just as firmly convinced of the long-term future of our daily newspapers. They are fighting the same problems of falling revenue that smaller weeklies are up against. They, too, are finding various solutions. They have had many battles and crises in the past. They have survived them and they'll survive this one. Many a newspaperman has watched, or been involved in, a struggle for survival in the past such as the Tenby crisis in 1978 in which my son Owen and I both played a part.

## The Tenby story

The Tenby Observer is a small independent weekly. It became famous when it led the fight, supported by Lord Northcliffe and much of the Press of the time, to achieve the passing of the Admission of Press to Meetings Act 1908. Seventy years later in 1978 it was in another fight, this time for its life. The first I saw of it was an announcement in the Daily Telegraph that the Observer had published its last issue. I rang the Receiver that morning and then left for Tenby.

I said to the staff: "I can only buy this paper if it doesn't miss an issue. You are a greatly reduced staff and we only have 48 hours left if we are to get a paper to press this week. Can you do it?"

"We'll do it," they all said with one voice.

I asked the editor and staff if they could get the paper to press in two days with every line strictly about Tenby or Narbeth, instead of the whole of West Wales, and every photograph to be strictly local.

The depleted staff worked like Trojans for 48 hours. The paper came out on time, its title returned to Tenby Observer. It was turned round into profit in six weeks and has remained healthily profitable for the following 38 years.

We treasure the Tenby Observer and I treasure that first issue we published in 1978 which I still have on my office wall. The resuscitated Tenby Observer almost doubled its circulation in the five or six years following its concentration on the town and nearby Narbeth.

**This is 10 Downing Street**

Local papers have a very special place in their own communities. They can at times be an essential part of it. A campaign we carried out from 1985 attracted the attention of the Prime Minister, Margaret Thatcher, who took a personal interest.

In 1984 the country began to feel the effects of a recession. The number of unemployed in our circulation area grew noticeably. This was unusual for our towns.

What could we do to help those made redundant and who were still out of work?

At the Farnham Herald we came up with an idea. We purchased an empty industrial building and, with the help of volunteers from the paper, we partitioned the building into small segments and then offered these areas, through the paper to those unemployed who wanted to start a business. No rent or rates or other charges were to be made, then or at any time.

The editorial people made the offer widely known and also asked for volunteers from the community to assist the unemployed with advice on how to get started. The scheme was taken up immediately by the unemployed. The whole building was soon filled completely.

Our particular scheme appealed to those made redundant because it solved the biggest problem facing would-be start-ups. To rent premises can mean needing a deposit and signing say a three or seven year lease. Very few unemployed could go along this route.

One day my telephone rang. A voice said: "This is 10, Downing Street. The Prime Minister has heard about your scheme for helping the unemployed. Could she please come and see it?"

She arrived for a 40 minute visit. She stayed four hours! She spoke to every unemployed person on the premises. When she left she said to me "This is the answer. Can you do nine more centres like this one?" We opened nine more.

**The Isle of Man purchase**

Several people have asked why I bought the three weekly papers on the Isle of Man in the summer of 2016. First of all they are very good papers – with clearly superb management, excellent editors and obviously a first-class staff. Secondly, they go back a long way. They are even older (by six years) than the Farnham Herald which was launched in 1892. Thirdly, I am convinced all established local papers will survive and prosper but these Isle of Man examples were particularly attractive and had a good record over the years. I doubt if there's a better investment obtainable these days than good local papers.

To a very large extent the Isle of Man papers will be managed locally. Half the board of this company is now and while in our ownership will always be made up of local people we believe this I.O.M. company will fit in happily with our philosophy.

## Head office

This philosophy of papers being managed locally means my deputy, Wendy Craig, and I endeavour to run the group HQ with only a small staff. Wendy and I have completed 100 years in local papers between us – 80 of them in Farnham. We have an excellent HQ staff of three ladies. We have five managing directors and 23 managers and publishing directors for our fully-owned 185 titles. We have two meetings a year of all managements and more frequent meetings of managing directors. Reports come in monthly and figures come in weekly.

We have kept Head Office small by keeping management mainly at local level and, in any case, we have always tried to keep costs down as far as we can. I started in newspapers with the £300 I received when I was demobbed after the Second World War and we've introduced no other capital into the business but have retained and used profits.

I've never had to borrow a penny to build Tindle Newspapers Ltd. We turned round some loss-making papers and used operating profits to buy or launch others. We now own all or almost all of the shares in the 185 local titles outright and have shares ranging from 6½% to 30% to 49% in another 200. We also own three very good profitable locally-managed and locally-chaired radio stations in Jersey, Guernsey and Tullamore and we have over 125 websites.

We've come through this dreadful seven year recession still not owing a penny and still not so far having made a single journalist compulsorily redundant. We've had some voluntary redundancy and we haven't automatically replaced those who have left and, of course, it should be said we are by no means at the end of this revenue downturn.

I am convinced local weekly papers will be with us for a very long time, though maybe with reorganised cost structures. Everyone wants to read about their own community, and they want to read about it in depth. That's what we do.

## Names, faces and places

When I joined the newspaper industry in the 1940s, I learned a great deal from the old hands. One said to me: "You can't go wrong so long as you fill your local paper with names, faces and places – that is, <u>local</u> names and <u>local</u> faces and <u>local</u> places." That's what we do. Our reporters and subs do it brilliantly.

We don't just take a photograph of one or two individuals, for example the Mayor handing a prize to a winner. We try to have them standing in front of the crowd of people present at such events so that we get lots of faces, not just two, one of which is, of course, in the paper almost every week!

## Great future ahead

With this in mind, and knowing as I do journalists on our weeklies as well as on the UK's excellent dailies are the best in the world, I have no hesitation in saying we have a great future ahead.

Our splendid journalists are backed by superb teams of advertisement and circulation staffs. They, together with our hard-working and loyal production, accounts and other personnel, publish daily and weekly papers which make us proud. Of course, other forms of media now exist. They will run alongside our newspapers but they will not supplant them. In the 70s and 80s we had new competition from local commercial radio and local commercial television and hundreds of new free papers covering the country but our best times for circulation and profit were in the Nineties and beyond despite all the new media.

At Tindle Newspapers we ploughed back the profit over 45 years to grow the group by purchasing and launching new titles so as to create a more secure situation for the group, for the papers and for the staff. The papers have helped each other through bad times.

## Changes

We make discreet changes to enhance our publications. We have changed some of our larger papers covering wide areas into a series of several smaller community papers making them closer to their readers and more effective for their small advertisers. At the same time some weeklies have formed area groupings – some groups including local radio. Different parts of the UK require different treatments, and we must ensure we are a medium effective for both small local advertisers and for the larger national ones. We need publicity and good campaigns to boost our effectiveness but this is in hand.

No doubt we'll be introducing further gentle improvements to make our papers even more attractive and viable and certainly making them even more essential to our communities. Newspapers have quietly changed and evolved over hundreds of years since 1643 or thereabouts. My friends in the local newspaper industry will, I know, join me in saying that with our excellent staffs we'll certainly complete many more years in our communities. If all staff are kept fully in the picture, they can and will work wonders in a crisis. I have seen this over my 70 years in the Press.

## Press will most certainly succeed

I am confident the Press will beat its current problems. In my lifetime I have seen us survive a World War and three recessions and the coming of new competitors – radio, local commercial television and hundreds of free newspapers. As I have said, (and it stands repetition), the highest circulation and the highest profits I have seen or heard of were <u>after</u> the recessions and <u>after</u> arrival of all these competitors.

Now we have the effects of a recession and of online shopping to add to everything else. The Press is fighting back – hard. In each newspaper journalists, newspapermen and newspaperwomen are working hard to produce even better and more attractive issues.

Yes, it's been a rough few years for the local Press but it is maintaining or returning to its strong position as a most effective marketing medium as well as the most acceptable way of conveying in depth reports of events happening locally and, for the daily Press, in the wider world. Digital ad spend in local media is forecast to grow faster than other published media – behind only video on demand out of all sectors measured - in 2016 (Advertising Association/WARC 2016). Signs for a good recovery and a long future are there.

I can only speak for myself as a local newspaperman but I know we have no comparable competitor when it comes to local detailed coverage of all that is happening and all that is important in our towns and in our lives.

David Newell, CEO of the News Media Association, commented: 'All sections of the press are working hard both individually and collectively to demonstrate the enduring effectiveness of the printed word. Newspapers' role has never been more important in helping to give identities to communities and to act as their champions. Newspapers have a unique ability to partner with businesses and advertisers to help grow their businesses. Their content is now available across many different platforms and this is ensuring that audiences are growing.'

## Fighting back successfully

Yes, the whole Press is fighting back – successfully. The Press will be here in the foreseeable future, and in growing strength, because newspapers are highly effective and are needed.

Even as I wrote these last few words for this chapter I asked a newspaper MD how things were looking for the next few months.

'The future', he replied 'looks very good indeed.'

## Note on the contributor

Sir Ray Tindle CBE founded of the Tindle Newspaper Group shortly after the Second World War. He was knighted in 1994 for services to the newspaper industry. On the occasion of his 90th birthday in 2016, Princes Charles thanked him for his hospitality on his many visits to Tindle Newspapers over the years and describing him as 'a legend'.

# The digital world is a bit more than local, but that's the space the internet giants are now trying to occupy

**We should reconnect with the past to understand the future, argues Steve Auckland, former chief executive of regional media companies Northcliffe and Local World**

My family has a long association with coal mining; they were there through the discovery of the first coal seams, through the nationalisation of the industry and eventually the pit closures. In those days of industrial revolution northern entrepreneurs made cloth or mined coal, global leaders in new ways of working, creating infrastructure and local communities around them. Now we face a new revolution led by technology, connecting people across the world and creating a globalised economy.

But whilst change is happening at the fastest pace in history, some things have remained unchanged. We will always need energy to supply heat and power, clothes to stay warm, and we will always need information to educate and influence. So what is the most effective way to consume information in 2016? I'm convinced whilst the internet is the new information provider of choice, print has an important long term role to play. Its future is not that of the coal industry, it will see a gradual resurgence similar to that of cinema, book sales or train travel, all of which are now growing, despite previous gloomy predictions. Important new research, current trends and my own experience all challenge this view.

The earliest newspaper owners were pioneers, like the publishers of the Stamford Mercury in Lincolnshire, which claims to be 'Britain's oldest continuously published newspaper', launched around 1710 and Rupert Wright who launched the Yorkshire Post from a small shop on Briggate in 1754 as the Leeds Intelligencer, one of Britain's first daily newspapers. Local advertising and news at the micro level made up the printed page of these early chronicles; bad debts created and paid, crime, health remedies and deaths. Journalism developed alongside the advertising as these early publications became more successful, widening readers views and opinions, as well as reporting local news.

So it should be no surprise it's to the local front that the newest entrants to the news and information sector have taken the battle. Like newspaper founders, Facebook and Google are seeing the benefit in going local, providing tips and encouragement to start up local Facebook groups to share hyper-local community news and targeting local chambers of commerce with marketing services training including the use of Facebook self-serve advertising or Google Ad Words, gradually invading the space previously occupied by local press and aggressively pedalling a message they can out-perform local news brands. They were once the new kids on the block, but in 2016 they control 75 per cent of all internet advertising revenue growth.

## Media conglomerates

The power of the news magnates such as Rupert Murdoch are being replaced with Mark Zuckerberg and Sundar Pichai. In many ways their influence is more insidious: creating algorithms which control the dissemination of information, a lack of regard to public scrutiny, and collecting data by stealth. Ask yourself what are they giving back to local communities and the state? Just look at how much tax they pay.

## A realisation of the value of local

The Brexit vote once again showed us how important local regions and communities are, and you underestimate them at your peril. As the world becomes more globalised a sense of belonging to a community is becoming more, not less important, reflecting who you are and what you stand for. The growing desire for recognition of the differences between north and south, and between rural and suburban communities is an important trend which is influencing our politics, our media consumption and our personal identity. Regional businesses run from London with a centralised diktat struggle to appreciate a wet, cold night in Hull, Stoke or Wigan.

So the first challenge for the established news brand industry is to take reporting and advertising generation back to its roots, celebrating and supporting local communities with a genuine desire for their success. Short cuts like content sharing across increasingly larger regions and running local news brands from 30-50 miles away are simply not working. Local consumers cannot be fooled so easily. Staff also need to feel they can make a difference to the communities where they work and live. One of the solutions is for senior newspaper executives to recognise the benefit of, and speed up, the generation of quality journalism via curation, a skill which few of the large UK publishing groups have pulled off successfully yet. In America this is bread and butter for many news sites.

## Take on the fight

Secondly, take on the fight, have more mettle. Champion the need to have greater regulation of the internet giants and punish misdemeanours. Even more importantly we need to promote the strengths of the newsbrand industry more effectively. When I returned as the MD of Metro in 2014 I started a big pro-print PR campaign and the result was a 17 per cent upturn in revenue. Other publishers were concentrating on their web presence and the size of their digital audience. Metro was a product unashamedly print focussed, built on the back of a unique reputation for developing high quality, bespoke creative advertising solutions which made brands stand out. Most advertising agency staff and brand marketeers understand print is a powerful communication tool, so they found it refreshing I was championing the value of print and its ability to drive results. After all, where would you want to place your business? With someone who plays down the product which generates 80+ per cent of their turnover, or with someone who recognises its importance and value? Free is being consumed by more readers than ever.

## Contrary to common belief, print is consumed by millennials

You only need to ask the UK's largest national free newspapers what the demographic profile of their readership is to understand it's not print millennials are turning their back on, it's paying for content. The average age of a London Evening Standard and Metro reader is between 34 and 36. Likewise regional press publishers who have switched some of their distribution to free have seen the same swing in reader age. The Yorkshire Evening Post in Leeds moved 3,000 copies to free handed out copies at Leeds railway station in 2016 and noted those actively seeking a copy from a distributor were predominantly younger than 30.

The growth of smaller, niche print products targeting millennials is also quietly expanding. In Leeds a local digital publisher reversed its model by launching a monthly lifestyle guide, aimed at the under 30s, called The City Talking. Four years later it has expanded successfully into five other cities with another three planned. So the third challenge for print publishers is to find a way to fund free distribution to widen the audience demographic to reach a greater numbers of millennials, and to use niche, targeted print products to attract communities of under-30s.

## Print is undervalued – research shows it creates greater emotional response than digital

WPP's Sir Martin Sorrell was interviewed last year by Johnny Hornby of The&Partnership and said: "The pendulum has swung too far away from print." After a recent interview by the London Evening Standard, Sir Martin asked for a copy and was referred to the website. His response? He wanted to be sent a copy of the paper so he could see it in print. This from the largest media buyer in the world.

The facts back up his response. There is increasing evidence print creates greater emotional engagement than digital and information consumed in print is more likely to be retained.

## Print works for advertisers... and readers

Neuroscience research shows paper-based content and ads offer special advantages in connecting with our brains. Rather than an all-digital world, it appears a multi-channel approach which leverages the unique benefits of paper with the convenience and accessibility of digital will perform best. The latest data from UK-based NMA shows the effectiveness of a digital campaign can be enhanced by up to three times by the addition of print advertising.

The most recent work supporting paper-based marketing in the US and Canada is a study sponsored by the Canada Post and performed by Canadian neuromarketing firm TrueImpact. It compared the effects of paper marketing, direct mail pieces, in this case, with digital media such as email and display ads. Perhaps the most significant finding from the Temple study was paper advertising activated one area of the brain more than digital media. A previous study of successful ad campaigns found this area was an indicator of desire and valuation.

While not quite the mythical 'buy button', activity in this small brain structure had the highest correlation with advertising effectiveness. Some of their key conclusions were:

- It has a meaning, and a place. It is better connected to memory because it engages with its spatial memory networks.
- Physical material involves more emotional processing, which is important for memory and brand associations.
- Physical materials produced more brain responses connected with internal feelings, suggesting greater 'internalization' of the ads.

I recently read in The Observer, the printed version naturally, on average Americans read 12 books a year and there has been no change in the numbers preferring to read a book rather than on a tablet since 2012, it's still 65 per cent. So print is far from dead, neither are cinema, train travel or book shops.

Digital channels are constantly evolving, so local publishers are constantly trying to find ways to balance the books by providing both print and digital options.

## Entrepreneurial spirit

They are minnows compared to Facebook and Google, but by finding ways to re-engage with local communities and inspiring an entrepreneurial spirit within their teams, they can create a niche which will help to reconnect some outstanding and trusted brands with local people.

The industry needs to find ways to fund print, where margins are still higher than digital and at the same time to court millennials. That often requires allowing an entrepreneurial approach to local management which can initially be expensive and not always easy to control. But that type of management in the long term reaps rewards. Most great inventions and creativity come from teams who play with products after work, look at how the Golf GTi was created.

The entrepreneurial spirit we tried to encourage and engender within Northcliffe produced excellent results for us, doubling profits in two years. I was often asked at that time what it was like steering an ocean liner. My answer was we were not a liner but the mothership, a base point for 12 independent speedboats which set out every day to create business. Each had many similarities but it was down to the skill and freedom of each of the captains to create results. That success was shared with their teams and ideas freely passed between all the captains.

## Confidence in their power to persuade

Newsbrands need to lead the fight to create a more appropriate legislative framework to ensure Facebook and Google behave responsibly, and pay taxes. They also need to have more confidence in their ability to influence and create an emotional response. A great case study to demonstrate this was while I was at the Evening Standard. The editor and I met the CEO and PR executive of Gatwick Airport to review their position in light of a Government report from the Airports Commission regarding airport expansion. This report firmly indicated Heathrow should be awarded the extra runway. Gatwick worked with us though a mixture of balanced editorial comment and a simple, hard hitting and effective advertising campaign. They tripled the amount they were going to spend which resulted in the Government delaying their decision and Gatwick being positioned as a credible and effective option. They swayed public, business and Government opinion by using print as the lead medium.

More recently the way in which Brexit played out across the print media is a classic demonstration of their power to persuade. The challenge is to take out a more confident and positive message promoting the unique role which print can play in brand building; to the decision makers at brands, advertising agencies, and most important, their own teams.

## Twenty years' time

Newsprint and local are here to stay. The case study in 20 years' time will be how publishers evolved to embrace both the agility of digital, and the impact of print. How they used the entrepreneurial spirit of the first publishers to reinvigorate their teams to face the challenges of today. How they were the medium of choice for local information and commerce through the digital revolution.

## Note on the contributor

Steve Auckland has managed national, regional, local, international, free, paid-for and subscription brands ranging from daily national newspapers to local TV. His last full time position was at ESI Media where he successfully re-engineered the business to demonstrate growth on all revenue lines. Prior to this, Steve was managing director for Metro, which is part of DMG media. Before that second period at Metro, he was part of the team that created Local World, as Group CEO from January 2013 – November 2013. Prior to this he was Group CEO of Northcliffe Media for 21 months. Before this he had his first stint as managing director of Metro, joining in 2002, and then becoming

MD of Associated Newspapers Free Division in 2005. Steve began his career at Yorkshire Post Newspapers in 1981, moving to the Lancashire Evening Post in 1985. He returned as sales director to Yorkshire Post Newspapers in 1989, later becoming MD for Yorkshire Post Newspapers and Yorkshire Regional MD for United Provincial Newspapers (UPN) before moving on to DMG.

# The collapse of the business model of regional newspapers has been far greater than previously stated and is undermining public sphere journalism

Local and regional newspapers have suffered a devastating destruction of their business model over the past decade, leaving them a shadow of their former selves. Revenues have collapsed by more than 80 per cent and the number of journalists has fallen by upwards of 70 per cent.

Newspapers all over the country would have gone bust if it wasn't for swingeing cuts, but one cut in particular has undermined local democracy and the principle of open justice. The move to a single overnight edition, with the axing of geographic editions, means hundreds of towns across the UK have been abandoned by their local daily newspaper, leaving a gaping hole in the coverage of local councils and courts.

This detailed study of individual newspaper accounts, by former regional newspaper editor Keith Perch of the University of Derby, along with the preparation of staff lists for various years, interviews with 40 current or former court reporters, and a brief study of the change in content in local newspapers from 1995 to 2015, shows the devastating effect of the changes – and underlines why local journalism will not go back to its heyday.

## The scale of the collapse

The Leicester Mercury has been one of the largest and most profitable regional newspapers in the UK. At its peak, it sold more than 150,000 copies a day (Peplow 2012), six nights a week, and declared more than £12m profit in a single year. It was the fifth biggest selling regional paper in Britain and was one of the most profitable in the country. In 1996, it brought in almost £59m revenue and employed 581 staff (Leicester Mercury Group Ltd 1996). By 2011, its revenues had plummeted to £16m and it employed just 107 staff (Leicester Mercury Media Group Ltd 2011). Circulation has fallen from a high of 157,000 a day in 1984 (Hudson 2014) to just 29,317 in the six months to July 2016 (ABC 2016).

In real terms, the company's revenues had dropped more than 82 per cent, a figure matched almost exactly by the fall in staff. Those figures hide a myriad of complexities which highlight the problems of studying company accounts, particularly those of a business which is part of a huge multi-national outfit. The Leicester Mercury was owned by Northcliffe Newspapers, which, in turn was owned by the Daily Mail and General Trust. In December 2012, it was sold to a newly-formed company, Local World (Local World 2013). Until October 2011, the Leicester Mercury operated as a distinct company within Northcliffe, producing its own statutory accounts. For the 16 months until it was sold in January 2013, it was folded into a single national company, Northcliffe Media, and produced no accounts specific to the Leicester Mercury. Its new owners, Local World, reported revenues continued to fall, leading to further cuts in staff numbers. In November 2015, the paper was sold to Trinity Mirror. As a result of this, detailed figures of what happened at the Leicester Mercury are available until October 2011, but not afterwards. What is clear from that detail is the Leicester Mercury reflected the depth and severity of the monetary collapse of local newspapers in Britain.

## Revenues fell by 80 per cent

The profits recorded by companies in their annual accounts can be very misleading for a number of reasons. There are a number of variables which have nothing to do with the actual day to day running of the business which can have a very significant effect on the profit declared and, indeed, companies sometimes deliberately manipulate profit figures. At a tax tribunal hearing in 2012, for example, newspaper publisher Yattendon said it had deliberately under-stated its profits to avoid having to pay bigger pay increases to its staff (Tax tribunal 2012). For this reason, revenues tend to give a clearer picture of what is happening at a business. There is much less room for manipulating the stated revenues in annual reports and, because the revenues at a newspaper business are directly related to both the advertising and newspapers sold, they are a good indicator of the health of the business.

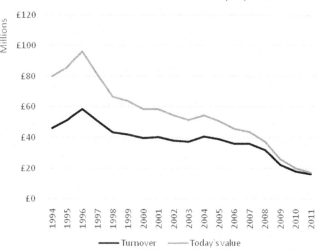

LM Revenue: Actual vs today's prices

As can be seen in the chart above, the revenues of the Leicester Mercury have fallen significantly since their peak in 1996. When the figures are converted to current values (June 2014), it can be seen they have come down from £96m to £17m, a fall of 82 per cent. The main falls came in two different periods: the late 1990s and from 2005.

In 1994, reported revenues stood at £46m. Over the next two years they jumped to £58m, before dropping back to the mid-40s again two years later. This was because in 1995, the company bought a chain of newsagents which brought with it revenues of about £20m a year. In mid-1997, the newsagents were moved out of the Mercury's business into another subsidiary of DMGT. Discounting the newsagents, revenues remained reasonably flat for the decade between 1994 and 2004 at about £40m. However, in the following seven years, revenues collapsed by 60 per cent and they are still falling today[1]. This collapse was caused by a fundamental shift in the marketplace which has seen the business model of local and regional newspapers significantly undermined.

## How newspapers made money

To understand why so much of local newspapers' revenues disappeared, it is important to understand the make-up of those revenues. Johnston Press (JP) is one of the UK's largest local newspaper publishers, owning 13 paid-for dailies, and 195 paid-for weeklies, along with 40 free titles and 198 news websites (Johnston Press PLC 2015). It gives very little detail in its annual reports for individual newspapers, but, at a group level, it breaks down its revenues to give a clear picture of where the money comes from. Looking at the figures in aggregate reveals what was happening across the industry and across the country. JP spent the decade to 1997 buying newspaper businesses wherever they came up for sale, growing from a relatively small owner of weekly newspapers, to one of the country's largest publishers, owning some of the UK's best-known regional and local titles, including the Yorkshire Post, The Scotsman, Edinburgh Evening News, and the Belfast News Letter (Johnston Press PLC 2007, 50-52). The numerous acquisitions make annual comparisons difficult, but the buying spree had tailed off by 2006 and the fall in revenues from that point is clear.

The first thing to note about local newspapers is the traditional make-up of the revenues. They tended to come from four areas: advertising, newspaper sales, contract print, and 'other', which might include events and photo sales, for example. Since the turn of the century, local newspapers have also started to grow digital sales on their websites, but this growth has been slow and, even today, represents a relatively small amount of revenues.

## Revenue categories JP 2007

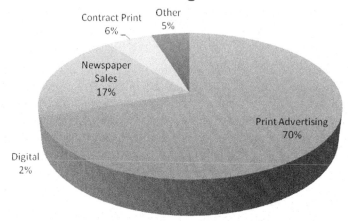

As can be seen in the chart above, the vast majority of revenues at JP in 2007 came from print advertising. A figure of about 70 per cent was typical for local and regional newspapers. It was this reliance on advertising which was to prove catastrophic for local newspapers when the internet really took off in the early 2000s. What exacerbated the situation was the categories of advertising on which local newspapers relied.

### The threat to local newspapers

The print advertising was broken down into two categories: classified and display. In 2007, classified made up 71 per cent of the total advertising at JP, amounting to £296m, compared with £120m for display. Just how much local newspapers relied on classified advertising can be seen from the fact it represented almost 50 per cent of the total revenues coming into the JP business. By the end of 2014, almost three-quarters of this revenue would disappear, bringing it down from £296m to just £79m – a fall of £217m.

Where did it go? The first issue was the UK had moved into a period of economic decline. Local newspapers had always experienced cyclical revenues: when the economy was strong, there were more advertisements placed, particularly for jobs, cars, and houses. At times of economic downturn, as businesses find it harder to sell their goods, they tend to cut back on their marketing and advertising spend, reducing the number of advertisements placed in newspapers. Most of those adverts for jobs, property and cars appeared in local newspapers. Why? Because people tend to move jobs locally, buy houses close to their current homes, and buy cars from local garages. It is a point which JP made much of in its often stated philosophy 'life is local'. Before the arrival of the internet, there was no choice: if an advertiser wanted to reach a local market, the only option was the local newspapers.

## The *real* threat to local newspapers

The UK was in full recession by 2008, but, the economic downturn for newspapers began before that. The reason for this was there was a more fundamental change disrupting the day to day business of newspapers and it was felt particularly hard in the classified areas of the business. As use of the internet grew, it became obvious classified advertising worked better online where it was fully searchable, always available and, relatively, cheap or free. This clearly posed a serious threat to newspaper revenues. Their fate was sealed when traditional newspaper executives were slow to understand the nature of the threat or the opportunity of online classifieds.

Take property advertising, for example. In the very early 2000s, newspapers thought they had a head start on all the internet start-ups which sought to steal away the property revenues. Newspapers already had a good relationship with thousands of estate agents throughout the country and, already gathered details and a photograph of hundreds of thousands of properties from them for advertising every week. Moving this online and making it searchable would keep them ahead. But, the newspapers were an intermediary and did not understand either the internet or the business of estate agents. In newspapers, space was at a premium. As a result, advertisements for houses tended to include just one photograph and very limited details of the property. In 2000, four of the largest estate agency companies in the UK came together, cut out the middleman and launched their own online property site, Rightmove (Rightmove PLC 2015). The estate agents were quick to realise the internet offered them the chance to put full details, and lots of photographs of every house, online, giving them rich data which was searchable at any time. They had access to the data via their members and could attract a direct audience without the need for newspapers as intermediaries. From that day to this, the newspaper companies have been playing catch-up, and failing.

## Newspapers got it wrong

Newspapers believed they owned the property advertising market. JP stated in its 2007 annual report (p23): 'We expect our newspapers to continue to be the main source of promotional and marketing activity for the majority of estate agents.' They were wrong. In the previous 12 months, JP had taken £80m in revenue for property advertising. In 2014, it took just £22.5m. In the same period, Rightmove had gone from zero revenue to more than £167m (Rightmove PLC 2014). Another online property site, Zoopla, which did not launch until 2008 (Zoopla Plc 2015), has seen its revenues grow to more than £80m (Zoopla Plc 2014). In the eight years after Zoopla launched, the two internet-only businesses grew online revenues to £247m between them: in contrast, JP grew its online property share to just £1.3m. This startling disparity illustrates clearly the biggest issue for local newspapers was not economic downturn, but the shift of key revenues to online businesses. The destruction of newspaper classifieds has reached such a level that Ashley Highfield, chief exec of JP, commented: 'The shift has been that we are not in the classified business, we are in the display advertising business' (Johnston Press Plc 2014). That is an extraordinary change from the days when classifieds represented a full 50 per cent of all revenues at Johnston Press.

Why can't newspapers compete with the online businesses when it comes to classified advertising?

1. Classified advertising simply works better online. It is searchable and always available. There are few space restrictions, meaning multiple photographs and lots of detail.

2. Newspaper advertising is costly. The newspaper model is based on using advertising revenues to fund journalism. This means their charges have to be high enough not only to cover the cost of publishing the classifieds, but to fund the journalism which brings the audience to the classified. New, pure-play digital classified businesses, do not have this cost.

3. The internet has also severed the link between advertising and news. The fundamental change brought about by the internet is one of unbundling: somebody looking for a house to buy online will not go to a news site, they go directly to a property website, possibly directly to an individual house, found via a search engine. Traditionally, the news has created an audience for the advertisers to sell to; now, the customer goes direct to the advertisers.

**Newspapers attempt to stem the tide**
Of course, the newspapers could (and, indeed, did) set up stand-alone property websites, but these are businesses in their own right and are unlikely to be used to fund journalism. The Daily Mail group, in particular, went about buying or building classified advertising sites, but they were run as separate businesses (Sweney 2014). The importance of classified to DMGT can be seen in the acquisitions it made in a single year: 2006. Having already bought recruitment website, Jobsite, in 2004, it bought a further two recruitment sites; property site Primelocation was bought in January; utility switching company SimplySwitch was bought in August; the UK's biggest online dating company, Allegran, was bought in March; Data Media and Retail, a company in the online motors category in February; Autoexposure, another motors-related online business, in June. The group's chief executive, Charles Sinclair, wrote in the annual report (DMGT PLC 2006):

> 'We intend to defend the Group's advertising base and to extend it, regardless of format. ... Associated has invested £155 million in pure play digital businesses since 2004 with the objective of being the number one or two player in each chosen market.'

However, DMGT soon realised building and running classified advertising sites online was not its core business. It had spent £90m buying Jobsite and several other online jobs businesses, but in May 2014 the company announced it had sold them all. It is not that they were not profitable: in the previous year, the recruitment sites had revenues of £78m and operating profit of £11m. Kevin

Beatty, CEO, of DMG media, said the sale would complete the company's exit from the digital recruitment market, "enabling DMG media to increase its focus on the core Mail businesses" (DMGT PR Newswire 2014). Classified advertising had been an essential part of local newspaper businesses. DMGT sold its local newspapers in 2013 and, a year later, it was clear although classified businesses were profitable, they were not a core part of a national newspaper business.

## Catastrophic decline

In the Leicester Mercury's accounts, it can be seen, while sites like Rightmove were rapidly growing their revenues, property revenues were declining at an alarming rate. The 2008 accounts record property revenues fell by 27 per cent during the year. The following year, property revenues fell by a further 50 per cent with the accounts stating the decrease was 'approximately in line with industry declines due to the economic climate.' (Leicester Mercury Media Group Ltd 2009, 4) In total, the Mercury had lost 63 per cent of its property advertising in just two years. Yet, despite the economic climate, Rightmove was seeing rapid growth. So, while the newspapers believed the decline in classified advertising was largely due to the economic downturn, there was, in fact, a much more fundamental shift going on. It was not just property advertising. In the four years to 2011, the Mercury lost 77 per cent of its recruitment advertising – the most expensive and profitable advertising it sold. The end result was in just four years, the newspaper lost almost 50 per cent of its total advertising revenues. In 2007, the paper had £22.5m advertising revenue. Just four years later, it had £11.4m.

All other revenues were also falling. Newspaper sales – the money from selling copies of the paper – came down from £5.7m to £4.3m. The presses had closed in 2009, bringing revenues down from £6.5m in 2007 to zero in 2011. And 'other' revenues fell from £1.6m to £500,000 in the same period. In all, revenues had fallen by £20m from £36.3m in 2007 to £16.2m four years later. The sheer size of the £20m fall was catastrophic when compared to the company's annual profit. In the 15 years to 2007, the company had declared £7m-£10m profit – without drastic action, the company would have been making significant losses by 2009 and would have lost at least £10m in 2011. But the company had seen all the signs in 2006, and it set about slashing costs.

## The newspapers' reaction

In common with local and regional newspapers across the country, the Leicester Mercury set about cutting costs in all departments and areas.

- Reduced the number of staff from 508 in 2005 to 107 in 2011
- Reduced the number of editions printed, from seven a day, to just one
- Moved to overnight printing at a printing press in Luton
- Closed its distribution arm, sending papers out with a wholesaler instead
- Reduced the size of the printed page
- Reduced the number of pages in the paper

## Reducing the staff

Leicester Mercury: revenues and staff

The company had seen its revenues fall 82 per cent from their peak and this was matched almost exactly by the cut in staff numbers. Staff numbers fell from 516 in 1996 to just 107 in 2011 and these cuts were made across the company. For example, the annual accounts show in 1995 the company bought a chain of newsagents and this was reflected in the staff numbers which rose to its peak of 581 in 1996. A year later, the newsagents were moved out of the Mercury business and staff numbers reduced back to 507, just one fewer than the number employed immediately before the newsagents were bought.

Traditionally, the Mercury had its own presses in the building on St George's Street and, in 2003, the number employed to operate these was 118 (Leicester Mercury Media Group Ltd 2003), but in 2007: "All staff relating to print division of the company were transferred to Harmsworth Printing (Leicester) Ltd, a fellow DMGT company." (Leicester Mercury Media Company Ltd 2007). As a result, in the accounts of 2008, the number employed by the Mercury in the print division has fallen to zero.

However, the purpose of this research was to detail the fall in editorial jobs, and specifically which editorial posts have been cut. The information given in the Mercury's annual accounts on the number of people employed in the editorial department is patchy, but it is possible to form a picture of what happened, by combining the statutory data with interviews with staff, both past and current. Details on staff numbers given in the annual accounts varies by year: between 1994 and 1999, the reports simply state the overall number of employees, but for three years (2000 to 2002) we see a more detailed breakdown, allowing a glimpse of how the staffing was made up. In 2002, for example, the annual report shows there was total staff of 561, of these, 181 worked in advertising, 114 in the printing, 61 in circulation – and there were 116 listed in editorial. The editorial staff numbers had risen from 108 in 2000, to 109 in 2001, and then to 116 in 2002. In personal correspondence with the author, a former senior member of the editorial team says the number then rose to 123 in 2003. By 2011, there are no details given in the annual reports, but the overall number of staff in all areas was down to 107.

In early 2012, a letter released by the NUJ at Leicester suggested 11 jobs were about to be cut, bringing the number of journalists down to 44 (Press Gazette 2012). Press Gazette later confirmed the jobs were lost when it interviewed one of those who left, the Mercury's award-winning feature writer Adam Wakelin (Press Gazette 2012a). This would suggest the number employed in the editorial department fell from 123 in 2003 to 44 in 2012. However, interviews with staff who left at that time, suggest the number of staff employed in the editorial department (June, 2014) was 46.5. Numbers have fallen further since then with most of the features department being made redundant (Ponsford, Press Gazette 2016), along with four of the six photographers (Ponsford, Press Gazette 2016), bringing editorial staff down to 35, according to Ponsford.

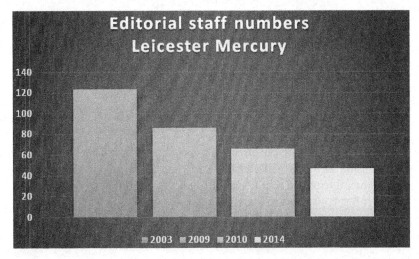

## Editorial cuts

While the figures may be out by one or two at either end, it is clear the editorial team has fallen by more than 70 per cent in the past 13 years. Interviews with current and former journalists at the Mercury's sister paper, The Nottingham Post, support this, showing the number working in the editorial department had fallen from more than 120 to 46.8 by June 2014. Both newspapers were previously owned by Northcliffe Media Group, before transferring to the newly formed Local World group in 2012. As most cost-cutting was driven centrally by group directors, it is likely the two newspapers – which were similar in both size and geography – would have been treated in much the same way as each other.

### The editorial department:

The important question is: which jobs have disappeared? Newspaper publishers like to say they have protected the news gathering side of their business, re-inventing the production side to allow cuts in that area, leaving reporters on the ground to cover their local communities. One editorial director put it to me this way in private correspondence: "In every restructure we've undertaken, we've tried to preserve content-gathering resource as much as possible. That's not to say numbers haven't reduced, they have, but less so than in the back-of-house areas of editorial."

The figures do bear this out, but only just. At the Leicester Mercury, in the ten years to June 2014, overall editorial staff fell by 63 per cent, the number of reporters reduced from 30 to 14.6 (about half). As noted above, the number of editorial staff has continued to fall since then.

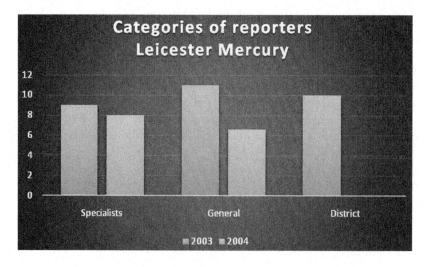

Reporters are the people responsible for the public interest reporting – the people who underpin local democracy and uphold the principle of open justice, or, at least, they should be. It can be seen the number of reporters has fallen by half, from 30 to 15, but closer investigation shows certain areas of reporting have been far harder hit than others. While the number of specialists has hardly changed, the number of general reporters has almost halved, and the number of district reporters has fallen to zero. This is a pattern repeated at dozens of local newspapers across the country. Putting aside the specialist for now, it can be seen the number of reporters on the Leicester Mercury fell from 22 to just seven.

## Public interest journalism: the courts and council

So, how has the fall in the number of reporters affected coverage in the paper? In 2015, thanks to a bursary from the University of Derby, undergraduate student Pete Salter interviewed about 40 current and former court reporters to find out how court reporting was changing. Almost all of those asked, said there were now fewer reporters in court than there were five years ago. In Leicester, for example, the Mercury had a full-time magistrates' court reporter until about six years ago. He then went part-time and, now, he is no longer used as a specialist court reporter, covering general news instead. Even in the Crown Court, where they still have a full-time specialist reporter, there have been cut-backs. The court reporter, Suzy Gibson, says when there are too many important cases for her to cover on her own, she rings the newsdesk and asks for help. "Increasingly, with staff being reduced, there isn't always anyone available to come and cover the other thing."

In the survey almost every court reporter said the number of journalists in court had reduced in recent years. Almost all agreed this meant important stories were missed. In a survey by the Press Association and the Justices' Clerks Society in 2010, almost 80 per cent of clerks said local newspaper coverage of their courts had declined, and almost two-thirds said they 'rarely' saw a reporter in their court (Johnston 2015).

Although it is clear the Mercury's coverage of courts in the city of Leicester has reduced over the past five years, they still have a full-time crown court reporter and occasionally send a general reporter to the magistrates' court. However, another cost-cutting measure has had a far more drastic effect on the coverage of courts up and down the country. As noted above, the number of district reporters employed by the Leicester Mercury has fallen from 10 to zero since 2009. This is as a direct result of the newspaper moving from producing several editions a day to a single edition printed overnight.

Traditionally, local evening newspapers had two sorts of editions: timed editions in the core circulation area; and geographic district editions. The district editions would usually carry the main news from the core circulation area, along with several change pages (usually including the front page) dedicated to news from the given district. To produce this, most evening newspapers had their own presses and would take much of the day printing the various editions and distributing them. As we have seen, the Leicester Mercury closed its presses in 2007 (with the loss of 117 jobs) and switched its printing to Derby and Cambridge, and then later to Luton. However, the Mercury was not the only newspaper closing its presses. Papers in Hull, Grimsby, Lincoln, Liverpool, Aberdeen and numerous other cities did the same. Former newspaper editor and owner, Chris Oakley, said: "Centralising printing at as few sites as possible brings immediate large cost savings and ensuring the press runs for 24 hours a day is the most cost-effective use of an expensive resource, even though it almost inevitably means titles have to be printed at inappropriate times and with deadlines that will, over time, damage sales." (Linford 2012)

The issue this created was the few remaining print centres were now printing multiple daily papers and the only way to do this was to reduce each paper to a single edition as it was time-consuming, and expensive, to stop and start a press several times for different editions. As a result, geographic district editions have all but disappeared throughout the UK. As newspapers reduced to a single edition, news from outlying areas was perceived as not interesting enough to be carried in the newspaper where most readers were in the core city area. As a result, the news from district areas – and the people who provided it – lost value. In Leicestershire, for example, district reporter Shirley Elsby had worked for the Mercury for almost 35 years. She spent more than 30 years at the paper's Hinckley office, but, in 2011, she was made redundant and the Hinckley office was closed. Elsby had gone to Hinckley Magistrates Court at least twice a week, and told us in an interview:

> "The daily paper is not covering the town. I think with the Mercury their city readership is still relatively strong but certainly in this district it is negligible, I would say. They don't cover the courts, they don't cover the councils unless a big story comes to their attention and it is strong enough for them to be bothered."

This is borne out by a study of the Mercury's coverage of Hinckley. It would appear the newspaper did not attend a case at Hinckley Magistrates Court for more than 12 months. The few cases which were covered were re-writes of council press releases. We found a similar story when we looked at coverage of the local council. Elsby said: "I don't think anyone is keeping an eye on the court and council to hold them to account."

This is a story repeated up and down the country. Gordon Wilson, who recently retired after spending more than 35 years in the local press, had carried out various senior roles at the Derby Telegraph, latterly as night editor. In an interview, he told us regional dailies had 'retreated and gone back to their core areas.' He added: "The level of news in the Derby Telegraph circulation area, be it Belper, Melbourne or Ripley, is far more superficial than it was 20 years ago when we did specific editions."

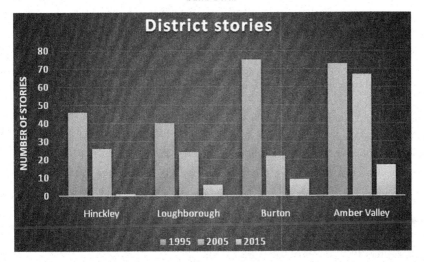

In a review of content in the Leicester Mercury, the survey found the number of court, council and crime stories from Hinckley during the same week in 1995, 2005, and 2015, had fallen from 46 to 26 to 1. The situation was similar for stories about Loughborough, falling from 40 to 24 to 6. A look at the Amber Valley district area of the Derby Telegraph, found the number had fallen from 73 to 67 to 17. The decline was similar in Burton (75 to 22 to 9). Across the four areas in the two newspapers, the number of stories had fallen from 234 in 1995, to 139 in 2005, and just 33 in 2015.

## Conclusion

It is clear the catastrophic reduction in the key revenue categories for regional papers has forced them to cut staff numbers by far more than has previously been reported. This, combined with other cost savings, particularly the closure of district editions, has led to hundreds of towns up and down the UK losing their daily newspaper coverage, with the number of stories falling by more than 85 per cent. The migration of revenues away from newspapers is a systemic change with little or no chance of local newspapers ever being able to afford to return to a situation where they can cover district towns as they did until ten years ago.

## Acknowledgements

With thanks to Peter Salter, Mat Twells and Richard Bowyer for help with research and the University of Derby for grants to help fund research.

## Notes

[1] The annual accounts for Local World for the year to December 2014 show that print advertising revenues fell by a further £12 million across the group, circulation revenues fell by £2 million, while digital revenues grew by just £4 million.

## References

ABC. *Leicester Mercury*. September 2016. http://www.abc.org.uk/Products-Services/Product-Page/?tid=20906 (accessed August 31, 2015).

BBC. *James Harding - 2014 Revival of Local Journalism Conference*. 26 June 2014. http://www.bbc.co.uk/mediacentre/speeches/2014/james-harding-local-journalism-conference (accessed July 24, 2015).

DMGT PLC. "Annual Accounts." 2006.

DMGT PR Newswire. *Disposal of Jobsite*. 22 May 2014. http://dmgt.g3dhosting.com/content/disposal-jobsite (accessed July 6, 2014).

Hudson, Nick. *Freelove or hate ... reports of the death of news are greatly exaggerated*. 10 March 2014. https://duncandanley.wordpress.com/2014/03/10/3162/ (accessed July 24, 2015).

Johnston Press PLC. *About Us*. 2015. http://www.johnstonpress.co.uk/about-us (accessed July 24, 2015).

Johnston Press PLC. "Annual Accounts." 2007.

Johnston Press Plc. *Investors report*. 6 August 2014. http://www.johnstonpress.co.uk/investors/reports-results-presentations (accessed October 30, 2014).

Johnston, Tony. "Email." 2015.

Leicester Mercury Group Ltd. "Annual Accounts." 1996.

Leicester Mercury Media Company Ltd. "Annual Accounts." 2007.

Leicester Mercury Media Group Ltd. "Annual Accounts." 2009.

Leicester Mercury Media Group Ltd. "Annual Accounts." 2003.

Leicester Mercury Media Group Ltd. "Annual Report." 2011.

Linford, Paul. *Midlands dailies scrap city final editions*. 22 April 2009. http://www.holdthefrontpage.co.uk/2009/news/midlands-dailies-scrap-city-final-editions/ (accessed July 29, 2015).

—. *Oakley responds to Dyson questions over SoE speech*. 14 May 2012. http://www.holdthefrontpage.co.uk/2012/news/oakley-responds-to-dyson-questions-over-soe-speech/ (accessed July 29, 2015).

Local World. *Local World completes acquisition*. 7 January 2013. http://www.localworld.co.uk/blog/2013/01/07/local-world-completes-acquisition/ (accessed July 24, 2015).

Peplow, Gemma. *Tribute paid to a 'great editor'*. 31 October 2012. http://www.leicestermercury.co.uk/Tributes-paid-great-editor/story-17200462-detail/story.html (accessed July 24, 2015).

Ponsford, Dominic. *Press Gazette*. 1 June 2016. http://www.pressgazette.co.uk/the-leicester-mercury-features-team-have-dominated-the-regional-press-awards-for-a-decade-so-why-are-they-facing-redundancy/ (accessed October 1, 2016).

—. *Press Gazette*. 20 April 2016. http://www.pressgazette.co.uk/the-leicester-mercury-features-team-have-dominated-the-regional-press-awards-for-a-decade-so-why-are-they-facing-redundancy/ (accessed September 30, 2016).

——. *The Survival of UK Regional Dailies and their Digital Growth is the Great Escape Story of the Media Downturn.* 27 August 2015. http://www.pressgazette.co.uk/content/survival-uk-regional-dailies-and-their-accelerating-digital-growth-great-escape-story-media (accessed August 31, 2015).

Press Gazette. *Feature writer of year on why he took redundancy.* 3 May 2012a. http://www.pressgazette.co.uk/node/49240 (accessed July 30, 2015).

——. *Journalists at Leicester Mercury condemn 'cavalier attitude to axing editorial staff'.* 28 February 2012. http://www.pressgazette.co.uk/wire/8714 (accessed July 30, 2015).

Reeves, Ian. *Press Gazette archive interview: Rupert Murdoch tells all.* 1 December 2005. http://www.pressgazette.co.uk/node/32634 (accessed July 4, 2014).

Rightmove PLC. "Annual Accounts." 2014.

——. *Our history.* 2015. http://plc.rightmove.co.uk/about-us/our-history.aspx (accessed July 4, 2014).

Spilsbury, Mark. "Journalists at Work." *NCTJ.com.* February 2013. http://www.nctj.com/downloadlibrary/jaw_final_higher_2.pdf (accessed July 24, 2015).

Sweney, Mark. *DMGT confirms it is to float Zoopla.* 22 May 2014. http://www.theguardian.com/media/2014/may/22/dmgt-float-zoopla-daily-mail-jobsite (accessed July 4, 2014).

Tax tribunal. *Iliffe News and Media and HMRC.* 2012. http://www.bailii.org/uk/cases/UKFTT/TC/2012/TC02365.pdf (accessed June 17, 2014).

Zoopla Plc. *About us.* 2015. http://www.zoopla.co.uk/about/ (accessed July 29, 2015).

Zoopla Plc. "Annual Accounts." 2014.

Barthel, Michael (2015) State of the News Media 2015, *Pew Research Center*, 29 April, pp 27. Available online at: http://www.journalism.org/files/2015/04/FINAL-STATE-OF-THE-NEWS-MEDIA1.pdf, accessed 1 September 2016.

## Note on the contributor
Keith Perch is Head of Journalism at Derby University. He previously edited the Leicester Mercury, the Derby Telegraph, and the South Wales Echo, and was MD of the digital publishing division of the Daily Mail's internet business.

# Local papers – after the fall...

**By any measure of performance, the local press industry in the UK is in dire trouble. Falling sales, declining readership, reduced income, crashing share prices and to cap it all, rising costs. Can local print media survive? The answer is yes - but not in their traditional form. And getting from where we are now to where we need to be is a tortuous and difficult journey. Roger Parry writes from personal experience**

I had the educational and at times traumatic experience of being chairman of Johnston Press, one of the largest UK regional newspaper groups, for nine years. The first seven were wonderful. The last two, not so much. The combination of classified advertising migrating to the web and the UK financial crisis starting in 2007 wrecked the economics of the local newspaper industry and Johnston was in the vanguard of the losing battle.

## A gold plated business model
As a corporate memento mori I have, on my office wall, a 2003 graphic, from investment bank Merrill Lynch, showing Johnston Press as one of the best performing media stocks in Europe for the second year in a row. In the late 90s and early 00s the local newspaper business was beloved by the investment community. Classified advertising was booming on the back of strong economic growth. In the glorious days before the great crash of 2007/8 GDP rose year after year by 3 or 4 per cent. Investors love monopolies and most local papers were, in effect, near monopolies. If you wanted to buy or sell a house or car, list or seek a job there was, in many places in the UK, only one game in town. The local paper. The local press managers called these three classified markets - property, motors and jobs - the 'rivers of gold'.

Local papers also benefited from another thing investors liked, the roll-up or industry consolidation. If a big company purchased a small one they enjoyed immediate and substantial benefits of scale, shared printing, purchasing, management and distribution. City investors lobbied for more and more such deals. Each acquisition was celebrated. Banks were willing to lend vast amounts to the local paper consolidation story. Corporate debts mounted. City analysts applauded. And share prices romped upwards.

## Net Nemesis and Northern Rock

The assumption was it would all go on forever. By the early 2000s the web was hardly a hidden threat but it felt like someone else's problem. The potential to utterly lay waste to the economics of local classified advertising was simply not understood by most people. Johnston's stellar stock market performance in 2003 simply reflected the collective wisdom of investors and analysts. It would be three years before Rightmove would become a listed plc. Autotrader was still mainly a print business. Craig's List was losing money and had less than 20 staff in a rented house in San Francisco. Google was still a private company building its search technology. Google Maps did not launch until 2005. Mark Zuckerberg was an undergraduate in his Harvard dorm.

But less than ten years later the economics of Johnston Press and its industry was in ruins. The financial crisis – started in the UK by the collapse of Northern Rock in late 2007 was painful for all industries. For local newspapers, now feeling the full force of the internet, it was all but terminal.

## Long term decline in readership

Local newspaper readership had been in decline since the 1950s. Radio, television and local free magazines had taken their toll, as had the much reduced sense of the importance of 'my town' to a new generation of commuters who lacked the deep community roots and interests of their forebears. But classified advertising defied circulation gravity. Classified was judged by evidence that it worked not by readership data. The local car dealer or estate agent was less worried about fancy metrics like reach, frequency, awareness and cost per thousand than simple proof of vehicles purchased and homes sold.

Income from selling the papers themselves also had held up well. Buying 'the local rag' from the newsagent's along with the cigarettes and lottery tickets was largely a function of habit and availability. As readership fell amongst the young, lured by other media, cover prices kept going up as older people with the local paper habit, like smokers and drinkers, showed remarkable price inelasticity.

## Spiralling down

So it was all wonderful. Until it wasn't. By 2008 the UK economy was in freefall and classified advertising with it. GDP dropped by more than six per cent a year at its worst moment. And to add to the pain of 2008 it was the year Google introduced the ability for small businesses in the UK to bid for advertising words and when Facebook opened its European business in Dublin. The future had arrived, at speed, at the worst possible moment in the business cycle. With less money in their pockets even those loyal older consumers suddenly found those cigarettes and lottery tickets a little more necessary to them than the local paper.

It was the classic vicious circle. The heavy debts of the go-go years weighed down balance sheets. Pension liabilities, in what had been a traditional, unionised, high labour industry suddenly rocketed. Reduction in classified and sales income led to cuts in editorial budgets which led to reduced circulation, which led to cuts in display advertising which was linked to readership numbers.

The NUJ, not unreasonably but inaccurately, complained the industry was cost-cutting itself into oblivion by reducing editorial quality but the truth was more nuanced than this. The reality is that what most readers valued in their local newspaper was no so much the editorial content but access to their local market and services. People would buy the paper to see the cars for sale or the situations vacant or to indulge it a little light 'property porn' by checking out the value of their neighbours' houses. The activities of the local council and local personalities were covered in the paper and enjoyed but they were far from the main reason for buying a copy. Research constantly showed very few people purchased a daily local paper every day. Many bought it only on the day it contained the classified advertising they wanted to access.

It was true people loved seeing the professional photography, in the medium of newsprint, showcasing their kids' school plays and sports victories but now they could go to Facebook and Instagram.

It wasn't a lack of good journalism that did for local papers. It was simply one of the main reasons for their traditional existence, classified advertising, had gone elsewhere.

## Evolution not extinction

Students of media history enjoy the notion of Riepl's Law. Wolfgang Riepl was the editor-in-chief of the venerable Nurnberger Zeitung (it is still going). In 1913, pondering the arrival of radio, cinema and recorded music, he proposed a law that newly invented media do not replace old ones but simply merge with and modify them (Parry, 2011: 364). The car replaced the horse because it did the same job but better. But of course horses are still around. For local newspapers Riepl is being proven correct. Local news, features and advertising still matter but the way people will get them has changed. The role of print in delivering them has to be modified.

So is there a future. Yes. And in fact it is relatively easy to describe the business model most likely to work. But, for a traditional newspaper company it is very hard to get there from here.

## Subscribers not Readers

In 2004, as the board of Johnston Press, we started to worry about the internet. We were proud of reaching six million weekly readers. I remember a presentation about how this audience reach was growing and a question being asked: "How many of those readers do we have names and addresses for?" It took a month for the answer to come back "about 400,000". And therein lay the heart if the problem. Local papers in the UK simply did not know their customers. The purchase transaction, over the newsagent's counter, was, for the most part, casual and cash-based. No credit cards. No registration involved. Google, by contrast, knew your name, email, post code and buying habits. Of course they would come up with a superior advertising model. It all seems so obvious now. But back then the huge financial success of the local press industry had not required it to it collect reader data.

## A vibrant local media: Learn from the winners

The future of local media is a subscription-based relationship offering a multi-media solution. Work out what people will pay for, in terms of both content and format, and offer it to them. Easy to say. Hard to do. But what is clear is the daily publication, produced on newsprint and distributed by retail outlets is almost certainly not the answer. It just happens to be what the whole industry is set up to provide.

There are many formulae proposed for saving local media. My solutions are influenced by having been chairman of a magazine publisher, which fared somewhat better in the digital revolution than a newspaper owner, and by working for many years in advertising agencies which are undergoing their own digital transformation.

Learn from The Economist. It looks like a magazine but calls itself, and behaves like, a newspaper with a model built on subscribers paying for high quality, exclusive content. It deals with current events but it offers comment, analysis and opinions leaving breaking the news to others.

Learn also from The Week and Private Eye again they deal with current events but do so with summaries, satire and comment. Again they are subscription businesses with very low cost production.

Learn from the FT and The Wall Street Journal. Quality, targeted and exclusive content will encourage subscription. The print edition lends credibility, authority and lustre to the growing and more profitable digital offering.

Learn from Evening Standard or City AM, quality journalism does matter. It means readers actually do actually read - so advertisers actually do value the medium. But don't think you can go free in most markets. London is special.

Learn from online publications like Huffington Post and Raconteur. Use digital media well with clean simple editorial and non-intrusive sponsored sections. Avoid the horrible user experience of flashing banners, pop-up videos and columns of clickbait that make such a mess of many local newspaper sites.

Learn from Schibsted – the successful Scandinavian giant. In print they have achieved economies of scale through aggressive consolidation and near monopolies. Online they have highly functional market-leading classified services

## Curation not creation

Local news is expensive to collect. It is far better if you can get enthusiastic and skilled local people to do it for nothing. And they will. In 2014 The Independent (Burrell, 2014) reported on an experiment by Johnston Press in Bourne,

Lincolnshire, which resulted in 75 per cent of the content coming from amateur, unpaid, providers. Website traffic and print sales grew as a result.

Professional journalists still have a vital role to play in commissioning and curating this material, and in taking the lead on investigations and campaigns. But a small group of skilled and experienced 'hacks' working across a group of papers in a region can orchestrate a huge amount of quality output.

If presented with the opportunity, in the right way, people get a real satisfaction out of providing content (text, pictures and video) to their local paper. They are not being exploited. They are being recruited and involved. But the professionals have to make it happen.

## Publish in all media and charge for access

Your content is local information but let your audience decide how they access it. The printed weekly, the website, Facebook, the smartphone. Your readers will use you the way they want to. Just make sure any material offered free is on a pathway to creating a loyal subscriber. 'Free' is a sample offer, it cannot be the whole service. Despite what some at The Guardian once thought there is simply not enough advertising, certainly on a local basis, to pay for a quality product. Local media has to be multi-media to deliver what the audience wants, and on subscription to pay the bills.

## Don't compete - complement

Type 'plumber' or 'BMW 5 series' into Google and you know why classified, in the traditional sense, is never coming back to your local paper. The result is instant, comprehensive and displayed on a map. But all is not lost. Local sites can thrive alongside the digital giants. People like and trust local reviews and recommendations.

People also like features on home improvement and supplements on gardening. There is no reason why a large group of local papers cannot generate very high quality, exclusive syndicated content. One set of costs to serve hundreds of local titles, each, in effect, having an exclusive local offer. Jeremy Clarkson on motoring, Monty Don on gardening, Mary Berry on baking. Why not? Three million weekly readers reached through syndication across 200 local papers is just as good as a national publication.

## And the future looks like....

The local 'paper' of the future probably won't be on newsprint but will look far more like a magazine. Except in a very few major cities it will be weekly and the bulk of sales will be delivered to subscribers along with their groceries or by post. The paper will be just one manifestation of what the subscription buys.

In the UK most local papers will be owned by just two or three companies or if they are independent will have very strong links with one of those companies. The competition authorities, who have done so much damage to the local press, need to get out of the way

About a third of the editorial will be exclusive, high quality and syndicated. With the focus on home, gardens, cooking and lifestyle. This material will enjoy national distribution and will be linked with national display advertising. But will be experienced locally, on an exclusive basis, by local subscribers

News will come from a small team of professional journalists organised on a regional basis serving a dozen or more titles with a network of largely unpaid stringers and correspondents at a local and micro-local level. These regional news centres will enjoy a contracted annual income from the BBC in return for which they will supply audio and video news material. The printed weekly will be in a way an artefact, an object to have around the house which affirms membership of, and interest in, a local community. The way that Vogue or Country Life enhance a dentist's waiting room, or the FT and Wall Street Journal adorn an investment bank.

The weekly publication will not try to be particularly time-sensitive. Indeed the economics will depend of having many titles under common ownership spread across a six day week to allow the production teams to keep constantly busy.

The root of local newspaper problems is they have been addressed from the viewpoint of the producer: "What should I do with my lovely factory full of, nearly new, Goss Universal presses, my fleet of vans and my classified sales team?" Better to start from the perspective of the subscriber who may well ask: "Where do I go to find out if they going to build a new bypass? Who can I get to fix my boiler? Where can I buy a good second hand car?"

So local print will not vanish but as Wolfgang Rielpl predicted, it will find a radically new role as part of a multi-media offering. Easy to describe but very, very hard to deliver if you start with a 200 years old local newspaper business and own all those expensive four-high towers and print works.

## References

Parry, R. (2011) The Ascent of Media, London: Nicholas Brealey.

Burrell, I. (2014) 'The Dizzying Decline of Britain's local newspapers,' Independent, August 31, 2014.

http://www.independent.co.uk/news/media/press/the-dizzying-decline-of-britain-s-local-newspapers-do-you-want-the-bad-news-or-the-good-news-9702684.html

## Note on the contributor

Roger Parry CBE is chairman of MSQ Partners, Oxford Metrics and YouGov. He was chairman of Johnston Press 2001-2009 and Future Publishing 2001-2011. He was CEO of More Group 1995-1998 and Clear Channel International 1998-2006. Educated at the Universities of Oxford and Bristol he was a consultant with McKinsey and started his career as a reporter for BBC and ITV.

# The decline of journalism, the democratic deficit and why it should concern us all

**The best print journalism provides a service no-one else can match. Even in an era of wall-to-wall digital media, local journalism is the only watchdog holding the powerful to account in their own communities. It must survive for the sake of our democracy, says widely experienced regional newspaper editor Michael Gilson**

From her hospital bed Evelyn Kennedy looked up at her family and pleaded for help.

Two years on these are words her granddaughter Emily recalls every day. "I just feel so guilty we didn't do more," she says, "just pick her up and take her out of there."

Evelyn was 89 years-old when she died. The independent great-grandmother's fatal misfortune was to fall and hurt her hip. This would bring her into contact with a struggling institution, an underfunded, harassed sometimes mismanaged hospital from which she would never return. For all the dysfunctional structure it was also carelessness that did for Evelyn. She was a bewildered pensioner caught in a process, she had no voice. In the end they had even lost the wrist tag which identified her.

After the fall Evelyn was taken to the acute medical unit of the Royal Sussex Hospital in Brighton. In the last five years the Trust which runs the hospital has had a carousel of government-appointed trouble-shooting chief executives and directors brought in to sort things out. Just five days into her stay at the acute medical ward (AMU) Evelyn was lost. Dehydrated, soiled and with hideous sores in her mouth she was transferred to another ward but it was too late. She died five days later.

What the family didn't know and might never have is one month before Evelyn's death, in November 2014, the hospital received a letter from Brighton's coroner warning it she had serious concerns about the AMU. It was she said 'not fit for purpose'. The subject of the coroner's concern was the death of 55 year-old Linda Rignall in the AMU from an undiagnosed blockage in an artery.

The coroner was clear. Linda was showing enough signs to warrant immediate further investigation which could have saved her life. And this wasn't even the first time that such a letter arrived.

Evelyn Kennedy, Linda Rignall, Herta Woods, Stephen Palmer, Jane Tompkins. Five deaths in two years. All avoidable. How do we know this? One thing is for absolute certain. We do not know these names because the NHS Trust management decided openness was the best policy. The Kennedys received no apology at the time. Neither did any of the other families, some of whom found out the manner of their loved one's death months later. It simply hadn't occurred to them a hospital could be partially responsible for the deaths. This was a scandal about to fade, to disappear. Except…

Rachel Millard has a belief local reporters should hold the powerful to account, tell people things they didn't know, neither confirm prejudice nor write puff pieces. It is a philosophy perilously close to dying out in some parts. A source of Millard's had the details. She could be trusted. The story published last year in Millard's newspaper, The Argus, shocked families. Finally the hospital issued a statement which majored on the tireless work of staff at the unit but did say changes were to be made including a better staff-to-patient ratio, regular team meetings, the appointment of a matron and education for staff on dementia.

It was understandable if readers wondered why all this hadn't happened before. There was no expansion on why management hadn't acted on the coroner's warnings but there was finally an apology to the families. Emily Kennedy had a simple reason for talking to a reporter for the first time in her life: We just don't want this to happen to anyone else.

Ashley Hackett has been living on the streets of Brighton for the last eight years. Hackett, 34, has not always helped himself. With a long-standing drug addiction he has not been the most willing participant of the support networks and rehabilitation schemes which social services, charities, housing associations and the police operate in the city. Last November Hackett was reading a newspaper after an uncomfortable night in a doorway on Western Street when two smartly dressed men walked very slowly by. He got out his begging cup and asked for ten pence. Less than 30 minutes later he was at the central police station being charged under the 200-year-old Vagrancy Act. The men were plain clothes police officers deliberately targeting beggars. In the station he refused to take a drugs test which would have shown he had heroin in his body. At that moment he became a criminal.

Hackett was just one of 17 homeless people brought before the courts for begging after being arrested by undercover officers in two months around Christmas. A total of 62 were arrested last year. The previous 16 were all fined in cases which cost the tax-payer £16,000 to bring to court. The possible irony of fining homeless people for begging for ten pence appeared not to have been recognised. More than 60 per cent of those fined never have the money to pay a single penny.

Brighton's magistrates' building is a warren of corridors and functional court rooms. Harassed defence solicitors dash to and fro while their clients loiter around the vending machines. A court reporter could easily spend a day down there jumping between courts getting nothing juicy. Some days it's like digging for tin in an exhausted Cornish mine. Little wonder that fewer and fewer journalists are to be found there. So it was thin gruel the day chief reporter Emily Walker met defence solicitor Ray Pape in the corridor outside court 6. Pape mentioned he was concerned about the number of homeless people coming before the courts. He said magistrates had begun voicing their own concerns while being forced to bring in the only sentence they could. Trouble was without anyone witnessing these hearings on a daily basis it was a cry in the wilderness. Pape took Walker to see Hackett. The story which followed wasn't Watergate. It wasn't even the best story in Brighton that week. But it was important. That could be gauged by the reaction of the police. Senior officers were furious with the story claiming The Argus had presented a partial picture. The 'multi-agency' approach in Brighton had won awards. Homeless people being brought to court were thus forced to enter a rehabilitation system which might free them of drugs. Nothing was said about lawyers, magistrates and homeless campaigners who protested about the arrests nor of the 30,000 names who signed a online petition following Walker's story calling for the practice to end.

Two weeks after the story Hackett came before the courts. Prosecutors performed a volte-face telling magistrates the issue of bringing homeless people to court had become 'particularly sensitive' and they and the police wished not to continue. District judge Teresa Szagun told them: To proceed with this case is plainly not in the public interest. By refusing a drugs test Hackett has a criminal record and must pay a court victims' surcharge of £60.

A number of things troubled the newsdesk about the terrible death of Janet Muller, a German studying at Brighton University. Janet, who had suffered from severe mental illness for many years, was burnt alive in the boot of a car. Her killer, an unemployed drifter called Christopher Jeffrey-Shaw escaped a murder charge because the prosecution couldn't prove he knew Janet was still alive when he set fire to the car. The jury had to accept a fantastical alibi he and his victim were caught up with a drugs gang and she with an armed robbery which went wrong. Jeffrey-Shaw was convicted of manslaughter and will serve eight years in prison. Janet had been Sectioned under the Mental Health Act at a unit called Mill View in Hove run by the Sussex NHS Partnership Trust. While attention focussed on the motives for the killing Gareth Davies, a reporter on The Argus, began to ask the Trust questions. But this would take time, time few regional newsrooms have in these days of 24/7 news cycles and diminished numbers of reporters.

A Freedom of Information request revealed emails from a governor of the Trust to the chief executive in which she lamented 'another life had been lost from Caburn Ward' the female unit at Mill View. The chief executive promised a full inquiry but this had already taken place it appeared and would not be made public. Janet had left Mill View the day before she died by simply walking through the front door. She was found wandering the streets and brought back to the hospital where she was supposed to be supervised at all times. That night she simply climbed over a wall in the garden of the unit using vines from a creeper that had been allowed to grow and disappeared. Her charred body was found in the boot of the car two days later. A planning application to make the wall higher had been submitted the day before she fled.

There was more to come. Four patients under the supervision of Mill View had committed suicide the year before, one jumping from a block of flats while her carer was inside.

As far back as 2013 a report had recommended security measures be improved at the unit but little work had been undertaken. The Trust said lessons had been learned and extra training given. Findings of the inquiry had been shared with 'our partners'. These partners did not include any of the relatives of the dead patients. That job was left to the newspaper.

All these stories happened within 12 months in Brighton. They are perhaps not untypical of events which occur in towns and cities up and down the country every day. But what unites these stories and thousands of others like them in the communities in which we live is you might very easily not have known about them. The Brighton stories could easily have forever existed in a little orbit of their own, unheralded by anyone, unremarked. Journalists made sure this was not so.

The institutions of the state exist to provide checks and balances. Handsomely paid watchdogs look over the police, government departments, local authorities, our hospitals and a host of other organisations paid for by us and supposedly working on our behalf.

But who watches the watchers? Where do the concerns of the coroner of Brighton find space when even the watchdogs seem powerless? We know journalism is in crisis but very little has been said about the profound democratic deficit that would follow any meltdown?

Since 2008 more than 8,000 journalists have lost their jobs. Ironically this has not been deemed important enough a story. Newspapers have folded, commercial television news is decimated and only the BBC has staff in numbers even though at local level it still often feeds off what is left of private sector reporting. Just as in music and books digital technologies have driven a coach and horses through media company business models. This we know. Most news from traditional media is given away free online on a drive to build vast audiences, this we also know. Only recently have there been attempts at local level to redefine what is published online and where building mass 'drive-by' numbers sits with what some might say is old-fashioned journalism, in other words telling people things they didn't know and having to spend time finding those things out. The debate is still nowhere near exhaustive and urgent enough.

Does any of this really matter? Hasn't the explosion of democratising technologies swept away the old order so now even the back bedroom warrior can hold government ministers to account? Why do we need 'gatekeepers', salaried journalists and their editors, to filter what we should know? Aren't we all reporters now? In Brighton searing images and accounts of the Shoreham Air Show tragedy last year, as an out-of-control vintage aircraft sped from a clear blue sky into unsuspecting motorists on the A27, were online before journalists, photographers and writers, had even made it to the scene.

But we still need journalists with the time, training and passion to avoid this ever-increasing deficit. No amount of digitally empowered bloggers, many of them diligent thorns in the side on a range of issues, will make up for the loss of professional reporting. In some towns courts, council meetings and trust boards are all going unreported now. Meanwhile the explosion of press officers, more often journalists fleeing a shrinking industry and skilled at 'social engagement' now outnumber salaried journalists in many areas. In Northern Ireland the government employs 160 press officers, more than the entire number of private sector journalists in the province. This must be worthy of debate.

Digital technologies will continue to evolve, changing the world as it does. There is no turning back the clock. But society must have a discussion about direction of travel otherwise a pure technological determinism will hold sway. There are many issues now facing the print industry. It needs strong, passionate leadership more than ever before. For what is manifestly obvious, and surprises the outside world, isthe industry has a poor record in promoting its merits.

Many strategies are being devised to protect revenues and find new streams, largely on digital platforms. Yet efforts to promote the purpose of journalism and the printed product which still pays for the lion's share of journalist endeavour seem underwhelming. Industry bodies, companies and editors, perhaps wary of the standing of the profession in the post-Leveson world, have been too shy to conduct a sustained and coherent campaign about its importance to society. It all sounds too pompous and maybe even desperate. But has the industry really engaged the public in a debate that starts with what is blindingly obvious: if you don't pay you lose it?

Signs both at The Guardian and in the US, at big titles like the New York Times, that readers will respond, if only a trickle at present, to such a 'call to arms' are a start. Of course many will say the steep declines in newspaper sales figures are already the readers' answer to the question. And even if the question is asked loudly and clearly it may well be some titles have reached the point of no return. They simply aren't good enough to justify the cover price. But many still may be, providing they are producing the sort of journalism described above consistently enough.

This is the time for a concerted explanation, a campaign if you like, to tell society what we will all miss if the cull of journalists continues at the same pace. Only after such efforts, when the debate is fully aired, might we have to conclude print-based journalism has no place in the shiny future. We are not there yet.

It goes without saying digital journalism must continue to evolve quickly and meet the technological demands of its users. That is taken for granted. But that does not mean print journalism's decline should just be a matter of extending the graph until the figures fail to stack and crossing fingers hoping to get even that far. The printed product can be re-invented, or at least we must not forget it must remain an intrinsic part of the industry's evolving strategy. Long form journalism, analysis and investigation remain the best hope for the printed product on all levels. A journalism which eschews the helter-skelter 24/7 news cycle might still find a place in the market. This would often be less frequently, from daily to weekly or even monthly, and it would have to be unapologetically intelligent, commanding of premium cover price, targeted more carefully than the centuries-old scattershot distribution models we still use.

In the regional press the change from daily to weekly has often resulted in customers getting a sixth of the mediocre product they were offered before. This is nowhere near good enough. On a regional level, upmarket and intelligence is the target, losing readers who do not fit the profile might be collateral damage that will have to be borne. Cover price increase for quality product that delivers the right readers for advertisers is the goal.

Everywhere we will have to take what might be called the Private Eye/Economist test when talking about print products' role in any future. Is it exclusive, targeted and unavailable anywhere else? It will have to exist apart from its digital operations, a real Back to the Future move, or it might be it has to come from a new start company. But a compelling, in-depth, punchy, physical news product produced with panache which asks readers to invest time and rewards that investment might still have a role amid the communications white noise filling the air around us.

The democratic deficit is real and it is happening now particularly at the unheralded, unglamorous local level, where we all live. With Evelyn Kennedy, Ashley Hackett and Janet Muller in mind we should begin the debate now.

## Note on the contributor
In a long career in the regional media, Michael Gilson has been group editor of Newsquest Media (Sussex) Ltd, based at the Brighton Argus, and also editor of the Belfast Telegraph, The Scotsman, The News, Portsmouth, and the Peterborough Evening Telegraph He was one of only four regional newspaper editors to give evidence to the Leveson Inquiry in 2011-12.

# Baiting the reader: Identifying the newspaper version of clickbait

**Sean Dodson, postgraduate leader in Journalism at Leeds Beckett University, argues the phenomenon of listicles is doing nothing to help the woes of the regional press**

In July 2016, the Croydon Advertiser, a 123-year-old newspaper, published two lookalike stories on consecutive, facing pages. Headlined '13 things you'll know if you are a Southern rail passenger' and '9 things you didn't know about Blockbuster' the articles stood out for their striking similarity.

Both articles were an example of an editorial phenomenon more commonly associated with the Internet – the listicle. A portmanteau of 'list' and 'article', listicles are so incredibly popular right now (Edidin 2014), but also controversial. They are an anathema to some critics who prize traditional journalistic values (White 2014), while to others listicles are not even journalism but a 'kind of cheap content-creation' (Brauer 2013) and, to yet more, 'listicles are the inevitable result of cost-cutting (Dvorkin 2016). Indeed, the Croydon Advertiser's articles appeared after a newsroom restructure: one wag on Twitter called them 'Buzzfeed on paper', a reference to the highly successful social news and entertainment company (Buzzfeed 2015) that publishes thousands of listicles every week.

Listicles, like other forms of clickbait, assume the public want information in quick hits (Birthisel 2014) and 'prefer mindless fluff and trivia over hard news and heavy stories'. Listicles are far from new, however, The Ten Commandments are an early example, and they not exclusive to the Internet. Traditionally print journalism has used lists in distinct ways: either as an attendant to news and feature articles or as a standalone special (such as the Sunday Times Rich List); the convention has also been, because space is limited, that lists work best in denominations of 10. The '100 best free things to do this week' or '10 things we learnt about the Budget' and so on. But on sites such as Buzzfeed, such traditional conventions are ignored. Lists start and end where they fall, as did those in the Croydon Advertiser.

## Shifting powers

Use of listicles in newspapers is an example, moreover, of a shift in the power relations of print and online journalism. Today more journalists work online than in print and online ads are more valuable than display advertising (Thurman, Alessio, and Kunert 2016). It is significant, moreover, because the format is no longer dictated by the conventions of print, but mimic the looser set of conventions born of the Internet. As such, listicles form part of a wider phenomenon of clickbait (Seeberger 2016), a pejorative term used to describe web content designed to capture an online audience in the hope of generating advertising revenue, often at the expense of traditional journalistic values, e.g. accuracy, balance or fairness.

Clickbait – bait laid to lure clicks – is instead known for dubious quality, an absence of simple attribution and a scant appetite for exclusivity (you know, actual scoops, the stuff that counts). Facts are pulled, instead, from the web, then knocked together randomly, by 'contributors' doing unpaid work for sites such as The Huffington Post ('11 Products That Make Cats More Like Humans'), Buzzfeed ('29 Mind Blowing Ways You Can Eat Chips') and Upworthy ('This Story Is So Incredible, The English Language Does Not Contain A Superlative Fit To Describe It. So I'm Just Going To Make One Up. Fantaculous [sic]').

And now, more recently, clickbait formats have made the pages of established news organisations. The Independent has been much lambasted for resorting to the tactic of late (typical Indy click-bait headline 'Matt LeBlanc: I need to to [sic] get back into watching Game of Thrones... to see Emilia Clarke naked' (Independent, 2016). How soon a respectable newspaper of the centre-left can be transformed into a less-respectable chronicler of clickbait.

Moreover, media commentators believe that clickbait lacks 'merit' (Ponsford 2016) and that it is 'rarely newsworthy' (Dvorkin 2016). Katherine Viner (2016), editor-in-chief at The Guardian has written that 'chasing down cheap clicks at the expense of accuracy and veracity undermines the value of journalism.'

## Chips are down

A concrete expression of this came in April 2016. The Gloucestershire Echo featured a story about litter. One morning someone dropped a bag of fast food on the pavement in the centre of Cheltenham. Now, this wasn't an instance of an unusual type of litter or an epidemic of litter. It was ordinary litter, the sort seen on every high street every day of the week. Even so, the Echo published a photograph of the rubbish and used it as the basis for a story ('Entire KFC feast of fried chicken breasts and fries strewn across Cheltenham pavement this morning'). An online team updated an incredulous public with a live blog throughout the day. Other papers and websites followed, most notably Metro, a national daily.

Fast food must be easy pickings for time-strapped journalists. Trinity Mirror, the paper's owner, had been here before. In 2013, the Echo's sister paper, The

(Gloucester) Citizen, had run a news story asking 'Is this the biggest chip in Gloucestershire?' complete with a user-generated image of the admittedly prodigious slice of deep-fried potato. In Folkestone, meanwhile, The Herald caused a minor social media sensation with its front-page splash: 'Out-of-date-pasty is sold to young mum'.

And so consider, for a moment, that discarded fast food wrappers and stale pasties are simply not news. Not in any conventional way. Not as generations of reporters have understood news to be. There is widespread academic consensus on this. A solitary piece of litter or a big chip or a stale pasty does not register on any of the news values codified by either Galtung and Ruge (1965) or Harcup and O'Neill (2001). So not news, then, but clickbait. And if such 'tripe' (Ponsford 2016) is printed in the paper, it is a short reach to the phrase 'page bait'. Cheap, and trivial content designed to tickle casually at the ribs, without the rationale of attracting actual pay-per-click adverts.

The economics of the strategy, if one dignifies it, must be that publishers are able to reuse website content in print, instead of having to pay people to produce separate content (Jarvis 2016). The cost is further reduced if user-generated content can be used in the place of paying for original journalism.

## Amateur calling

Can we expect more? You bet. Regionals across the land are using ever more content written by amateurs. Not only to strafe bullshit across cyberspace in the hope of attracting enough pay-per-click advertisements, but also to fill newspapers under-staffed chronically by rounds of job losses.

In 2013, Johnson Press relaunched its Lincolnshire regional The Bourne Local, as a 'people's paper' featuring up to 75 per cent content supplied by the area's local people – unpaid of course. The experiment was repeated in Yorkshire at the Pocklington Post, initially reviving both paid-for titles. The experiment has not been extended to other papers in the group, yet, while more centralised media hubs where regional journalists work across greater geographic regions has been adopted across the group.

More recently, Trinity Mirror converted its regional titles into 'digitally-led news publications' (Reid, 2014) publishing on the Internet first and then shifting the content into the paper late afternoon. Further job cuts followed.

Surviving journalists were told to produce live blogs – everything from fascist marches to sporting events to, in one instance, the opening of a branch of KFC, 'the eighth in the county' (Norton 2015). In this model editorial work is first produced online and is then reformatted for the print newspaper later. The Wolverhampton-based Express & Star, the biggest regional newspaper outside London, opened a user-generated content desk to take further contributions from the public (Economist 2015).

## No news values

Fewer journalists, fewer scoops, fewer hard questions, less topicality and weaker attribution. It all contributes to the drip-drip-dripping away of seriousness and credibility in the regional newspapers of Great Britain. The idea of a critical-rational press so clearly defined by Jurgen Habermas (1991) cannot, surely, be consistent with editorial policy that counts generating click-bait as part of its schedule. And so, we see more listicles, more user-generated content, and more stories without any recognisable news value, whether industrial or academic. Just bait, more and more of it. The local paper scraping like a scavenger for content from the great scrap heap of the Internet and piling it to the old paper as a matter of grim routine.

"The future of local journalism cannot just be built on 'click-bait' stories," wrote Peter Barron, the departing Northern Echo editor early in 2016 (Sharman). "Local newspapers have a vital role to play in society and my parting wish is that they are given the time and support for quality, campaigning journalism that makes a difference to people's lives."

But even those who rile against clickbait, call them clickbait skeptics, the protest can prove futile. "We are not afraid of running the odd quirky story while not falling into the clickbait trap loved by many news organisations desperate for someone to read their content," wrote Lee Marlow (Ponsford 2016), and then the current regional features writer of the year in a column for his paper, the Leicester Mercury. "We avoid lists," he continued, "of the best places to go dogging or running stories about popular TV shows or naked pictures of celebs with no local link." The column was spiked. Room for such integrity in short supply at the 143-year-old newspaper. Marlow was made redundant shortly after, along with his team. The Mercury, the newspaper that awarded Donald Trelford his first byline, runs a feature desk today with just one journalist instructed to focus on "what's on style content".

## Ringfence hope
Don't despair. There is hope, though. Print is flourishing where skillful journalism is ring-fenced and professional work encouraged to a high standard. The Spectator is celebrating an all-time, 188-year circulation high. Its editor, Fraser Nelson (2016) attributes the success to "a perfect storm of print and digital". The Economist has seen its subscriptions rise – subscribers always pay for digital access. Private Eye has reached a 30-year high in circulation. It too restricts content online.

Regionals newspapers took another road. Each gave content away in the hope of clicks. Now they hope to subsidise those very clicks by sharing content with the paper and offsetting the cost of production. Newsroom restructures, involving staff layoffs, create further commercial pressures on journalists to produce quick copy on the fly, leading to the promotion of 'cheap' listicles and other types of clickbait of the type popular in the Croydon Advertiser.

Incidentally, '13 things you'll know if you are a Southern rail passenger' wasn't confined to the Advertiser. It appeared in the East Grinstead Courier (20 miles from Croydon) and in the Surrey Mirror that same week. The story repeated throughout the group wasn't even original, a very similar article had appeared on the Internet a week earlier, on Cosmopolitan.com, which managed not just 13 things about Southern, but 23 (Edwards, Capon 2016). We can, perhaps, expect more lookalike listicles appearing in the regional press as the same bleak certainty that a rail passenger awaits delays.

## References

Birthisel, J (2014) "'Too embarrassed to ask ": The pros and cons of foreign affair explainers in the Washington Post', The Bridgewater Review.

Brauer, S M (2013) 'Manipulative headlines and listicles: Upworthy and Buzzfeed are reshaping the internet', November 22. Available at: http://www.dvafoto.com/2013/11/manipulative-headlines-and-listicles-upworthy-and-buzzfeed-are-reshaping-the-internet/ (Accessed: October 10, 2016).

BuzzFeed (2016) About BuzzFeed. Available at: https://www.buzzfeed.com/about (Accessed: October 10, 2016).

Economist, The (2015) Stop press. Available at: http://www.economist.com/news/britain/21677662-local-newspapers-are-just-about-managing-survive-stop-press (Accessed: October 10, 2016).

Edidin, R (2014) '5 Reasons Listicles Are Here to Stay, and Why That's OK', Wired Magazine [US] (January).

Edwards, J, Capon, L, Jones, K, Lewis, A and Harvey-Jenner, C (2016) '23 daily struggles every southern rail passenger will feel (passionately)', *Reports* (July).

Galtung, J; Ruge, M. Holmboe (1965). "The Structure of Foreign News. The Presentation of the Congo, Cuba and Cyprus Crises in Four Norwegian Newspapers". Journal of Peace Research. 2: 64–91.

Harcup T and O'Neill, D (2001) 'What is news? Galtung and Ruge revisited', Journalism Studies, 2 (2), pp. 261–280.

Habermas, J (1991) The structural transformation of the public sphere: An inquiry into a category of bourgeois society. Cambridge: The MIT Press.

Jarvis, J (2011) 'Hard economic lessons for news — BuzzMachine', April 25. Available at: http://buzzmachine.com/2011/04/25/hard-economic-lessons-for-news/ (Accessed: October 10, 2016).

Newmark, C (2014) 'A case for old-school values in a click-driven journalism landscape', Business, September 10. Available at: http://mediashift.org/2014/09/a-case-for-old-school-values-in-a-click-driven-journalism-landscape/ (Accessed: October 10, 2016).

Nelson, F. (2016) 'Sales of The Spectator hit a 188-year high in "perfect storm" of print and digital  coffee house', Coffee House, 11 August. Available at: http://blogs.spectator.co.uk/2016/08/sales-spectator-hit-188-year-high/?_ga=1.100782145.1355062568.1470913739 (Accessed: October 10, 2016).

Oppenheim, M. (2016) Matt LeBlanc: I need to to get back into watching game of thrones... To see Emilia Clarke naked. Available at: http://www.independent.co.uk/news/people/matt-leblanc-emilia-clarke-naked-emmy-awards-game-of-thrones-comments-friends-star-a7315996.html (Accessed: October 10, 2016).

Norton (2016) See inside the brand new KFC in Cinderhill. Available at: http://www.nottinghampost.com/live-opening-kfc-cinderhill/story-29277918-detail/story.html (Accessed: October 10, 2016).

Ponsford, D. (2016) 'Spiked column by star writer on Leicester Mercury railed against "risible" standard of clickbait online journalism', August 8. Available at: http://www.pressgazette.co.uk/spiked-column-by-sacked-star-writer-on-the-leicester-mercury-railed-against-risible-standard-of-clickbait-online-journalism/ (Accessed: October 10, 2016).

Reid, A. (2014) 'How "newsroom 3.1" will change Trinity Mirror's local titles', Media news, March 26. Available at: https://www.journalism.co.uk/news/how-newsroom-3-1-will-change-trinity-mirror-s-local-titles/s2/a556221/ (Accessed: October 10, 2016).

Sharman, D. (2016) *Departing northern echo editor warns against 'click-bait' future - journalism news from HoldtheFrontPage*. Available at: http://www.holdthefrontpage.co.uk/2016/news/departing-regional-daily-editor-warns-against-click-bait-future/ (Accessed: October 11, 2016).

Seeberger, T. (1996) 'Listicles and clickbaits: The downfall of journalism', Available at: http://chimes.biola.edu/story/2016/sep/13/listicles-and-clickbaits-downfall-journalism/ (Accessed: October 10, 2016).

Viner, K. (2016) How technology disrupted the truth Katharine Viner. Available at: https://www.theguardian.com/media/2016/jul/12/how-technology-disrupted-the-truth (Accessed: October 10, 2016).

**Note on the contributor**
Sean Dodson is the postgraduate leader in journalism at Leeds Beckett University. He specialises in the study of editorial codes of ethics and is currently writing a PhD about how such codes work on the internet. He is a former judge of the Orwell Prize, the UK's most prestigious award for political writing.

# The clickbait debate – myths and realities

**Journalism's newest dirty word is clickbait, now shorthand for anything that isn't traditional, 'proper' journalism, especially but not totally confined to online media. But what is really going on deep inside regional newspaper websites? Alan Geere gets his hands dirty**

Departing Northern Echo editor Peter Barron warned the future of local journalism cannot be built on 'clickbait'. A spiked column by a star writer on the Leicester Mercury railed against 'risible' standard of clickbait online journalism. An online journalists' survey revealed: 'Public will soon live off attention-seeking, fact-free, gossipy clickbait'.

Once we had comment. Now we have clickbait.

## What is clickbait?

The academic community is surprisingly united in its definition of clickbait and its desired effects. "Clickbaits are articles with misleading titles, exaggerating the content on the landing page. Their goal is to entice users to click on the title in order to monetise the landing page. The content on the landing page is usually of low quality," say Biyani, Tsioutsiouliklis and Blackmer (2016) in their research paper 'Eight Amazing Secrets for Getting More Clicks: Detecting Clickbaits in News Streams Using Article Informality'.

Similarly Chen, Conroy and Rubin (2015) assert: "Clickbait refers to content whose main purpose is to attract attention and encourage visitors to click on a link to a particular web page and has been implicated in the rapid spread of rumour and misinformation online."

Chakraborty et al (2016) maintain clickbait exploits the cognitive phenomenon known as 'curiosity gap'. "Headlines provide forward referencing cues to generate enough curiosity among the readers such that they become compelled to click on the link to fill the knowledge gap."

**What are they saying?**

Peter Barron left the Northern Echo after 17 years as editor with a valedictory editorial. In it he reflected on his successes but cautioned readers as follows: "The future of local journalism cannot just be built on 'click-bait' – stories which attract the biggest number of hits online.

"There will be those who call me a dinosaur but if I see another 'stomach-churning compilation of the best spot-squeezing videos' on a 'news' website, I may well take a hammer to my computer. Exploding spots may get lots of hits, and that may attract digital advertising revenue, but it isn't news."

In the Midlands, Lee Marlow, the writer behind the hard-hitting Fred Leicester column, also wrote a piece when he was made redundant, but the editor at the Leicester Mercury chose not to run it.

Edited highlights of that column included: "We have a website which is updated all day, every day, constantly. Yet it's a website festooned with so many ads that you try to access it on your phone and it's barely readable.

"And on that website there will be not just all of the news from the paper, but other 'news', too. Stories about Apple iPhone batteries. Product recalls. Some stuff about how people are comparing Leicester City to Donald Trump. (No, really. Apparently, they are.)

"This is 'internet only' news. Clickbait. You may have heard of it. It doesn't have a good reputation and its reputation is deserved, if you're asking me.

"But you can also see how these stories have been shared. This one had been shared more than 8,000 times on Facebook and Twitter. Click, click, click, click. In this brave new world of digital journalism, this is what counts. The click is always King. It doesn't matter that your readers are laughing at you when they click. It just matters that they click."

In South London, reporter Gareth Davies took to Twitter after accepting his redundancy cheque from the Croydon Advertiser to bemoan the direction his old paper was going. "A paper with a proud 147-year history reduced to being a thrown together collection of clickbait written for the web," he tweeted.

He added: "What do readers get? A website focused on live blogging everything, with reporters told to 'write like they speak down the pub'. Well, it breaks my heart. I couldn't stick around to watch the paper be destroyed & I would not help them do it."

**The new numbers**

Online audience, not unsurprisingly, continues to grow while print sales fall.

The latest figures for daily average unique browsers in regional publications (Jan-June 2016) show Newsquest with the biggest group-wide jump over the six months to the end of June, with a 24 per cent rise year-on-year to 1.575m daily uniques, 23 per cent up on the last half of 2015.

Johnston Press was up by 22 per cent year-on-year while Trinity Mirror, which boasted the biggest number of daily uniques at 2.471m, was up 19 per cent year-on-year. The Local World Network, owned by Trinity Mirror, was up 13 per cent year-on-year to 1.393m daily uniques.

## The research

For the purposes of this chapter we returned to scene of the crimes above to examine the websites and determine just what sort of job they are doing. They are by definition a snapshot and concentrate on the 'splash' page or opening page of the site where by definition any clickbait would reside. Each site was monitored for quantity and quality with a verdict delivered at the end.

## The Northern Echo

Newsquest

http://www.thenorthernecho.co.uk/

Accessed Friday September 9 2016 at 09.12

Opening page has 25 news stories, four videos, 20 in the Most Popular column.

Sport – 17 stories

National sport – four stories

Four 'others' inc the infamous Headline Challenge started by Peter Barron, who lives on it its blurb [see illustration]

Ents (that's what it's called) - seven stories

Echo memories – seven

Business news - seven

Trending across the UK – seven stories from other Newsquest titles

National news – seven, although the most recent was nine hours ago

Most popular (again) – top 18

## Headline Challenge

The Headline Challenge is played out every weekday morning between The Northern Echo's editor Peter Barron and BBC Tees.

A story is selected and radio listeners try to come up with a better headline than the one published in the paper. Points

#headlinechallenge

Alfie Angry Shih Tzu
@alfieangry

@BBCTees @greenyfrom630
@amy_oakden Boom-a-rang Turn
#headlinechallenge

**ANDY RICHARDSON**
**Business Editor**

Follow @bizecho { 0 followers }

### Social media

Twitter: 41.4k followers, 29.6k tweets, Followers Per Tweet (FPT) ratio 1.4

Very handy Twitter directory of all staff, plus their number of followers, including the ex-editor Peter Barron leading the way with 13.9k followers. The current editor Andy Richardson is still listed as Business Editor with 0 followers, probably because the Twitter name given @bizecho links to a baby supply store in Indonesia.

**Toko Alat Bayi**
@BizEcho

Perlengkapan bayi lengkap degan harga dan rinciannya.
Produk berkualitas hanya di http://buahhatiku.com

· http://buahhatiku.com

FOLLOWERS 0          FOLLOWING 0

 **Toko Alat Bayi** @BizEcho
Semua yang Anda butuhkan mengenai perlengkapan bayi modern. Ada di sini
buahhatiku.com pic.twitter.com/YEM8R3nZDL
11.20 AM - 12 Aug 2016

23k Facebook likes

Verdict: Lots to look at and lots to read, a la DailyMail.co.uk, with a big landing page that takes quite a bit of scrolling through.

Clickbait score 0/10

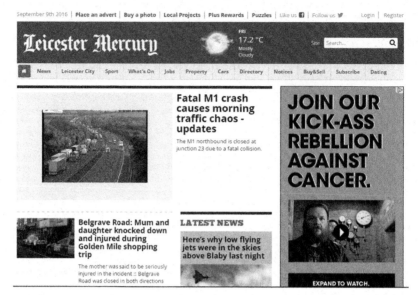

## Leicester Mercury

Trinity Mirror/Local World

Accessed on Friday September 9 2016 at 09.50

http://www.leicestermercury.co.uk/

The top of the opening page has three stories, which are not labelled, one Latest News and two Editor's Choices.

The lead is a timeline of a fatal crash on the MI, which happened that morning, lively updates with pix and maps.

Sport – seven stories (all Leicester City)

News – seven stories

Entertainments: Features - seven, events - five

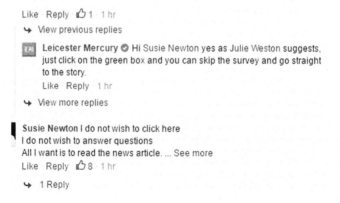

## Social media

Twitter: 72.7k followers from 75.3k tweets with a FPT ratio of 1.03

Facebook: 45k likes (although link takes away from website)

In common with all Trinity Mirror/Local World sites readers have to 'answer a survey question to continue reading this content'. However, the advice on getting around the survey is neatly provided by the paper on its Facebook page.

Verdict: Practical, purposeful and if anything, a little understated. Plenty going on, but nothing that jumps out at you. The ads are there but aren't intrusive.

Clickbait rating 0/10

## Croydon Advertiser

Trinity Mirror/Local World

http://www.croydonadvertiser.co.uk/

Accessed Friday September 9, 2016 at 08.40

Splash page has three stories plus another headlined Worth The Money?

The lead is a court story with picture taken by reporter

Sport – seven stories, all Crystal Palace

Editor's Picks – two

More news – six local stories inc 'The insane giant milkshakes you can now buy in Croydon' with one comment, which was spam

Most read – five stories (three Crystal Palace)

What's On - seven features, five events

'9 things you'll know if you were a regular at London nightclub Fabric' was more than 1,200 lovingly crafted words written by a staff member and actually deserved better than the lame listicle headline. Not local though.

**Social media**

Twitter: 11.8k followers. 15.7k tweets FPT ratio .75

Facebook 19k likes

Verdict: Plenty to read, well written and from a visit later in the day updated regularly. Sponsored content (Staples back to school), some ads but nothing obtrusive.

Clickbait score: 1/10 just for that '9 things' headline

In the interests of fairness, we also looked at titles from the other two big groups, Johnston Press and Archant – this time selected at random from a numbered list using random.org number generator.

**Norwich Evening News**

Archant

http://www.eveningnews24.co.uk/home

Accessed Tuesday September 6 2016, 12.34

Under 'Latest' 10 items – crime, news, views, education, motoring, all time stamped

Mustard tv promo

'More' – five items, one sport

Photo galleries – six items

More 'more'

Most read – top five

Revealed: The number of parents fined at every Norfolk school for taking children out of class was a super FOI story with comments, facts and figs

**Social media**, reached by big, bold links not the usual tiny symbols

Twitter: 39.7k followers, 59.6k tweets FPT ratio .66

Facebook: 13k likes

Verdict: Bright, accessible page. Interesting to see sport mixed in with other content, although readers can click through to a dedicated page.

Clickbait score: 0/10

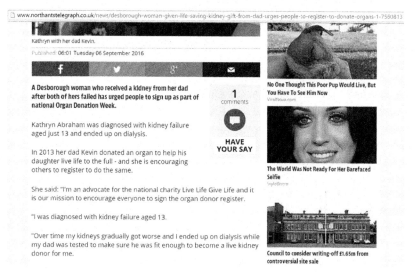

## Northamptonshire Telegraph

http://www.northantstelegraph.co.uk/

Johnston Press

Accessed Tuesday September 6 2016 at 14.36

Hot Topics – seven items

Followed by Sky promotion and 'Supermarket price war' credited to Offbeat

Sport – eight stories

What's on – three stories

Essential daily briefing from inews – five stories which open in new window

Lifestyle three stories (two local)

Trending now nine stories (all local)

Promoted stories (nine) 'Promoted link by Taboola'

**Get involved in the discussion and have your say ...**

SIGN IN

1 comment

Sort by: Newest to Oldest

**Name withheld**

3:31 PM on 30/08/2016

*This comment was left by a user who has been blocked by our staff.*

## Social media

Twitter: 12.1k followers, 39.2k tweets FPT ratio .31

Facebook 25k likes

Verdict: Register to leave a comment clearly is a put-off with just four comments on whole of news page. A neat story on organ donation surrounded by 'sponsored links'. Felt far more commercial than the other sites looked at.

Clickbait score: 2/10

## So, where are we with clickbait and the regional press?

As this research shows claims for the pervasive influence of clickbait appear to be exaggerated. All the sites visited showed an honest commitment to providing local news, sport, information, comment and entertainment to the highest standard.

If anything, they were somewhat prosaic, lacking the, er, buzz of buzzfeed.com, the sheer breadth and depth of dailymail.co.uk or the clickbait heaven (or hell) of cosmopolitan.co.uk.

Perhaps because of the eternal 'time constraints' or the effect of job cuts throughout the industry, engagement with the audience via website interactivity or through social media was low. Maybe it's time for the regional press to get off its high horse and start to realise the full potential of the 'new media' at its disposal.

## References

Biyani , Tsioutsiouliklis and Blackmer (2016) 8 Amazing Secrets for Getting More Clicks": Detecting Clickbaits in News Streams Using Article Informality. *Proceedings of the Thirtieth AAAI Conference on Artificial Intelligence (AAAI-16)* pp 94-100

Chen, Conroy, and Rubin (2015) Misleading online content: Recognizing clickbait as false news. *Proceedings of the 78th American Society for Information Science Annual Meeting: Information Science with Impact: Research in and for the Community* pp 15-19

Chakraborty, Paranjape, Kakarla and Ganguly (2016) Stop Clickbait: Detecting and Preventing Clickbaits in Online News *Media IEEE/ACM International Conference on Advances in Social Networks Analysis and Mining (ASONAM)*

## Note on the contributor

Alan Geere is a journalist, academic and international editorial consultant. He was editorial director of Northcliffe Newspapers South-East and, as editor, led the Essex Chronicle to two successive Weekly Newspaper of the Year awards.

As an editorial executive he worked in the UK, Canada, United States and the Caribbean and his consulting career has taken him into 200 newsrooms worldwide.

He was head of the Media, Communications and Journalism undergraduate degree course at Victoria University in Kampala, Uganda, and taught journalism at City, Westminster and Worcester Universities. Alan was also a member of the board of the National Council for the Training of Journalists (NCTJ).

# Can video save the former newspaper star?

**The business model of the local press appears to be broken. There is no quick or simple solution. But could online news video, distributed on social platforms and using native advertising and sponsored content be the answer? Are the printing presses redundant, set to be consigned to history, and replaced by the video camera, asks David Hayward**

"One minute of video is worth 1.8m words," says Dr James McQuivey of Forrester Research.

And 2016 has been heralded as the year news organisations really got to grips with the challenges of online news video. In Nic Newman's annual media journalism and technology predictions, he said:

"This year's key developments will centre on online video, mobile apps and further moves towards distributed content. Mounting problems around online display advertising will lead to a burst of innovation around journalism business models."[1]

It has become the key battleground for the most creative news organisations in the world. There can be no surprise, when you consider the demand for online video by a global and mobile audience. Nearly 400bn videos[2] are viewed every month on the four main social media platforms.

Facebook and Snapchat are both claiming 10bn video views a day. Meanwhile Cisco predicts 75 per cent of mobile data traffic will be video by 2020.[3]

While print editions of newspapers are coming to an end[4], digital native news companies, such as Vox, Vocativ, AJ+, NowThisNews, Fusion, Buzzfeed News and Vice News have emerged. They are creating innovative, distributed online video and reaching huge numbers of viewers.

To use just one example, NowThisNews, has an astonishing 1bn video views a month. It is getting such huge audiences because it is operating in a digitally native way and attracting digitally native viewers. To use a quote from the younger generation it is "…..smashing online news video."

"NowThis was one of the first publishers to post natively to Facebook – and was also one of the very first brand creators to deliberately use a lot of text overlay on its videos. It knew it needed a way to capture the viewer's attention on silent auto plays, a strategy which not only paid off very quickly, but one which thousands of other video creators adopted as a way of retaining viewers for as long as possible."[5]

These organisations are not looking to print; they are looking to video and investing heavily in it. The broadcasters and big global press are following suit.

The BBC, Channel 4 News, ITV, Sky, Washington Post, Wall Street Journal, New York Times and The Guardian are producing some interesting material. It's working for them and they are reaching vast new audiences and engaging with them in an entirely new and productive way.

Channel 4 News has a particularly successful Facebook strategy. They have reported a massive increase in its online news video – from 5m views in January 2015 to more than 200m videos viewed in June 2016.

"In the last year, UK broadcaster Channel 4 News has entirely stopped posting text and static photos to social media to focus almost exclusively on video. The move to video has paid off. Although half its Facebook posts were already video as of January last year, it netted a total of 5m views for the month. Today that monthly number is over 200m."[6]

In contrast to these market leaders and innovators, the local and regional press in the UK is lagging far behind. Unless it changes and changes fast, the industry is in serious trouble. Nic Newman quotes one anonymous editor in the Reuters Digital News report – but in so many ways, it reflects the wider malaise within the industry: "Video is a difficult area for former print groups. None of us is doing it well, we do not have in-house expertise (generally) and it is vastly expensive. We will proceed with caution in this area" (anon).[7]

There are bright examples. Trinity Mirror has announced[8] it is hiring local video producers and editors. It's clear there are some very good people thinking about the digital future of the regional press. But while the same parent company takes the unbelievably ill conceived decision to launch a paid-for print newspaper[9] in today's climate, warning bells must be ringing about how it intends to succeed in the future.

The prospect of a new collaboration with the BBC[10] could see much more access to online video for the regional press, with video banks being created to share material. But this is not enough. There needs to be a radical change at the heart of the local news industry. I'm afraid it doesn't revolve around print.

For more than a decade, video has been hailed as one of the saviours of the local newspaper industry. It was the reason the newspaper groups fought so hard to make sure the BBC local TV pilot was abandoned back in 2006[11]. But what has happened in the intervening years?

There has been a tacit nod to video, but in truth it's been largely ignored, or done very badly indeed, while there is a continued concentration on the core business of print.

Who can blame the regional press for this? Print advertising still holds the power; with digital spend taking some time to catch up. However, it is apparent that a new direction and a new start are needed.

The overwhelming evidence shows the audience is moving away from print. The metrics to measure the industry – the ABCs make very unpleasant reading, year on year and month on month decline.

The audience wants video that's not just an add-on or second thought. They want distributed online video that is central part of the news process, video that is re-versioned to suit different platforms and most importantly mobile. To do this, much needs to change.

## Cultural and structural change is vital
It is essential to rethink the entire news operation from the planning, to the production, to the staffing, even to the layout of the newsroom. This is an entirely different way of working. The workflow, structure and culture need to be overhauled. Digital and video needs to be at the heart of all stories from conception to publication.

## Training and skills
With the culture and structural change comes a need for training and new skills. Editorial excellence is still the absolute key, but it needs to be delivered in a new way. All staff need to be able to create and share compelling video. It can't be a separate, isolated group of video producers, set apart from the core business. It needs to become the core business.

The cost of technology is no longer a barrier. Journalists taught how to film and edit using their iPhones and smartphones can produce incredible material. If you combine this a team of high-end filmmakers and you have the ability to make all the video you need.

## Make digital native news video
Don't try to imitate television. The grammar of online video is very different to the grammar of traditional broadcast and TV news. The audience engages in an entirely different manner. It is far more active and depends on the screen and platform they are watching it on.

Video produced for Facebook on your mobile is a specific style, duration and impact – it doesn't work on the big TV screen in your living room.

In same way traditional TV news packages simply don't engage on mobile. You need to make video that appeals to your platform and audience.

## Re-versioning and distributing online video
Online news video is no longer about producing one piece of film to go on your website or TV channel. You need different formats, versions and clips that are appropriate for different platforms, apps and social media networks.

This is vital – to engage with the widest possible audience – and there is a massive potential audience here. Look at the most imaginative and creative teams in the digital news world.

"We are spending a lot of time trying to understand there is a certain type of person that watches video and there are lots of people that never watch video. The better understanding you have in terms of what to serve to whom, you're going to get smarter about the way you distribute,"[12] – the words of Lindsay Nelson, Global head of brand strategy at Vox Media.

Here Vox has specific groups, targeting and re-versioning film and video, to suit the audience and platforms. This needs careful consideration. It begins in the planning process and goes right through to the end production.

The footage required for Snapchat and vertical platforms is clearly very different to the footage you will need for your website, YouTube, Facebook and Instagram. This all needs to be taken into account from the very start.

## Business models and making it pay
Here comes the difficult part. As we are only too well aware, the media industry is in transition. Business models have not been fully developed, to simply step from one to the next. The legacy press continues to have expensive production costs – but they are needed because traditional advertising revenue is still way ahead of digital.

This is where the importance of video comes in. Advertisers go where the audience is and the audience is in video. We are still very much in the infancy of monetising video through social platforms but it's beginning to happen and definitely worth investing in.

So in many ways the success and sustainability of online news video rests on native advertising, Facebook Instant Articles, Twitter Moments, Snapchat Discover and Google's AMP

The media industry is at a tipping point with online news video. The received wisdom is that media outlets need it to survive. At the beginning of the 2016, 79 per cent of senior media executives said they would be investing more in online news video this year.

We all know the statistics about the importance of digital video

* By 2020 75 per cent of all mobile traffic will be video;
* Snapchat and Facebook get 10bn video views every day;
* US digital video ad spending is predicted to reach $28.08bn in 2020.

But here lies the problem. There is a big divide between the success of online news video, uploaded off-site to social platforms and linked video, hosted on news sites and apps.

The latest research from the Reuters Institute for the Study of Journalism shows a far lower than expected uptake of video on news sites.

In his latest – Future of Online News Video report, Nic Newman found

"....the growth around online video news seems to be largely driven by technology, platforms, and publishers rather than by strong consumer demand. Website users in particular remain resistant to online video news..."[13]

"Meanwhile, off-site news video consumption is growing fast… Some individual viral videos… have had 75–100m views, far more than they could ever have expected using their own websites."

This has serious implications and poses a very real quandary for publishers. Upload natively to social platforms and reach massive audiences, but you cede control of your content and, with it, much of the analytics and data surrounding them; or maintain control, upload to your news site and lose out on the potential audience.

The stakes are huge and clearly dividing the new and the old. The legacy publishers and broadcasters are unwilling to lose their websites. While the likes of AJ+, Vox, Vocativ and in the most extreme case, NowThisNews, have embraced social platforms fully.

In June 2016, Christian Bennet, Global Head of Video and Audio for the Guardian warned: "NowThisNews is taking one hell of a bet on Facebook monetising video – don't get rid of your website just yet."

Which of course is just what NowThisNews has done. They are gambling on making money from their vast audience. They claim to be getting 1bn video views a month. With these sorts of numbers, it surely must be possible to make money. The big problem is that no one has conclusively proved this yet.

It's clear the more traditional pre-roll and banner ads are failing, they act as a barrier. More than a third of people, in the latest RISJ study, said they were put off from watching online video, because of the ads. If you combine this with the rise of ad blocking and the future is bleak.

## Native advertising and sponsored content

But is there a shining knight on the horizon? Is this where native advertising and sponsored or branded content comes in?

There is hope and a lot a very interesting work being done here. As Philip Trippenbach from Edelman puts it: "There's only one answer to this: don't interrupt the content they're consuming with ads. Create The Content They Want To Consume."

The Washington Post, New York Times and NowThisNews are leading the way. They are eschewing the traditional adverts that don't work – and producing native, digital videos that do.

The most powerful example of native advertising I've seen recently is the "Let's Open Our World"[14] campaign for the travel firm Momondo. It's a brilliant piece of filmmaking and storytelling. People are watching it in the hundreds of millions – by choice – not because they are forced to before getting to the content they want to watch. It is the future.

This is clearly an untested landscape. Publishers and news organisations are waiting to see how Instant Articles, Discover, Moments and AMP work out. They and the increase in native advertising will play a vital role in the development of online news video over the coming months and years.

However, the issues of control remain a major concern. Any change in algorithm, like the move by Facebook to favour family and friends over news organisations, could have very serious consequences.

As with so many articles about online news video and making it pay, I'm afraid there is a certain the 'truth remains to be seen' element to this piece. But I do believe there is a clear case that a new form of native, digital advertising for native online news video is a far better bet than old fashioned, analogue adverts adapted and squeezed into the digital world.

Let's be clear, print is not dead just yet. It is sustainable in the short term but for how long? The regional press is certainly in need of radical change. That needs to happen now and creative online distributed video needs to be right at the heart of it.

## Notes

[1] Newman, Nic, Digital News Report Predictions, Reuters Institute for the Study of Journalism, January 2016. Available online at
http://digitalnewsreport.org/publications/2016/predictions-2016/

[2] Marshall, Carla, Top Online Video Creators Across Social, July 2016, Tubular Insights, August 18, 2016. Available online at http://tubularinsights.com/top-online-video-creators/

[3] The Network, Cisco, Growth in Smart Devices, Mobile Video, and 4G Networks to Drive Eight-fold Increase in Mobile Data Traffic Over the Next Five Years, February 2016, Cisco. Available online at https://newsroom.cisco.com/press-release-content?articleId=1741352

[4] Hayward, David, The last edition of the Indy, a sad demise, or phoenix rising from the ashes? The Memo, March 24, 2016. Available online at
http://www.thememo.com/2016/03/24/the-independent-last-edition-demise-phoenix-digital/

[5] Marshall, Carla, How NowthisNews become the most watched news publisher on Facebook, Tubular Insights, May 20, 2016. Available online at
http://tubularinsights.com/nowthis-facebook/#ixzz4K3EVXRHe

[6] Davies, Jessica, How Channel 4 News grew its monthly facebook views to 200 million, Digiday, August 9, 2016. Available online at http://digiday.com/publishers/channel-4-news-grew-monthly-facebook-video-views-200-million/

[7] Newman Nic, Digital News Report Predictions, Reuters Institute for the Study of Journalism, January 2016. Available online at
http://digitalnewsreport.org/publications/2016/predictions-2016/

[8] Higgerson, David, Taking video to a new level in the regional press, Personal Blog, January 2016. Available online at https://davidhiggerson.wordpress.com/tag/video-journalism/

[9] Greenslade, Roy, Why the New Day didn't work and had no hope of working, The Guardian, May 5, 2016. Available online at
https://www.theguardian.com/media/greenslade/2016/may/05/why-the-new-day-didnt-work-and-had-no-hope-of-working

[10] Sutcliffe, Chris, The BBC and local media: Collaboration is the key, Media Briefing, April 22, 2016. Available online at https://www.themediabriefing.com/article/the-bbc-and-local-media-collaboration-is-the-key

[11] Luft, Oliver, BBC local video branded very damaging by newspaper society, The Guardian, August 13, 2016. Available online at
http://www.theguardian.com/media/2008/aug/13/bbc.pressandpublishing

[12] Scott, Caroline, The challenges of making online video pay, journalism.co.uk, April 13, 2016, Available online at https://www.journalism.co.uk/news/the-challenges-of-making-online-video-pay/s2/a628295/

[13] Newman, Nic, Future of Online News Video, Reuters Institute for the Study of Journalism Report, June 2016, Available online at
http://reutersinstitute.politics.ox.ac.uk/publication/future-online-news-video

[14] Let's Open Our World, Momondo, June 2016 film available online at
http://www.momondo.co.uk/letsopenourworld/

## Note on the contributor

David Hayward is a journalist, writer, media consultant and Senior Lecturer on the Channel 4 MA in Investigative Journalism at De Montfort University in Leicester. He works with news organisations, governments, NGOs, charities and corporate clients all over the world, designing online video, digital media and communications strategies.

David was a journalist at the BBC for 18 years. He worked across the organisation, as a reporter, producer and senior editor, in network radio, TV and for the BBC World Service Trust in Bosnia, Albania and Romania. His last role at the BBC was head of the strategic Journalism Programme. The project was designed to keep the BBC at the vanguard of the digital news revolution.

He has a strong track record of leading teams at the forefront of the move into multi-skilled, multi-media working. He was editor of the first BBC multi-media newsroom and led several high-profile projects, including the BBC's Local TV pilot.

David now writes about ethics and the changing nature of journalism for several publications, including the BBC, the Memo, TheMediaBriefing and Thoughts on the Media.

# An international perspective

\* \* \*

# We are not alone… a partial picture of the world

**John Mair**

The decline/death of print is not a uniquely British phenomenon. In the rich First World the sales graphs are steadily and inexorably going down; elsewhere they go up in some places and down in others.

The spiritual home of much modern journalism is the United States. Newspapers were woven into the very fabric of the American way of life. No more. My chapter 'The long and not-so slow death of print in the United States' shows print journalism in the US has taken a battering over the last ten years. A tsunami of negative news. The big city papers have been hollowed out with hundreds of thousands of readers lost and thousands of journalists' jobs gone.

Using the respected Pew Annual State of the Media report and the Newspaper Deathwatch website, I tell the sad story of the cities now with one or no local papers; those that have gone weekly or digital; and the rise of the (US-based) aggregators Google and Facebook. Choice has increased for consumers, but employment of journalists gone seriously down (40 per cent) in the last decade.

As ever, there is no better prism to see this than the city of New York. That has proved a hell's kitchen for print. Former New York Daily News and Daily Post Managing Editor David Banks saw it in the glory days of the 1990s. Today, from his lair in the north east of England, he does some first-hand reporting – in reality chewing the cud – with some of his former senior colleagues and competitors.

The newsprint habit has been lost and they recognise it. Les Hinton was the deputy don of the Murdoch empire. He sees the decline as irreversible and the result of the fat cats not protecting their milk. Others do too. In the words of one of them, Ken Chandler, on seeing live reporting of the Gulf War on television in 1991: 'I knew then we were fucked.' His words have proved prescient with the exception of the digitally nifty New York Times (see Mark Thompson's chapter at the beginning of this book). The decline of print in NYC and the USA has not been a pretty sight.

Closer to home in the Republic of Ireland the story is much the same. Kathryn Hayes and Tom Felle tell the story from another battlefield filled with corpses. There was a newspaper gold mine in Eire; then the Celtic tiger was tamed and so was newspaper circulation. Between 30 per cent and 50 per cent of circulation has been lost, the biggest losers being the implant British titles with the Irish Daily Star, for example, tanking.

But the native papers, too, have not fared brilliantly. As in the UK they had their foundations and advertising lifted from them by digital sites – Daft for property and Done Deal for classifieds. Digital news though has shown remarkable growth in Eire, yet the digital cents do not make up for the lost print euros. As they conclude: 'It is not that news has suddenly become unfashionable, it's that making money out of news is proving increasingly difficult.'

Surprisingly, even with a market of 1.4bn, print is not thriving in China. Two scholars, Xin Liu and Dong Dong Zhai, from the leading journalism school the Communication University of China look at three news groups and show that all is not rosy in that garden. They report that 2015 was a bad year for advertising and, as the Chinese economy continues to slow down, the situation is not that much more hopeful.

Even the revered People's Daily, the organ of the Chinese Communist Party, has had to face the future and go digital to some extent. All face the dilemma of the First World – go digital or die. As Liu and Zhai conclude: 'We believe newspapers will not die, but they need to find a mode of sustainable development in the converging media environment.'

Finally, some good news for inkies. India with 1.2bn people is the world's largest democracy. Newsprint and newspapers are booming there with 250 per cent growth between 2004 and 2015. As Savyasaachi Jain in his chapter puts it: 'The Indian media, especially the news media, is characterised by rapid growth, high energy and a spirit of adventure. There are virgin lands still to be claimed and frontiers to be expanded. Indian newspapers draw upon a combination of aggressive pricing, geographical expansion and localisation to capitalise on demographic and economic trends.'

Readership is going up (one title, Dainik Jagran, has 16m readers!); there are 800m literate people in the country, a quarter of those added in one decade, and newspapers are dirt cheap at two-four (British) pence per copy. The market may be booming, but it is still ripe for rationalisation and consolidation. Jain concludes: 'Newspapers are not dead in India. To the contrary, they are very much alive and kicking, and determined to stay that way.'

So, the picture, even from this partial snapshot, is mixed worldwide. The future is clear, but maybe taking a long time to arrive in some places.

# The long and not-so slow death of print in the United States

**Print journalism in the United States has taken a battering over the last ten years. The big city papers have been hollowed out with hundreds of thousands of readers lost and thousands of journalists jobs gone. John Mair charts how and where the decline has taken place**

It has been a bitter decade in the newsrooms of the big city papers in the USA. Relentlessly sales have tanked, so too advertising and so too employment.

This chapter attempts to chart that decline by dipping into the annual respected Pew State of the News Media reports (each year the Pew Research Centre in Washington undertakes a forensic analysis of the US news media on various platforms and their state of health (http://www.journalism.org/2016/06/15/state-of-the-news-media-2016) and the Newspaper Deathwatch website (newspaperdeathwatch.com) dedicated to just that. That is a sad graveyard of newspapers and their mastheads and personnel.

By necessity this is just a snapshot of the war zone. Pew provides the big picture, Deathwatch the names of the tombs in the graveyard.

## Year-by-Year: A Decade of Decline 2007-2017

### 2007

On the last day of December 2007, The Cincinnati Post closed.

'The Post newspapers printed their final editions Monday, ending a 126-year run. However, the final editions also carried some news... Originally called The Penny Paper when it was started in 1881, the paper was renamed The Penny Post by E.W. Scripps, who assumed control in 1883. The newspaper became The Cincinnati Post in 1890, when its Kentucky Post edition began'. (Deathwatch 1)?

### 2008

In January 2008 The King County Journal in Seattle closed:

'The King County Journal will put out its last issue on Jan. 2... Circulation of the Journal, which has been losing money since 1994, has fallen to 39,100. It is the region's fifth-largest daily paper. Forty full-time employees will be laid off.' (Deathwatch 2)

Pew tried to make some sense of the carnage in its annual report:

'...another rough year (2007) for newspapers, and an even worse one expected in 2008. Advertising revenues fell by an average of more than 5 per cent. Hardest hit has been classified, most of all employment. In 2007 alone, job ads were down 20 per cent.'(Pew 2008)

That decline was reflected in company share prices:

'The stock prices for newspapers for the year fell 42 per cent, after drops of 11 per cent and 20 per cent the two previous years. Profits, though were still twice the average of other American industries but the print gold-rush was coming to an end.' (Pew 2008)

Modern capitalism almost fell apart in 2008. A worldwide banking and stock market crisis, banks being rescued on both sides of the Atlantic and governments barely holding it all together. It was the start of the closest we have seen to the Great Depression.

In the UK, the bank cash machines nearly did not open one Monday, in the US the descent into hell of print continued:

'A single statistic provides a good illustration of how bad 2008 has been for newspapers. In 2006, total industry advertising was $49.3bn. In 2008, it was about $38bn (estimating fourth-quarter results) – a decline in the two years of 23 per cent.' (Pew 2009)

Stock prices once again reflected this:

'Newspaper stocks, which had lost 42 per cent of their value from the start of 2005 to the end of 2007, lost an astonishing 83 per cent of their remaining value during 2008.' (Pew 2009)

Signs of future trouble were well signalled. Advertising was moving online, readers too but not necessarily together...

'The crisis in journalism, in other words, may not strictly be loss of audience. It may, more fundamentally, be the decoupling of news and advertising.' (Pew 2009)

The business model that had sustained newspapers-revenue from sales and advertising – for well over a century was starting to show signs of simply being broken.

Newsrooms by now were 30 per cent smaller than in 2000.

Consumers were not spending long on the new websites either. Just three minutes and four seconds on average apart from on the New York Times that was a minute longer. Oligopoly was taking over in cyberspace. The top seven per cent of the nearly 5000 newspaper websites garnered 80 per cent of the traffic.

In December 2008 the Detroit Free Press went (largely) online:

'We could almost see the collective eyes rolling in the newsrooms of the Detroit News and Detroit Free Press today as the newspapers' holding company announced a 'bold transformation' that will cut home delivery to three days per week and move the bulk of editorial content online.

'A daily electronic edition will also be introduced for people who want to do their printing at home. "These are exact copies of each day's printed newspaper and can be easily navigated and printed from readers' computers," the press release says. This means that the $170m printing plant that the newspapers built in 2005 will now be nearly idle four days a week while printing is outsourced to the readers. There is no research we're aware of that supports the assumption that readers are interested in printing their own newspapers.' (Deathwatch 3)

## 2009

In February 2009 the final bell tolled for the Baltimore Examiner:

'The Baltimore Examiner will close on February 15th, ending its three-year-run as the city's second newspaper. Launched by a company controlled by Denver billionaire Philip Anschutz, the free daily had been troubled since the beginning. Parent company Clarity Media Group had cut newsroom staff by half since launch and reduced home delivery from six to two days per week last summer. A spokesman blamed the closure on a lack of national advertising. The AP report said the newsroom was shocked by the news, a surprising reaction considering that the Examiner had been on the market for months. About 90 people will lose their jobs.' (Deathwatch 4)

Like autumn leaves, newsroom jobs just kept disappearing, too. The monthly rates of job loss in the journalism industry was reported to be 22.23 per cent compared to the average for the rest of industry of 8.1 per cent according to the US Bureau of Labor Statistics (BLS 2010). Pew estimated 1000 to 1500 newsroom jobs had been lost in the year gone.

'When the final tally in online ad revenue in 2010 is projected to surpass print newspaper ad revenue for the first time. The problem for news is that by far the largest share of that online ad revenue goes to non-news sources, particularly to aggregators.' (Pew 2010)

The march of Google and Facebook had started. It was never to stop.

In May 2009, the Honolulu Advertiser had the its rites read:

'Hawaiians are preparing to be one newspaper poorer. Gannett officially exited the Hawaiian market where it has played for nearly 40 years. The company signed over ownership of the Honolulu Advertiser to the owner of rival Honolulu Star-Bulletin, bringing an end to a brutally competitive battle. The Star-Bulletin plans to merge the two papers into the Honolulu Star-Advertiser sometime in the next 60 days, cutting about 300 of jobs in the process.' (Deathwatch 5)

Advertising revenue had gone online, but not to newspaper websites.

'Already in 2011, five technology companies accounted for 68 per cent of all online ad revenue, and that list does not include Amazon and Apple, which get most of their dollars from transactions, downloads and devices. By 2015, Facebook is expected to account for one out of every five digital display ads sold.' In 2011, losses in print advertising dollars outpaced gains in digital revenue by a factor of roughly ten to one, a ratio even worse than in 2010. When circulation and advertising revenue are combined, the newspaper industry has shrunk 43 per cent since 2000. (Pew 2011)

## 2012

The circle of newspaper death spread to the US Deep South – the New Orleans Times-Picayune goes to three days a week

'The New Orleans Times-Picayune, a fixture in the Big Easy since 1837, will slash its staff and production schedule, going from seven to three days a week beginning this fall. The body count isn't known yet, but estimates are that at least a third of the staff will be fired. Those who stay are expected to take pay cuts… All the spin-doctoring in the world doesn't change the fact that New Orleans will soon become the second major US city without a daily newspaper.' (Deathwatch 6)

Pew chronicled the decline and some attempts to arrest it:
'Newspaper ad revenue is now down 60 per cent compared to a decade ago. The number of US news jobs is likely now below 40,000, compared to the historic high of 56,900 in 1989, a 30 per cent decrease overall. (Pew 2013)

However, 'after years of decline, total daily circulation in 2012 stayed even with 2011, falling only 0.2 per cent, according to an estimate by Rick Edmonds of the Poynter Institute. Much of this is tied to new digital pay plans, with the number of newspapers implementing them now up to 450, more than double a year ago.' (Pew2013)

Analogue dollars were converting to digital cents. The bottom line was bleeding.

According to data from the Newspaper Association of America, 'in 2012, for every $16 in print ad revenue lost, only $1 in digital ad revenue was gained. That was even worse than the $10-to-$1 ratio in 2011.' (Pew 2013)

In 2012, total [online] traffic to the top 25 news sites increased 7.2 per cent, according to ComScore. And according to Pew Research data, 39 per cent of respondents got news online or from a mobile device 'yesterday,' up from 34 per cent in 2010, when the survey was last conducted." (Pew 2013)

The world had shifted from paper to the mobile phone screen.

Full-time professional newsroom employment declined another 6.4 per cent in 2012 with more losses expected for 2013. Total newspaper advertising revenue in 2013 was down 49 per cent from 2003. (Pew 2013)

## 2013

The loss in papers, titles, regularity, and journalists and, therefore, the quality of product did not pass un-noticed by the customers:
'Nearly one-third –31 per cent – of people say they have deserted a particular news outlet because it no longer provides the news and information they had grown accustomed to, according to [a] survey of more than 2,000 US adults in early 2013.' About half of all people surveyed said news stories are not as

thorough as they were previously. Of the consumers who reported abandoning certain news outlets, 61 per cent said the decision was based on issues of quality, while 24 per cent said there were not enough stories.' (Pew 2014)

The Cleveland Plain Dealer goes half time …as the managers sold it (badly) to the readers:

'The Plain Dealer will continue to publish in print and online seven days a week. The newspaper will be delivered to homes three days a week, including Sunday. The paper will continue to be available daily at thousands of locations across the region. An electronic edition of the newspaper also will be available daily. The e-edition looks just like the printed newspaper and can be read on your desktop, laptop, tablet or smart phone.' (Deathwatch 6)

## 2015

Yet more woe…

'In 2015, these (newspaper) companies experienced their greatest decline since the recession years of 2008 and 2009. In 2015, advertising revenue fell eight per cent, while circulation revenue was stable (up one per cent). The decline in 2015 was nevertheless far less than what was seen in 2008 (-15 per cent) and 2009 (-27 per cent).' (Pew2016)

The overall newsroom workforce experienced its sharpest decline since 2009. According to the American Society of News Editors' Newsroom Employment Census (ASNE 2015) after falling six per cent in 2012 and three per cent in 2013, overall newsroom employment was down ten per cent in 2014 to 32,900. Between 1994 and 2014, the profession has shed more than 20,000 jobs, representing a 39 per cent decline.

## 2016

May 2016 The Tampa Tribune died.

'The Tampa Tribune is no more The rival Tampa Bay Times said on Tuesday that it has purchased the 121-year-old Tribune and shut it down, converting subscribers and advertisers to the Times. The Tribune published continuously from 1895 until this week. Long owned by Media General, it was sold to an investment capital group in 2012 for $9.5m. That company nearly doubled its money when it sold the Tribune's headquarters building last July for $17.75m, but the Tribune can hardly be considered a winning investment. The owners had reportedly borrowed more than $37m over the last two years.'

And in a rich piece of irony, look who bought it and closed it…

'The Times is owned by the Poynter Institute, a non-profit school and journalism think tank.' (Deathwatch 8)

## Stop Press:

## September 2016

Pittsburgh loses its last paper the Tribune Review

'We're going to call a time-of-death on the Pittsburgh Tribune-Review, despite the fact that the newspaper says it'll live on with a website. Everyone says that these days. The more important news is that the 24-year-old daily will shutter its print edition and lay off 106 staff members. It will maintain an online-only edition, but most dying newspapers say that. Our favorite quote comes from Jennifer Bertetto, president and chief executive of Trib Total Media, which owns the Tribune-Review: "Our commitment to covering news in Pittsburgh and Allegheny County will not change." Right. We'll just do it with 106 fewer people. (Deathwatch 9)

The decade 2007-2017 has been a decade of inexorable, sometimes slow mainly fast, decline in the American newspaper print industry. Large cities have been left with just one or sometimes no daily paper. Times have changed. Readers have gone online through various platforms, the advertisers have followed too.

Some more prescient titles have been able to moderate slow death through paywalls (metered or otherwise) but the real winners have been aggregators Google and Facebook who have achieved commercial nirvana – huge audiences, huge advertising revenue following them and very little costs of acquisition. They are baking and selling bread with stolen (or at best borrowed) flour. Some say the real casualty has been not just journalists out on the street but journalism itself.

**Notes and sources**

Deathwatch: http://www.nbcnews.com/id/22452666/#.V8HNK5grK00 Accessed October1, 2016 .

Deathwatch 2: http://www.seattlepi.com/business/article/King-County-Journal-to-close-1223641.php Accessed October 1, 2016

Deathwatch 3: http ://newspaperdeat:watch.com/panic-in-detroit/ Accessed October 1, 2016

Deathwatch 4: http://newspaperdeathwatch.com/rip-baltimore-examiner/ Accessed October 1, 2016

Deathwatch 5: http://newspaperdeathwatch.com/r-i-p-honolulu-advertiser/ Accessed October 1, 2016

Deathwatch 6: http://newspaperdeathwatch.com/times-picayune-eliminates-daily-frequency Accessed October 1, 2016

Deathwatch 7: http://blog.cleveland.com/upd ates/2013/04/a_letter_our_readers.html#incart_big-photo Accessed October 1, 2016

Deathwatch 8: http://newspaperdeathwatch.com/r-i-p-tampa-tribune Accessed October 1, 2016

Deathwatch 9; http://newspaperdeathwatch.com/Accessed October 3, 2016

BLS 2010 http://www.bls.gov/ooh/media-and-communication/reporters-correspondents-and-broadcast-news-analysts.htm

ASNE 2015:http://asne.org/content.asp

**Pew Research Centre's Project for Excellence in Journalism, Annual State of the Media Reports**

Pew 2008; http://www.stateofthemedia.org/2008/

Pew 2009; http://www.stateofthemedia.org/?s=2009+state+of+the+media

Pew 2010; http://www.stateofthemedia.org/2010/

Pew 2011: http://www.stateofthemedia.org/?s=2011+state+of+the+media+

Pew 2012: http://www.stateofthemedia.org/?s=2012+state+of+the+media

Pew 2013: http://www.stateofthemedia.org/2013/overview-5/

Pew 2014: http://www.stateofthemedia.org/?s=2014+state+of+the+media

Pew 2015: http://www.stateofthemedia.org/?s=2015+state+of+the+media

Pew 2016: http://www.journalism.org/2016/06/15/state-of-the-news-media-2016/

All accessed October 1, 2016

**Note on the contributor**

John Mair has taught journalism at the Universities of Coventry, Kent, Northampton, Brunel, Edinburgh Napier, Guyana and the Communication University of China. He has now edited 18 'hackademic' volumes over the last seven years, on subjects ranging from trust in television, the health of investigative journalism, reporting the 'Arab Spring', to three volumes on the Leveson Inquiry.

In a previous life, he was an award-winning producer/director for the BBC, ITV and Channel 4 and a secondary school teacher. He is lead editor of this book.

# Why are the US big city papers dying?

**The story of US newspapers offers little cheer on this side of the pond, says former Daily Mirror editor and US veteran David Banks... and several of his very well-informed friends**

In the chilly pre-dawn hours of January 17, 1991, two CNN journalists huddled in their overcoats on the roof of the Hotel al-Rashid in Saddam Hussein's Iraqi capital awaiting a US-led blitzkrieg. Six thousand miles east of Baghdad, in Boston, Mass., where Eastern Standard Time ran eight hours behind the small hours darkness of Iraq, British-born Boston Herald editor Ken Chandler was designing the tabloid front of next morning's newspaper. "Turn up the CNN monitor!" a City Desk voice commanded as the TV screen changed from US anchor to a static library image of night-time Baghdad, accompanied by the gravelly tones of broadcaster Bernard Shaw voicing the biggest breaking story of the new year.

"This is Bernie Shaw. Something is happening outside. ... Peter Arnett, join me here. Let's describe to our viewers what we're seeing. . . the skies over Baghdad have been illuminated. . . we're seeing bright flashes going off all over the sky."

Those historic words and the exclusive live pictorial coverage that soon followed guaranteed Shaw, Arnett and their colleagues top table seats in the foreign correspondents' Hall of Fame. It was an international scoop that instantly repositioned Ted Turner's foundling network firmly alongside the USA's Big Three networks. It also produced a queasy foreboding in the pit of Ken Chandler's stomach.

"It was about eight o'clock in the evening," former New York Post editor Chandler recalls, "and as I began to work on page one I realised I would be asking our readers to pay 50 cents next morning to read about something they had seen with their own eyes 12 hours earlier. I knew then we were fucked."

Broadband, the super-dooper fuel that was to rocket the internet instantly along every Main Street in North America only to be credited with (and blamed for) dealing a mortal blow to the newsprint media, was still ten years distant. In those early Nineties, the World Wide Web limped along on dial-up. According to Chandler, television was first into the bullring and rolling news played the part of picador, whose jabs and thrusts wounded and weakened a doomed media Minotaur.

Four years or so after that 'Baghdad blitz' scoop , another old hot metal man – an adversary of Chandler's from ding-dong Eighties battles between the rival tabloids they had edited in New York City – was falling for the lure of the looming Digital Age. After seven years at the Daily News, ex-editor/publisher Jim Willse had, like most of his peers, flirted with new media but it was not until the mid-Nineties, when he began editing New Jersey's Star-Ledger, that he really caught the bug.

"I would read half-a-dozen papers every morning but I couldn't get all of them delivered as early as I wanted so I'd drive into town at 6am and lift what I needed from the bundles sitting in front of the local drugstore (I left money), then bring them home. After a while it dawned on me I could accomplish the same thing without leaving my bed by reading all the papers on my laptop. From that point on, I never again read a physical paper until I got to the office."

## 2015: The industry's worst year

Anecdotal maybe, but in examining the recent deaths of dozens of America's city newspapers big and small I trust what men like Willse and Chandler feel and believe over the evidence of volumes of spreadsheets charting the decline and fall of print media: I worked for both during my years in New York, they taught me how to be an editor. I share their regard and concern for the survival of readable, honest journalism over any abiding nostalgia for newsprint. I admit, however, some kind of grasp of the figures helps provide a framework for the problem, so the latest report from the Pew Research Centre, which describes itself as 'a nonpartisan fact tank', seemed a good place to start.

That majordomo of the media mansion, former Guardian editor Peter Preston, summarised the Pew view of 2015 thus in an Observer column as possibly 'the worst year for newspapers since the Great Recession and its immediate aftermath'. Daily US circulation fell by seven per cent, the most since 2010, while advertising revenue at publicly traded newspaper companies fell by eight per cent. There was no hope to be had for the newspapers' online arms from the digital advertising which had supposedly promised to be the industry's salvation.

"Almost two-thirds of $60bn in digital advertising spending (65%) went to just five technology companies: Google, Facebook, Yahoo, Microsoft and Twitter," Pew reported. At the same time. overall digital ad revenue FELL by two per cent in 2015.

The same thing is happening around the rest of the English-speaking 'rich world', Preston pointed out: digital ads draining away, growth hopes stalled, branding and the importance of running your own website diminishing as

Facebook and Google mop up the stories they like, with hardly an 'own brand' reporter on the ground. Add to that Pew's contention 'most consumers are still reluctant to pay for general news online, particularly in the highly competitive English-speaking world (nine per cent average). Interestingly, twice that number in smaller countries, protected by language, is likely to pay'.

According to Pew, four-in-ten Americans usually get their news online. Digital is second only to TV news as the preferred platform. Nearly twice as many adults (38 per cent) get news online than in print (20 per cent), and while almost all young news seekers turn mostly to the web for their news, older Americans rely heavily on TV. Mobile phone use is increasing fast, even articles of 1,000-plus word length attracting more phone readers than ever before.

Social media, particularly Facebook, is now a common news source. Overall, 62 per cent of US adults get news on social media, and 18 per cent often do so. However, news plays a varying role across the social networking sites studied. Two-thirds of Facebook users (66 per cent) get news on the site, which amounts to 44 per cent of the general population. Nearly as many Twitter users say they get news on Twitter (59 per cent), but due to Twitter's smaller user base this translates to just nine per cent of the general population. The number of Americans who enjoy reading 'a lot' – 51 per cent in a recent Pew poll – has changed little over two decades but a declining proportion does its newspaper reading from newsprint. So many have 'gone digital' that in the last ten years the percentage reading a newsprint daily has fallen by 18 points, from 41 to 23 per cent. Somewhat more (38 per cent) say they regularly read a daily newspaper, although this percentage also has declined, from 54 per cent in 2004.

## I, too, am a dinosaur

Substantial percentages of the regular readers of leading and even 'legacy' newspapers now read them digitally. Currently, 55 per cent of regular New York Times (NYT) readers say they read the paper mostly on a computer or mobile device, as do 48 per cent of regular USA Today and 44 per cent of Wall Street Journal (WSJ) readers.

But let's get real here. I'm writing a thesis on why America's big city newspapers are rapidly reiterating the fate of the dinosaur, yet I'm a dinosaur myself: although I worked at executive level on both major New York tabloids I quit that continent in the late Eighties, first for Australia and later the UK's Daily Mirror editorship. It's difficult to be a commentator without first-hand experience, and newsprint was still thriving on both sides of the Atlantic and would do so for another ten years after I quit both continents to head Down Under.

So, as any journalist knows, this chapter cannot be an opinion piece, at least it cannot be **MY** opinion. Therefore, I turned reporter again and sought the views of editor friends who stayed and watched helplessly as the giants of the American newspaper industry fell. What my research turned up was a kind of patchwork conversation between half-a-dozen of us (all men, sadly) which I have stitched together from a series of individual conversations.

**LES HINTON**'s career with Rupert Murdoch's News Corporation spanned more than 50 years as a reporter, editor and executive in Australia, the United Kingdom and the United States, culminating in his appointment as CEO of Dow Jones in December 2007.

To the question 'Is news finished as a distributed newsprint product?' the one-time associate editor of the Boston Herald and editor-in-chief of Star magazine replied: "Whether or not the decline in print is terminal may be an open question but there's little doubt it is going to continue and the decline is essentially irreversible.

"Print is losing the battle for people's time and attention because there are so many more vivid and digestible demands upon that time. The distribution of news and information is a pyramid that has been turned on its head. Once, a tiny few (like us) controlled what the mass of people consumed, whether it was daily newspapers or limited spectrum TV. Now the base of the pyramid has been inverted and billions of individuals have an infinite choice of words and images to choose at will. Old style 'Big Print' is done for."

Did **JIM WILLSE**, former editor of the Star-Ledger and. before that, editor/publisher of the Daily News, agree?

"Yeah, I think daily print is pretty much dead, with a couple of possible exceptions," he said. "Weeklies that 'own' their local markets and have buttressed print with online and national chains like Gannett that are heavy into online and have cut costs by centralising everything from payroll to copy desks. Then, maybe, a couple of the big boys, like the New York Times, Wall Street Journal and Washington Post.

## Too much cost, too little revenue

"But even Gannett and the Big Boys won't keep printing daily indefinitely – there will be a time when the remaining print audience dies off. There might just be enough advertising left to support weekend-only editions. As for all the big metropolitan papers, the likes of Los Angeles, Chicago, Boston and the New York tabs? Fuhgeddaaboutit!. Too much cost, too little revenue."

**MARTIN DUNN**, former editor of UK's Today newspaper and Willse's successor at the Daily News, laments that newspapers resolutely refused to imitate TV's eagerness to plunder rich historic resources which Street Smart Video, the production company he founded, is now doing by inviting newly-redundant print journalists to turn their lifetime of great stories from treasured contacts into TV documentaries.

"The WSJ and NYT and the like are somewhat protected by their status as 'legacy' journalism," he says, adding: "Popular newspapers here have a century and more of resources which they never tapped. They have learned the hardest way that it simply wasn't and isn't enough to publish yesterday's news today." Dunn's production company does just that, he says, "using traditional journalism techniques and paying redundant reporters and feature writers to trawl their years of contacts for yarns which we research then turn into television specials.

"When I edited the Daily News we published '100 Years of Yankee Stadium', a six-parter which was a sensational success in terms of sales, sponsorship and ad revenue. That kind of legacy journalism will still sell, even in print," he insisted

**KEN CHANDLER** adds: "I disagree with Martin when it comes to 'legacy' print journalism. I wish he was right. Manufacture the very finest horse and buggy you like, kitted out with all the bells and whistles, but it won't sell if consumers have moved on to automobiles. Same with print. . .

"Even the Washington Post and the NYT, who still produce excellent products, will go down without some billionaire philanthropist bailing them out. The WashPo is lucky, they have [new owner] Jeff Bezos. Let's hope he doesn't get bored. But metropolitan papers elsewhere are undergoing a slow, painful death."

Halfway through this series of interviews I took a call from a great friend, **MURRAY FORSETER** in New York, a more commercially-minded kind of journalist who, until retirement, was editor/publisher of the influential US trade magazine Chain Store Age which keeps an itchy trigger finger on the pulse of America's biggest advertisers, the retailers.

"Don't let those 'fancy Dans' fool ya," said Forseter. "It was the loss of advertising from mainstream print to hundreds then thousands of dedicated websites that put paid to newspapers: cars, realty, lonely hearts, job ads... . it happened almost overnight!"

**HINTON**: "Agree! The big metropolitan moneymakers were fat and lazy enterprises nourished by vast amounts of classified advertising, up to 70 per cent of total revenue in their heyday. Circulation income would never sustain them, so advertising always mattered more than readers.

"They became dull and self-indulgent, counting their success in Pulitzers more than readership. Cue the advent of low-cost advertising sites and their revenue was screwed, the bosses of these companies lost in the storm, their competitive instincts dulled by years of easy pickings."

### News coverage without journalists: immediate, raw, exciting
**BANKS**: So we are where we are, is there a future for print? And if not print, what?

**CHANDLER**: "Newspapers are finished (mostly) because people have lost the habit of buying them. It's just easier and more convenient to find what you need by staring at a smartphone where the information is up-to-date, not 12 hours old. On my morning commuter train no one under the age of 70 reads a newspaper."

**DUNN**: "Newspapers, it seems to me, now want to staff their newsrooms with (young) people on 25 grand a year who can just trawl the web, post stuff online and do a quick rewrite for the following day's paper. Tragic, it really is. Ken's right: commuters read cellphones, tablets and just the occasional serious broadsheet. It's over."

**WILLSE**: "A couple of days following the Boston Marathon bombing [April, 2013] cops began a pursuit of suspects after midnight, well past most print deadlines. The chase was followed by Twitter users, including someone in whose backyard one of the suspects hid out. It was news coverage without journalists: immediate, raw, exciting. I remember thinking, this is how big stories are going to be reported from now on.

"I do think microjournalism can help fill the gap, 'micro' as in one town or one neighbourhood. Groups of 'micros' could put some money in the pot to have someone cover city hall, like a 'new form' Associated Press. There are already optimistic examples of such non-profit undertakings in places like Texas, Minneapolis and San Diego and, I hope, with my guys in New Jersey.

"How will we train future journalists? If there are enough really small, online-only newsrooms to augment larger, civic-minded online endeavours like Pro Publica and slimmed-down chains like Gannett, plus a few surviving Big Boys, then maybe there's a place for a young journalist who still wants to accomplish what we all thought was our goal – finding out things so the public could make informed decisions. But it won't be in print."

Last word to **LES HINTON**: "The extent to which 'print' and its associated brands can transmute to digital is still open and, in the case of most publishing companies, highly doubtful. Certainly the old profit margins and monopoly power are gone forever.

"Meanwhile, the average punters who care about the world around them are in clover. The quality may vary but they've never had more to choose from topically, geographically, and ideologically. And because of the great idiocy of newspapers around the globe it's mostly free, although newspapers everywhere, finally, are struggling to change that. As an avid news consumer, I love it!"

**Sources**
Pew Center

**Note on the contributor**
David Banks is a former editor (1992-94) and editorial director (1992-99) of the Daily Mirror and assistant editor of the Sun in the UK, managing editor in New York of both the NY Post and the Daily News, editor of the Sydney Daily Telegraph and deputy editor of The Australian. He is now an occasional broadcaster and edits the website www.voiceofthenorth.net.

# Going digital or going free? Ireland's newspapers struggle for digital success as the print cliff looms

**Ireland's newspapers are proving remarkably resilient, while audiences are in decline in print they are growing digitally. The problem, as ever, is paying for the journalism because revenue from digital is so far miniscule, write Kathryn Hayes and Tom Felle**

Never have so many people been interested in news. And never have so few people paid for it. At a time when many Irish news organisations are recording double digit digital growth, all Irish newspapers, not unlike their counterparts across the UK and elsewhere, are haemorrhaging print circulation. And despite the fact print remains profitable, print advertising rates are declining year on year, and circulation drops averaging five per cent per year are now standard across the industry. A number of local and national newspapers in the Republic and in Northern Ireland have already closed, and more are likely to follow.

At the same time, almost all Irish newspapers are recording extraordinary growth in digital traffic. This chapter looks at the Irish case, first with an overview of the national picture in the Irish Republic. Secondly through a case study in Limerick, where a legacy Johnston Press-owned title the Limerick Leader, producing both daily and weekly editions, is battling for survival with local free rivals. While its online presence is healthy, revenue returns are tiny. Its struggle is a case study for what is happening elsewhere in the Irish market.

## The Irish newspaper landscape

For generations Ireland's newspapers were steady as she goes. Both local and national titles were largely family-owned affairs, though the biggest selling newspaper group, Independent Newspapers, had been taken over in the 1970s by Tony O'Reilly, who later owned the separate, UK-based Independent. The newspaper business was always profitable, though profits were usually single-digit returns. Then the Celtic Tiger came along in the early 2000s and changed everything. The main Irish titles – the market-leading Irish Independent, the upmarket The Irish Times and the Cork-based Irish Examiner, all boomed, as did the Irish editions of the British red tops. The Daily Mail launched in Dublin in 2006, following The Sun, The Daily Star and The Daily Mirror, all of which had highly profitable Irish operations.

Family-owned local newspapers were bought out by larger newspaper groups. Johnston Press spent more than £200m buying Irish assets (Flanagan, 2013). By 2007, almost 75 per cent of the market was owned by a handful of major players including Independent News and Media, Thomas Crosbie Holdings, Celtic Media and Johnston Press (Felle, 2012: 42-49).

For a short while, it appeared newspapers had a licence to print money as double digit ad growth fuelled almost exclusively by Ireland's out-of-control property market continued unabated. But it all came to a sudden, shuddering, halt in 2007 when Ireland's Tiger economy collapsed, plunging the country into the deepest recession in its history. There were, of course, external factors such as the worldwide slowdown contributing to the collapse, but Ireland's heavy reliance on its property market exacerbated the difficulties considerably (O'Toole, 2009). For newspapers, the house of cards their future circulation projections and ad growth assumptions had been built on simply crumpled.

The collapse in sales circulation, even by international standards, has been extraordinary, though the pattern is repeated in the UK, the US and elsewhere. Local and national titles have lost between 30 and 50 per cent of their circulation in the decade since 2007. While circulation drops have steadied at about five per cent per year, few are celebrating. The following tables show the circulation drops of the major Irish titles between 2006 and 2016:

**Table 1: Irish Daily Newspaper Circulation, 2006-2016**

| Newspaper | 2006 | 2016 | decline |
|---|---|---|---|
| Irish Independent | 162,582 | 102,537 | 37% |
| The Irish Times | 117,797 | 72,011 | 39% |
| Irish Examiner | 57,217 | 30,964 | 46% |
| Irish Daily Mirror | 73,754 | 38,355 | 48% |
| Irish Daily Star | 104,054 | 53,945 | 48% |
| The Irish Sun | 110,191 | 60,371 | 45% |
| Irish Daily Mail | 58,335 | 46,544 | 20% |

*Source: Audit Bureau of Circulation, 2006-2016.*

*Figures for January to June each year are used as a basis for comparison*

**Table 2: Irish Sunday Newspaper Circulation, 2006-2016**

| Newspaper | 2006 | 2016 | Decline |
|---|---|---|---|
| Sunday Independent | 287,588 | 199,210 | 31% |
| Sunday World | 274,143 | 162,938 | 41% |
| Sunday Business Post | 55,876 | 31,364 | 44% |
| Daily Star Sunday | 56,548 | 15,067 | 73% |
| News of The World/Sun On Sunday | 160,935 | 57,820 | 64% |
| Irish Sunday Mirror | 46,398 | 26,628 | 43% |
| The Mail on Sunday | 127,399 | 83,335 | 35% |
| Sunday Times | 108,071 | 77,455 | 28% |

*Source: Audit Bureau of Circulation, 2006-2016.*

*Figures for January to June each year are used as a basis for comparison*

**Table 3: The worst performing local newspapers, 2006-2012**

| Newspaper | Decline |
|---|---|
| Leinster Leader | 53% |
| Leinster and Offaly Express | 46% |
| Donegal Democrat (combined) | 40% |
| Limerick Leader | 38% |
| Nationalist & Munster Advertiser | 38% |

*Source: Audit Bureau of Circulation, 2006-2012*

*Annual figures are used as a basis for comparison. Up to date reliable figures for local newspapers are not available, as most regional titles have stopped auditing their circulation and now publish claimed figures.*

The decline in popular titles' circulation across both daily and Sunday titles has been pronounced, almost 50 per cent Monday to Saturday and 40 per cent on Sundays. Quality titles have fared slightly better, with drops of about a third Monday to Saturday and Sunday respectively. Irish titles do not publish details for Monday to Friday only versus Saturday circulation via their audited ABC circulation, so the Monday to Friday circulation decline is likely to be bigger.

The total market for daily circulation in Ireland in 2006 was 713,000. In 2016, just 428,000 newspapers were sold daily. On Sunday, more than 1.25m titles were purchased each week in 2006. That has dropped to just over 700,000 in

2016 (ABC, 2006-2016). The UK 'red top' tabloids have all fared badly in Ireland. Most have seen close to 50 per cent declines in their circulation between 2006 and 2016 (ibid).

Among the legacy Irish-owned groups, there have been mixed fortunes. Thomas Crosbie Media, owner of the Irish Examiner, went into receivership in 2013 (RTE, 2013), and was taken over by Landmark Media. The company owns a number of regional titles and local radio stations, as well as a digital news service and a recruitment website. Circulation declines continue and the company lost its celebrated editor, Tim Vaughan, in 2016 (Shanahan, 2016).

Independent News and Media, owner of the Irish Independent, Sunday Independent and various other local and national titles, went through a prolonged period of restructuring but has largely weathered the storm and has announced in 2016 it will use cash reserves to buy digital assets (O'Donovan, 2016). It reported further declines from both print advertising and circulation in its first half results for 2016, though recorded digital revenue growth (RTE, 2016). Print circulation of its flagship Sunday title, the Sunday Independent, dropped below 200,000 for the first time in 2016. Its daily market leader, the Irish Independent, recorded daily circulation of 102,000 in 2016, down almost 40 per cent from its peak. However, ABC audited figures show this figure is generously massaged – 80,816 were actively purchased at the full rate, with almost 17,000 bulk sales, and a further 4,000 below full rate sales (ABC, 2016). The Irish Times is owned by a complex trust. It remains profitable but cash reserves have been largely depleted. It introduced a paywall in 2015, though significant revenue growth from digital remains elusive (O'Hora, 2016; Slattery, 2016).

At the local level consolidation continues. Johnston Press left the Irish market in 2014, selling to Malcolm Denmark's Iconic Newspapers for just £7.2m. Independent News and Media announced in September 2016 it was to purchase a number of regional titles from Celtic Media, further consolidating its grip on the regional market (O'Donovan, 2016)

However, while print circulation declines continue, all the main Irish newspapers have recorded significant increases in digital traffic, and in some cases subscriptions. Digital revenues are also increasing. In fact among some publishers the audience for digital content has increased exponentially. All major Irish news titles have extensive digital operations. They compete with broadcasters and new digital-only entrants, however. Table 4 (below) demonstrates the digital penetration of major Irish news titles.

## Table 4: Digital penetration of Irish news websites

| Website | Digital penetration |
| --- | --- |
| independent.ie | 548,228 unique daily browsers (audited by ABC) – free access |
| irishtimes.com | 9,873 paid subscribers; claims 7.5m monthly users – leaky paywall |
| examiner.ie | 2m (claimed) monthly visitors – free access |
| thejournal.ie | 430,000 (claimed) monthly visitors – free access (digital only) |
| rte.ie | 6.3m (claimed) monthly visitors – free access national broadcaster |

Sources: Audit Bureau of Circulation; title websites

### The battle for survival: a case study in Limerick

Ireland's mid-west region offers a good case study for what is happening to the news media in Ireland generally. The regional capital, Limerick, is a traditionally working class city, the home of the iconic Munster rugby team, though it has historically had a major image problem, with organised crime gangs and a high murder rate. Much has changed in recent years, with a major regeneration of the city underway. The region has two main competitor newspapers, the legacy Limerick Leader group, and freesheet tabloid, the Limerick Post. Both have suffered during the post-Celtic Tiger recession, though circulation for the Post has grown in recent years. The region also has two hyper-locals, the Weekly Observer and the Vale Star, as well as a News Corp-owned regional commercial radio station, Live95FM; the base for national classical music radio station Lyric FM; a bureau for national broadcaster, RTE, and ITV subsidiary UTV Ireland. All national news media have had correspondents based there. A number of competitor titles opened during the boom years, including a mid-west edition of the Landmark Media owned Evening Echo, but all have since closed.

The Limerick Leader, founded in 1889, is one of Ireland's oldest local titles. It is owned by Malcolm Denmark's Iconic Newspapers, having survived tumultuous years of ownership by Johnston Press. Though currently not audited the combined circulation of its main weekly broadsheet editions was just under 13,500 in 2012, down from 21,600 in 2007 (ABC, 2007-2012) and likely to be less in 2016. At its height, when the paper was a fully operational printing hub, it employed up to 100 staff. Today the figure is in the low 30s, with staff working in editorial, advertising IT and finance. The paper publishes two city tabloids on Mondays and Wednesdays, and the Limerick Chronicle, a freesheet, on Tuesdays, as well as three main editions on Thursdays and Fridays. Its newsroom also runs a thriving news website, which is one of the most successful in the country. According to Alan English, a former sports editor of the Ireland edition of The Sunday Times, and Leader editor for nine years before being recently appointed

Iconic Newspapers Group Editor, the paper has been keeping a close eye on the digital space since the early days of its primitive website in the mid-1990s. "From those early beginnings it's definitely the case… [we took] online seriously; in part because Limerick is such a great news patch but also because there's been a belief there's an audience out there who are not going to buy our print products and we can't afford to ignore that audience, as has happened in quite a lot of provincial papers. So we have operated on the basis there's a print audience and there's a digital audience," (English, 2016).

The Iconic group owns 13 local newspaper titles in Ireland and has aggressively pursued a digital strategy. So, while print circulation is declining, digital circulation is growing steadily. "It is not an empty boast to say the Limerick Leader has more readers now than at any time during its 127 year history – that's a fact and it has comfortably the biggest audience of any local newspaper website in the country," claims English.

The Leader produces both freesheets and paid-for titles, charging £1.90 (€2.25) for its weekly broadsheets. In the long run it may decide to go free to protect its circulation base. "It's a business decision at the end of the day. If we felt the paper would be more profitable free, as was the case of the Evening Standard in London, there's absolutely no reason not to do it and you would do it, but at the same time the cover price is generating very good cash income for us and you have got a massive head start every week over a free paper that has so many overheads before it can turn a cent of profit. But if the day comes when we feel the paper can be more profitable free than as a paid-for title then we would do it instantly," says English.

The Leader's main competitor is the Limerick Post, a free weekly newspaper, distributed throughout Limerick with an audited weekly circulation of 50,000 (ABC, 2016). Publisher Will Ryan believes the freesheet model hasn't been as hit by digital as paid-for titles because digital advertising is not luring advertisers. "Research has shown the vast majority of ad clicks are by accident. There is no ad blocker you can put on a paper, people are seeing your ads and it's more organic; it's a nicer way they like to be associated with the local paper. If your ad pops up while you are searching for something else online it is nearly invasive," (Ryan, 2016).

The Post launched an iPhone app in 2010 but later dropped it because it wasn't producing revenue. It recently modernised its website, adding video, polls and a new digital edition, and is launching a new mobile app at the end of 2016 in partnership with another company to produce a new revenue stream. The Post is also growing its digital audience, though the printed edition is its main focus. Ryan says he is curious about the revenue model from digital.

So for now, print remains profitable for both rival titles, but revenue from digital remains elusive and the biggest challenge facing both local newspapers is developing new revenue streams. The Leader has looked at a number of models including paywalls, though they have dismissed it because of the scale required to make a paywall operationally successful. For all titles, the scale required to make a reasonable return from CPM (cost per thousand – how advertisers measure and buy digital advertising) means small publishers are going to struggle unless new revenue models can be developed.

English believes just like in print, news sites need to become the 'go to' site for audiences if they have a chance of developing a successful revenue stream from digital. "Nobody has the answers. I think the smart phone is the future and partnerships with businesses who need an audience. If you can become the 'go to site' for your area across a whole range of subjects, news and sports being just two." Mobile apps, location-based, are showing potential but its early days, he admits.

Ryan is more circumspect. Audiences are strong both in print and online, but while demand from advertisers, in terms of what they are prepared to pay, remains strong for print, but is "not there" when it comes to digital. "From a business standpoint there is no revenue there. There is no demand for it. If we were to rely on the digital revenue to produce our paper we wouldn't pay our electricity bill there's that much of a contrast." Notwithstanding this Ryan is interested to see if the new app will generate a new revenue stream. For both, then, the biggest challenge facing the newspaper business is revenue not audience.

## Conclusion

For more than 100 years Irish newspapers controlled the news and advertising markets, but digital technology has changed everything. Newspapers were too slow to react to classified sites such as CraigsList and Gumtree – in the Irish case it was Daft, the property website, and Done Deal for classifieds - and lost the market. At the same time titles have haemorrhaged circulation as news, once a prized commodity, is now freely available on a diversity of sites. Legacy news organisations initially gave everything away for free online, naively assuming their brands were invincible and digital advertising would simply replace print loses. But digital revenue is hard won, and while online revenues are growing, the growth has up until now been unable to offset the decline in print advertising and circulation.

Trusted and verified news costs money, there is no getting away from that. The hard truth is journalism has for some time been in an existential crisis: revenue to news organisations has fallen off a cliff over the past decade and up until recently no clear business models had emerged to sustain news in the digital era. The good news for Ireland's news organisations is readers are not abandoning journalism, they are converting from print to digital. And digital revenues are growing, but from a tiny base.

But while media companies are still making significant revenues from print, any revenue from digital, while impressive in growth terms, remains for now small by comparison. Free content supported by advertising is also profitable, though precarious. Mid-market popular newspapers and tabloids, with a heady mix of 'gotcha' journalism, crime stories, celebrity and entertainment news, have proved a recipe for huge popular success in the UK and Ireland, though they have the least loyal audiences. They are losing most in the print circulation battle, and while celebrity and entertainment stories offer high-volume returns in terms of views on social media, the revenue returns have not as yet followed.

While many UK news titles have successfully transitioned into global brands, with significant international digital readerships, for Irish newspapers, economies of scale may mean their potential audiences are too small to monetise via digital advertising alone. Niche brands - The Sunday Business Post and the Irish Farmers Journal - both charge for content, and The Irish Times reintroduced a leaky paywall last year. For now the Irish Independent remains free. All are profitable. The provincial press, despite years of struggle, survived the recession and many are dipping their toes in the digital water, diversifying their commercial activities, and are also making money.

Quality and trusted journalism is still being produced. Newspapers which have survived are profitable and audiences across print and digital are growing. But the elephant in the room, the decline of print and the lack of any sustainable business model to support good quality journalism in the future, looms large. It is not that news has suddenly become unfashionable, it's that making money out of news is proving increasingly difficult.

## References

Audit Bureau of Circulation 2006-2016. Various audit reports. Available at www.abc.org.uk

Felle, Tom (2012) 'From boom to bust: Irish local newspapers post the Celtic Tiger' in Mair, John, Lance Keeble, Richard and Fowler, Neil (eds), *What do we mean by local? Grassroots journalism, its death and rebirth*. Bury St Edmunds: Abramis

Flanagan, Peter (2013) 'Johnston Press is expected to fetch €8.5m for papers it bought for €300m' in Irish Independent, 20 December, available at http://www.independent.ie/business/irish/johnston-press-is-expected-to-fetch-85m-for-papers-it-bought-for-300m-29854346.html, accessed 16 September 2016

O'Donovan, Donal (2015) 'Post-Brexit uncertainty means INM won't rush deals', in Irish Independent, 28 August, available at http://www.independent.ie/business/media/postbrexit-uncertainty-means-inm-wont-rush-deals-35000258.html, accessed 30 August 2016

O'Hora, Ailish (2016) 'Irish Times to introduce a paywall next week, costing €50 a month' in the Irish Independent, 17 February, available at http://www.independent.ie/business/media/irish-times-to-introduce-paywall-next-week-costing-up-to-50-a-month-30998124.html, accessed 30 August 2016

O'Toole, Fintan (2009) *Ship Of Fools*. London: Faber and Faber

RTE (2013) 'Receiver appointed to publisher of Irish Examiner as part of restructuring' in RTE News, 6 March, available at http://www.rte.ie/news/business/2013/0306/374490-thomas-crosbie-holdings/, accessed 2 September 2016

Shanahan, Catherine (2016) 'Irish Examiner editor to leave for new challenge' in Irish Examiner, 3 August, available at http://www.irishexaminer.com/ireland/irish-examiner-editor-tim-vaughan-to-leave-for-new-challenge-413811.html, accessed 30 August, 2016

Slattery, Laura (2016) 'Newspaper circulation declines in first half of 2016' in The Irish Times, 18 August, available at http://www.irishtimes.com/business/media-and-marketing/newspaper-sales-decline-in-first-half-of-2016-1.2760884, accessed 30 August 2016

## Interviews

Interview with Alan English, Group Editor, Iconic Newsapers, Limerick, August 8, 2016

Interview with Will Ryan, Publisher, Limerick Post, Limerick, August 8, 2016

## Note on the contributors

Kathryn Hayes is a lecturer in journalism at the University of Limerick, and a former regional correspondent and news agency chief. Her email is kathryn.hayes@ul.ie. Tom Felle is a lecturer in journalism at City, University of London, and a former newspaper journalist and foreign correspondent. His email is tom.felle@city.ac.uk

# Chinese newspapers look for sustainable development in the new world

**The challenges facing print in China are just as real as those in other parts of the world. Xin Liu and Dong Dong Zhai examine three cases of different news groups trying to find a strong future and ask whether the industry will die or if it can reform to adapt itself to the new environment**

The advent of the Internet age has brought both unprecedented challenges and opportunities to the newspaper industry. High speed, wide coverage and strong interactivity and other advantages of network media place the newspaper industry at a disadvantage when facing the challenges. Many newspapers have to deal with the circulation reductions and the decline in advertising because of the loss of audience. China is no different.

Throughout the world, the newspapers of Europe and the United States and other developed countries suffered a turning point at the end of the 20th century, and entered a historical period of decline. For the development of China's newspaper industry, the actual turning point of the decline occurred in 2005, which became the worst year ever for China's newspaper industry[1] (Chen Yi 2015).

In this year the former General Administration of Press and Publication of the People's Republic of China started the digitalisation of the newspaper sector. There has been change but there is still a long way to go.

Newspaper profits have continuously fallen since 2012 with revenue downturning dramatically (see Figure 1) in 2015, because of a sharp decline in advertising (see Figure 2).

According to the Analysis Report of Chinese Newspaper Advertising Market released in February 2016, traditional media advertising market fell by 7.2 per cent in 2015. The decline in newspaper advertising accounted for the largest proportion among traditional media (35.4 per cent of the overall loss), with advertising space of advertising falling by 37.9per cent. This is the driving force for newspapers[2] to change (Tang Xujun & Wu Xinxun & Huang Chuxin et al 2016).

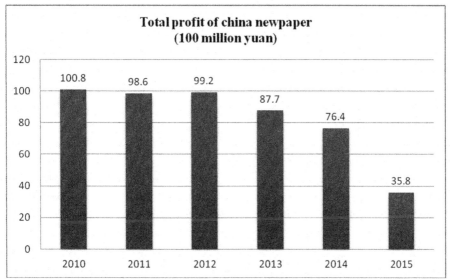

Figure 1: Total profit of Chinese newspaper and media in 2010-2015, it can be seen from the chart that the profits of newspapers in 2015 fell significantly. Data source: based on the data of the report of press and publication industry analysis (2011-2016).

## Comparison between Internet advertising and traditional media advertising

### Units: m Yuan

|  | Year 2013 | Year 2014 | Year 2015 |
|---|---|---|---|
| Internet | 1100 | 1540 | 2096.7 |
| Television | 1101.1 | 1278.5 | 1219.69 |
| Newspaper | 504.7 | 501.67 | 324.08 |
| Radio broadcast | 141.18 | 132.84 | 134.30 |
| Magazine | 87.2 | 81.62 | 65.46 |
| Total revenue of traditional media advertising | 1834.18 | 1994.63 | 1743.53 |

Figure 2: Advertising revenue of competing media in 2013-2015. The data shows Internet advertising revenue in 2015 exceeded the revenue of traditional media advertising with the advertising revenue of newspapers showing the most obvious decline. Data source: based on relevant data from The State Administration of Radio Film and Television, CRT and iResearch.

## Chinese newspaper groups

Consolidation now shapes China's newspaper industry. Chinese newspaper organisations began merging from 1996, resulting in the current 39 groups. In the digital age major newspaper groups also share resources actively. They understand the importance of the convergence with Internet media and are trying hard to find a suitable direction for future development.

Nanfang Daily Media Group is a typical business. Nanfang Metropolis Daily, Nanfang Weekly and 21st Century Economic Report are its main newspapers. They are also the most influential domestic newspapers in China in terms of authority, credibility and high quality reports.

In 2003 The Beijing News was jointly created by Nanfang Media with Guangming Daily Media Group. Then it moved aggressively into the Beijing newspaper market, becoming the model of cross-regional media business in the country.

Other newspaper groups have also looked for breakthroughs. In 2010 Guangzhou Daily was listed on the Shenzhen Stock Market. Its new media businesses including its website have merged into Yue Media in order to create better development through the capital market along with new governance and management.

In 2012, the Zhejiang Daily Press Group acquired games companies Hangzhou Bianfeng and Shanghai Haofang, owned by Shengda Network Games, for RMB 3.19bn Yuan. These two businesses became the key profit source for Zhejiang Daily soon afterwards.

In 2015 many media organisations including Beiguo Media of Liaoning Press Group, Longhoo website (from Nanfang Media Group), and Shun Network Media established by Jinan Daily Press Group scrambled to list on the NEEQ (National Equities Exchange and Quotations). Press groups trying to be listed as public companies became a norm for them to strengthen their ability to compete in the competitive media market.

## State-owned newspapers

There is a certain relationship between the delay in the decline of Chinese newspapers and the immaturity of the Chinese media market.

State-owned newspapers and business newspaper have different distribution channels. State-owned newspapers are sold mostly through subscription, while business newspapers are completely dependent on the open market. The integration and transformation of state-owned newspapers is the result of 'proactive transformation + policy initiative', while the reason for the transformation of business newspaper is market pressure. However, both state-owned newspapers and business newspapers face the common problem of how to reverse declining profits while embracing new media.

The reform of the People's Daily is an example. First, it initiated changes in layout and content. It expanded from 16 pages to 20 and then to 24 in 2010 with the promise of 'no price mark-up with added pages'. Second, in terms of content, the People's Daily has gone through an unprecedented content change. It is developing towards more factual and serious content.

After its expansion, the People's Daily launched a new edition on new media on every Tuesday. The new edition, jointly edited by people.com.cn and the

People's Daily, focuses on a variety of topics and pays attention to the feedback from readers and users, which is a new attempt at newspaper-network integration[3] (Gong Yong 2011).

The People's Daily has also tried with other new media techniques. In 1997, the web edition of the People's Daily officially published on the Internet. People's Daily Online Co Ltd was founded in 2010, and was listed as a public company on the Shanghai Stock Exchange in 2012, becoming China's first news website with the overall listing of A shares.

In 2015, daily average visitors to People's Daily Online exceeded 400m. In 2012, the People's Daily launched a micro-blog, and now its micro-blog fans on Sina reached 47m, ranked first in the media micro-blog sector.

In 2016, the all-media platform of the People's Daily was formally launched. The all-media platform of the People's Daily is also known as the 'central kitchen', which has involved rearrangement of the traditional editorial staff. The reform of the People's Daily in the newspaper and new media sector enables it gradually to explore a media integration road to assist in growth and development.

**Business newspapers**

In undertaking change, metropolitan daily The Paper is one of the best examples. In 2015, a number of newspapers made efforts to develop an independent digital news style. New media appeared independently instead of relying on source newspapers. These independent news outlets such as The Paper but also Shangyou News and Bingdu News grew in popularity.

The Paper is a key new media project launched by Shanghai United Media Group after its creation in 2013. In July 2014, The Paper was officially launched with the slogan of 'the open media platform dedicated to politics and ideology', and it claimed to 'become China's Number1 brand of political news' in its official micro-blog.

It is an important new media project from Shanghai United together with Shanghai Observation and Jiemian News. Its editorial team comes from the Oriental Morning News, which provides original content. It has successfully combined this original content with digital distribution. In terms of profit, the problem of The Paper lies is that it fails to move out of the traditional media income model: 'quality content → accumulation of users → the re-selling → advertising revenue'[4] (Zhu Chunyang & Zhang Liangyu 2014 ).

The success of Facebook, Google, Twitter, Apple and other technology companies in developing their own news businesses is being mimicked in China by organisations such as Tencent News, Netease News and Sina News.

As technology companies, they are actively seeking cooperation with traditional newspapers, such as Tencent working with Nanfang Media Group to launch the gd.qq.com, and with Shanghai United Media Group to launch the sh. QQ.com. Alibaba's acquisition of the South China Morning Post and others all show the ambitions of network media to be in newspapers business.

## Where will it end up?

In the 1990s, debate about whether the newspapers would die out had already begun. Currently nothing has changed. Circulation is dropping, display and classified advertising revenues are drying up, and the industry in recent years has experienced an unprecedented wave of layoffs.

In traditional media newspapers have suffered more than radio and television. Newspapers must make a choice of adapting to the new communications environment and Chinese newspapers have responded. They are trying to pursue a path of new development.

Currently, the newspaper is still an important part of China's mass media. Newspaper groups are actively implementing change, and there is still room for profits. We believe newspapers will not die, but they need to find a mode of sustainable development in the converging media environment.

## Notes

[1] ChenYi (2015) The new media transformation of People's Daily and other reviews, *Youth Journalist* Vol. 21, No.3 p53.

[2] Tang Xujun & Wu Xinxun & Huang Chuxin etc. (2016) *Annual Report on Development of New Media in China 2016*, Beijing: Social Sciences Academic Press.

[3] Gong Yong (2011) All media path of People's Daily, *News and Writing*, Vol. 28, No.2 p20.

[4] Zhu Chunyang & Zhang Liangyu (2014) The Paper: Shanghai Model of Political Newspaper-New media integration, *China Newspaper Industry*, No.8 p46-48.

## References

Chen Guoquan (2012) New media rescues newspapers? Guangdong: Nanfang Daily Press.

Chen Guoquan (2008) A new strategy of newspaper industry transformation, Beijing: Xinhua Press.

Chen Yi (2015) The new media transformation of People's Daily and other reviews, Youth Journalist Vol. 21, No.3 p53.

Gong Yong (2011) All media path of People's Daily, News and Writing, Vol. 28, No.2 p20.

Tang Xujun & Wu Xinxun & Huang Chuxin etc. (2016) Annual Report on Development of New Media in China 2016, Beijing: Social Sciences Academic Press.

The State Administration of Press, Publication, Radio, Film and Television of the People's Republic of China(2015)Analysis Report of 2015 News Publishing Industry Available online at http://www.gov.cn/shuju/2016-08/08/content_5098276.htm accessed on September 14, 2016

Yang Yinjuan (2010), The incremental reform of media: an empirical study of Guangzhou Daily and Nanfang Daily Press Group. Journal of International Communication, No.11 p77-82.

Zhu Chunyang & Zhang Liangyu (2014) The Paper: Shanghai Model of Political Newspaper-New Media Integration, China Newspaper Industry, No.8 p46-48.

**Note on the contributor**
Xin Liu is a postgraduate student at the School of Journalism of Communication University of China majoring in New Media Journalism. Her interest lies in new media technology and how it changes the news environment and especially how the structure of the online group structure affects communication efficiency.

Dong Dong Zhai is also a postgraduate student of School of Journalism of Communication University of China majoring in New Media Journalism. Her research interests focus on the convergence of tradition media and digital media and its influence on journalism, and online group dynamics with relations to the communication effectiveness.

# India: You ain't seen nothing yet

**The Indian media market serves a sixth of the planet's population and is still growing. In this chapter that will give hope to all those with ink in their veins, Savyasaachi Jain examines how newspapers are not only holding their own against digital upstarts in the market but also continuing to grow.**

To call India the Wild West of the media world is to stretch the metaphor only a little, and that too mainly because the geographical indicator is not appropriate. For the most part, the metaphor applies.

The Indian media, especially the news media, is characterised by rapid growth, high energy and a spirit of adventure. There are virgin lands still to be claimed and frontiers to be expanded. Indian newspapers draw upon a combination of aggressive pricing, geographical expansion and localisation to capitalise on demographic and economic trends. Their strategy has allowed them to shrug off the effects of newer media and remain confident of continued growth in at least the medium term.

The growth of Indian media is one of the great untold – or less told – stories in the study of media. Indian media have not received academic attention commensurate with their size and reach, but there is no doubt they are significant. They serve one of every six humans, the largest democratically governed population on the planet. Their scale and energy are unparalleled, and their structure complex. The Indian media system is not one homogenous entity but a conglomerate of thriving media systems in nearly two dozen languages differentiated by diverse historical, political, linguistic and cultural traditions but simultaneously linked by cross-holdings and a common legal and regulatory framework (Jain, 2016).

Even with low penetration rates, newspapers reach more people than in any other country; India overtook China as the largest newspaper market in 2010 (WAN-IFRA, 2011). At a time when newspaper circulations in many countries were in decline, Indian newspapers grew more than 250 per cent between 2004 and 2014. *The Times of India*, with 7.6m readers, is the second largest circulated quality English-language newspaper in the world (WAN-IFRA, 2015) but it is by no means the largest in India. Seven newspapers in other languages have far greater reach (Table 1).

## Table 1: Top 10 dailies in India

| Average issue readership (AIR) in '000s | | | |
|-------------------------------|------------|----------|----------|
| **Publication** | **Language** | **IRS 2013** | **IRS 2014** |
| *Dainik Jagran* | Hindi | 15,527 | 16,631 |
| *Hindustan* | Hindi | 14,246 | 14,746 |
| *Dainik Bhaskar* | Hindi | 12,857 | 13,830 |
| *Malayala Manorama* | Malayalam | 6,565 | 8,803 |
| *Daily Thanthi* | Tamil | 8,156 | 8,283 |
| *Rajasthan Patrika* | Hindi | 7,665 | 7,905 |
| *Amar Ujala* | Hindi | 7,071 | 7,808 |
| *The Times of India* | English | 7,254 | 7,590 |
| *Mathrubhumi* | Malayalam | 6,136 | 6,020 |
| *Lokmat* | Marathi | 5,601 | 5,887 |

Source: Indian Readership Survey, 2014 (IRS measures readership, not circulation)

Many of the numbers for Indian media are an order of magnitude larger than other countries, and rising steadily. There are, for instance, more than 800 television channels in about two dozen languages, of which about 400 are news channels. There are 105,443 publications registered with the Registrar of Newspapers for India at the end of March 2015 (Registrar of Newspapers for India, 2015), rising from 99,660 the year before and 94,067 in March 2013. Other media show similar or higher growth figures in terms of numbers of outlets and audiences as well as revenues. As a result, India hosts the largest and most vibrant media system in the world.

## A brief history

The first printing press arrived in India with the Portuguese in 1556 and was largely used for the printing of religious literature by Jesuit missionaries based in Goa on the western coast of peninsular India (Vilanilam, 2005: 51). The first printed newspaper dates back to 1780, during the colonial period, when an Englishman, James Augustus Hicky, launched the weekly *Bengal Gazette*, also known as the *Calcutta General Advertiser*, in Calcutta (now Kolkata). *Hicky's Gazette*, described as a 'witty and scurrilous newspaper' (Parthasarathy, 1997: 19), lasted less than two years. Hicky was sued for defamation by the Governor-General of Bengal, Warren Hastings, fined, imprisoned and subsequently deported.

However, within a few years, Calcutta had four weeklies and a monthly and in the next half century there were nearly 50 publications in different parts of the country. The first newspaper in an Indian language, *Digdarshan* [World Vision], was launched in 1818 by missionaries and it was soon followed by others in a number of languages.

Newspapers in colonial, pre-1947 India displayed three strong, persistent trends – those of resistance to oppressive legal and governmental regimes, furtherance of social reform campaigns, and a strong tradition of political activism. Each of these has persisted in different forms, emerging as watchdog journalism, development journalism, participation in the nation-building project, and the use of newspapers for mobilisation and activism during the freedom struggle. Several contemporary newspaper titles have been in existence for 150 years or more but they have seldom, if ever, experienced the growth that they have enjoyed in recent years.

The first half of the 1990s was an inflection point for Indian media. If one were to conceive of phases of Indian media, there is no question that this period was the beginning of a new and distinct phase that continues to the present time. This phase represents a far-reaching qualitative change, driven by a sustained and rapid quantitative change. This phase is simply described here as the phase of explosive growth. The markers of the phases of Indian journalism proposed here are:

i) The *formative phase*, extending from the first newspaper in 1780 to 1919, encompassing social and spiritual as well as political concerns.

ii) The *nationalist phase*, from 1919 to the attainment of Indian independence in 1947, marked most prominently by anti-colonial, pro-independence activism. Numerous political leaders including the Father of the Nation, Mohandas Karamchand Gandhi, were editors of newspapers.

iii) The *nation-building phase* from 1947 to the end of the Emergency in 1977, marked most prominently by concerns of development, governance and secularism.

iv) The *aggressive journalism phase* from 1977 to the early 1990s, marked most prominently by activism, investigative journalism and an assertion of the media's role in demanding accountability.

v) The *phase of explosive growth*, a substantive disjuncture from the past in numerous dimensions, including practices, structures and norms. This phase began with economic liberalisation in the early to mid-1990s and has shaped today's media system.

## Drivers of growth: Population, literacy and the economy

Although newspapers in India are growing slower than television, radio and online media, they still achieve enviable growth rates. Projections by industry analysts suggest that the print industry will continue to grow at nearly 8 per cent over the next five years (Figure 1).

## Figure 1: Growth of the Indian print industry

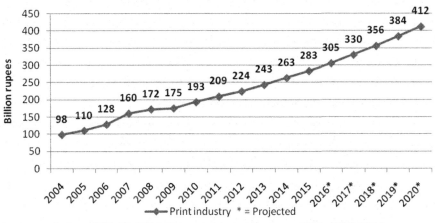

Source: KPMG, 2016; PricewaterhouseCoopers, 2008, 2009, 2011

This growth is partly rooted in demographic factors. India has a population of 1.21bn (Census of India, 2011) that is growing, becoming more urbanised and also more literate. India's people are slowly moving from its 640,867 villages to nearly 8,000 urban settlements, making it easier for them to access media. Greater Mumbai has a population of more than 18m, and there are 53 cities with more than 1m residents. The share of population living in towns and cities increased from 25 per cent in 1991 to 31 per cent in 2011, adding up to an urban population of nearly 400m. Simultaneously, the literacy rate rose to 74 per cent in 2011, up 22 percentage points in 20 years, adding a pool of readers larger than the populations of most countries. Figure 2 shows the explosion of newspaper readership in the first decade of this century.

## Figure 2: Literate population aged more than seven years

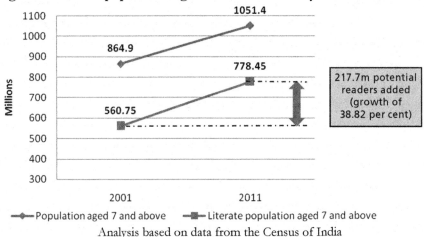

Analysis based on data from the Census of India

At the same time, the penetration of newspapers in India is still relatively low, higher than the US and other developing economies such as South Africa and Brazil, but substantially lower than many others (Figure 3). This also goes to explain why newspaper publishers are confident of sustained growth in the medium term.

**Figure 3: Comparative newspaper reach**

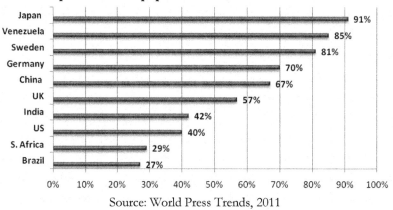

Source: World Press Trends, 2011

The mushrooming audience base has had the effect of moving relationships between media beyond the zero sum game that exists elsewhere. Growth of other media does not necessarily draw readers away from newspapers or, if audiences do desert newspapers, fresh entrants to the pool compensate adequately. The rise of private news television in the mid-1990s, for instance, is credited by industry insiders with increasing the appetite for news, which is vividly illustrated by data on newsprint consumption (Figure 4).

**Figure 4: Newsprint consumption in India**

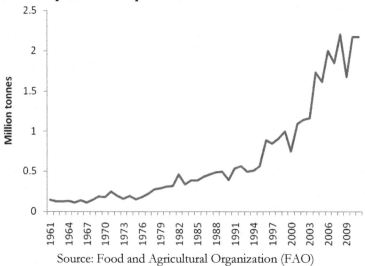

Source: Food and Agricultural Organization (FAO)

The backdrop to India's media growth is provided by economic growth. India overtook China to become the fastest growing major economy in 2015 with a growth rate of 7.6 per cent, and is projected to maintain pole position by growing at 7.4 per cent over the next two years (IMF, 2016). A growing economy has meant greater advertising support for media, even though advertising spend, at 0.34 per cent of GDP, remains at about half the level of Western Europe and one-third of that in the US. Although poverty is widespread, GDP growth has meant greater disposable income and purchasing power, as shown in Figure 5.

**Figure 5: Relative growth of GDP and population**

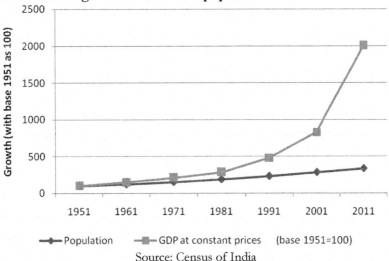

Source: Census of India

## Business strategy

However, India's newspapers have not grown by passively waiting for readers to be ushered through the door by demographic and macroeconomic drivers. They have adopted a range of aggressive – and effective – business strategies in terms of their offering, footprint and pricing.

Most large newspaper groups now offer advertisers '360-degree solutions' drawing upon diverse media holdings and their distribution networks. They aim to provide a one-stop solution to advertisers, including a variety of print titles catering to different linguistic and regional audiences and other media outlets ranging from online media and radio and television stations to outdoor advertising. In effect, they try and capture as large and varied an audience as they can to offer to advertisers.

In a market that is crowded in terms of numbers, expansion into fresh geographical areas and media has become as much a strategy of survival as a sound business plan driven by advertiser interest in rural and semi-urban areas which now exhibit buying power (Jain, 2016). Digital technology has facilitated rapid expansion of newspapers through facsimile and remote editions that offer customised and localised newspapers for relatively small geographical areas, sometimes as small as one small town or one district (India's 29 states and seven union territories have 687 districts). *The Times of India* multiplied from 12 to 33 editions in the four years from 2010 to 2014, and the publishers of the Hindi newspaper *Dainik Jagran* have enlarged their footprint from one newspaper in one language in one state to more than 130 editions across 11 titles in five languages reaching 69m readers in 15 of India's 29 states.

Even though big players such as *The Times of India, Hindustan Times, Dainik Jagran, Dainik Bhaskar* and *Malayala Manorama* dominate their home markets, they often struggle in the fresh markets that they seek to enter. The strategy of choice is to hurt existing market leaders in their wallets by starting a price war. Soon after Rupert Murdoch initiated a price war in the UK by dropping the prices of *The Sun* and *The Times* in the early and mid-1990s, *The Times of India* also dropped its price in Delhi, where it was trying to unseat *Hindustan Times* as the market leader (Whitaker, 1994).

Today, price wars, especially when an outside newspaper attempts to break into an established market away from its home, have become an integral element of the strategy of expanding into new geographical and linguistic markets. Newspaper cover prices have settled at levels that are sustainable only by the leaders in each market, the top two or three who attract the bulk of audiences and an even larger proportion of the advertising.

In India, the price for a 24- or 32-page broadsheet newspaper delivered to the doorstep is typically between Rs.2. and Rs.4. At the equivalent of £0.02–0.04, that is 2–4 British pence at pre-Brexit exchange rates, the selling price barely covers the cost of the printing ink used. Each copy is sold at a substantial loss, and the more copies that sell, the more money the publisher loses. Probably the only reason newspapers are not given away free is that they would disappear during distribution and would not reach the reader, being sold instead in bulk for recycling (in India, the price for newspapers as 'raddi' or scrap for recycling has varied between Rs.3 and Rs.5 per kg over the last two decades).

## Questions of sustainability

Although the Indian newspaper market is undoubtedly expanding rapidly in reach and numbers, its health is more questionable. With more than 105,000 publications and growing, the advertising pie is being sliced ever thinner. Newspapers that were settled in regional linguistic markets are threatened by larger national players seeking to expand into fresh territory. The result is an intensely crowded and competitive environment. In each specific linguistic or geographical market, the top two or three can be wildly successful, but hundreds of other players barely survive.

The downward pressure on cover prices has also meant that the balance of revenue is shifting towards increased dependence upon advertisers (Figure 6). Many in the newspaper industry believe the business model is broken because it renders publications overly vulnerable to economic downturns that might result in downturns in advertising. Others have expressed concern that the strong dependence on advertisers renders newspapers susceptible to editorial pressures and that this in turn impacts editorial values.

**Figure 6: Print industry – advertising and circulation revenues**

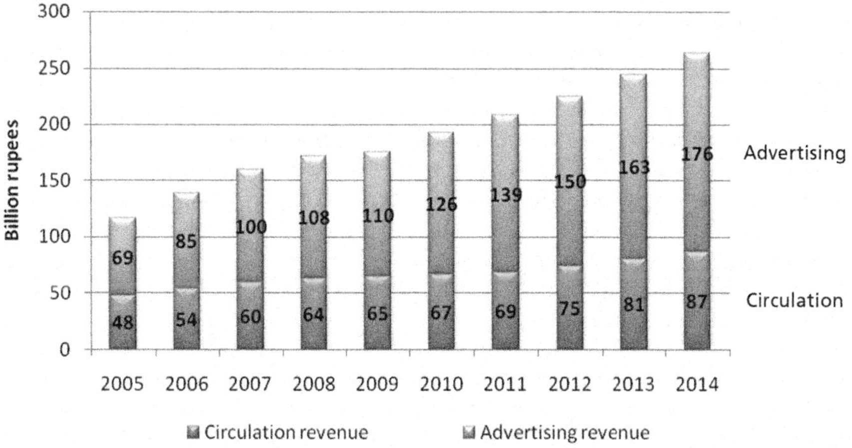

Source: KPMG Analysis

Indian media, in its current phase of explosive growth, has experienced unprecedented expansion over the last two decades, but this has also created distortions in the business models and practices of newspapers. A shakeout and subsequent market consolidation have long been anticipated, but the flow of fresh entrants remains unabated. Newspapers in India exist in an intensely competitive space, one that requires constant tactical and strategic refinements to survive and grow. Large and diversified players dominate the market, but not without having to exert themselves.

All the same, there is little doubt that newspapers are holding their own against other media. Their continued growth is fuelled by a mix of demographic and macroeconomic factors, as well as by low market penetration that provides scope for substantial further growth. Newspapers are not dead in India. To the contrary, they are very much alive and kicking, and determined to stay that way.

## References

IMF (2016) World Economic Outlook Update, International Monetary Fund, July. Available online at https://www.imf.org/external/pubs/ft/weo/2016/update/02/, accessed on 23 September, 2016.

Jain, S (2016) *Characterising Media Systems: Insights from a Case Study of Paid News in India*. Unpublished PhD thesis, University of Westminster, London.

KPMG (2016) *The Future: Now Streaming. KPMG-FICCI Indian Media and Entertainment Report 2016*. Mumbai: KPMG.

Parthasarathy, R (1997) *Journalism in India: From the Earliest Times to the Present Day* (4th edn). New Delhi: Sterling.

PricewaterhouseCoopers (2008) *The Indian Entertainment and Media Industry: Sustaining Growth: Report 2008*. New Delhi: PricewaterhouseCoopers.

PricewaterhouseCoopers (2009) *Indian Entertainment and Media Outlook 2009*. New Delhi: PricewaterhouseCoopers.

PricewaterhouseCoopers (2011) *India Entertainment and Media Outlook 2011*. New Delhi: PricewaterhouseCoopers.

Registrar of Newspapers for India (2015) *Press in India 2014–15*. New Delhi: Ministry of Information and Broadcasting.

Vilanilam, J.V (2005) *Mass Communication in India: A Sociological Perspective*. New Delhi: Sage.

WAN-IFRA (2011) World Press Trends 2011. World Association of Newspapers.

WAN-IFRA (2015) World Press Trends 2015. World Association of Newspapers.

Whitaker, R (1994) Newsagents Knocked Off Their Bikes in India's Own Price War. *The Independent*, 12 July. Available online at
<http://www.independent.co.uk/news/newsagents-knocked-off-their-bikes-in-indias-own-price-war-1413260.html>, accessed on 20 September, 2012.

## Note on the contributor

Savyasaachi Jain is a senior lecturer at Swansea University, where he is programme director of the Erasmus Mundus MA in Journalism, Media and Globalisation (War and Conflict specialism). Formerly a journalist and documentary filmmaker, he researches journalism, conflict, media ethics and media systems. He has trained journalists in 18 countries and supervised numerous documentary co-productions on behalf of international, intergovernmental and UN organisations.

# Niche journalism

\* \* \*

# What's my niche?

**Neil Fowler**

Niche is good but is it too small? This section looks at how acute specialisations have found success in the storm of media upheaval. Is this the real answer for the print industry?

Barry McIlheney, CEO of the magazine industry trade body the Professional Publishers Association, an organisation that thrives on niche, has no doubt about the future of ink and paper.

'Is print dying?' he says. 'No. Will print ever die? No. And is right now the best time ever to use that print base to build a greater all-platform audience than ever before? God yes. So let's get cracking.'

His is both an optimistic and offers a challenging view which heads this part of the book and looks at how a keen focus can bring continued success for journalism.

Joely Carey, whose career spans national newspapers and magazines and who now works as an award-winning digital content specialist, says magazine publishing in particular has stared death in the face. But it has hope. The sector has seen what it has to do to survive, she says, and it is starting to fight back with passion, skill and determination. But is it too late? She hopes not.

Car magazines were once big, says automotive writer and research specialist Richard Aucock. But the best have business units bigger than the print title ever was – and, he believes, the magazine is the halo product which adds the authority to the brand. But there is a rider says one of his sources. 'Print has a future… if you're selective.'

And this look at motoring is supported by Bauer's Tim Pollard who explains how Bauer Media seized the digital moment and invested in its digital motoring brands not just to save old titles but also to create vibrant new businesses.

Many niche publications exist in the business-to-business sector and Clive Couldwell argues over the last decade and a half many B2Bs failed to innovate and their publishers viewed online as a form of cost cutting. But it doesn't have to be so, he says, there is a mix to be had and this sector can lead the way.

Niches exist in many forms, of course and the alternative, activist press is one where there remains huge life – with many progressive groups still producing their own journals. Lincoln University's Professor Richard Lance Keeble looks in depth at two such publications and finds out from their editors their strategies for survival.

And Channel 4's and City University's David Lloyd believes print media, and in particular national newspapers, should learn to exploit their great specialist journalist assets. Brilliant critics and columnists whose detailed knowledge of specific subjects is invaluable are being given away for free. That must change, he says.

As traditional media businesses have reduced the numbers of journalists in their employ, so has come the rise, albeit slowly, of the specialist agency covering areas that might have been the preserve of these businesses in the past – one clear example being investigative journalism.

Napier University's Eamonn O'Neill outlines why broadcast audiences for dynamic and revelatory reporting from news organisations might be the saviour of their newsrooms, while Rachel Oldroyd, of the Bureau for Investigative Journalism, looks at how the rise of not-for-profit agencies, is adding another ingredient to the mix of 21st century journalism.

But how big, or small, can these audiences be? Catalina Albeanu, of Journalism.co.uk, asks what communities suddenly finding themselves no longer served by a local news outlet can do. And she finds people without formal journalism training are stepping to fill the gap. She takes a look at two organisations which have flourished in recent years doing fundamental journalistic tasks their founders thought were lacking from larger media outlets.

And her look at the growth of such smaller businesses is supported by Andy Williams and Dave Harte, who outline the findings from a major research project by academics at both Cardiff and at Birmingham City University looking into the success and future of hyper-local, community journalism.

Is niche, of whatever kind, the future? Read the follow-up to this book in ten years!

# Oh no it isn't!

Let's all grow up and stop fighting, says Barry McIlheney, CEO of the Professional Publishers Association (PPA). Everybody wins when content and format create that sweet spot together...

I have kindly been offered 3,000 words here to tackle the question of Is Print Dying? ...And How To Avoid It. Leaving aside the fact that the second part of that statement seems to prematurely – and in my view entirely wrongly – give an answer to the first part, you will be glad to know that I need nothing like 3,000 words to take down this ridiculous notion. Not only is print not dying, ladies and gentlemen, but in so many different ways it has in fact never ever been more alive and kicking.

Let's start right here right now. I do hope that you are reading this chapter in print and on paper in what we still like to call a book. Why? Because that is the best way to read it. There, I said it. Shoot me now officer, I'll go quietly. One of the many oddities of this so-called digital age is the fear that so many folk still seem to have of speaking this bald truth to Silicon Valley power. What are we all so frightened of? That they might defriend us on Facebook? Block our tweets? Not accept our LinkedIn request when that dark day finally comes and we are all in the increasingly cramped consultancy space? Steal all our beautiful content and all the lovely advertising that likes to follow that content wherever it may reside? Hmmmm.

## Holiday reading

So I shall say it here loud and clear. A book is always best read in print unless you are packing for your holidays and don't want to fall foul of Ryanair, in which case a Kindle is clearly the smart way to go. Personally I do both. A magazine is always best read in print unless you are on a business trip somewhere where they don't sell your favourite magazine, in which case the tablet is clearly the smart way to go. Personally I do both. A newspaper is always...you get the picture I'm sure.

If the good people behind this book want to alert people to its very existence, I would suggest that they send out some tweets. Set up a Facebook page. Form a LinkedIn group. Ask the various authors to tell them their Desert Island Disc – Teenage Kicks by The Undertones now you ask – and put out a Spotify playlist. Get together some of the bigger names involved and get them round a table to do a podcast. Pick the three best pieces and put them out there in a neat digital format and see if you can get a few thousand people to pay for those pieces and those pieces alone using one of those really cool micropayment systems. Do all that till the proverbial cows come home, but sooner or later the people still have to read the bloody book. And a book – please see above – is always best read in print.

## Content and context

For me, as the boss of the Professional Publishers Association, the network for all UK consumer magazine publishers and Business Media companies, I always assume that the content in any magazine produced by any of our members will be of the highest possible standard. The platform on which I choose to read this world-class content is then all about the context. Most of the time I will choose to read long-form content in printed form because I think that this is the way God meant it to be. Anything under say 400 words I find that it matters less. Much of the time I am alerted to this brilliant content by links posted on various digital and social networks. So here's the shocking news just in: it's never been about print versus digital, it's always been about print *plus* digital. Plus social plus live events plus carrier pigeon plus whatever else might have been invented by the time I finish this piece. They are all just ways of getting the lovely content out there to all those lovely people who are just gagging to get it down them.

We folk in the media have always loved nothing more than a good scrap between the seemingly different platforms – usually technologically driven – on which any form of content can be consumed. Desktop versus mobile! Print versus digital! Video versus cinema! The latter is particularly poignant for me in that it almost scuppered the launch of Empire magazine, of which I was lucky enough to be the Editor from its launch in 1989 through to 1992, by which time – despite the fact that it very nearly never launched due to the declining number of people going to the cinema at that point and because video was therefore about to kill cinema – it was selling more than 100,000 copies every month. By which time cinema audiences were rising again anyway, a trend that continues to this day. The fact is that nobody *needs* to go to the cinema any more to see a film, yet more people do so than ever.

## The phoney platform wars

We now live in a world blessed with an ever-increasing number of formats and an ever-expanding volume of content. What I love the most about this blooming ecosystem is when these two strands combine to be more than the sum of their parts, creating that fabulous and truly memorable spark of magic. It's that moment when you're transported away, goggle-eyed, by the latest blockbuster on the big screen in all its sumptuous glory; it's that feeling when you're standing in a muddy field as the bass thumps through your veins; and it's that unparalleled sensation of sinking deep into the pristine pages, beautiful colours, and wonderful words of an expertly-crafted magazine.

If we want progress, we must of course encourage and welcome new formats and all the opportunities that they bring in their wake, but the sad truth for all big fight fans out there is that most big platforms never actually die. Sure, they might ebb and flow in popularity when the new kid on the block comes along, but then it all settles down again until the next one arrives. Look at radio. Dead as a dodo surely when that radical new thing called television came along. No, not really. Look at television. Kaput surely when that interweb thing came along. No, not really. And look at printed magazines. Six foot under surely when those new tablet editions would sweep the world. Er, no, not really.

We all really do need to grow up and to work together. This stuff will still be here when we are all gone, and that's the end of it. New platforms don't kill old ones, they merely expand the potential audience for all that beautiful content. It's really hard to expand this notion into a PowerPoint presentation, never mind 3,000 words, but here's the truth of it. People still listen to the radio and watch TV and read consumer magazines because they *like* to. They may not *need* to, but that's a different story. There is still a town crier making a decent living up in Derbyshire for God's sake, and we haven't needed one of those for a very long time. Apparently people just like the way he looks and the tone of his voice. It might be stretching it to call it content, but I rest my case.

## Paid content

The final reason why print will never die is that an awful lot of people are still prepared to pay an awful lot of money for it. With the exception of the burgeoning freemium market where if anything the content works even harder to earn its keep, we still ask people to part with hard-earned coin of the realm to partake of all that lovely magazine content, week-in-week-out, month-in-month-out. And still they do it in their hundreds of thousands, year after year. Some of our PPA members' magazines have fewer people buying their printed editions than they once had. Some of them have more. All of them now reach a greater audience than they ever have done through their modern potent cocktail of print, digital, social, broadcast, and live events. More than half a million people still buy Radio Times *every week* – and the clue to the veracity of some of the general points made earlier here is in that particular title – with that number more than doubling when it comes to the legendary Christmas edition, now as much a part of that festive season as mince pies and a great song being ruined by John Lewis. The Great British Public buy it, then keep it close to them every day to check what is on and whether or not it is worth watching. Day after day after day.

Excuse me if I turn up the volume here for a second, but which advertiser with a half a brain and a beady eye on his client's money is ever going to ignore that incredibly deep level of rich engagement to opt instead for popping up next to a ten-second clip of a monkey soiling itself on a skateboard? Don't get me wrong, I am one of the many millions of clowns who like nothing more than wasting my time on this sort of free rubbish – and by the way have you seen the one of the dog running into the sea *shot from the dog's POV* – but let's call it for what it is. It's rubbish and it's free and it's already over in the time it takes me to write this sentence (it's so funny I'm watching it again). Therefore I don't really mind that it's rubbish and if it stops me having to contemplate the meaning of life for a few more seconds then that's all well and good. But please let's not confuse it with paying actual cash every month to be transported to another world for days on end by the latest issue of Vogue or Empire or Wallpaper* or BBC Good Food or The Economist or any other of the hundreds of titles I could list here. And any advertiser who makes that mistake should personally be forced to pay back the money that they have just wasted to their client. Thankfully, the smarter ones such as Sir Martin Sorrell are starting to realise the error of their ways and are beginning to row the boat back towards their spiritual home. And a home – thanks to the huge investment made by publishers in ABC and PAMCo – that can actually tell them in more detail than they might ever want just exactly how many people have seen all their lovely ads in all those lovely magazines. Rather than just thinking of a number and doubling it, which would be nice, but which seems to be the preserve of merely the shiny and the new. And which should of course be stopped with immediate effect.

## A final word from Felix

I shall close by referencing the late great Felix Dennis, as close to a genius as anyone I have had the good fortune to come across in all my time in this caper. Not content with making close to a billion dollars from his unlikely beginnings as the publisher of some Bruce Lee partworks, Felix also had that unique ability, always the hallmark of a very clever person, to hold two totally conflicting ideas in his head at the same time. One of these ideas, which I first heard him expound upon in 1997, was that print was dying, was destined to become 'mere roadkill on the information superhighway', and would as sure as eggs is eggs be dead and buried 20 years from now. This, of course, was roughly around the same time as Felix was gradually developing his interest in a title called The Week, one of the greatest printed magazine success stories of the early 21st century. Talk about hedging your bets to quite spectacular effect. As for Felix's more general Mystic Meg-style predictions from 20 years ago for 2017, I will simply report two notable events from this year. The first is that Vogue magazine celebrated 100 years as a printed magazine with its biggest-ever issue of all time. And the second is that Dennis Publishing, now led by PPA Chairman James Tye, won both Specialist Consumer Magazine of the Year and Digital Publisher of the Year at the annual PPA Awards. Is print dying? No. Will print ever die? No. And is right now the best time ever to use that print base to build a greater all-platform audience than ever before? God yes. So let's get cracking.

**Note on the contributor**
Barry McIlheney began his career in magazines at The Hot Press and Melody Maker before being appointed Editor of Smash Hits and going on to become launch Editor of Empire, Publishing Director of Emap's music and film titles, and Managing Director of Emap Metro. In 1999, he led the launch of heat magazine before moving to Paris to oversee the launch of FHM France. He returned to the UK to become Chief Executive of Emap Elan and in 2003 became Editor-in-Chief of Emap Consumer Media. Barry was appointed CEO of the PPA on February 1, 2010.

# The magazine market isn't dead, it's different

**Death by a thousand cuts: Is the women's magazine industry really destined for a papery grave, asks Joely Carey**

Firstly, let me firmly state that I heart magazines. I really love them. I'm also very fond of newspapers but mags: those luscious, heavy, beautiful, glossy works of genius are what makes my professional heart swell with happiness.

And so, for the last few years, I've been in professional mourning for an industry that has been ripped to shreds and left to slowly, but oh-so-surely, bleed to death in an all too crowded papery gutter.

Today's mag-land, specifically women's mag-land is considered a shadow of its former self. The celebrity and lifestyle sector, once a behemoth within the publishing world is – from a circulation perspective – a limp, lacklustre version of what it was once was. It's like the media equivalent of the Sex and the City movies.

Or The Hangover Part II. Or The Hangover Part III. Oh, how the mighty have fallen. Look at these headlines, taken from trade press following the 2015/2016's Audit Bureau of Circulation (ABC) results.

1. "60 out of 442 titles grow sales" sang one. (Press Gazette)

2. "Mag ABCs: Price-cut and give-away copies help Cosmopolitan lead growth in women's fashion and lifestyle titles" reported another Press Gazette article a day later.

It's clear the trade title was putting a positive spin on a set of figures showing the appetite for magazines, and in particular for women's magazines, is fading. It's sad times, indeed, when you can legitimately crow about price cuts and giveaways being the formula to circulation gains for your brand. Or, when the overwhelming number of titles in existence show either zero growth year on year, or worse, significant losses.

Perhaps we should rewrite those headlines without the desperate positivity?

1. Just seven per cent of UK magazines show any readership growth in the last 12 months

2. Millions of readers lost as publishers resort to price cuts and freebies to lure readers to the newsstand

The story suddenly seems a much sorrier one, doesn't it? Because, for the past five years, not only has the women's magazine market lost readers and lost titles – it's also lost its nerve. Magazines are still being read in the millions – although they are not the traditional newsstand titles. Top of the magazine tree are those being given away by The National Trust to its members, or by retail giants such as Tesco and Asda, who both produce monthly magazines for their customers to pick up in store.

The paid-for titles holding on to prime positions in the ABCs are, without exception, TV listings magazines, with TV Choice topping the list at 1.2m (up 0.2 per cent year on year). The sector hardest hit by declining sales? Paid-for celebrity and lifestyle titles. These beauties have taken such serious body blows in recent times, some may never recover, some have already gone. Goodbye Company magazine and InStyle is now a digital-only product.

Endless hand-wringing in publishing offices can't get away from the fact the publishing business model of old is broken. There's no hiding from it. The ABCs twice-yearly reports tell it like it is. So why are sales plummeting when people still want to access the same kinds of stories they always have? I believe the mass market women's magazine sector is perhaps at its most vulnerable because digital content and digital distribution models are killing it one click at a time.

I spoke to a number of editors, anonymously, from titles in the specialist, weekly and monthly sectors and despite the variety in their titles, they are all facing the same problems – restricted budgets, reduced resource and, in the main, sliding sales.

Is magazine content already a print Dodo? Consider the MailOnline – now the home of all celebrity news – has a global audience of 14.8m unique visitors a day – it's clear the appetite for standard celebrity content has never been stronger. The difference is the distribution of this content and the way the audience can access it have changed considerably.

I believe the publishing industry failed to understand just how important emerging technology and global competition could (and would) be to their age-old business model. They failed to understand the impact of how digital accessibility to words, pictures and videos would change and, consequently, devastate the glory days of sell-out issues and circulation figures that regularly bust the 1m mark – a week.

This isn't purely with the benefit of hindsight. I worked within the industry as digital content slowly took over from its print predecessors. The emergence of digital technology was a turning point for magazine content and magazine journalism. The art of storytelling was changing: the tech was there, the talented teams were there, but to deliver strong digital content wasn't without a heavy price tag and for many the change never happened. Many weren't convinced they could make digital publishing pay in the same way that print has in the past.

So, the wilderness years ensued, many magazine titles were left floundering in a tide of technology eating away at their sales. As a result, they lost part of their sass and balls because of just how quickly the reader landscape was changing. They didn't grasp just how quickly this tech was going to rip out the paper hearts of their beloved magazines without as much as a backward glance.

For an industry whose brilliance was rooted in the ability of great creative minds to start each and every issue with a blank front cover and an empty flat plan – ideation and innovation seemed to not just stall, but to stagnate. Instead, many seemed to hope their loyal readers would stay and their quality content would be protected. In fact, most titles stood like rabbits blinking in the glare of the oncoming digital headlights.

For years it had been declared 'print was king' when in fact 'content was king' and as technology seeped into every corner of daily routines, readers changed their behavior when it came to consuming content. As the internet became the new distributor for journalism, bravery, commitment, cash and creativity were needed to ride and embrace this new technology, to plug it into the heart of existing print brands.

But who was up for that? Step forward Martin Clark, tabloid to his core and the brains behind what became MailOnline. It launched in 2003. For three years it languished and then in 2006, Clark became editor and then publisher in 2008. The rest is history.

He brought his unique tabloid take on showbiz and celebrity to the site and the audience grew. He got more investment – while the UK celebrity magazine market stayed stagnant – and his audience grew even bigger. The MailOnline's showbiz section became renowned as the sidebar of shame. It became everyone's guilty pleasure. It became a runaway success. It had beaten the women's magazine market at its own game.

Turns out the audience was always there. It was only ever going to be bigger than the print audience because online content allows people to access what they want when they want it. And the MailOnline stole readers away from their natural magazine heartland. By now women's celebrity magazines were caught in a financial catch-22 – they were losing sales, so advertising dipped. As a result, the established business model was breaking up.

Talented teams did their best to push out quality magazines, but on a smaller budget, with fewer staff and on poorer quality paper, it became an almost impossible task. Loyal audiences trickled away, those obsessed with tabloid celebrity gossip and fodder that had been the very lifeblood of the women's weekly magazine market found it elsewhere. It was available for free, 24/7 at Mailonline.co.uk and any other online offering. Some dismissed MailOnline as a consistent threat because its sidebar of shame wasn't overly skilful, or clever or even exclusive, but it was accessible and it was free.

The arrival, and 'thrival', of the internet as a news provider and the growth of social media as a news distributor meant anything in print was under threat. Those at the helm needed to find a new way to succeed in the journalism arena. As our phones became the digital companion to our lives, they became the access point for our storytelling, too. The magazine industry's circulation figures and future now lay, literally, in the hands of an increasingly fickle audience happy to flip between Facebook, MailOnline, Twitter and back again. And it seemed the death of magazines was within sight. It broke my professional heart to watch as the women's magazine industry, once a hugely powerful force, was staring at a bleak existence.

In the 90s and 00s publishing houses launched new titles with passion and fervor. The competition was fierce, exciting and spawned talented editors, writers and terrifying publishers. Then, the only thing holding you back from launching a new magazine or growing your existing brand's popularity was the increasing cost of the paper needed to print it. Now, the cost of paper was miniscule compared to the cost of reinventing a brand for an increasingly digitally savvy audience and investing in it. As publishers fought to find a way to survive, there was an element of chaos as the two worlds of print and digital struggled to find a way to work together in the same arena. It became a world of us versus them and it was bloody.

Ad revenues were tricky to find for emerging digital platforms – advertisers were nervous of spending big bucks on relatively new offerings. The audience was different, the time spent with content was shorter. It was a new dawn, but no-one felt comfortable with it.

I've asked many former colleagues, award-winning editors, journalists, and editorial directors why our industry stalled so badly. And the answer is that, as the digital revolution hit, publishing seemed to lose its nerve. There was a palpable sense of disconnect from the reality of grass-roots content consumption and magazine production. The publishing landscape had changed, but the publishing model had stayed rooted in the past. As magazine launches became less frequent, talent stagnated. Budget cuts meant teams were reduced. Staff had to do more with less and eventually quality began to suffer.

For a while the real-life sector had boasted huge circulation numbers when Take a Break, under the legendary John Dale racked up over a million sales a week, followed by That's Life!, Bella and Chat. The magazines weren't sexy, but they were gripping and their fans were loyal, and less likely, for a while at least, to jump ship and spend all their time online. Now, Take a Break is still the highest selling real-life magazine, but with latest figures posted of just over 500k sales a week.

These magazines gave ordinary people with extraordinary stories a voice to be heard, to share their life stories, when other news outlets weren't interested. Then along came Facebook which gave everyone the chance to share their stories, their photos, their life moments and hey, real life became every-day content in our news feeds.

In all, the UK magazine industry was running scared while MailOnline had a runaway winner on their hands. The brand launched in America, then Australia. It seemed to be on an unstoppable global rampage.

It was clear to anyone who cared that the industry had reached a critical moment. Digital publishing continued to be frenzied with online editors desperate to publish first and fast. This desperation created a culture of 'churnalism', celebrity articles were barely stories, but elongated picture captions. They were sloppy, lacked skill, precision and wit.

But the readers barely noticed. Martin Clark once said he produced 'journalism crack' for MailOnline and he was right. The emergence of digital content consumption was an industry game changer. The culture it created also spawned a new dawn for journalism. As audiences were drowning in a sea of curated content – varying from sometimes brilliant, but often banal, user-generated content, to social clickbait – the mood seemed to trigger a desire for something else, something better.

Although consumed by millions, in time, the Mail's sidebar of shame and its ilk were often ridiculed for the choice of subjects and inane style of writing. Those who had kept their finger on the publishing pulse could sense the digital content revolution had actually helped create a new need – and new audiences.

Content was everywhere but good content wasn't and that was the jewel in the publishing crown. Digital think tanks reported back to the front lines that time was ripe for change. Although certain content delivered quick hits and 'social drive-by eyeballs' that tore through celebrity content on offer for free, there was a desire for quality long-form journalism, both online and… in print.

While many had claimed the digital revolution was the death of the magazine industry – it wasn't. In fact, what the internet – and later social media platforms – did for magazine journalism was give it a swift, hard, forceful kick up its backside.

Magazine digital offerings had to up their game. Be smart. Lure audiences, old and new, back into the fold. The rise of social media meant everyone had a voice and a means to communicate to the world, if you were a fan you could see into their lives via Twitter and Instagram. Sure, it was controlled access but hey, it was ultimate voyeurism.

Social media also meant magazine offerings were under extreme scrutiny. Incorrect facts were swiftly highlighted in 140 characters or less on Twitter. Get a celebrity magazine cover story wrong and the subjects, the celebs themselves, took to social media to denounce it. You lost credibility and readers in an instant.

With the stakes higher than ever before we lost Company, Bliss, Sugar, More, FHM, Zoo and Nuts. Others are struggling – Time Inc's Now magazine is one of those crawling to the next circulation dip: last ABCs saw it post 109,661 – a dip of 21.8 per cent year on year.

And, although Bauer's Heat magazine has also dropped from the dizzying heights of 700k plus a week in its heyday, to now posting ABCs of 144,074 – a drop of 22.3 per cent, year on year, it has nailed the brand extension survival path. While others were playing at it, Heat launched its own online offering, Heatworld, alongside a radio and TV station. Such foresight should ensure the brand lives on, even if the print product continues to falter on the newsstand.

The last year (2015/16) has seen some magazines truly evolve into the digital content arena: Hearst's Cosmopolitan saw its US issue strike a deal with Snapchat and the UK title followed suit. Its editor says many of the audience who find their content on Snapchat Discover don't even know a magazine exists. But, if they engage with their content on that social platform, perhaps that doesn't matter.

Bauer's Grazia has also struggled with falling sales figures – the last ABCs recorded 138,992 but, as a brand, it is still powerful and is forging ahead with digital innovation, launching shopping apps, running Facebook Live events and, like the 'freemium' giveaway Stylist, is also maximising its fashion credibility by hosting events around fashion – its playing to its strengths and I hope it wins out.

The digital revolution also created a new publishing model: launch online then go into print. But it's not for everyone. This model works well for niche markets. End of.

Square Up Media is a classic example of a runaway specialist interest success story. Foodism launched first as a website in 2013 and in 2014 later launched as a stand-alone glossy print magazine. Recent ABCs showed it had a circulation of 109,296.

American music site Pitchfork started life as a website – it is now also available as a quarterly print magazine.

The quality end of the market is also faring well: Vogue and Elle are holding their own. The ever-useful Good Housekeeping is unbreakable and special-interest magazines are shifting significant numbers, too.

In recent years magazine launches have been in the specialist/niche sector - from the multi-platform health and fitness title, Coach, from Dennis publishing, to Puzzler Media launching Candy Crush in print (yes, really), to News UK pushing out a monthly film magazine, Popcorn, in association with Sky.

The common strand with these and all the other magazines is they aren't the multi-million pound glittery launches of old. They're appealing to a smaller, highly engaged, often commercially sweet, audience and so their profitability and their chance of success is a little brighter.

Online lifestyle launches aimed clearly at modern women such as The Pool – which is faring well with a sturdy 500k uniques less than a year since launch – and Bauer's The Debrief is also a success (albeit on a smaller scale) for the no-bullshit 20-something city chick.

So, the magazine industry isn't dead. It's different. Budgets will never be what they once were because advertising is also different. Media spend, once clearly defined and split between TV, print and commercial radio. Now? Now it's split across so many distribution channels – Facebook, Twitter, YouTube, Google,

TV, digital TV, radio, bloggers, vloggers… it's a bloody battle to secure decent ad revenue.

Any print title has to be strong online, in print and on social. Modern journalists must be multi-talented story-tellers – able to envisage how to bring their words to life in a way that is far beyond just words. They must be able to write brilliantly, report on camera, shoot their own images, edit and crop their own footage and write copy that works with both SEO and social in mind.

Publishing, and magazine publishing in particular, has stared death in the face.

It's seen what it has to do to survive and at long last the fight-back it starting with the kind of passion, skill and dogged determination that makes it such a stimulating industry to work in.

## Note on the contributor

Joely Carey has worked across a number of newspaper and magazine titles including the News of the World, The Sun, The Sun on Sunday, Chat magazine, That's Life!, and was Editorial Director of News UK's award-winning Fabulous magazine. She has also worked as a specialist digital content consultant for Trinity Mirror and Bauer Media's portfolio of print and digital titles. She now works as Editor in Chief for an award-winning content agency based in Soho, London, where she develops, launches and runs digital platforms for brands, and as a digital content consultant and social media strategist for brands. In 2016 she collected the award for Content Initiative of the Year for Sainsbury's latest food platform, which was also shortlisted in the website of the year category. She was shortlisted as Editor of the Year (Branded Consumer) by the British Society of Magazine Editors.

# If print is dying, nobody's told the car mags

**Car magazines were once big. Today, they are not as big. But the best have business units bigger than the print title ever was – and, according to Richard Aucock, the magazine is the halo product that adds the authority to the brand**

Michael Ward is upbeat. He edits Auto Italia magazine, a long-running title for enthusiast of Italian cars. The title is about to mark its 250th edition with a 44-page boost, taking it up to its biggest-ever pagination. He says sales are up to 10,000 a month. Advertising is up. Newsstand sales are up. Is print dying, I ask him? Far from it, he replies. And he's so positive about the future of the magazine brand, he's just bought the company.

This is the surprising story coming from some titles in automotive publishing. Far from fading away, specialist titles continue to draw readers and continue for now to earn their place on the newsstands, not least the supermarkets, which these days stock a range of niche titles almost unimaginable in previous years (and we know how mercenary supermarkets can be).

If print is dying, nobody's told these car mags.

Of course, reality check: motoring magazine sales are not what they were. Indeed, they are half what they were. The big weeklies could claim 80,000-100,000 a decade ago. The numbers were multiples more before then. A popular car monthly could even sell 250,000 issues.

Autocar, however, recorded 33,521 in ABC January-December 2015, and Auto Express had a certified readership of 45,150 between July-December 2015. The weeklies used to be clear of the monthlies, but today they are similar: 43,564 for CAR, 40,215 for Evo, 39,371 for Octane. Two stand out: Classic & Sports Car on 67,356 and Top Gear on 114,973. The classic car industry is thriving at the moment, and Classic & Sports Car is a title with heritage; Top Gear, well, is a brand in its own right.

The decline is being arrested, though. 'Print is definitely not dead,' says Steve Fowler, editorial director at Dennis Motoring. 'We have a loyal subscriber base and, although news-stand sales are tough, we are holding our own.'

Steve Cropley, editor-in-chief at Haymarket's Autocar, agrees that while it depends on whom you talk to, there are successes. 'What Car? posted a circulation increase recently, after we redesigned it and did some judicious promotion, including on the What Car? website.' It does depend on whom you talk to. He adds: 'Other well-known and long-lived magazines are finding the decline is lessening, though not all of them by any means. But there's no pretending we're going back to some golden age of printing pages.'

The reality in the automotive industry, that sales aren't what they were and declines may continue, is recognised. However, there's almost surprise amongst some, and certainly gratification, that the business case for print remains strong. It's ageing, but not dying.

**Offline to online**

As soon as you mention print's decline, publishers reference their websites, which these days complement print rather than just recycle it. The big titles have readerships of millions, giving automotive more exposure than it's ever had. They are not simple news and review sites, either. They have ever-sophisticated buying tools alongside editorial content. Increasingly, bigger titles are exploring broader ecommerce opportunities, even car sales.

Dennis Motoring owns Buyacar. James Tye, CEO of Dennis Publishing, told Media Briefing[1] that Buyacar was purchased initially to generate valuable leads for new car sales which could be sold to manufacturers, but it quickly developed into a transactional product. 'If you transact cars, that generates a lot of revenue, because they're big ticket items.'

The Media Briefing explained that, while Dennis still saw the lion's share of its revenue coming from print focused brands, the balance was shifting as a result of ecommerce growth. 'At Dennis and other successful publishers, there are no hard-and-fast rules for the platforms on which its brands need to exist. Gradually, that culture of a print/digital divide is disappearing.'

Top Gear magazine is a striking example of this. A combination of online and 31 international print editions gives it a readership of more than 9m globally: there are almost 2m readers in the UK alone, coverage that you could only dream of solely with print – but which is well supported by the high-quality print title that often commands such a prominent position on the news-stands. Top Gear also has a successful quarterly reviews magazine, the print-only New Car Buyers Guide, giving it added presence on the shelves and appealing to in-market car buyers who may not know what's best to buy, but do know Top Gear and use it to help them.

Of course, Top Gear sales generally go up when the TV show is on: such casual readers will not necessarily stumble across a website, but a magazine with a strong cover carrying the stars of the show is bound to appeal. Do not underestimate the power of a strong brand when selling print magazines. Fowler concurs. 'With Evo, we have a high quality, very focused magazine with a strong brand. We know the core market and the magazine succeeds because of this.' It's those titles without a strong brand that will struggle, he warns.

## The promotional power of print

One of the first rules of magazine publishing, that of a good front cover, is more important than ever today, say those in automotive. Ward cannot stress highly enough the appeal of a strong cover with the right type of car, which can make or break monthly sales. Cars are emotive subjects and readers are enthusiastic people: the sheer diversity of motoring means the breadth of appeal and ability to make an instant impact with art-form vehicles is high, particularly within the right brands with the strongest enthusiast followings, undoubtedly helping fuel magazines' continued news-stand presence.

Fowler believes print has a key role to play in brand promotion. 'Magazines do your marketing for you. The front cover is your weekly or monthly billboard of real estate in high footfall places such as supermarkets. They advertise your product. Even if readers don't buy the print magazine but later search for a car and see content produced by a magazine they've heard of, that adds authority.' Magazines today are partly about revenue but also act as part of your wider content offering, he says. 'There are clear benefits from a brand marketing point of view.'

Perhaps partly because of this, the appeal of print to advertisers is another reason why car magazines are not dying just yet. The automotive sector is one of the biggest marketing spenders and a prominent DPS, inside front cover or back page in a car magazine can still command rates publishers cannot ignore.

Tony Whitehorn, president of Hyundai Car UK, admits that marketing spend has shifted. The firm used to allocate 80-85 per cent of its budget on traditional media, including print. Today, that's more like 60 per cent. There's now more social, more search, more sponsorship.

But automotive manufacturers do still value print because of its enthusiast readership. If you are reading a car magazine, you are likely to be an influencer and car manufacturers still want to reach you. Indeed, there's perhaps more conviction about the continued value of automotive print within manufactures than in the agencies that place their campaigns, grumble some. And it's agencies doing the buying, not the manufacturers.

It's undeniable that print is harder to track than digital. You can't target reader profiles in anything like the way you can with programmatic. You won't receive reports. You have no idea on exposure times or whether readers saw your ad and then went onto the website to find out more. But the same applies for all print publications. Automotive's advantage is its specialist audience. 'Car companies still see the loyalty car enthusiast have for magazines like Autocar, and continue to want to appeal to these people,' confirms Cropley. It's a matter of making sure the agency lets them.

## From classifieds to native

But what about making money from magazines? One traditional profits-driver of some car magazines, classified ads, is now dead, says Cropley, killed by websites. There are still successes – 'Our Classic & Sports Car is still very successful, because its readers like small ads.' The same applies for niche specialist titles. But although advertisers in general still see value, it's generally less than it used to be.

Gone are the days of the deathly dull advertorial, with car magazines frequently now offering visually alluring and, dare I say it, genuinely appealing branded content. The maturity of online native is fostering creativity in print as well, activating a rich new revenue stream that can ensure car magazines still earn their keep.

Cropley does sounds a warning here, though: 'A gigantic challenge is maintaining the editorial purity.' This is probably one of the biggest challenges for motoring magazines today, he says. It's vital not to blur the line between editorial and advertising for money. 'Such activities ease the difficulty of delivering the big profits successful publishers have traditionally been used to, but in our experience they are disliked by readers who are sensitive to this stuff and disapprove. They value editorial probity, and we'd better remember that.'

One way to demonstrate your independence is with awards. All the major titles run them, and their associated awards events are highly profitable. Car manufacturers like awards from recognisable titles as they can use them in advertising and PR. Cue the news-stand presence of print, guaranteeing far greater recognition amongst casual car buyers than online titles. It's back to what Fowler says about the supermarket and newsagent being your billboard – and, perhaps, revenue from successful awards events helping sustain this presence.

## Remember your reader

How else can you continue to survive in such a marketplace? Firstly, by being realistic, advises Fowler. 'The car enthusiast is changing' he says. 'People like us are fewer and fewer between. Today, there are more everyday enthusiasts – people who love cars but don't want to hear about every tiny detail. They want more bite-sized content that will leave them informed without forcing them to read an eight-page feature.'

Those who fail to consider their reader will struggle to survive. An obvious lesson? Perhaps not when editorial teams are such hardcore enthusiasts, says Fowler. 'Focus on what your customer wants. All too often in this business, people create magazines for themselves rather than their audience.' It's a matter of natural enthusiasts thinking more like businesspeople. Easier said than done.

Ward could not agree more. 'We're a specialist magazine and we're close to our audience. We know what works. The bits that we don't know, the sales figures soon tell us. Our core audience is loyal but we'll get more readers if we put an Alfa Romeo on the cover than a Lancia.' The car geek in Ward might tell him to put a Lancia on the cover but, although it's his magazine, it's not for him. An Alfa Romeo it is, then.

Co-existing with other channels is also crucial for magazines. Cropley says Haymarket's titles do this pretty well: 'Better than logic suggests they should, given that one of them is a freebie. All staff members work for both media in our place, and we promote one in the other when we have something sensible to promote. You'll find a "What's on the site" section in the mag, and vice versa. It's worth doing.' Just remember your editorial purity, stresses Cropley. The people who have handed over their hard-earned for your print title 'value editorial probity, and we'd better remember that'.

## The authority on cars
With seemingly more car magazines on the shelves than ever before – and certainly more car magazines in high-footfall locations such as supermarkets than ever – print in automotive seems not to be dying just yet. Yes, it has declined. But stronger titles are now arresting that decline and continue to hold their own.

Both Cropley and Fowler agree that there remains a core readership who simply prefer reading a magazine on the train. If someone picks Auto Express up at Waterloo, reads it and then leaves it on the seat for the next person, says Fowler, that's a result. Don't forget the people in the bath either, adds Cropley. 'These people perceive that while websites are great for info, magazines still have value for leisurely reading.' The lifestyle content of automotive lends itself well to this.

Cropley continues: 'We hear more and more from an "I-like-print" faction who would like to see us invest in the products, even if we have to charge a bit more for them. There are some examples of this and it has worked. You have to examine each case individually, but some people still like print.'

Then there's the authority that you still get from being a magazine. 'Print publications are still perceived, even by those who run radio and TV media, as the senior partners when it comes to comment,' says Cropley. 'That's why radio, web and TV still have "What the papers say" sections, which have a good following.' During the Volkswagen emissions scandal, which erupted in September 2015, Autocar editors appeared frequently on TV and radio offering opinion – as authoritative experts. Brand exposure, plentiful promotion. The UK automotive industry is among the country's biggest, employing 900,000 people. It's a core of UK plc and mainstream media will thus seek regular commentary on it.

The same is true at automotive manufacturers. Copies of influential car magazines are still delivered to the desks of senior executives who, in turn, use the British press as a bellwether. The power of the leaders of car companies seeing value in what you do is not to be underestimated.

One person from a UK car importer told me that as soon as a new car is reviewed by the British press, the Asian HQ will get in touch with them to analyse in detail the results. UK motoring reviewers and titles command authority within car companies. Publishers need to consider how to capitalise on this to help print survive.

## Conclusion

Not all car magazines will survive. It will be a struggle for some, says Fowler. News-stands are competitive places and you need a core, consistent customer base because 'if retailers get more from selling tins of beans than your magazine, they'll take it off the shelves'.

For this reason, it will be particularly tough for once-larger titles that are now smaller titles, set up without the ultra-niche infrastructure that makes more specialist titles financially still viable. Fowler predicts that there almost certainly will be fewer car magazines in the future.

And there's no one answer. The business changes fast. Out of the blue during writing this, Haymarket announced the sale of its entire motorsport magazine division which has been a part of the group for almost half a century. It's a seismic event that shows how quickly things evolve.

Cropley stresses: 'This is an evolving situation. There are no absolutes. It could be very different as soon as next year.' The art of running Autocar and What Car? – 'and the Facebook, Twitter, YouTube and Instagram outlets we also maintain – is to be ready to change emphasis'. But the emphasis is not going to shift from print for it just yet. 'For now, print remains very profitable per unit of effort, so we continue.'

As for Ward, he's already planning what else he can do with his new business. But everything has print at its core. That's what makes the money, so that's where his efforts will be going. It's not easy, and it's harder work than ever, but other publishers of strong titles share his optimism. It's those with weaker titles and brands that will suffer first.

'I'd say print has a future,' says Cropley. 'If you're selective.'

## Notes

[1] See https://www.themediabriefing.com/article/dennis-publishing-s-james-tye-on-culture-change-in-consumer-publishing

## Note on the contributor

Richard Aucock is an automotive writer with two decades' experience in the industry. After studying Mechanical Engineering at Birmingham University, he wrote for motorsport magazine Autosport before joining content experts Motoring Research. Today, he is Managing Director of the company, which provides copy, data and services for clients such as Microsoft, Top Gear, Pistonheads, City A.M. and others. Autonomous technology and the business side of the automotive industry are key specialisms. For 2017, Richard is a juror on the World Car Awards.

# From rags to niches: the Bauer way to avoid death by print

**Tim Pollard explains how Bauer Media seized the digital moment and invested in its digital motoring brands to create vibrant new businesses**

It will come as no surprise to anyone reading this book to be told that we are living through a period of intense change transforming the media landscape. My two decades in journalism have witnessed the industry turned inside out and upside down, cajoled this way and that by external forces well beyond the control of any publishing executives in Fleet Street, Wapping or Peterborough.

When I joined Cardiff Journalism School in the newspaper course intake of 1996, we were launching our media careers in the calm before the storm. The Daily Telegraph's first website, the Electronic Telegraph, had launched quietly in November 1994. We still used manual typewriters and a waxing machine took pride of place in course tutor John Foscolo's production cupboard. But there were ranks of beige Apple Macs too, sporting early desktop publishing software such as the bafflingly basic Talbot Newswrite. Though we didn't know it, we were about to witness the changing of the media guard.

Come graduation day, every one of us landed a job in real journalism; the majority on local or regional newspapers, a couple joined national magazines and the lucky few waltzed straight onto Fleet Street. Nineteen years later and at least a fifth are no longer employed in journalism, the lure of PR dollar, less stressful, more dependable careers outside the media or family duties bringing journalistic roles to an end. Many blame the uncertainty of the media revolution for their exit. We have truly lived through – and continue to experience – significant structural change.

But one hack's change is another's opportunity. There is reason to be optimistic: successful journalists with chameleon-like tendencies have a knack of reinventing themselves. I heartily believe there is space in the new media landscape for old-fashioned journalistic graft and editorial nous; for scintillating subbing and headline writing skills to lure in casual browsers; and for publishers adept at building communities of readers and communicating with them

289

regularly – just online, rather than on paper. Where there's audience, there's commercial opportunity.

That's my experience working at Bauer Media for the past decade. Allow me to explain why we believe we are building successful digital publishing businesses around highly targeted, niche audiences, designed with longevity to weather the storms gripping our industry. Here's what I've learned.

## 1) Know your mission statement

It sounds obvious, but so many publishing enterprises either lose sight of their original mission statement or never had one in the first place. Any successful web publishing business should be able to write on a beer mat their *raison d'être*. Ours at Parkers.co.uk is dead simple. We want to help Britain's car buyers find the best possible vehicle for their needs and budgets. It really is that simple.

This focus is instilled across the team and underpins everything we do. We even plastered the mantra across a giant 65in screen above the editorial desks. A motivated, focused team is a much easier one to pull in the right direction, after all.

At Parkers that mission statement is used to sense-check everything we do: from daily editorial conference, where every story is cross-checked for user-usefulness, to commercial brainstorms and development road maps. If any plan doesn't feel like it is helping the great British public buy their next car, the chances are it's not going to improve our business.

## 2) Understand your digital audience

This is as fundamental as understanding your mission statement. Knowing your reader has long been a staple of print publishing – and it's even more important in digital publishing. But there's one crucial difference: we have all the data in the world to deepen our understanding of how real people actually behave.

Anyone who has worked in print publishing will be familiar with the beard-stroking and black art of interpreting magazine or newspaper ABC sales data. Guesswork is another way of describing some of what I have witnessed in print. Why did one issue sell, when another flopped? The honest answer is, you often have no idea. Yet senior publishers concoct elaborate theories, blaming rival cover stories or promotions, unseasonal heatwaves or the competitive landscape to support gut instinct and/or political back stories. There's nowhere to hide in digital publishing, where the raw stats are available for all to see.

At Bauer Media we open up analytics to the entire team – everyone from junior staff writers to the board has access to data. It's unforgivingly transparent. We all see which stories sizzle, and which sink. The popular content with huge dwell times and long scroll depths, as well as the pages which disappear without trace, sparking a woefully high bounce rate. Knowing your readers inside out is much easier when you can see what floats their boat.

One of the most valuable lessons I have learned is this: digital publishing is devilishly simple: see what works – and then do more of it. Ditch what isn't popular and learn from your mistakes. Research every decision with analytics, train your team in data interpretation and surround yourself with team members who see data as their friend, not their enemy. Too many journalists are suspicious of analytics, although that is slowly changing.

### 3) Hire creative advertising geniuses

So you have found yourself a genuine user need that you are uniquely placed to answer. You are convinced you stand a good chance of building a strong community whose needs you can service brilliantly, repeatedly and – hopefully – uniquely. Now the hard part. How on earth do you monetise this audience? Especially in an age when ad rates are collapsing through the floor, as agencies become more sophisticated with micro-targeting, programmatic ad networks depress the prices commanded by once-valued audiences and technology such as ad-blocking create new headaches with every passing month.

Who would want to be in digital sales with that cursed backdrop? Fortunately for us, Bauer Media – and other publishers – are slowly building an army of salespeople who have taken the leap alongside their editorial counterparts into this new data-driven world. The risks are huge online, but rewards can be significant too, especially if you come up with a compelling content proposition that rivals cannot match.

It's true to say that the rules of online advertising are even more fluid than in print. The days of the humble leaderboard, MPU and skyscraper ad are well and truly past, complicated by the addition of multiple ad placements, sticky display units, Google ads, third-party sponsored content networks, takeovers, MPU2s, retargeting on- and off-site plus all manner of disruptive methods designed to give advertisers stand-out in a crowded marketplace.

It takes skilful teams to tiptoe the line between helping users with useful, carefully targeted advertising and the aesthetic mess that'll result if you overload the page with too many commercial interruptions. The best digital ad sales people understand this tension and can think laterally around the problem – using data at the heart of their arguments. Unlike in print, you really can micro-target exactly the audience a client wants online and we are getting better and better at doing that.

Bauer has invested heavily in new ad platforms on both Parkers.co.uk and Carmagazine.co.uk, where we can serve adverts not just against a given manufacturer's models, but also against its rivals'. Right down to the level of detail where it can promote against competition's hybrid petrol-electric estate cars but not the diesel ones. Plus we have added new services so we are less dependent on advertising money: vehicle valuations, used-car classified adverts, leasing deals and insurance quotes all help diversify our revenue streams.

### 4) Go social: Thinking outside your own walled garden

Gone are the days of relying solely on people coming to our websites to consume content. We have to market the hell out of it – and the journalists themselves are the brand's marketers-in-chief and social media warriors. Understanding your user and how to talk to them on social media is a crucial skill nowadays, and we are constantly striving to spark the conversation online across social platforms to drown out our competition's buzz and get our own stories noticed.

We have had great success in this area, growing CAR's Facebook audience from 350,000 in 2014 to 1.2m in 2016. And that's 100 per cent organically, with no paid-for followers, just from publishing compelling picture galleries, posting irresistible links and engaging heavily with our users (not something many traditional print journalists enjoy doing). Combined with a growth spurt on Twitter (we have doubled in the same period to 122,000 followers), it means we are speaking to more people than ever before. At its peak, we were driving nearly 10 per cent of the website's entire traffic from social media.

But it's not just about on-trend social platforms. We have also engaged with our own in-house audiences, accessed from across the Bauer Media portfolio. Parkers' audience development strategy saw it partner with our female-focused sister titles, producing motoring content in association with Grazia, Closer, the Debrief and Mother & Baby. It's a move that other publishers will struggle to replicate and taps into a female audience that car makers are eager to speak to. Publishers who can drive audience around their own portfolio successfully will stand a better chance of winning.

## 5) Scale is important

Big is beautiful in the web world. The biggest advertising wins are reserved for the select few at the top of the ratings lists, with slim pickings for smaller fry. And with the likes of Google and Facebook hoovering up ever more ad money, it's hard work keeping the revenues rolling in.

Parkers.co.uk is consistently one of the UK's biggest motoring editorial websites, drawing 2.5m users a month, consuming some 20m page views (August 2016). At that scale, we are generating revenues well into seven figures annually, making this Bauer's biggest and most profitable website in the UK.

This is the classic business conundrum: the larger, most successful websites attract the lion's share of investment. But there's a need to invest equally in the smaller, more niche brands we publish too. You can't have all your eggs in one basket. The internet has a habit of building up successful brands only to knock 'em down again in remarkably short order. Anyone remember Friends Reunited?

## 6) Know that the only certainty is uncertainty

The pace of change in digital publishing is mind-boggling. Online specialists have to adapt continuously to new working practices, ensuring we meet new demands from search engines such as Google and quickly assimilating new technologies such as Accelerated Mobile Pages (AMP) and the rise of ad blockers. By the time you read this, there will doubtless be even more developments rewriting the rulebook all over again.

Let's drill into one example in more detail. The battle to be at the top of search engine results pages means that digital publishers worship at the altar of Google more than any other service. Around 80 per cent of our traffic arrives at our sites from the search giant and we spend an inordinate amount of time to ensure our stories rank higher on Google than rivals' pages.

But Search Engine Optimisation (SEO) moves at a frightening pace. Best practice evolves weekly and our editorial teams have to adapt constantly to remain relevant. Back in 2014, we realised that we could play Google's results by ensuring writers built Google+ profiles with a picture byline. Result? Any search results page plugged our story with a photograph of the journalist, lending extra authority, stand-out attention and – ultimately – a higher click-through rate to boost our traffic.

Once everyone cottoned on to this, Google unsurprisingly stopped placing author bylines on its results pages. A cynic might suggest it had encouraged hordes of reporters to sign up for profiles on its struggling social network, Google+. But it was certainly another example of how the competitive landscape is forever changing. There are myriad other tricks we now pursue instead, such as researching keywords with sophisticated tools, improving our domain authority and honing every article's metadescriptions to ensure our content wins the all-important click from Google.

## 7) Be prepared to fail

You have to be prepared to push the boundaries in this brave new world of digital publishing – and that can mean occasionally getting things wrong. Contrary to recognised publishing best practice, we are trying to accept that this is fine. The digital mindset should embrace failure as a route to improvement.

It's all to do with risk and reward, and making the most of our agility as digital-first operators. We can conceive ideas, implement, publish and test in less than 24 hours – with reams of data points to guide us whether the development has worked or not. We A/B test often, by concurrently publishing two variants of the same feature to see which one responds best, meaning we can test in real-time different headlines, or colours of tint boxes or navigational signposting around the website. Beta testing is a great way of making informed business decisions.

The important thing is to recognise when failure has occurred, learn from it and remember this when you are planning your next development. In the fast-moving world of web publishing it's all about new ideas. Come up with 20, launch the best 10 and maybe half will work. One might even be a game-changer. But unless you try all of them, and see some flop, you'll never know.

So be prepared to fail. Just make sure you do it quickly, and smartly, using all the tools at your disposal. You'll emerge stronger, and wiser, if you do.

## 8) Focus. Focus. Focus.

How on earth do you retain focus in a world in which you are continually expected to launch new ideas, develop your website and publish a steady flow of compelling written, video and audio content – as well as produce a printed magazine or newspaper, curate all your brand's social media channels and maybe even build a few apps and iPad tablet editions for good measure? No wonder journalists have little time to frequent the pub nowadays.

It's hard to keep all those plates spinning at the desired quality levels in a typically busy modern newsroom. But having the team resolutely focused on the overarching mission statement – it's back to point 1) above again – is crucial for the best chance of success.

Bauer Media came up with a simple way of ensuring there is 100 per cent focus on its digital objectives: it hived off the web publishing team into a new division, named Bauer Xcel. This is a structure unlike many rival publishers in the motoring space, and means that the editorial staff running the websites do not report into the magazine editors, but into a new digital operation. It has increased focus on digital. It has accelerated the pace of change in our websites. And it means that online is not held back by any lingering print-first mentality.

## 9) Employ the smartest journalists

For all the strategic thinking and digital black arts we have discussed, there is one exciting truth at the heart of modern web publishing: brilliant journalism still sells.

The best stories and scoops will generate more clicks than any Facebook quiz or Google page-rank. I am always heartened to see a genuine scoop fly to the top of the analytics feed, proof that good, old-fashioned journalistic graft and story-telling is at the heart of what we do.

So invest in your journalism. Online publishing should not be about churnalism – unique content, brilliantly researched and written is the best single marketing tool any website can have. I firmly believe there will continue to be a demand for fabulous editorial that speaks to real readers' needs, whether it's in print, on a laptop screen or a smartphone. It's what separates us from the mere bloggers.

Digital publishing is at its most exciting when it mixes old-school journalistic insight with the new-tech tools which tell us how people research their next car purchase, what they are searching for and the exact phrase they put into Google. Marrying up the two skillsets, ancient and modern, that's where the magic lies.

## Note on the contributor

Tim Pollard is the Digital Editor-in-Chief of Bauer Media's motoring titles, leading the 14-strong web team on Carmagazine.co.uk and Parkers.co.uk, the publisher's flagship automotive titles. A print veteran turned digital warrior, he studied newspaper journalism at Cardiff Journalism School and started out on the Cambridge Evening News and the News in Portsmouth before switching to magazines and finally digital, via stints on What Car?, Autocar and Microsoft, where he ran four of MSN UK's web channels.

# Make audiences the purchase, not the platform

**Clive Couldwell questions whether the dying print versus today's all-digital debate is a valid one as we begin to understand the fallout from the major changes that have scythed through the business-to-business publishing industry**

Over the last 16 or so years, many business-to-business (b2b) magazines too numerous to mention just didn't innovate and their publishers viewed online as a form of cost-cutting. But print isn't dying. It's one of a number of channels we should be using as part of the modern multimedia publishing model.

Former b2b editor (PC Magazine) and BBC TV Click producer Chris Long says: "Early magazines reinforced opinion of the people reading and writing them. Fast forward to the 1920s where a plethora of magazines cater for all sorts of interests. Reading is part of the culture – partly because there isn't much else.

"All this has changed by the end of WW2. Within 20 odd years, TV, radio and cinema are already ahead of print. Reading for pleasure is still happening but reading for information is dying off," he says.

Incidentally, newspapers were fighting a decline that actually started around 1965. Although, interestingly with the Daily Mail increasing its circulation in 1992 and then coming down to where it started by 2015, everyone else in the UK just slowly switched off newspapers.

However, Long maintains when we talk about 'publishing' these days we should really be saying 'making money out of engaging people'. Publishing isn't about print, it's about monetising a product you can either sell or sell adverts around to make a profit. It has nothing to do with printed words on any kind of page. The problem is 'print people' don't understand this.

"These people are so hooked up on 'print' – from printing on paper to printing on screen – they miss the obvious. Print (printing on paper) was a technology which persuaded people to part with cash to make money for those who produced it, but now they can do the same thing and look at pictures or listen. Printing on paper is old technology for what the publishers were doing. Its day has gone," says Long.

The new publishing paradigm will almost certainly use reading as part of its game plan, but not what people used to call 'print'. And here is the big reveal according to Long. When people talk about print they don't include 'read' in its meaning.

"They talk about distribution, colour pieces, knowing the audience, and so on. This is the gargantuan failure of thinking from those in the print business. Reading is at the core of 'print' - how people read, why they read, their reading ability, reading age, vocabulary. They were at the heart of the mechanism of selling magazines, papers, books, whatever. Alas the print types made so much money from print they forgot the key principal of the exercise (quite literally in as much as energy expended) is getting people to read. What if they are no longer as interested in reading their words?

"Books sales keep up because books are fun, and radio, goodness, radio is going through another golden age – and you can see why? It is simpler to listen to for information or just have in the background so you listen to that rather than go to a magazine or newspaper.

"And because of this drift away from getting your information from the traditional delivery systems, the internet steps up, because these internet people aren't in publishing or 'print' they are an information diaspora doing it for the craic, doing just what print people did, but to much smaller groups and not so much with the words," Long continues.

"So now you have a fragmented readership being sated by idiots of varying degrees on the web. They are doing just what papers used to do, engage people, but they are doing it for free and instead of talking to millions they talk to hundreds, or thousands or hundreds of thousands... but there are lots of people providing this information, and people are learning to not bother with the reading of the papers and magazines but go online for their hit of information," adds Long with some passion.

"It's pretty simple," he says. "If there is a way to scratch the itch newspapers et al have been creating, it doesn't involve sitting down and concentrating on something printed. Publishing means entertainment, like just about anything else. The platform for that entertainment will develop with the culture. To try and define it with words and concepts from old technology is to court disaster.

"The term 'multimedia publishing models', when used by print people, makes the same mistake. They mean something with a bit of video, audio, some pictures and print, not realising the print bit doesn't attract the growing number of people who wouldn't dream of reading a 3,000 word article – even on Taylor Swift."

### Exploring different b2b sectors...

Some turmoil came from certain print publications not realising how quickly the mix of internet, tablet computers, reasonably priced 4G data packages along with extensive Wi-Fi would allow consumption of online publications virtually anywhere.

And if a competitor offered more extensive, cheaper or free information online the original print publication would suffer. Once newspapers realised the importance of online the question for most became whether it had to be provided free or could be charged for, says Matthew May, Director of the Media Arm consultancy and former b2b editor (What Micro, Information Strategy) who ran The Times technology sections in the 80s and 90s.

"That jury is still out with The Times struggling to succeed by charging for its online (The Sun has given up trying) and The Guardian suffering heavily from being unable to attract enough advertising to make its free online news work. It is now resorting to the equivalent of a begging letter on its website. "If you use it, if you like it, why not pay for it? It's only fair. Give to the Guardian."

Broadsheets were typically assumed to get half their production costs from advertising, unlike tabloids where circulation figures tended to be a multiple of the broadsheets and so the revenue from the cover price was far more significant.

"The decline in broadsheet readership has become a vicious circle that means their print versions are unlikely to make long term commercial sense unless they want to print them as a loss leader and marketing tool for their online versions," says May.

"For b2b publications wanting to charge subscriptions the growth of online meant the question of whether nearly identical information was available for free elsewhere became even more important. It was not just b2b. Private Eye, for example, has never put its content online and is sufficiently unique that print sales have steadily increased.

"Other b2b publications, such as Total Telecom, used online as an opportunity to increase the amount of daily news and press release information available such that a subscription service worked. It is still able to charge nearly £500 a year. Similar information is available online for free but one important factor is the time saving for telecom industry executives from its collation to a single source accompanied by an easily searchable archive," adds May.

Many other b2b publications are unable to attract sufficient subscriptions to make charging work. In this case both web and print may have to become a branding and marketing tool for events such as conferences, exhibitions, and seminars. Just as music makers can no longer make money from selling albums many can survive from the ticket prices when playing live.

"But free print can sometimes now work better than charging as many readers will increasingly not pay for what they can read for free on the web. Yet new free daily city newspapers and free local papers have appeared. But they have to be produced with far less staff to make economic sense," adds May.

"The problem for b2b, as elsewhere, is that cost cutting usually leads to a drop in quality and that can become a vicious spiral of perpetual reductions in costs resulting in a weaker and weaker product that eventually becomes extinct."

## Looking at other fundamentals

Going back to the very early days of the internet all publishers – both b2b and b2c - saw the internet rather like a supplement to the main/original brand and as such thought it would be purely ad funded.

"Most put the main effort into the print products and sold the internet as an add-on, inadvertently starting a problem still playing out now – open web sites, with an ad funded model," says John Barnes, chief digital officer at Incisive Media, Director and former chairman of the Association of Online Publishers (AOP).

This was best exemplified by recruitment as most early digital recruitment advertising was bundled free with print to keep up market share and win business.

"If you think about the positions both Computer Weekly and Computing held in the recruitment space it is extraordinary to now see them both with no recruitment revenue at all. In the day Computing/Computer Weekly would be £12-15 million per annum each. Weekly exited the space before Computing, having struggled with the shift from print recruitment ads to digital recruitment ads," recalls Barnes.

"Advertisers initially welcomed free internet as a sweetener. As the internet started to pull more results and was trackable this allowed recruiters to measure return on investment and they started asking for internet-only prices. As print revenue was significant, the price was often quoted as the same, but the problem was it had been positioned as free initially so advertisers said they wanted it for very low cost, and worse, new online-only players, such as Jobserve had launched and slashed prices to win business, offering job listings for as little as £5, when a single job ad in print may have been as much as £5,000 a page. First to go online only was contract jobs then inevitably full-time roles followed."

Barnes uses this example not because it is how all recruitment went - we still have strong positions in many markets but nothing like the revenues in the late 80s and mid 90s – but it is indicative of the issue which digital still faces, that it is seen as cheaper because often it was positioned as free initially. In some respects you are still seeing this playing out with the paywall/freemium debate and all the issues facing publishers around ad blocking, data collection and privacy.

## So why did some magazines go to the wall and others didn't?

The main reasons according to Barnes are:

1. Some markets, such as technology, were in the eye of the storm, recruitment and comparisons/reviews combined with tech-savvy early adopters

2. Others had weak print positions exposed by the web goldrush

3. Many publishers had poor data strategies so could use alternatives such as email or direct marketing to fill in revenue gaps

4. Lots didn't innovate at all or fast enough

5. US players land grabbed UK/Europe having adopted internet earlier

6. Not enough invested and saw internet as a cheap way to make bigger profits.

**So those which survived and succeeded more or less did the opposite:**

1. They did innovate and developed multiple revenue streams

2. They invested in tech and digital people early on and built a reputation for innovation and career development that attracted and retained good people

3. They almost certainly went through a period of having digital-only teams competing with print for budgets/revenue/best people/content

4. They developed their niche well and made it easy to understand and buy

5. They launched new products/solutions for old models and redefined what their media offer was

6. They acquired more able publishers and brands.

"Over the last 15 years digital and print teams have been combined, separated, put in different locations even and have over the last three to five years slowly come back together," says Barnes. "This is true of what we have done at Incisive/VNU and best exemplified by our flagship brand, Risk.net. We expressed this as the print tail wagging the digital dog, the shift from offline to online had been so immense our organisation and focus didn't reflect this. I think this is true of many b2b publishers and something I have witnessed time and time again at the AOP."

With now more of a focus on one team producing content for multiple channels (print, web, mobile, tablet editions email services and audio/video), as well as taking on the role of content marketers, using social media channels such as Twitter, Facebook, YouTube and Linkedin, with some now also including pinterest and Instagram (both used extensively by the FT, Economist and Forbes), print and digital sit happily together.

Most publishers who have a well rounded strategy see web as the main publishing medium, and apps and print as curated editions. Simply put the web is unfinishable in that most sites house tens of thousands of articles and add to this archive daily, so the web is either used by readers to find content they need, searching for relevant articles, or use it to keep abreast of what is happening in their markets, much as the old weekly trade press was used.

"This in turn has led to many weeklies going through a cycle of reducing pagination, paper quality and ultimately frequency to monthlies. These monthlies usually have bigger paginations and investments have been made in print quality and paper stock," continues Barnes.

A good example of this is Barnes' Post Magazine http://www.incisivemedia. com/our-news/insurance-post-embraces-digital-first-world-enhances-offering-first-class-monthly-print-magazine/ or Computing). In effect they are long-form reading vehicles, where the web is much more short-form, and are curated by editors to give readers, who are usually also web subscribers/visitors the must-read articles.

"Most also look at the concept of 'finishability' in that too many pages are seen by some subscribers as a bad thing and they can't read it all. The Economist has done a lot of work in this area and concluded there is an optimum issue size, and if it was regularly exceeded subscription renewals fell.

"It is also the criticism leveled at the Sunday papers with too many sections." (http://www.niemanlab.org/2015/04/the-economists-tom-standage-on-digital-strategy-and-the-limits-of-a-model-based-on-advertising/).

So what this has led to is seeing different channels offering different usage and reading behaviours as per this slide below:

## Making audience the purchase, not the platform

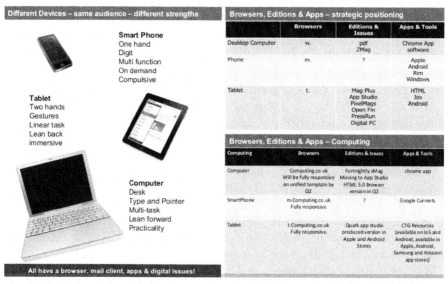

"Given this shift to digital, print-only businesses are seen as much less valuable and print-only businesses would expect a four-to-six times valuation on profit whereas digital-only businesses will be seen as 10 to 20 times and a blended model something like nine to 15 times," maintains Barnes.

"As such most businesses are trying to have a strong digital focus, use print tactically for this curated role alongside apps, and many are investing in print as it is seen as a valuable subscriber benefit, but equally effort is directed to selling digital subscriptions or collection of deep data on users as this paid subs model, as well as deep knowledge of users, is seen as the real value. As such b2b publishers are well placed as data has always been our thing."

Finally, according to Aly Warner, freelance PR consultant, b2b journalist and editor (Marketing, Marketing Event, Promotions & Incentives, and Luxury Travel): "The vast majority of b2b magazines now have a website for their publication, but it appears the chief concern for editors I speak to is how to use that portal, either as a means of news distribution or for advertising revenue and enquiries. Giving away free news online remains their chief concern I feel. And the debate about who writes the online news, print journalists or web editors, is a hot potato too."

"The eco argument against print appears to be strong, with email messages invariably urging recipients not to print their message, underlining the impression in everyone's mind that print is a bad thing and certainly not for the Green enthusiasts.

"I think the subject of a magazine has a great deal to do whether it will survive in print. Some target audiences are still averse to new technology and prefer the magazine form.

"The future of print is assured for at least the next generation, for example, my own 18 year-old daughter is obsessed with her mobile/laptop but curiously won't use a Kindle, prefers the touch and feel of a printed book, and is aware of the health implications of too much work on screen, which she has taken on board as a healthy lifestyle."

## References and sources

http://www.incisivemedia.com/our-news/incisive-voted-best-digital-publisher-uk-peers-record-third-time/

http://www.niemanlab.org/2014/05/the-leaked-new-york-times-innovation-report-is-one-of-the-key-documents-of-this-media-age/

https://www.theguardian.com/media/2016/aug/21/newspaper-magazine-abcs-gawker-trump-bannon?CMP=share_btn_tw

https://www.themediabriefing.com/article/what-is-the-point-of-the-news-media

http://www.thedrum.com/opinion/2016/07/28/times-editor-john-witherow-how-its-paywall-paying-and-why-he-thinks-guardian-will

http://fortune.com/2016/08/08/john-oliver-newspaper-journalism-investifarted/

## Note on the contributor

Clive Couldwell is a UK-based consultant, editor, journalist and published Formula One author. He is also a former editor of Which Computer? magazine who launched and fronted the first business TV service for the Information Technology (IT) industry, The Computer Channel. Currently, he's editing the leading industry title for the audio visual industry, AV Magazine and its digital service, avinteractive.com.

# The progressive left: Better read than dead

**The alternative, activist press is certainly alive – with many progressive groups still producing their own journals. Richard Lance Keeble focuses on the London-based Peace News which has been publishing since 1936, and the Washington-based news website CounterPunch.org. And he interviews PN's joint editor Milan Rai and CounterPunch's editor Jeffrey St Clair on their publishing strategies**

Walk into Housman's Bookshop, at 5 Caledonian Road, North London, just round the corner from King's Cross station, head for the back and there before you is shelf upon shelf bursting with newspapers and magazines. Every branch of the progressive, international left appears to have its own journal: there's the glossy New Internationalist, Race and Class, Morning Star, Socialist Worker, Red Pepper, Palestine News, The Chartist, Marxist Revival, The Humanist, Peace Matters, International Socialist, Monthly Review, New Left Review – to name but a few. So print is certainly not dead yet on the left!

Keeping afloat amidst that tidal wave of titles is Peace News which carries the logo prominently: 'For non-violent revolution'. First published in 1936, its 24-page tabloid August/September 2016 edition (Nos 2596-2597) splashed on the front page with 'Brexit: Reasons to be cheerful: Let's use this upsurge of energy to root out racism and classism'. Headlines indicating important stories inside confirm the lively, newsy, informed, international feel of the journal: 'Chilcot: What they left out', 'Post-Brexit: How to get the bomb out of Scotland', 'Orlando: It's when we're winning…' According to joint editor Milan Rai (2010: 211):

> For *Peace News*, citizen journalism has meant activist journalism, with self-reporting by large numbers of social movement activists through the years… Throughout the past 30 years, a staple of PN coverage has been self-documentation by members of various peace camps around Britain, most famously Greenham Common Women's Peace Camp in the 1980s

and now including Faslane nuclear submarine base in Scotland and the Atomic Weapons establishment in Aldermaston, Berkshire.

Drawing from the 'propaganda model' of Noam Chomsky and Edward Herman (1979: 69-79), Rai suggests there is considerable room for 'leakiness' in the corporate media and for 'small fragments of disruptive information to bob up in the onrushing river of propaganda' (ibid). Accordingly, he says Peace News promotes an important form of 'counter journalism':

> The purpose of journals such as Peace News, then, is precisely to search the output of the mass media with diligence and a sceptical eye, cutting through the mass of misrepresentation and fraud to discover nuggets that can help citizens to better understand – and to more effectively alter – the world in which we are living and acting (Rai 2010: 217).

Interestingly, Peace News also runs a lively, attractive website (at http://peacenews.info/), complete with a supportive quotation from the American maverick intellectual and political activist Noam Chomsky: 'Peace News has compiled an exemplary record ... its tasks have never been more critically important than they are today.'

To explore the issues more generally, I recently interviewed Milan Rai on why print has survived at Peace News.

**RLK**: Tell us, Milan, your thinking behind PN's decision to continue printing hard copies of the newspaper.

**MR**: Well, *PN* began in 1936 as a weekly with around 12 to 16 pages. During the war, we had to shrink right back to being a four-page, very small edition. Actually we achieved our peak circulation figures then – nearly 20,000 – so we were a publication clearly very much needed and desired at the time. After the war we became a fortnightly magazine and then in the 1980s a quarterly. During the 1990s, we went through some difficult times and actually suspended operations for a while. We re-opened as a War Resisters' International quarterly – an international glossy magazine but with a UK-focused Non-Violent Action insert. In 2002, it was decided to refocus PN on the UK – with 10 issues a year and in newspaper format on the roughest newsprint of them all. I became editor in 2007, and kept the format. Activists who know PN as part of their cultural corner were glad it had refocused on the UK and welcomed the newsiness as part of the package. Now we publish six times a year: of the 3,000 printed, 1,400 go to subscribers.

**RLK**: I guess the newspaper is good for distributing at demonstrations and peace events?

**MR**: Yes: we also do some street selling. And it's £2 when we sell. A lot turns on the message of the front page lead story: if it's in tune with what people are thinking then we are more likely to sell. I think the paper version is important for promoting a set of values as well as keeping an activist culture alive. And with the print version you have a product on which you can base face-to-face interactions – and which you can physically take away as a tangible mark of that conversation.

**RLK**: Your website largely reproduces the content of the print copy.

**MR**: Yes: and in addition there are blog postings and events listed. When we revamped the operation in 2010 we had two models in mind. There was the Catholic Worker (catholicworker.org/) model in which everything is available for free on the paper version and website, though it is also available on a voluntary level of subscription. Then there was the model of CounterPunch.org, the excellent, investigative Washington DC-based website. They put up a ton of stuff up for free on the web and alongside that produce a 36-page magazine six times a year carrying entirely original material which is available to subscribers: $35 for the digital edition; $85 for the print edition mailed to the UK; $90 for print and digital editions. After a while some at PN lost faith in the Catholic Worker 'trust in the universe' approach and we moved to a £15 'minimum donation'-based system.

**RLK**: How can you survive on that kind of funding system?

**MR**: In the 1950s, an Anglican priest inherited £5,000 (the equivalent of £100,000 today) and sent out an invitation to progressive groups to present a proposal on the way in which they could use that money. They all thought: there's no point in thinking about it – it's never going to happen. But Peace News proposed using the money to purchase a property to make its HQ and as a base for other progressive groups – and they got it! With the money 5 Caledonian Road, London N1 9DX was bought. We rent it out way below even activist levels – and from that get an annual grant of £31,000 with which we can pay our staff and produce the paper.

**RLK**: How do you see the future of Peace News?

**MR**: Print will definitely provide a crucial function for a project like PN. It will be unavoidable part of our future. But on whether it will remain as a regular two-monthly I'm uncertain. Maybe we will become more occasional, appearing for specific purposes, for particular events. We are certainly going to have to be flexible over our publishing strategy to match the demands of the kind of world we are entering.

## Exploring the *CounterPunch* publishing model
I began my interview with Jeffrey St Clair by asking him to outline the thinking behind CounterPunch's publishing strategy which had so impressed Milan Rai.

**JStC**: We started publishing CounterPunch in 1993, as a six-page newsletter published twice a month. It was modelled on the newsletter of I. F. Stone, whom I had gotten to know a little bit in college, when he was learning classical

Greek for his book on the trial of Socrates. We were relatively latecomers to the web, in large part because both Alex Cockburn [joint editor from 1993 until he died in 2012] and I were basically Luddites.

Around this time, a CounterPunch subscriber actually bought the domain names for CounterPunch.org and CounterPunch.com and donated them to us with a note saying we were too stupid to do this for ourselves. He was probably right. Once we had the domain and a server we didn't do much with it. But the real question was: what the hell do we put up on the site? Our view at the time was we couldn't put fresh writing on the site because who would then purchase subscriptions for the newsletter? So we posted a lot of old writing. Not surprisingly, these pieces drew only minimal traffic and did nothing to dissuade us from our view that the web was a distraction from our real work.

Then, in 1999, Clinton's war on Serbia broke out and events were out-pacing our publication schedule, so we started posting pieces online and the website sprang to life. At the time, CounterPunch probably had 4,000 or so print subscribers. But during the Serbian war we were getting 30,000 to 50,000 visitors to the site each day! This opened our eyes a little bit, but not much. Soon after the cruise missiles stopped hitting the bridges and buildings of Belgrade, we lapsed back into our coma. We threw something new up on the site once a week or so and, predictably, the traffic collapsed. Then came 9/11. I called Cockburn early in the morning to tell him (he hadn't paid his cable TV bill) and we wrote something and put it up on the site. Within 20 minutes the story had more than 75,000 page views. Since then we've published a new slate of stories every weekday and a much larger weekend edition. We were, of course, very glad to have the larger audience of web readers but now the question was reversed. What the hell were we going to do with the print newsletter? CounterPunch was entirely funded by subscriptions and donations to the newsletter. How could we survive financially if we migrated to the online world, especially when we were opposed to selling advertising on the website? Our decision was to keep a wall of separation between our print stories and the pieces we run online and we've more or less abided by this rule for the past 15 years.

**RLK**: How many subscribers do you have?

**JStC**: At its peak, CounterPunch newsletter had about 4,200 subscribers. Now we have about 3,700 or so. And we've changed our print strategy several times. First, we doubled the number of pages in the print issue. Then, shortly after Cockburn died, we switched from a newsletter format to a magazine format, which allowed us to incorporate photos and graphics and bring on board new writers and columnists. In a sense, we were trying to make the magazine a little more like the experience readers get in the Friday online edition of CounterPunch.

**RLK**: How important do you think print is to the progressive left?

**JStC**: Personally, I prefer the magazine format as an editor. There's something more permanent about a magazine that you can walk around with, sit on the toilet and read, annotate, pass around to others and use as a fire-starter. It seems weightier and more substantial. The magazine/newsletter/pamphlet also has such a rich history on the left, going back to Tom Paine, to Marat and Hébert in the French Revolution, Hazlitt, Lamb and Blake in England to the American anti-slavery movement and Prairie populists to the Catholic Workers and then Stone. It's a tradition Cockburn and I saw ourselves as a part of and didn't want to renounce entirely for the 'new thing'.

Of course, the 'new thing' also seems to be always morphing and changing. Online journalism is captive to the latest trends in technology, in software, and tech gizmos. Once you're online you have to continually upgrade and update. It's expensive and time-consuming. Plus, you begin to feel that you're catering to the latest fetishes of your readers. For example, now about 40 per cent of CP's online readers access the site through cellphones. In fact, we had to redesign the website to make it cellphone compatible. The technology also dictates reading habits. For social media purposes, each story now requires a photo to encourage 'sharing'. Because so many people are 'reading' on cellphones the trend is to keep stories short, 500 words or so. It's the revenge of USA Today. We haven't succumbed to this trend yet, though we are under constant pressure to do so.

**RLK**: How global is your audience?

**JStC**: Unlike many left and progressive publications in the States, we do have a global audience, with a large readership in England, Ireland, Scotland, France, Germany, Spain, India, South Africa, Japan and Australia. In part this is because we've always written about international issues. In part it's because we've worked at it. Alex and I both travelled and spoke abroad frequently and regularly did interviews on international TV and radio. About 10 per cent of CounterPunch's print subscribers live outside the US. About 25 per cent of the traffic to the website comes from outside North America.

## Conclusions

Newspapers and magazines have for decades played crucial (though largely under-researched) roles in progressive movements – in the campaigns for trade union and women's rights, for African liberation, for peace during the First and Second World Wars, in the anti-Vietnam war movement and so on. Today, the internet has helped in the revival of the progressive left internationally. This chapter has shown the continuing value of print publications as campaigning tools in the UK and US. But there are many other examples globally: for instance, Frontline, in India (www.frontline.in), Green Left Weekly, in Australia (www.greenleft.org.au) and Politis, in France (www.politis.fr). All of them continue to challenge the lies and mystifications of the warmongering, imperial powers. There are, indeed, reasons for optimism!

## References

Rai, Milan (2010) Peace journalism in practice – Peace News: For non-violent revolution, Keeble, Richard Lance, Tulloch, John and Zollmann, Florian (eds) Peace Journalism, War and Conflict Resolution, New York: Peter Lang pp 217-221

Chomsky, Noam and Herman, Edward (1979) The Washington Connection and Third World Fascism, Boston MA: South End Press

## Note on the contributor

Richard Lance Keeble, Professor of Journalism at the University of Lincoln and chair of the Orwell Society, has written and edited 35 books and on a wide range of topics: including peace journalism, literary journalism, media ethics, newspaper writing skills, humour and journalism, the coverage of US/UK militarism and the secret state. He is also the joint editor of Ethical Space: The International Journal of Communication Ethics and George Orwell Studies. He would like to thank his son, Gabriel Keeble-Gagnère, for introducing him to CounterPunch all those years ago.

# Is the muckraker as dead as a dodo?

**Eamonn O'Neill scrutinises investigative journalism in an era of shrinking print sales**

Investigative journalism in the UK in recent years has been a patchy tale of successes and failures. This is particularly amplified when played out against the shifting context of print sales within the UK press sector. The traditional support of tabloid editors has either shrunk or, indeed, vanished (e.g. the News of the World) for populist stories with a tinge of investigative techniques, whilst larger cross-border stories (e.g. the Panama Papers) have grabbed global headlines. Is there a general trend towards less investigative journalism in print? Or are there exceptions in other parts of the UK media landscape which give us clues to how this genre can survive and even thrive?

## How can we spot investigative journalism?

Investigative journalism by its very nature is sometimes a difficult beast to nail down. Definitions of the genre have been thrown around for decades both in the USA (where it was more established in a codified form) and the UK (where it was practised widely but the use of the term itself was resisted until relatively recently). Most serious practitioners tend to agree with Robert Greene (see below) that the most comprehensive definition is his three-point criteria that:

- it must use the author's own work (i.e. not what Nick Davies would have termed 'churnalism');[1]
- it must be journalism which others want concealed;
- finally, it must have a measurable impact (e.g. someone could be fired or there could be legal fallout from the story being published).

Additionally, the core aspect of what James Ettema and Theodore Glasser noted as a 'morally engaged voice' should also be considered.[2]

As this author has written elsewhere, even senior members of The Sunday Times's 'Insight' team in the heyday of legendary editor Harry Evans, did not know where the basic term 'investigative journalism' actually came from. Phillip

Knightley, who worked on the much-vaunted thalidomide scandal in the 1970s, explained that he had had no clue who 'coined the term'. Indeed, to him it was simply a matter of doing tough reporting on stories that mattered to society at large and their readership in particular. The term itself may possibly have emerged during the 1950s and early 1960s when journalists like the late Robert Greene were bringing journalism approaches into congressional investigative committees when they were examining links between labour unions and the 'rackets' under the auspices of Robert F. Kennedy, then US Attorney General. Greene told this author:

> There were major investigative reporters around doing investigative reporting, we maybe hadn't defined it but you knew it by what you were doing. ... I was giving seminars at the American Press Institute for reporters and editors, on what I called 'investigative reporting' in the 1960s. ... That was before Watergate. ... I was using techniques I had used in the Senate Rackets Committee to form a squad, a group of reporters.[3]

Back in the UK, the idea that for The Sunday Times the pursuit of investigative journalism through a dedicated team was a particular selling point of the publication was never recorded and no mission statement placing investigative journalism at the heart of that newspaper's business strategy was ever noted. Yet, decades later the story of the story became the subject of a critically acclaimed documentary which reached a global audience in 2016 to inspire a new generation of journalists to think of investigative practices as one of the highest forms of their professions.[4] The documentary and the charismatic style and approach of Evans underlines research findings from this author which indicate a strong correlation between the emergence of editors who believe in the benefits of investigative journalism and its appearance under their management. This challenges other studies which argue that the shifting economic patterns of societies account for the ebb and flow of investigative journalism's fortunes and profile.

Recent studies, however, have indicated that the inclusion and encouragement of investigative journalism in news organisations' output can help buck the trend when it comes to print sales and online profile. This, in essence, suggests that investigative journalism may be a regarded as a 'silver bullet' in terms of adding value to a news product and encouraging new consumers to engage with the output and, indeed, stay loyal.

## Decline of newspaper print sales in the UK and Scotland in 2016

As part of this research for this chapter, the author undertook a qualitative examination of the trends in newspaper sales within his home country, Scotland. This methodology was determined as much by the access to current data as by the fact that the general trends in Scotland are also broadly applicable to the rest of the UK.

The most recent PAMCO (Publishers Audience Measurement Company) statistics for print press sales in the UK in February 2016 (and for which 30,000 people across the country were surveyed) indicated a complex picture across the country.[5] Its finding included:

- Sun readers stayed loyal with a monthly readership of 4.45 million for print, though that was a decrease of 16 per cent year-on-year.

- The Daily Telegraph remains the most-read broadsheet daily newspaper in print at 1.17 million; however, that figure also marks a 2.3 per cent year-on-year decline.

- The Daily Express incurred a huge loss of readers, down 28 per cent from 1.079 million to 777,000.

- The survey noted that 12 other print newspapers also saw double-digit readership losses, including the Daily Star which was down 20 per cent to 808,000 and the Daily Mirror, down 19 per cent to 1.85 million.

- The major casualties in the Sunday titles print market were the Sunday Mirror (down 23.9 per cent to 1.87 million); and Trinity Mirror stablemate, the Sunday People (down 23 per cent to 526,000).

None of these newspapers pushed their own investigative journalism teams as being crucial to their mission and/or 'brand' with readers. Articles which might meet the criteria of investigative journalism only appeared very occasionally. Few, if any, had investigative teams or, indeed, a house commitment to carrying this genre of journalism out or training their staff in new and emerging techniques and approaches.

One of the few exceptions which perhaps proves the rule is the Guardian which was the only daily newspaper to show an increase in print readership, up 8.8 per cent to 814,000 in 2015. This was before and during the departure of its iconoclastic editor Alan Rusbridger who was committed to and expanded its arena of investigative reports under his stewardship before handing over to Katharine Viner.[6]

One of the most notable findings from this PAMCO study, however, was the fact that 74 per cent of the 30,000 respondents consumed their news via a PC, laptop, tablet or handheld phone rather than via traditional newspapers. This accounts for a 5 per cent rise in digital, mobile and, arguably to a lesser extent, print, consumption.

Magazines, which somewhat buck the trend, recorded a 21.4 per cent increase in monthly readership. Nicholas Coleridge, the president of Condé Nast, recently explained in a public discussion how magazine sales were not only holding steady but in many cases, increasing:

> To prove his point, he [Coleridge] listed figures for three of his company's titles. Vogue, which sold 135,000 copies a month in 1989, is now selling more at 200,000; Tatler has risen from 25,000 to 85-90,000 copies; and GQ is up from 40,000 to 120,000. In addition, said Coleridge, the March issue

of Vogue had sold more advertising that any other March issue in its 99-year history.[7]

Notably one of the key components of the Condé Nast flagship, Vanity Fair, is a regular commitment to and publication of, investigative journalism pieces. These have featured writers such as the late Dominick Dunne on crime to more recently Michael Lewis on the antics of Wall Street traders.[8]

The Scottish print journalism scene is no less complex nor fascinating than the rest of the UK's. The Audit Bureau of Circulations (ABC) figures delivered in the same month as the PAMCO survey revealed a precipitous fall in print sales for several long-established titles.

- The Glasgow-based Sunday Herald title, for example, dropped to 25,000 in the second half of the year against 32,200 in the same period in 2014.
- The Scotsman's sales figures fell as low as 14,000 copies at full price, while bulks and give-aways made up the rest of the 22,740 circulation for the second half of last year. This is down from 23,700 in the first half and 26,200 in the second half of 2014.
- Scotland on Sunday has dipped to 22,060 from 24,100 in the first six months of 2014 and 27,500 in the second half of the same year.
- The Herald's six-month sales figure was 32,141, compared to 34,300 in the previous six months and 37,000 in the equivalent period a year earlier.

## US study suggesting investigative journalism can save newsrooms
A study from 2013 delivered findings which suggested an overwhelming demand from broadcast audiences for investigative journalism. The findings were delivered via the Investigative Reporters and Editors organisation and website in a presentation titled: 'Can Investigative Journalism Save Your Newsroom' which underlined the demand for original, dynamic and revelatory reporting from news organisations.[9]

In 2014, this trend towards using investigative journalism as both a print and digital driver for sales and enhanced quality was underlined by the growth of new digital entities like Buzzfeed using investigations as a key component of their corporate strategy.[10] By 2016, major news groups such as Gannett were also using investigative journalism as a core USP, hiring new talent with award-winning experience in the genre to help grow and expand their sales and reputation.[11] Notably, this model focused on utilising existing talent, current networks and ambitious targets, whilst delivering a stated goal of original investigations and projects both in print and online.

## Scottish investigative journalism reveals a shifting perspective
If the picture from across the Atlantic shows a new growth in investigative journalism in both print and online sectors, then the picture currently emerging in Scotland adds an important dimension to the shifting and, at times, contrasting patterns within this genre.

The PAMCO findings indicated that more consumers are accessing their news online and via handheld devices like tablet and mobiles. This is precisely the territory of the Ferret, a new online-based investigative project in Scotland run on a co-operative basis.[12] Utilising both established and new talent, this online project is similar to Pro Publica in the USA and the Detail in Northern Ireland in delivering a wide array of articles focusing on both indigenous and international issues for its readers who crowd-fund its endeavours. Regularly reaching out to its audience for both support and ideas represents a new model for media operations. In April 2016, it held a very successful and well-attended conference at the University of Strathclyde which afforded its readers to engage face-to-face with the editorial staff and discuss, its plans, achievements and aims. This initiative was unparalleled in Scottish journalism and marked the dawn of a new directions for investigative journalism in the country in a turbulent political and economic era. Peter Geoghegan, founder of the Ferret, told this author:

> Investigative journalism is in a paradoxical position. On the one hand legacy media and TV seem to be pulling funding from longer term investigative work, but new outlets – Buzzfeed, in particular, springs to mind – see investigative journalism as a way to build their brand as a 'serious' news organisations so are investing in it. Also, in the digital age, investigative stories can have a much longer shelf life: I'm thinking of the Guardian's work on Sports Direct and Buzzfeed on Asos. Both are stories that Channel 4 Dispatches covered before, but both stories had a huge online reach, built week-on-week and, in the case of Sports Direct, had real effects.

The accessibility which the Ferret's predominant online presence affords was something the founders had anticipated and exploited. Geoghegan explained:

> Being online-only has been a huge advantage. Costs are greatly reduced, so the barrier for entry is very low. We launched the Ferret with just a £1,500 grant. But online gives our stories the opportunity to have a much longer shelf life. Some of our most popular stories this year are tales published last year. Also, online we can share all of our source documents and other materials which is really useful for building relationship with our audience.

However, research for this chapter also uncovered a remarkable success story of a very different variety which suggests old fashioned print publications may have a sustainable future too if they tap into the right market. The Glasgow-based, the Digger, is a small print-run publication which has managed to use investigative journalism techniques to present fresh stories that connect with its loyal readership in recent years. Exploiting the manifestly paltry court coverage at the city's busy legal parishes, the magazine regularly recounts grisly details involving errant criminals, drug dealers and paedophiles in the pages of its small-format A5 magazine.

Its founding editor James Cruikshank retains a low profile and has gained something of an iconoclastic status within the city's media community. Whilst it has sometimes run afoul of the legal process is covers intensely, the magazine continues to manage to shift enough copies that prove it is able to punch well above its low-scale operation weight.[13] A former employee of the magazine who is now a widely-respected senior broadcast journalist with BBC Scotland explained to this author how the magazine operated:

> The success of the Digger is rooted in the way it was founded and grew at the outset. The magazine was founded by its editor when he lived in the Possil area of Glasgow as a self-published newsletter focusing on housing primarily, but also crime. It was sold at local markets and eventually some local shops and by locals keen on pushing local issues. The reputation of the magazine was solidified through coverage of the trial of Robert O'Hara, where the emphasis was on the impact on the communities of the drug operation laid bare in the case.

> As it grew the focus shifted more towards crime. The publication of Sheriff Court indictments became the fixed point in the magazine and created a tangible link between the magazine and its readership, since the cases often emanated from their communities. The magazine continued to grow and then took in Glasgow High Court cases. But the magazine also followed cases on a weekly basis, despite constant antagonism between it and the court authorities. As coverage expanded, the more contact from communities in the North, South West and eventually East of Glasgow – where readership was highest – came in furnishing more stories and detail, as well as complaints (which are in themselves always a rich source of information.)

> The secondary focus of the magazine was to cover any stories which highlighted the problems associated with poverty in the city, from housing association failures to fraud and even the withdrawal of community resources by churches. Unfortunately, through covering crime the magazine gained an unfair reputation as being obsessed with 'naming and shaming' paedophiles; an unfair reputation since cases covered were only ever those which appeared in the courts. Also very important to its success was the organisation of distribution. The print run changed on a weekly basis in reaction to the feedback received from the shops it was sold in and with whom we had a weekly contact. Because we did our own distribution we came face-to-face with shopkeepers and got regular feedback from them, rather than just a list of returns. In many respects our distribution system was amateurish but that amateurism was also in some ways a strength.

> Lastly, we carried no advertising. Revenue was entirely derived from over-the-counter sales – with a handful of postal subscriptions – so there was

never any basis for the accusation levelled at other local papers in Glasgow that they daren't criticise the City Council or local business for fear of losing advertising revenue. It also meant that people knew that every inch of every page of the magazine was made up of editorial, and not advertising, copy. All of these points taken together meant that during my time at the magazine, sales went from just over 2,000 to more than 12,000 distributed through over 200 shops across the city.

I remain convinced of my principal belief about print journalism and publications based on my experience at the Digger: print stories that mean something to the people and they will buy your papers. ... It is massively important that the readership felt that the stories they read were about them, their situation and their communities; that they were relevant. So no advertising, no repetition, relevance to readership and a determined, understandable focus made the publication attractive to more and more people at a time when sales for established print publications were collapsing.

## Conclusions

Investigative journalism remains a potent, indeed necessary, force in the new media landscape in the UK. The roots may lie in the era when print publishing was the norm and Harry Evans was the gold standard, but it has evolved and grown into a new form in the modern era. Whilst retaining its power, its practitioners still thrive in areas where economic realities might mean glossy magazines from the Condé Nast stable can fund their work or, indeed, encourage them to try the crowd-sourced route as well. There is no one quick, cheap and easy fix for this genre of journalism.

Recent research like IRE's and sales figures from both the broadsheet sector and magazine sector, indicate that investigative journalism *can* contribute to a new flourishing within newsrooms and news organisations in an era when 'churnalism' is freely available to consumers. This requires vision, commitment and the hiring of respected talent by organisations such as Gannett/USA Today to reverse the trend. The use of examples from the Scottish media sector, at a time when news-consumers in a post-2014 independence referendum are amongst some of the most engaged nationally and internationally, suggests original investigative journalism is still a much-valued product. Sales figures and crowd-sourced financial commitments to online sites like the Ferret and print publications such as the Digger suggest audiences are keen to seek out and stay loyal to investigative journalism initiatives whether in print or online.

## Notes

[1] http://www.nickdavies.net/2008/02/05/introducing-flat-earth-news/

[2] See The Reporter's Craft as Moral Discourse, Custodians of Conscience: Investigative Journalism and Public Virtue by James S. Ettema and Theodore L. Glasser (New York: Columbia University Press, 1998) pp 3-4.

[3] Bob Greene interview with author, July 2006.

[4] See this Guardian interview for a summary of the film and comments from Harold Evans.

[5] http://www.newsworks.org.uk/pamco.

[6] https://www.theguardian.com/media/greenslade/2016/oct/06/who-are-the-new-kids-on-the-block-in-investigative-journalism.

[7] https://www.theguardian.com/media/greenslade/2016/apr/15/why-our-magazines-are-defying-digital-erosion-by-conde-nast-chief.

[8] http://www.vanityfair.com/style/2014/01/crime-reporting-archive.

[9] http://ire.org/events-and-training/online-training/webinars/can-investigative-journalism-save-your-newsroom/.

[10] http://www.usatoday.com/story/money/columnist/rieder/2014/02/03/buzzfeeds-investigative-unit-taking-shape/5084213/.

[11] http://www.niemanlab.org/2016/07/as-usa-today-network-builds-its-investigative-ambitions-it-looks-to-keep-things-in-the-gannett-family/.

[12] https://theferret.scot/.

[13] http://www.vice.com/en_uk/read/the-digger-glasgow-patrick-ferry-720.

## Note on the contributor

Dr Eamonn O'Neill is Associate Professor in Journalism at Edinburgh Napier University. Over a career spanning 27 years he has been honoured internationally for his investigative journalism in both broadcast and print, in, amongst others, the British Press Awards, BAFTAs and the Paul Foot Award. In 2008, he became the first British recipient of an Investigative Reporters and Editors Award (Special category – Tom Renner Award) in one of the USA's premier peer-judged honours for his work investigating miscarriages of justice. In 2010, 2011 2012, 2013, 2015 and 2016 he received honours in the University of Strathclyde Excellence in Teaching Awards following nominations by students. His work appears in broadsheets throughout the UK and he regularly broadcasts on BBC Scotland. He is married to an American artist and has twin sons.

# Foundations and the foundation of a new way of funding journalism

**Not-for-profit journalistic organisations are springing up around the world and producing stories of huge value. Rachel Oldroyd looks at their role and whether they can take the place of traditional print outlets**

In early January 2016 one of the United States' oldest newspapers, a once hugely profitable and highly regarded enterprise, was turned into the American equivalent of a charity. The financial situation had got so bad at the Philadelphia Inquirer that its 85-year-old billionaire owner Gerry Lenfest decided its best chance of survival was to transfer his ownership along with that of its sister paper, the Daily News, in to a newly created non-profit organisation.

'Of all the things I've done,' said Lenfest, 'this is the most important because of the journalism.'

Ask anybody working in the newspaper industry why the decline in print sales is such a matter of concern and the response across the board will be something to do with the importance of journalism. The huge impact of the decline raises worrying commercial concerns, but even among those responsible for the business side of newspapers there is a strong understanding that the problem has a much wider implication. Without robust financial returns serious journalism is threatened – and in the current media landscape that threat seems very serious indeed.

It is a well-rehearsed argument: journalism is a vital part of any functioning democracy. A country without a strong and free press is a much poorer society. An independent press informs, educates, scrutinises and questions. It provides the facts that help citizens better understand their world and it holds to account those that wield the power.

So if the commercial model is no longer working – or if alternative commercial models have not yet been found, non-profit status perhaps provides a way of saving journalism. The Inquirer's Lenfest is not the first to think so.

In the US there are more than 150 non-profit journalistic enterprises. A study by the Pew Research Centre in 2013 looked at the rise of this alternative funding model[1]. It found a healthy, optimistic and growing sector. Many of the organisations it reviewed were still small entities employing fewer than five journalists. But the sector was diverse in its interests and spread widely across the US. Another study by the Investigative Reporting Workshop run out of American University found operating budgets in the largest 60 of these organisations amounted to $86m.[2]

Some of the largest have news teams that are starting to equal those of many papers both in scale and numbers. The Center for Investigative Reporting (CIR)[3] in California, for example, has a budget of more than $10m and employs nearly 80 people. On the east coast Propublica[4], which was set up in 2007 by Paul Steiger, former managing editor of the Wall Street Journal, operates at a similar scale.

Both Propublica and CIR pursue investigative reporting. Other non-profits operate in more niche areas such as the well respected Marshall Project[5], which focuses on injustices, and InsideClimate[6] News that reports on climate change issues. Others such as the Texas Tribune[7] and Voice of San Diego[8] have taken over local patches left by now extinct print products.

The ability to focus purely on journalism – rather than clickbait (the latest obsession in news rooms desperately chasing elusive digital advertisers) is a huge draw – leading some of the US media's brightest young and some of the country's most senior journalists to this new model. Go into their newsrooms and there is a buzz, an enthusiasm that has long evaporated from many of the traditional print establishments. And this is leading not only to gap plugging, but to fantastic stories and powerful journalism as highly regarded New Yorker writer Nicholas Lemann noted in an article earlier this year: 'Their work is always good, and sometimes spectacular.'[9] Propublica, it is worth noting, has already received three Pulitzer prizes – the highest honour in American journalism – in its short nine-year existence.

Earlier in 2016 a relatively small Washington-based non-profit announced a global tax story based on the biggest leak of information ever received by the media. More than 100 teams of reporters, mostly working in traditional newsrooms across dozens of countries, were pulled together to work on this leak, known as the Panama Papers. It was to be the biggest global story of the year and it was pulled off by a non-profit – the International Consortium of Investigative Journalists[10].

The old print publications are benefiting too, with many commercial news organisations now partnering with non-profit media both in the journalism and the story publication. The ICIJ for example partners largely with commercial interests as it seeks out well-placed publishers in each country.

The enthusiasm for this new model is, perhaps most importantly, also there among those able to provide the financial backing. The sector has blossomed because the funds have been readily available, with some of the country's largest foundations putting up increasing levels of support.

The Ford Foundation, the Knight Foundation, the Bill and Melinda Gates Foundation, the Reva and David Logan Foundation all pour millions into journalism each year. And as quickly as the old, traditional print models have tumbled into ever more chaos, the commitments of the funders have risen. The MacArthur Foundation, for example, enhanced its commitment in 2016, providing $25m to 12 journalistic non-profit organisations[11]. The Reva and David Logan Foundation[12] committed funds to help launch Reveal, a new investigative radio strand produced by CIR.

The success of the non-profit model in the US has not gone unnoticed in the wider world. In 2010 in the UK philanthropists David and Elaine Potter launched the Bureau of Investigative Journalism. Elaine had a good sense of what was being lost as the global financial downturn started to bite. As a former Sunday Times journalist she had been part of the team that investigated thalidomide, a pharmaceutical drug that was discovered to cause defects in unborn babies if taken in pregnancy. David was behind the Psion computer and then mobile phone technology Symbian.

Like many of the US non-profits on which the Bureau was modelled, the remit was to pursue in-depth investigative journalism in the public interest. The desire from the start was ambitious stories that mattered, stories that revealed a hidden and important truth, stories that could have an impact and lead to change.

Large subjects have been tackled. Examples include the waste and corruption inherent within European Structural Funds; the use of drones and targeted killings by the CIA; secret lobbying of the UK government; party political funding; failings in the care system; the lack of provision of affordable homes; the cause and impact of antibiotic resistance; military contracting; and unaccompanied asylum seekers. To properly investigate these topics requires months of work and a team of reporters. It is the privilege of time – so rarely available in now slimmed-down traditional newsrooms – that the non-profit model has been able to provide.

The environment in the UK is very different to that in the US. To get the tax advantages offered by non-profit status in the US an organisation has to become a charity. But while there is no rule against journalism being funded charitably in the UK, it has proved difficult for organisations producing news to fit within the charitable description in the Charities Act 2011, as it does not recognise journalism as a charitable endeavour. The Bureau has applied twice for charitable status and has on both occasions been turned down. It is set up as a company limited by guarantee – and all revenue is ploughed back in to its journalism.

Foundations in the UK have also been slower to recognise the social impact of the disruption to the traditional newspaper model perhaps because UK newspapers initially proved more resilient to falling circulations than their US counterparts. The BBC with its requirement to provide public service broadcasting also meant the democratic deficit resulting from the reduction in print journalists was less marked. In 2015 and 2016, however, market conditions deteriorated fast and virtually every newspaper group cut journalist posts quite dramatically.

Over the past three years the Bureau has expanded both the number of funders and the level of its funding. It now has nine different backers and over the past three years has increased its funding by more than 40 per cent. In 2017 the Bureau will launch a data journalism project for which it has also received substantial funds from Google's Digital News Initiative[13], a €150m fund aimed at encouraging innovation among European media companies.

The hurdles in the UK have not stopped other journalistic organisations adopting the model too. Open Democracy[14], Bellingcat[15], the Ferret[16] and the Bristol Cable[17] are all producing fantastic journalism through non-profit structures. And in wider Europe a number of journalism teams have set themselves up in similar vein – CorrectiV[18] in Germany and the Organized Crime and Corruption Reporting Project in Eastern Europe[19].

In fact the model is not that new in the UK. Back in 1936 John Scott, the then owner of the Manchester Guardian, came to the same realisation that the Philadelphia Inquirer's owner Gerry Lenfest did 80 years later.

The Manchester Guardian (now The Guardian) had gained an international reputation under long-serving editor and owner CP Scott. When he retired he passed control to his two sons, John and Ted. The death three years later of CP Scott and Ted within three months of each other brought a very real threat to the paper. Upon John's passing the Inland Revenue would claim substantial sums in what were then death duties and this threatened the independence of the paper. In order to prevent this John transferred all his and his family's interests in the paper to a group of trustees – the Scott Trust, effectively creating a very early non-profit model. The trust, though, is not a charity but a company limited by guarantee (the trustees are the shareholders) whose main aim remains the continuation of The Guardian in perpetuity.

Of course this model has not protected The Guardian from the recent, and most ferocious of financial storms to hit the print industry. The losses on the paper have become so enormous that even the Scott Trust does not have the resources to keep it alive in the long term.

This illustrates an important point. Non-profit status does not guarantee success. Organisations have to be run well, they need to develop structures, accounting and fund-raising practices.

Even in the US where there are many more foundations offering funding to journalism, the pool is still relatively small and, as few of the new non-profit models have well developed publishing platforms, raising funds from the general public is a difficult task for many. These factors make the sector inherently fragile and long-term sustainability far from guaranteed.

Yet despite the issues those running and working in the sector are determined to make it work – and for no other reason than a belief in the importance of journalism.

With the latest crisis to hit the print industry these ambitions among those running non-profit newsrooms are more important than ever. Newspapers had hoped that as their print circulations declined they could pick up readers on their websites and then persuade advertisers to migrant their spending to their growing online presence. The problem is that the digital advertising revenues that were expected to follow the growing online clicks have not materialised at the levels required and are rapidly evaporating. Many newspaper groups are finding themselves now fighting on two fronts – stretching their shrinking resources still further.

Foundation-supported journalism has not and probably will not take the place of traditional media – even if print declines to nothing. It is not a silver bullet, but it is a force for good. And in the storm that is blasting across the traditional media landscape it has to be a welcome part of the mix.

## Notes

[1] www.journalism.org/2013/06/10/nonprofit-journalism/

[2] http://investigativereportingworkshop.org/ilab/story/second-look/

[3] www.revealnews.org/

[4] www.propublica.org/about/documents/

[5] www.themarshallproject.org/#.KFWhfjpbc

[6] https://insideclimatenews.org/

[7] www.texastribune.org/

[8] www.voiceofsandiego.org/

[9] www.newyorker.com/news/news-desk/a-code-of-ethics-for-journalism-nonprofits

[10] www.icij.org/

[11] www.macfound.org/press/press-releases/macarthur-expands-its-commitment-journalism-and-media/

[12] www.loganfdn.org/index.html

[13] www.digitalnewsinitiative.com/

[14] www.opendemocracy.net/

[15] www.bellingcat.com/

[16] https://theferret.scot/

[17] https://thebristolcable.org/

[18] https://correctiv.org/

[19] https://www.occrp.org/en/

## Note on the contributor

Rachel Oldroyd is Managing Editor of the Bureau of Investigative Journalism, a UK-based non-profit news organisation. She joined the Bureau at launch in 2010 as a reporter, becoming its Deputy Editor six months later and its Managing Editor in 2014. She joined the Bureau from the Mail on Sunday where she worked for 13 years first as a reporter and then as a commissioning editor.

# The rise and rise of hyper-local news in the UK

**Andy Williams and Dave Harte outline the findings from a major research project by academics at Cardiff and Birmingham City universities looking into hyper-local, community journalism**

As conventional local print journalism is in decline, a new sector of hyperlocal, community journalism is growing. This covers everything from local blogs to regular printed press – but produced within the community it serves – sometimes on a voluntary basis but increasingly as commercial printed newspapers and magazines as well. Cardiff University has developed a Centre for Community Journalism which, with colleagues from Birmingham City University, undertook a major survey of this new sector. The results suggest that although it is a growing and dynamic area, it is sustained mainly by volunteers, is as yet small, and has uncertain prospects for scaling up or becoming financially sustainable.

## Who are the community journalists?

Part of our research involved mapping out broad trends in this developing and emerging sector, and we thought it was important to determine how hyperlocals see themselves, how they self-identify. Seven out of ten respondents to our survey of publishers consider what they do as a form of active community participation, over half as an expression of active citizenship and over half as local journalism (Williams et al 2014). It is often assumed that this is a sector made up of citizen journalists and amateurs, but that is not the case in the UK; almost half have some mainstream journalistic training or experience (ibid.). That said, apart from a growing professional and professionalising minority, this *is* a sector dominated by volunteers who are not primarily motivated by making money from what they do.

## What is community news good for?

Many community news publishers serve areas which have been hit by the closure of a local newspaper, or where there was never much commercial news coverage to begin with. Where legacy local news organisations continue to publish they often do so at a distance – the industry has seen the closure of many local offices, and the news has become less local in its orientation (Franklin 2006). By contrast, hyperlocal news is almost always produced by people who live in the communities they serve. A large proportion of stories focus on covering banal everyday local community activities and events which are often considered too local in their orientation for professional journalists seeking wider audiences. This can give readers rich information about local community life not available elsewhere (Williams et al 2015).

You also see a lot of stories about local government and the services it provides – so a lot of information that could be high in civic value. We know from existing studies (Franklin 2006) that more established commercial local news tends to be authority-oriented in sourcing strategies, sometimes at the expense of lay voices. Official sources also get plenty of coverage in hyperlocal news, but the role afforded to members of the public and to people from local community groups is proportionally greater (Williams et al 2015). All of this is important for fostering and enabling informed local participation and citizenship, as well as for representing communities to themselves, helping forge shared local identities, both key democratic functions of local news (McNair 2002).

Informing local communities is one thing, but how about playing watchdog or advocacy functions? Holding local elites to account, or standing up for communities when things get tough is arguably more difficult, but there are signs they are often done very well. Almost half of survey respondents had 'started a campaign where the site has sought to change things locally in the last two years' while almost three quarters had publicised the campaigns of others (Williams et al 2014). Investigations are time-consuming and often risky, but still almost half had carried out an investigation which had helped uncover controversial new information about local civic issues or events in the same period. Issues covered can be very small (relating to minor planning complaints, a surfeit of dog poo) or pretty big, addressing issues in the public interest (tackling cuts to public services, major developments, accountability or corruption).

## Does community news strengthen communities?
As well as assessing community news in relation to established social and democratic functions, we have tried to understand hyperlocal news content and practices in relation to newer notions of interactivity, participation and collaboration. Journalism practice has changed considerably since the advent of new media, but research suggests that news audiences, and the content they provide, tend to be understood by legacy news companies in a few dominant ways: as untapped commercial opportunities (with UGC to be 'harvested') (Freedman 2012); and/or quantifiable units in the attention economy (news 'users' whose clicks can be monetised) (Anderson 2013). Local legacy media experiments with community news have, correspondingly, often been found

wanting (Thurman et al. 2012; Baines 2010). Our research suggests, perhaps because of the scarcity of commercial motivations among producers, much UK hyperlocal news is more horizontal, dialogic, rooted in physical and online local everyday community spaces and based on more equal and socially embedded reciprocal exchange relationships (sometimes in new ways, sometimes in ways which evoke residual, but disappearing, professional journalistic practices such as walking local news beats) (Harte et al 2016). We also find that hyperlocal news production practices often blend on- and offline, journalistic and community activist, practices in mutually re-enforcing ways (facilitating community appeals, creating 'school uniform exchanges'; setting up social media surgeries). All of this suggests that much hyperlocal journalistic activity is effective at strengthening community bonds and encouraging direct, indirect, and sustained reciprocity which Seth Lewis and colleagues have linked to increased community cohesion and social capital (Lewis et al 2014).

## How is hyperlocal funded?

Despite the impressive social and democratic value of hyperlocal news content, community news in the UK does not generate much money and is dominated by volunteers and hobbyists who cover their own costs. For example, only around a third of survey participants make money and most of these only quite modest amounts; only one in ten say they generate more than £500 per month in revenues. There is a small but growing group of professional and professionalising entrepreneurial local news startups (Williams et al 2014). Those who seek to monetise typically employ a mixture of revenue streams including:

- online advertising (although this is hampered by moribund and wary local markets, and the limited reach of many sites);
- crowd-funding (time-intensive and short-termist but can help increase audiences and foster loyalty);
- audience co-operatives (also very hard work, but can guarantee medium-term income, and effectively engage audiences by recruiting them as owners, producers, and editors);
- grant money (organisations such as Nesta and the Carnegie UK Trust have provided valuable, but short-term, targeted funding);
- charity funding through local community development trusts (such as the long-standing Ambler, in Amble, Northumberland, where one person is paid to produce a news website and printed paper, and to co-ordinate broad community participation);
- cross-subsidy with other streams of income; and, increasingly
- print advertising models using free newspapers (this can increase readerships and visibility, and it is easier to convince local advertisers to buy into print) (Radcliffe 2015).

The overall picture is mixed. The data suggests that while the market may sustain *some* hyperlocal outlets, under *some* conditions, it is currently unable to sustain this kind of news on a large scale consistently across the country (Williams 2016). Still, many community news sites are thriving, which is testament to producers' drive, and to the public appetite for local news, which remains strong despite economic and technological upheavals.

## How sustainable is community news?

In a sector largely underpinned by volunteer labour, sustainability is not only a question of money, and we have highlighted the precarious nature of many community news operations. People's professional and personal circumstances change, many 'burn out' and output can vary because of this (Harte et al 2016). Many interviewees independently raised the spectre of their site disappearing should they 'get run over by a bus'. Often it takes less catastrophic personal changes (moving house, a change of job, a divorce) for news provision to fluctuate (Williams 2016). Widespread voluntarism is currently sustaining the largely non-institutional community news sector, but this is a fragile foundation on which to base something as important as the generation of local news. Some argue volunteer labour can underpin this field in much the same way as it already does with other areas of public life (e.g. school governors, elements of the justice system). Even supercharged by the affordances of freely-available digital media, however, this may not be enough to sustain community news in the long term. Local news has always had the backup of strong institutions which offered support mechanisms and the social capital and power of editors and newspaper offices.

Without the profits needed to remunerate people the sector may be too precarious to sustain the kind of institutions which have previously been prerequisites for strong, independent and critical local news. Another limitation is the sector's reach and scale relative to the historic strength of commercial legacy local news publishers. In terms of the *numbers* of news producers, and their *capacity* for (mainly part-time) work, community news can only very partially plug growing local news deficits caused by the widespread withdrawal of established local journalism after decades of (widespread) job cuts and (more limited) newspaper closures (ibid.).

## Conclusion: The future of UK hyper local news

The research to date outlines three broad groups of community news outlet:

- first, a relatively small group of precarious but, crucially, economically viable community news services. This a rare good news story about local news in the UK, and as a society we should do everything we can to foster and support them, as well as to encourage others to join them;

- second, a number of sites run by hobbyists who are now trying, in difficult market conditions, to professionalise and/or commercialise in different ways; and

- third, a larger pool of volunteer-led sites that have no commercial ambitions, who will carry on doing this as long as they want to, before closing their site or transferring it to somebody else to run and produce.

Players in all three groups are producing public interest news, often of impressive quality and quantity. Many are also playing new, less traditionally journalistic, community-building roles both on- and off-line. But those seeking to make money face serious challenges and a tough market dominated by established newspaper and online news publishers.

What does all this mean for the established printed newspaper industry? There are some indications in our interviews that legacy local news companies have seen community journalists appearing on their patches as a threat, while others have embraced hyperlocal news providers as partners, sometimes sharing content or employing them as part-time local correspondents. In limited ways many commercial community news operations are undoubtedly providing competition to established local newspapers (for advertising revenues, for audiences, for stories). And, more troublingly, they often do so in ways which undermine the previously established economic and professional value of local journalism (*pro-bono*, volunteer-led news operations are hard to compete with). But whether relationships with newspaper companies are hostile or collaborative, it is clear that community news is now a small but well-established sector of the diversified local news and information ecosystems which have emerged since the advent of blogging and social media cut the costs of communicating with publics so substantially.

We believe that our combined collective knowledge of the residual mainstream, and emergent community, news sectors allows us to see local news in the UK as a public good: something that society needs, but which the market can no longer provide in sufficient quality or quantity. This logic arguably underpins existing public subsidy to local newspaper groups, but we now have a paradoxical situation where our local news policy currently protects entrenched interests on declining print platforms (for instance, with statutory notices in printed publications), while not supporting or encouraging new local news start-ups, no matter how beneficial they may be to the communities they serve. We think that to protect, support, and encourage local news as a public good in the 21st century we will need a re-evaluation of local news policies to encourage newer entrants to the market, to foster experimentation with different funding models, and stimulate independent and plural local news in print *and* online.

## Sources

Anderson, C. W. (2013) Rebuilding the News: Metropolitan Journalism in the Digital Age, Philadelphia, PA: Temple University Press

Baines, David (2010) Hyper-local: Glocalised rural news, International Journal of Sociology and Social Policy, Vol. 30, Nos 9/10 pp 81-92

Franklin, Bob (2006) Attacking the devil? Local journalists and local papers in the UK, Franklin, Bob (ed.) *Local Journalism and Local Media: Making the Local News*, London: Routledge

Freedman, Des (2012) Web 2.0. Misunderstanding the Internet, Curran, James, Fenton, Natalie and Freedman, Des (eds) London: Routledge pp 69-94

Harte, Dave, Turner, Jerome and Williams, Andy (2016) Discourse of enterprise in hyperlocal community news in the UK, Journalism Practice, Vol. 10, No. 2 pp 233-250

Harte, Dave, Williams, Andy and Turner Jerome (2016) Reciprocity and the hyperlocal journalist, *Journalism Practice*, web first

Lewis, Seth C., Holton, Avery E. and Coddington, Mark (2014) Reciprocal journalism, *Journalism Practice*, Vol. 8, No. 2 pp 229-241

McNair, Brian (2002) *Journalism and Democracy: An Evaluation of the Political Public Sphere*, London: Routledge

Radcliffe, Damian (2015) *Where Are We Now? UK Hyperlocal media and community journalism in 2015*, Cardiff and London: Centre for Community Journalism and Nesta. Available online at https://www.communityjournalism.co.uk/wp-content/uploads/2015/09/C4CJ-Report-for-Screen.pdf

Thurman, Neil, Pascal, Jean-Christophe and Bradshaw, Paul (2012) Can Big Media do Big Society? A critical case study of commercial, convergent hyperlocal news. *International Journal of Media and Cultural Politics*, Vol. 8, No. 2 pp 269-285

Williams, Andy, Barnett, Stephen, Harte, Dave and Townend, Judith (2014) The State of Hyperlocal Community News in the UK: Findings from a Survey of Practitioners, Cardiff and London: Cardiff University and Westminster University. Available online at https://hyperlocalsurvey.files.wordpress.com/2014/07/hyperlocal-community-news-in-the-uk-2014.pdf

Williams, Andy, Harte, Dave and Turner, Jerome (2015) The value of UK hyperlocal community news, *Digital Journalism*, Vol. 3, No. 5 pp 680-703

Williams, Andy (2016) UK Hyperlocal Community News: Five 'Ws' and an 'H'. Keynote address: MECCSA Conference 2016, Canterbury Christ Church University, 6-8.January

**Note on the contributor**
Andy Williams is a senior lecturer at the School of Journalism, Media and Cultural Studies at Cardiff University where he teaches and researches about local news, the relationship between news and public relations, and news media coverage of science, the environment, and health.

Dave Harte is a senior lecturer in Media and Communications at Birmingham City University. His main research interest relates to the role of online community news in fostering citizenship. He edits a hyperlocal news website for Bournville in Birmingham, UK.

# Inside the organisations plugging the gaps

As some communities suddenly find themselves no longer served by a local news outlet, and some topics remain unexplored in detail by stretched newsroom staff, people without formal journalism training are stepping up to the job. Catalina Albeanu of Journalism.co.uk takes a look at two organisations which have flourished in recent years doing fundamental journalistic tasks their founders thought were lacking from larger media outlets: verification and local investigations

Newsrooms nowadays can take many forms. Some have recently been reshuffled to enable more collaboration. Others operate entirely online through communication tools such as Slack, and some do not contain even a single reporter or editor with formal journalism training.

Journalism as a profession has become 'fully academised' (Thurman, Cornia, Kunert, 2016).

A survey of 700 UK journalists found 98 per cent of those who had begun their career between 2013 and 2015 had a bachelor's degree (Thurman, Cornia, Kunert, 2016). While this sample may not necessarily have studied journalism, those who get hired in the larger newsrooms in the UK increasingly tend to have some formal education in journalism.

And then there are those who develop an interest in a subject area or a conviction about the role of media in society, and armed with the technology now available at almost everyone's fingertips, decide to figure out a way through to the world of investigative journalism.

Some start on their own, diving into an obsession which will soon become their specialism and bring other like-minded people to them. Others find a team of people who are on the same page and start learning together, with the goal of producing the type of journalism they wish they could read but do not find in the traditional media.

In this chapter, we take a look at two organisations which do not conform to the traditional idea of a media outlet, founded by those who discovered underused technologies and under-served communities.

## The citizen investigative journalists who run training in newsrooms

In 2011, Eliot Higgins worked in financial administration. In his spare time, he monitored the conflict in Libya and the Arab Spring, discussing information which came out of the area on various forums and liveblogs, debating what could be true and what could be misinformation.

He figured out he could try to verify the photos and videos he found online by using satellite imagery to identify the location where they were taken. A year later, he started a blog as a hobby to outline his practices and process, noticing there was no other media outlet doing the same at the time.

He ran the blog, called Brown Moses, for two years, and noticed the community around this type of work, using open source tools for investigations and verification, was growing. In 2014, Higgins opened Bellingcat, a site 'by and for citizen investigative journalists'. He aimed to offer a platform to others who were doing similar work but had a smaller audience, as well as to create resources for those who were interested in learning how to use these tools.

The tools are available to everyone online, and include well known programmes such as Google Earth, Google Streetview or Yandex Maps. According to Higgins, the main characteristic needed to succeed in this field is to be obsessive about the subject.

"I would find obsessiveness is quite useful, because you have to search for a lot of stuff that's irrelevant. But also at the same time you need to temper that using common sense about a lot of stuff, because I do see a lot of people who are a little bit crazy when they start doing this work."

Bellingcat now has a few dozen contributors, some regular writers and some who have only written one or two pieces for the site. "They come from a range of backgrounds," Higgins explained. "A few are journalists who are working freelance and just want to do more in depth pieces they know wouldn't really be published in a mainstream publication. Others are people who have worked in conflict investigation and just have an interest in it as a hobby, like I did."

Bellingcat also has a core investigations team, which grows or shrinks depending on circumstances, but largely developed in the aftermath of the downing of flight MH17 in Ukraine. The team published a series of posts verifying related images posted online, detailing their workflow and the thought process behind their conclusions. As a result of this work, Higgins was interviewed by both the Dutch and the Australian police as a witness in the inquiry which followed, prompting him to consolidate Bellingcat's investigations team as its work was proving valuable.

Bellingcat articles are naturally often picked up by Russian language media, but its work has also been featured by media outlets in the UK, such as The

Guardian which has covered the team's reports on MH17. (Borger, Higgins, 2015; Luhn, 2016; Agence-France Presse, 2016)

The open source investigations community has been growing in the last few years, a growth mainly driven by Russian-language groups. The next step for Bellingcat is to start focusing more on training and strengthening ties with other media organisations.

Higgins adds: "Not just giving people a one-day workshop, but training them for several days and then working with those organisations we've trained to develop stories. Our value is we can teach other people to do it, but also offer our assistance with other organisations.

"And because now there's more investigative journalism organisations run more like NGOs rather than for-profit companies, we work with those more and collaborate with them."

With all things going according to plan in terms of funding, Bellingcat will have close to ten investigators as well as new projects in the near future. Its first 18 months were supported through a crowdfunding campaign, while funding for 2016 came from Google, covering a salary for Higgins, one other member of staff, and expenses for running the site. In November 2016, Bellingcat was also awarded funding through Google's Digital News Initiative to support The Archive for Conflict Investigation, a platform establishing a set of tools and methodologies for journalists.

## Reaching people in media deserts with local print journalism

Alon Aviram graduated with a degree in international relations in 2013, and set up the Bristol Cable with two other co-founders that summer.

He says: "As a reader rather than a professional journalist initially, there was a frustration there were a lot of challenging ideas and journalism of high quality which just weren't really permeating beyond quite narrow confines. There's so much information and investigative journalism which doesn't really have an impact in communities across the UK."

The Bristol Cable functions as a media co-operative, where members can pay from as little as £1 per month to fund what the team hopes is a new style of local journalism, focused on independent investigations.

"In order to improve the quality of content, make it more engaging, make it more interesting, make it relevant to everyday people's lives, there needs to be a direct connection between the reader and the producer and what better way than to create a democratic cooperative,"Aviram added.

"Essentially we thought this could be a model which would democratise media by having the reader or the user participating in content decisions as well as wider strategic decisions regarding our business operations, and would also be a way to fund the model as well."

Aside from Aviram, who worked a freelance journalist for a short period of time, the founding team (Alec Saelens and Adam Cantwell) had no formal journalism training or experience before deciding to set up the Cable. They came up with a skeleton idea for the organisation in the summer of 2013, and sought support from journalists, filmmakers, lawyers and other people in the community to shape the idea.

The team raised £3,000 through crowdfunding to get the project off the ground. The money was spent on training for the core team at the Cable as well as around 300 people in the community who were interested in learning more about media law, writing, or using social media as a journalist.

"The sessions were useful to get the brand in front of potential members," explained Aviram, "but also to offer the co-founders a chance to really get to grips with what they were trying to do."

It took the Bristol Cable four months to publish its first edition, but now it publishes stories online every day with a free quarterly print edition.

The print edition enables the organisation to reach more people with its journalism, and Aviram believes simply promoting the Cable's website through social media would not have been enough to cut through the noise that exists online.

Some 30,000 print copies of the Cable are distributed every quarter, through local pubs, cafes, places of worship, community centres and public areas.

"You can put a copy in someone's hand who would never have otherwise engaged with you on social media because they have no connection with the circles in which you might be operating. So that has been a crucial way of getting the brand out, getting a diverse membership, sourcing stories as well."

Print also enables the team to reach communities that exist in what Aviram calls media deserts. "They can feed us really interesting stories which then get taken up and published in future editions and online."

The stories the Cable publishes are sourced in three main ways: commissions from the organisation's media coordinators; submissions from members of the public; and content production with an 'educational twist'.

The latter approach means the Cable spends time with members of a particular community to both source stories and collaborate with them during the newsgathering and production phases. The organisation continues to host workshops on subjects from information security to feature writing, the basics of film production and photography.

"We will often sit with someone who has no prior experience in producing journalism and work with them to produce a piece of content. That could take a couple of days just online or it could be a person comes into our office over a period of a couple of months and researches and develops a piece. Because our journalism is slower, we have the space to be able to really nurture people's development."

The Cable's media coordinators also spend time collaborating with local communities which would otherwise never produce their own journalism. The team has co-authored pieces with the Kurdish community in Bristol showing how regional developments in the Middle East are affecting them here in the United Kingdom (Saelens, Cantwell-Corn, Aviram, 2014; Amin, 2015).

The organisation has also worked with a Somali teenager to place freedom of information requests about deportation rates and investigate how they impacted on the Somali community, a story which was published both in English and in Somali (Mohamed, 2015). Aviram explained their approach stems from an effort to reimagine how local journalism works and even what type of content can be considered local journalism.

The Bristol Cable's strategy for reaching out to people and converting them into members relies on the community's understanding that legacy local media can no longer deliver the type of journalism needed to hold local authorities and corporations to account. The team ties the local situation in their area to national and international trends to get people to sign up.

The long term goal is for the Cable to become sustainable – 12 team members are now paid on a part- or full-time basis, but there is still some way to go. But Aviram believes their model can work in other parts of the country where local journalism has suffered from cost-cutting, and where other media deserts have formed.

In fact, he plans to create a package documenting their experience, highlighting what they have done well and what could have been done better. With some start-up capital and a local network of experts to support them, like-minded people in other areas could replicate and evolve their model.

"There's been so much innovation on a national and international level but barely on a local level. Most people find local journalism boring as hell and rightly so. There is a way in which we can reimagine what local journalism looks like and actually make it interesting."

## References

(2016) MH17 crash: Dutch investigators to assess new study implicating Russian soldiers, *Agence-France Presse*, 4 January. Available online at https://www.theguardian.com/world/2016/jan/04/mh17-dutch-investigators-to-study-citizen-journalist-claims-over-russians-involved-in-crash accessed on 10 September 2016.

Amin, Esam (2015) Why are Bristolian Kurds boycotting new year celebrations?, *The Bristol Cable*, 18 March. Available online at https://thebristolcable.org/2015/03/why-are-bristolian-kurds-boycotting-new-year-celebration/ accessed on 11 September 2016.

Borger, Julian and Higgins, Eliot (2015) Russia shelled Ukrainians from within its own territory, says study, *Guardian*, 17 February. Available online at https://www.theguardian.com/world/2015/feb/17/russia-shelled-ukrainians-from-within-its-own-territory-says-study, accessed on 11 September 2016.

Luhn, Alec (2016) MH17 report identifies Russian soldiers suspected of downing plane in Ukraine, Guardian, 24 February, Available online at https://www.theguardian.com/world/2016/feb/24/mh17-report-identifies-russian-soldiers-suspected-of-downing-plane-in-ukraine accessed on 10 September 2016.

Mohamed, Abdi (2015) Will Somali voters determine Bristol's 2015 General Election, *The Bristol Cable*, 5 May. Available online at https://thebristolcable.org/2015/05/somali-voters-eng/ accessed on 11 September 2016

Saelens, Alec and Cantwell-Corn, Adam and Aviram, Alon (2014) 'We are not allowed a state on the ground, so we created one online', *The Bristol Cable*, 21 October. Available online at https://thebristolcable.org/2014/10/kurdish-debate/ accessed on 11 September 2016

Thurman, Neil and Cornia, Alessio and Kunert, Jessica (2016) *Journalists in the UK*, Reuters Institute for the Study of Journalism

## Note on the contributor
Catalina Albeanu is international editor at Journalism.co.uk, which is a one-stop shop for all things digital journalism, publishing news on all of the latest innovations changing the industry, providing training and experience-sharing events to help people and companies improve their digital skills, and hosting journalism's leading jobs board. Before joining Journalism.co.uk, Catalina covered London's start-up scene and media industry events after graduating with a journalism degree from City, University of London.

# Death and transfiguration
(with apologies to Richard Strauss)

**Print can have no hope of arresting the dominance of broadcast news and current affairs, but can nonetheless learn to accommodate to it, argues David Lloyd from his former long-time vantage position as Head of News and Current Affairs at Channel 4. The way to do it, he says, is for newspapers to monetise more aggressively the value in their critics and columnists**

Does a case study about a successful commercial television company have any relevance in a book about the future of print journalism? It is a reasonable question and precisely the one the editors of this book asked themselves before including this chapter. You, the reader, will be the judge whether we have made the right decision, but the fact that it still seems a reasonable question to ask shows how far apart in some ways print and broadcast remain and how little they know (or understand) one another.

"Print? You know nothing whatsoever about it. You've never even worked in it." That was my wife's instinctive response to the prospect of me writing this chapter, a view that will no doubt be echoed by many more objective souls. It is true, if only up to a point. However, I do believe I have something to offer from a parallel experience of journalism practised over the years.

My entire journalistic career has been spent in broadcast media rather than print. I was briefly the cricket correspondent for my university newspaper, *Cherwell*, but sacked for inadequate attendance at the matches. I can only lay claim therefore to the journalistic life-skill of substituting reminiscence and reflection for reportage.

Nevertheless I have witnessed at first hand the leading edge of journalism shift towards television and, from my ringside seat, can boast a minor role in this process. Such are my credentials, and I shall carefully join up the dots of my own experience to advance some thoughts for print's salvation.

## More journalism, not less…

None of us should derive any joy from the travails of print; a free society needs as versatile and robust a journalistic culture as its citizens can deliver to it. My prescriptions are focused on expanding the many journalistic corps, not cutting them back in a continuing series of redundancies for short-term financial advantage.

## Online – just a temporary stay of execution?

Newspaper groups' attitudes to online content clearly vary. It therefore must be time to declare only a paywall/subscription approach holds out any prospect of salvation. Not for the first time Rupert Murdoch got this right – and early in the game – and The Guardian's attitude, by contrast, seems ruinously ideological.

Some half-way house may be on the cards for The Guardian. This could be news material being offered freely but with subscription income being derived from premium material, which may follow the model that David Abraham has introduced at Channel 4. Here All4 subscribers offer both sophisticated demographic data and, with subscription income, even out the boom and bust of the advertising market in the process. (See chapter 7 for more discussion of Channel 4)

Sadly, the free online broadsheet offer is currently only reducing costs, rather than enhancing revenues. My reading is that advertising revenue for online is simply cannibalising possible revenues to the printed paper, and both are being taken to the cleaners by social media.

## Premium for what?

The easy but as yet untested answer to this quandary would seem to be to charge for premium material offered under the group banner of a newspaper's columnists.

But is there really a single columnist at any newspaper that possesses a primacy of opinion-forming who could, in a few hundred words, change the political or social weather? If this challenge is thought too rhetorical, it would still be possible to monetise the output of a newspaper's most trusted critics – rather in the manner of 'high-end' TripAdvisor apps – whether on theatre, film, rock or restaurants. But this would again demand some serious re-thinking of a newspaper critic's role, taking them from the margins to the core of a newspaper's operation.

Perhaps the best example of a critic used and supported to this kind of advantage, but yet to be adequately monetised could be Simon Calder, Travel Editor of The Independent. He has been nurtured and branded from the paper's inception as 'the man who pays his way' and has gradually assumed the status of the guru of the weekend break. With similar support there seems no reason why that status cannot play to equal advantage for other newspapers with other critics in other areas of interest.

More pertinent than critics, though, to any newspaper's branding are its columnists; can serious analysis demonstrate how much subscription income they can generate, and how great a re-thinking of their role that may demand?

The Guardian clearly offers one such example. Devotees of a Rawnsley, Hutton, Younge or Monbiot could surely be persuaded to subscribe to their next big book in extract form, pre-publication, just as Hardy or Dickens released their novels in the late 19th century.

And it might even be possible to conjure some income from Seumas Milne's 'Corbyn, my part in his rise', simply because we may all want to know how on earth this turns out. For other titles, of another hue, please read a Parris, Cameron (Sue) or whomsoever accordingly.

Without a fundamental re-think of the role of columnists within a newspaper, it seems that the only premium content that newspapers can currently stake an ownership to is the high-end news on which they are precisely losing ground to broadcast media. But the reasons they are losing this ground need first to be analysed in greater detail, and can be addressed under several distinct headings, of which reader trust surely plays an important part.

### Standards…and trust

This is admittedly a heading that applies almost exclusively to the red-top tabloids and it would be unfair to suggest that the entirety of broadsheet print titles has been tarred with their brush. Nevertheless, it's fair to point out that, at an early stage of the Coalition, the Daily Telegraph's attempt to deploy moles posing as constituents at one of Vince Cable's surgeries to elicit disquiet at the Government's performance was a fishing expedition that would never have been allowed in television.

Even if the enterprise succeeded in hanging Cable out to dry, the end did not justify the means. Ofcom guidelines demand prima facie evidence of behaviour, or intention to commit such, against the public interest, before any undercover sting can be entertained.

In effect, secret filming or recording on television is only an on-camera confirmation of evidence already gleaned – a not unreasonable bar to vault given the sheer power to destroy that miniaturised technology offers.

Throughout the Leveson enquiry too little account was paid to the context rather than the detail of declining press ethics at the tabloid end of the market, yet this is surely integral to that self-same collapse in sales, even of the market leaders.

It is perhaps no wonder that this tabloid culture sought to arrest that loss of cover price income with ever more dramatic stories, obtained by any ethical short-cut that would fit.

Some of the grossest invasions of privacy betrayed an ignorance of the law among some senior editorial staff – something first highlighted in the Channel 4 weekly programme Hard News.

In the circumstances the self-serving bickering that attended the formation of any one recognised regulatory body after Leveson had ruled seems to be a clear symptom of empires in terminal decline (cf Rome, Austro-Hungary, Ottoman, Ancient Athens, Incas even), behind the protective windshield of vaunted 'press freedom', when regulation of standards – of truth, accuracy, fairness and due impartiality – has worked very well and constructively, indeed creatively, for many years in broadcast.

## Form and content...

The competitive challenge for high-end news content, both tabloid and broadsheet, appears at its most visible in its distribution; small vans trundle bundles of newsprint round the country from the early evening in a vain attempt to compete with digital broadcast transmission, and the content of the television Ten O'clock Newses. The wonder, perhaps, is that this ritual is still played out nightly.

But if there is financial or cultural value, beyond mere consumer habit, in preserving the model of printed content on paper (and the success of the I as a printed news precis of record suggests that there is indeed), there are surely some lessons of distribution that newspaper managements could learn from their television competitors.

Newspaper dissemination is defined by having all the smart technology – of assembly of both content and advertising, and printing them in tandem – at the production end, whereas newsagents, large or small, simply receive and distribute their quota of copies of each title without any smart technology at all.

Television, on the other hand, places its smart technology at both ends of the process – at transmission and, with Freeview, Freesat or subscription boxes, at the point of reception.

## Lessons from TV?

Can newspapers learn from this model? It cannot be beyond the wit of newspaper managements and strategists to invest in reception 'hubs' that can print and reconcile copy with advertising in a finished assembly at various strategic locations around the country.

Time was when public libraries, or possibly Post Offices, would have been the obvious location for such hubs, but it still might be that placing them there – in the heart of the community – could lead to the regeneration of all concerned.

## Find the advertising

Integral to this model of distribution is the search for a new advertising dynamic. With an estimated 70 per cent of all advertising income enjoyed annually by network television, it is clear that national newspapers are not a must-place for national advertising. No single broadsheet delivers a critical mass of readership to deliver what national advertisers really need, but the same difficulty need not apply to regional or local customers.

Part of Channel 4's success in attracting advertising income has been in offering space on both a network and regional basis.

Whatever rates newspapers could command for such smaller opportunities, they would at least represent a new outlet in the market and any such idea must surely better the current daily haemorrhage of production cost over income.

## Content and form plus technology?
Aside from distribution the more intractable and subtle challenge for print lies in the way that the visual media can now tell their stories.

At City University I attempt to introduce broadcast journalism students to the grammar of television narrative as it has developed, under the rubric that in news 'script leads, and visuals follow', whereas in current affairs the roles are reversed.

This covers their origins in print and then harnesses digital editing to deliver dramatic reconstruction and low-cost and versatile graphic explanation.

I show them a copy of the first-ever Dispatches from 1987, an excellent and prescient piece of journalism on the black market for plutonium. It comes across as an illustrated version of print rather than a television experience in its own right. Many able television producers and directors have laboured to this end in the intervening years, and their testimonial is the gap that has been opened up – with print trundling along in their wake.

Brokering the advance of digital technology to achieve a genuinely accessible and engaging narrative has had its effect on print writing styles, particularly in the case of pro-active investigative journalism, in which – I would judge – Dispatches continues to lead the way.

But, in the case of hard, reactive, frontline news, television has also achieved a primacy by means of the portability of broadcast-quality cameras, and the enhancement in the edit suite of citizens' smartphone material. The most potent metaphor for this could be seen on the occasion of the November 2015 Paris Jihadi attacks when virtually all news outlets, both print and television, came to rely on adventitious smartphone video purchased from bystanders by Le Monde.

More sadly, an equally potent metaphor lies in the death of the Sunday Times' distinguished war correspondent Marie Colvin, killed in Syria, in a no-man's land civil war without recognisable front lines, but worse, in the service of a deadline likely to be scooped by the most rookie of TV freelancers. The decline of print is not without victims, and needless ones at that.

## The road to salvation?
It's unlikely, coming from television, I alone possess the philosopher's stone that has eluded a majority of newspaper managements. Yet, at the same time, some thoughts do suggest themselves that could at least be woven together into some sort of plan of redemption. My mantra is based on the fact that television, for its starting points and agendas, relies far more on print journalism than it likes to admit and that the journalism profession needs greater security of employment,

across all genres and outlets, than it currently enjoys, supported by a more expansive business mind that can deliver it a proper robustness.

## In the TV beginning...

First, some history. Throughout the 1950s and 1960s British cinema audiences fell in the face of television until hitting their lowest point in, I think, the early 1970s. The response of Rank and EMI was to regard television as an unqualified enemy, and to make no concessions whatever to it, including holding back TV screening rights for films for as many as seven years after the first cinema release.

The turnaround came not only through the arrival of Hollywood hits like Star Wars and ET, and Steven Spielberg in general, but when the exhibitors started to make concessions to television by reducing the screening delay and even using their foyers to sell videos.

In such an accommodation there surely lies a lesson, and one that could be brought to bear upon the strategy of newspaper managements. It involves them re-assessing the value of their key assets, their journalists, rather than cursing them as a cost round their necks, to be made redundant wherever possible. And it involves them retracing steps to some of their own pasts, when Observer Films – to name but one – added greatly to the Guardian Media Group's profits with commissions from the BBC and Channel 4.

It surely cannot be beyond the wit of newspaper chief executives to replicate this success on behalf of other titles, and might even press the case for a more uniform regulation across all journalistic media, while following television's lead.

## Follow the money to television...

With so much advertising directed to television, it must surely make sense to monetise journalistic assets by pitching ideas to television, on a global basis, both in strict news and current affairs and specialist factual-even factual entertainment, if available.

Of course, the television industry has changed greatly in the last decade, since Observer Films succeeded so markedly, but any profitable use of one's staff surely must be better than online videos that attract no advertising or subscription.

What is it that prevents newspaper managements from forming the next super-Indie? If Elisabeth (daughter of Rupert) Murdoch and her company Shine can do it, why not others?

And yes, there is a delicious irony available in this plan, too. If a significant proportion of journalistic output is transmitted via television – or broadcast – we might all benefit from a more coherent and cohesive level of regulation, and an enforced rise in standards and trust.

I've no doubt that my smorgasbord of prescriptions may be of more use, and more relevant, to some titles than others; these ideas are certainly not mutually exclusive. A long, high paywall, protecting all output, is hardly desirable and may not be sustainable in the long term. Better to introduce subscription in a new model and attitude as I have outlined.

There may be significant evidential gaps in what I have written, but in catalytic terms, if any one spark ignites a discernible change of thinking and saves a single journalistic job, my time at the keyboard will have been worth it.

## Note on the contributor

David Lloyd joined the BBC as a general trainee in 1967, rising to edit The Money Programme, Newsnight and Breakfast Time, before moving to Channel 4 in 1986. There he was Head of News and Current Affairs he originated Dispatches and Unreported World and was responsible for the development of Channel 4 News for nearly 20 years. He is currently a visiting professor in television journalism at City University of London, teaching long-form television documentary to MA students.

# The future

\* \* \*

# The future is young – and it's pop up, too!

**John Mair**

So should be all just pack up our bags and leave the journalism field? Is there any future? Is it universally depressing? Maybe, maybe not.

The patterns of journalistic work may be changing but still the young keep coming into the trade. Journalism courses have been one of the growth areas in higher education in the last decade – in the vernacular, plenty more bums on university seats. But just who are the wannabe hacks entering HE?

Mark Spilsbury has undertaken a unique piece of research. With financial support from the National Council for the Training of Journalists (NCTJ), he has mined (for this book) the stats from the Higher Education Statistics Authority (HESA) for 2014-15, the last full year available. Some very interesting results, too.

More than 12,000 now study journalism at post and undergraduate levels in the UK. The majority are female, especially amongst postgrads; the vast majority are state-school educated at both levels (96/97 per cent); middle class; and white. Diversity has not taken hold – just eight per cent are black and four per cent of Asian origin. They do get jobs though; 22 per cent of undergraduates and 45 per cent of postgraduates are in journalism jobs six months after leaving university.

But the many courses maybe are not needed. Two thirds of those in journalism jobs six months on, according to HESA, had not studied the subject; nearly a fifth had studied languages of all sorts. A journalism degree, though, does make your employable in a wide area. Story-telling skills travel.

But where do these young people get their news?

In another piece of original research Tor Clark and I undertook a dipstick exercise with a semi-qualitative study of freshers (and a few recent graduates) at three UK universities. The findings are not good news for inkies. Students are abandoning print for online as it is easier to access and free. Less than ten per cent admit to buying a printed national paper regularly. A quarter never buy one. More than half never read a local paper. They are out of the habit of buying printed journalism or maybe these millennials simply never had it.

The present and future for them are digital platforms like Facebook and Twitter, which do bounce them to trusted news sites like the BBC and The Guardian. But news is also now expected to be free. So none of this augurs well for current business models.

The future is, however, entrepreneurial. Social Darwinism rules in the digital as well as the analogue sphere. Success comes to the quick and brave. Vide the rise of The New European.

This isn't just the story of the fastest national newspaper launch in UK history, though that's a story worth hearing in itself. The New European is a story about how print still has the power to capture the imagination and trigger the kind of emotional engagement for which we are all striving. And it's a story about teamwork, about how setting the right organisational structure and management ethos empowers a business to achieve what others would have seen as impossible.

Archant CEO Jeff Henry tells it for the first time in his chapter. It started with an email in the post-Brexit vote depression from one Archant executive to another: 'Jeff, I realise this will sound a little crazy but if ever there was a perfect time to launch a new national newspaper, this is it. There are 16.5m people out there feeling really hacked off and I can't think of any newspaper that properly represents that sense of anger many of them are feeling. A pro-European newspaper for the 48 per cent. Wdyt?'

Henry thought 'Why not?' In under two weeks his company launched the paper to capture (some of) the spirit of the age but, as Henry puts it: 'The point about zeitgeists is they disappear as quickly as they surface. Today's zeitgeist is tomorrow's fish and chip paper.'

Archant had found gold in the base metal of the Brexit debacle. The paper needed to sell just 15,000 copies to break even. It did. The four-week trial run became eight then 12. Today (late November 2016) the paper is offering subscriptions and trips to the place we will have to learn to call Europe.

So there is hope…it is digital, young, and it is pop up.

# The next generation of readers prefer online access

**A survey of students shows younger people are increasingly abandoning print for online formats, with ease of access and cost the main factors, says journalism lecturer and former newspaper editor Tor Clark**

If the future is in their hands, it's looking bleak for print journalism. That's what a small scale survey of students exclusively for this book has shown. The survey showed students largely didn't read hard copy local newspapers any more and very few regularly read national newspapers.

There was better news for magazines, with equal numbers of students saying they read printed magazines and saying they preferred their online versions.

A total of 67 mostly undergraduate journalism students in three UK universities were asked to complete a questionnaire about their consumption of printed national newspapers, local newspapers and magazines, in September and October 2016. They were mostly aged 18-20, but the inclusion of a handful of postgraduate students meant their ages ranged up to 32.

### Hard reading for the nationals

For national newspapers the findings are depressing, with only six students, or nine per cent, admitting to regularly buying a printed national newspaper. A quarter of them said they never bought a printed paper. The largest group, 44 out of 67 or 65 per cent, said they 'occasionally' bought a national.

All students said they used digital sources for accessing news more regularly than any other platform. Those who never bought a daily paper noted the ease of access of digital platforms as the biggest draw, but also preferred not to have to pay for news.

Interesting additional comments from those who only occasionally bought national newspapers included they didn't like the political bias in traditional national papers and many didn't think there were enough articles aimed at their own age group. Many did say they would buy national newspapers when they were covering a major event or big story.

## Gloom for the local press

The steep decline in circulations of local newspapers is well documented in section four of this book, but the results of this survey suggest the regionals have no hope of replacing the lost readers with those from the next generation. More than half of the students surveyed (55 per cent) said they never read a local paper.

Only four students (six per cent) said they regularly read a local paper with 26 of them, or 39 per cent, occasionally reading one. Many of those surveyed did check out local news through online portals, but they also offered a weird and wonderful variety of ways of keeping up with local news. A number said their most regular source for local news was 'word of mouth', many noted social media as a regular provider and, asked for her best source for local news, one student responded: 'The Co-op'.

## The longer form holds onto its readers

There was some cheer for enthusiasts for hard copy journalism from the students' responses to their consumption of magazine journalism, where 37 per cent said they regularly read mags and the same number said they never read printed periodicals. In the middle 22 per cent occasionally picked up a weekly or monthly mag. In all three categories all students said they consumed magazines digitally.

Those who never read printed magazines divided between those who liked magazines as a format, but only online, and those who had no interest in magazines at all. Interestingly a very small number still liked to collect high-end magazines, such as Vogue.

## Views on the future

Asked what they thought the future held for printed news most of the students were pessimistic, saying the format was doomed by the ubiquity and ease of access of online journalism, though some did feel some printed forms of journalism might survive.

Whether they regularly, occasionally or never consumed printed journalism, all respondents did access journalism by a variety of digital platforms. BBC News, as website and app, and social media were popular destinations for news fans.

## Weighing up the survey results

Today's students are obviously digital natives. They all carry mobile devices on which they access a variety of platforms, mostly for social purposes, but also to keep in touch with news. It is interesting to recall that ten years ago students did regularly buy newspapers and bring them to journalism classes but that now they never do. In their defence, you could as 'why should they?' when all the news they will need is available at the swipe of a finger, but nevertheless they are not even out of the habit of buying printed journalism, because most of them have never had the habit.

They all noted ease of access and (lack of) price as telling factors in their consumption of news, which does not offer much comfort for those who hope the answer to paying for digital journalism might lie in subscription models.

Of course these students are at the beginning of their careers and will certainly consume more and specialist media as they develop their studies and then their careers, but they want that journalism easy and they want it free.

This was a small survey, not big enough to draw definitive conclusions on the future of printed media, but it was indicative of wider trends among the young, trends which do not offer any cheer to publishers of printed journalism. And, at the risk of appearing even more alarmist, we must remember these students are firstly intelligent and educated and secondly, most worryingly, given their lack of uptake of traditional journalism, they are all very interested in journalism because they are all journalism students. If journalism students won't read printed journalism, what hope is there of getting anyone else to?

## So what does it all mean?

There are many chapters elsewhere in this collection of fascinating articles that offer success stories in printed journalism, stories of survival, of successful niche publishing, of subscription success and, in one notable case, of the launch of a new national newspaper to a receptive market.

This survey is small in scale and very narrow in its geography and age range, but given all participants are studying journalism at degree level, it does not offer much hope that people will still want to consume printed journalism in future, with regional publishers being the hardest hit by the audience's abandonment of the printed form.

## Note on the contributor

Tor Clark is Principal Lecturer in Journalism at De Montfort University in Leicester, UK. Previously he was a journalist in the UK regional press, working as a political reporter, news editor and, lastly, as editor of two regional newspapers. He is co-editor of this book.

# Who studies journalism and why?

**Despite concerns about over-supply of journalism courses and the disruption to 'traditional' patterns of employment in the industry caused by the introductions of digital technologies, Journalism students remain very employable, reports Mark Spilsbury**

## Introduction

Much negative publicity surrounds the newspaper industry and the employment of journalists, yet there appears to be no shortage of people wanting to study journalism. This chapter examines who studies journalism and why, using data provided by the Higher Education Statistics Authority. The availability of this data has been made possible by funding from the National Council for the Training of Journalists (NCTJ), as part of its wider research programme looking at the diversity of the journalism profession.

## Numbers studying journalism and type of study

For the most recent year that data is available (2014/15), there were just over 12,000 students studying on a Journalism course at one of 72 Higher Education Institutions in the UK. These are 'all students' (i.e. including students on each year at a university): there were 5,280 students in their first year of Journalism study (split between 1,525 at postgraduate level and 3,755 at undergraduate level).

The majority (83 per cent) are studying at an undergraduate level. 95 per cent are studying full-time courses, with 5 per cent on a part-time basis. Journalism students are:

- more likely to be studying at an undergraduate level (83 per cent compared to 76 per cent of all other subjects), and

- more likely to be studying full-time (95 per cent compared to 75 per cent).

## Table 1: Numbers studying journalism and mode of study

| | Studying Journalism | | Studying all other subject | |
| --- | --- | --- | --- | --- |
| | n | % | n | % |
| **Level of study** | | | | |
| First degree | 9,920 | 82 | 1,514,305 | 67 |
| Other undergraduate | 150 | 1 | 203,520 | 9 |
| Postgraduate (taught) | 1,830 | 15 | 423,440 | 19 |
| Postgraduate (research) | 125 | 1 | 112,790 | 5 |
| | | | | |
| **Mode of study** | | | | |
| Full-time | 11,460 | 95 | 1,685,690 | 75 |
| Part-time | 570 | 5 | 568,360 | 25 |
| | | | | |
| **Total** | **12,030** | **100** | 2,254,050 | **100** |

*Source: HESA, Student Record 2014/15*

The patterns within this are the same for Journalism as for other subjects – those studying at an undergraduate level are more likely to be studying full-time (97 per cent compared to 85 per cent of those studying at a postgraduate level).

### Who is studying journalism?

HESA collect a range of data on students studying in Higher Education and this allows us to understand the nature of students studying Journalism and (as important) how this compares to the characteristics of students on other courses. In this section, we separate this analysis between undergraduates and postgraduates to make sure that we compare, as far as possible, like with like. This data shows that for undergraduates:

- the majority of Journalism students are female (57 per cent), but that this is little different from the figure across all other subjects (56 per cent);

- 82 per cent of Journalism students who gave their ethnicity were white, with 8 per cent black, 4 per cent Asian and 6 per cent 'other'. This is a higher proportion of white students than for all other subjects (79 per cent) and a lower proportion of Asian students (10 per cent) for all other subjects);

- 9 per cent of undergraduate Journalism students are known to have a disability, which compares to 12 per cent of students across all other subjects; and

- 73 per cent of undergraduate Journalism students were 20 and under, 22 per cent aged 21-24, with small proportions in older age groups. This is a different pattern to those studying all other subjects where far fewer (52 per cent) are aged 20 and under and higher proportions are at older age levels.

The make-up of postgraduates shows that:

- the majority of postgraduate Journalism students are female (62 per cent compared to 38 per cent of men);
- the majority of postgraduate Journalism students are white 86 per cent – a higher proportion than for postgraduates studying all other subjects;
- 7 per cent of postgraduate Journalism students are known to have a disability, which is the same as postgraduate students across all other subjects; and
- the majority of postgraduate Journalism students are aged 21-24 (61 per cent) with 20 per cent aged 25-29. Some 18 per cent are aged 30 and over. This compares with 33 per cent aged 21-24 for students of all other subjects, 25 per cent aged 25-29 and 42 per cent aged 30-plus.

This difference in age distribution is of interest: it may suggest that people are more likely to study postgraduate journalism immediately (or soon after) after their first degree rather than waiting later, as seems to be the case for other subjects. It has been suggested elsewhere (Journalism at Work[1], 2012, published by the NCTJ) that entry into a journalism job is increasingly dependent of individuals having a postgraduate qualification and this may be what is being reflected in this data.

## Table 2: Personal characteristics of Journalism students

| | Studying Journalism | | Studying all other subject | |
| --- | --- | --- | --- | --- |
| | | | | |
| | **n** | **%** | **n** | **%** |
| **Undergraduates** | | | | |
| **Sex** | | | | |
| Male | 4,295 | 43 | 752,995 | 44 |
| Female | 5,770 | 57 | 964,575 | 56 |
| | | | | |
| **Ethnicity** | | | | |
| White | 7,180 | 82 | 1,151,400 | 79 |
| Black | 690 | 8 | 98,430 | 7 |
| Asian | 375 | 4 | 146,265 | 10 |
| Other (including mixed) | 515 | 6 | 69,775 | 5 |
| | | | | |
| **Disability** | | | | |
| Known to have a disability | 955 | 9 | 202,295 | 12 |
| No known disability or unknown | 9,120 | 91 | 1,515,530 | 88 |
| | | | | |

| Age | | | | |
|---|---|---|---|---|
| 20 and under | 7,345 | 73 | 893,440 | 52 |
| 21-24 | 2,170 | 22 | 425,465 | 25 |
| 25-29 | 305 | 3 | 126,880 | 7 |
| 30 and over | 250 | 2 | 271,825 | 16 |
| | | | | |
| **Total** | **10,070** | **100** | **1,717,575** | **100** |
| | | | | |
| **Postgraduates** | | | | |
| **Sex** | | | | |
| Male | 740 | 38 | 234,335 | 44 |
| Female | 1,215 | 62 | 301,770 | 56 |
| | | | | |
| **Ethnicity** | | | | |
| White | 870 | 86 | 259,120 | 81 |
| Black | 35 | 4 | 18,300 | 6 |
| Asian | 55 | 5 | 228,540 | 9 |
| Other (including mixed) | 55 | 6 | 14,165 | 4 |
| | | | | |
| **Disability** | | | | |
| Known to have a disability | 145 | 7 | 36,030 | 7 |
| No known disability or unknown | 1,815 | 93 | 500,195 | 93 |
| | | | | |
| **Age** | | | | |
| 20 and under | 25 | 1 | 2,660 | 1 |
| 21-24 | 1,200 | 61 | 175,880 | 33 |
| 25-29 | 390 | 20 | 132,825 | 25 |
| 30 and over | 340 | 18 | 224,750 | 42 |
| | | | | |
| **Total** | **1,955** | **100** | **536,105** | **100** |

*Source: HESA, Student Record 2014/15*

*Note: bases are adjusted for each category to remove those who did not provide data so that all percentages add to 100*

So, in terms of physical characteristics, Journalism students look very much like the rest of the student body: a little more likely to be from white ethnic groups, less likely to have a known disability and (considering those on undergraduate courses), more likely to be young., but overall not in marked differences. Other areas of concern do not relate to physical characteristics, but background – the issue of diversity and the impact of social class on studying Journalism.

It is worth noting that when collecting details on education and socio-economic class, the HESA data has a reasonably high proportions of gaps, with respondents refusing to answer or just because of missing data. In these cases – shown in the table below – we have shown the distributions with this missing data included and with the table re-based to remove them from the percentages. These data gaps are particularly severe for students studying at postgraduate level. We have no way of knowing if there is any significant bias in these non-responses: whether, for example, people from the privately-funded education sector or higher socio-economic classes are more (or less) likely to report their school type or socio-economic class, so on this basis we assume that they have the same distribution as those who have given a response.

The first thing to note is that the data on 'school type' does not show the pattern that we may have expected. Research from the Sutton Trust[2] has previously shown that half of 'leading journalists' were privately educated: we might also expect, therefore, that we would see a preponderance of privately-educated students studying Journalism, but the opposite is true for the undergraduate level. The data shows that 82 per cent of Journalism undergraduates were funded in the state system, with only 3 per cent being educated privately, although we have to bear in mind that there is missing data for a significant 16 per cent. If we remove these from the base, the data suggests that 97 per cent of undergraduate Journalism students were state-educated. The comparable proportions for undergraduates studying all other subjects are 91 per cent state-educated and 9 per cent from the private system.

The data for postgraduates is similar: removing those for whom there is no data, it suggests that 97 per cent of those on a postgraduate Journalism were from a state school or college, with 3 per cent from a private school. This is broadly similar to the data for all other postgraduate subjects, where 99 per cent were state-educated.

In terms of socio-economic class, the re-based data shows that 63 per cent of undergraduate students studying Journalism were from socio-economic groups 1-3, similar to the 65 per cent of students studying all other undergraduate subjects. For postgraduate study, 66 per cent of those studying Journalism were from socio-economic groups 1-3 (compared to 74 per cent for all other postgraduate subjects) and 29 per cent in Groups 4-7 (compared to 24 per cent for all other postgraduate subjects).

## Table 3: Education and socio-economic class of journalism students

| | Studying Journalism | | | Studying all other subject | | |
|---|---|---|---|---|---|---|
| | **n** | **%** | | **n** | **%** | |
| **Undergraduates** | | | | | | |
| | | | (excluding DK's) | | | (excluding DK's) |
| **School type** | | | | | | |
| State-funded school or college | 8,220 | 82 | 97 | 1,133,810 | 66 | 91 |
| Privately funded school | 285 | 3 | 3 | 114,395 | 7 | 9 |
| Unknown or not applicable school type | 1,565 | 16 | n/a | 469,615 | 27 | n/a |
| | | | | | | |
| **Socio-economic class** | | | | | | |
| 1-3 | 4,635 | 46 | 63 | 634,265 | 37 | 65 |
| 4-7 | 2,645 | 26 | 36 | 335,330 | 20 | 34 |
| Never worked & long-term unemployed | 45 | 0 | 1 | 6,310 | 0 | 1 |
| Not classified | 2,275 | 23 | n/a | 399,200 | 23 | n/a |
| Unknown | 470 | 5 | n/a | 342,720 | 20 | n/a |
| | | | | | | |
| **Total** | **10,070** | **100** | **100** | **1,717,825** | **100** | **100** |
| | | | | | | |
| **Postgraduates** | | | | | | |
| | | | (excluding DK's) | | | (excluding DK's) |
| **School type** | | | | | | |
| State-funded school or college | 165 | 9 | 97 | 71,615 | 13 | 99 |
| Privately funded school | 5 | * | 3 | 1,005 | * | 1 |
| Unknown or not applicable school type | 1,785 | 91 | n/a | 463,610 | 86 | n/a |
| | | | | | | |

| Socio-economic class | | | | | | |
|---|---|---|---|---|---|---|
| 1-3 | 95 | 5 | 66 | 43,290 | 8 | 74 |
| 4-7 | 40 | 2 | 29 | 13,990 | 3 | 24 |
| Never worked & long-term unemployed | 5 | * | 5 | 1,000 | * | 2 |
| Not classified | 290 | 15 | n/a | 71,475 | 13 | n/a |
| Unknown | 1,525 | 78 | n/a | 406,470 | 76 | n/a |
| | | | | | | |
| **Total** | **1,960** | **100** | **100** | **536,105** | **100** | **100** |

*Source: HESA, Student Record 2014/15*

## Why do they study journalism?

Individuals will have many reasons for going into Higher Education to study Journalism (or, indeed, any other subject). However, it is generally assumed that some of the main reasons are to (i) secure a job at the end of it and (ii) get a job in a field that they want. HESA again provides us information on these aspects via its 'Destinations of Leavers Survey' which follows leavers from HE six months after they have graduated. Again, we can compare Journalism students with students studying all other subjects.

On the first of these Journalism students are likely to be in work and more likely to be in work than leavers who studied other subjects. Some 82 per cent of Journalism students are in work (64 per cent full-time, 17 per cent part-time and 1 per cent 'primarily' in work), compared to 75 per cent of students of all other subjects (60, 12 and 3 per cent respectively). Journalism students are less likely to have continued their studying (6 per cent compared to 16 per cent). They are, however, more likely to be unemployed: 7 per cent compared to 4 per cent.

There is a distinction between employment rates of undergraduate and postgraduate Journalism students. Some 89 per cent of postgraduate students were in employment six months after graduation, compared to 77 per cent of undergraduate Journalism students. The difference is almost all made up of the differing proportions who have moved into further study (9 per cent of undergraduates, 1 per cent for postgraduates).

**Table 4: Current activity**

|  | Journalism students | | All other subjects | |
|---|---|---|---|---|
|  | *n* | *%* | *n* | *%* |
| Full-time work | 1,695 | 64 | 236,245 | 60 |
| Part-time work | 460 | 17 | 47,925 | 12 |
| Primarily in work and also studying | 25 | 1 | 12,820 | 3 |
| Primarily studying and also in work | 25 | 1 | 10,000 | 3 |
| Full-time study | 115 | 4 | 47,010 | 12 |
| Part-time study | 15 | 1 | 4,460 | 1 |
| Due to start work | 30 | 1 | 3,420 | 1 |
| Unemployed | 175 | 7 | 16,975 | 4 |
| Other | 125 | 5 | 17,830 | 4 |
|  |  |  |  |  |
| **Total** | **2,665** | **100** | **396,680** | **100** |

*Source: HESA Destinations of Leavers Survey 2014/15*

As to whether this is a job the individual wanted, this is more difficult to assess. Our main guide here is the occupation the individual is doing some six months after graduation – which in the HESA data is coded to the Office for National Statistics Standard Occupational Classification. From this we can see, in broad terms, what the individuals who studied journalism are doing in work. This shows that 22 per cent of those who studied Journalism at university were working as a journalist some six months later, with a further 5 per cent working in the (perhaps related) field of Public Relations. If we again remove the 'Don't knows' from the data, this suggests that over a quarter (26 per cent) of those leaving university after studying Journalism are working as a journalist, with a further 6 per cent working in PR.

The assumption here is that someone who studied Journalism at university will want to become a journalist when they leave – which is an assumption which may not be true. It may not be the case that a decision taken at the age of 18 to study Journalism will result in a decision three years later to become a journalist. A wider measure, perhaps, is the extent to which those who studied Journalism are working in 'graduate level' jobs, loosely defined as being those in the higher level occupations (coded 1-3 in the SOC). On this measure, it was nearly three quarters (73 per cent).

Here though, we should note a clear distinction between the proportion working as journalists from postgraduate and undergraduate courses. The data shows that 45 per cent of employed leavers from postgraduate Journalism courses were working as journalists (which increases to 50 per cent if the 'don't know' data is removed) compared to 14 per cent of employed leavers from undergraduate courses (18 per cent when the 'don't knows' are removed).

Evidently (and perhaps not surprisingly), postgraduate Journalism courses are more likely to lead to employment as a journalist than undergraduate journalism courses.

## Table 5: Occupation of Journalism leavers

| Occupation | | n | % | % |
|---|---|---|---|---|
| **Code** | **Description** | | | **Excluding DKs** |
| 11 | Corporate managers and directors | 40 | 1 | 2 |
| 12 | Other managers and proprietors | 25 | 1 | 1 |
| 21 | Science, research, engineering and technology professionals | 45 | 2 | 2 |
| 22 | Health professionals | 5 | * | 0 |
| 23 | Teaching and educational professionals | 40 | 1 | 2 |
| 24710 | Journalists, newspaper and periodical editors | 575 | 22 | 26 |
| 24720 | Public relations professionals | 140 | 5 | 6 |
| Others in (24) | Business, media and public service professionals | 55 | 2 | 2 |
| 31 | Science, engineering and technology associate professionals | 20 | 1 | 1 |
| 32 | Health and social care associate professionals | 15 | 1 | 1 |
| 33 | Protective service occupations | * | * | 0 |
| 34 | Culture, media and sports occupations | 295 | 11 | 13 |
| 35 | Business and public service associate professionals | 360 | 13 | 16 |
| 41 | Administrative occupations | 120 | 4 | 5 |
| 42 | Secretarial and related occupations | 30 | 1 | 1 |
| 51 | Skilled agricultural and related trades | * | * | 0 |
| 52 | Skilled metal, electrical and electronic trades | * | * | 0 |
| 53 | Skilled construction and building trades | * | * | 0 |
| 54 | Textiles, printing and other skilled trades | 15 | 1 | 1 |
| 61 | Caring personal service occupations | 30 | 1 | 1 |
| 62 | Leisure, travel and related personal service occupations | 15 | * | 1 |
| 71 | Sales occupations | 205 | 8 | 9 |
| 72 | Customer service occupations | 65 | 2 | 3 |
| 81 | Process, plant and machine operatives | * | | * |
| 82 | Transport and mobile machine drivers and operatives | 5 | | * |
| 91 | Elementary trades and related occupations | 5 | | * |
| 92 | Elementary administration and service occupations | 120 | 4 | 5 |
| | | | | |
| Unknown/ not applicable | | 450 | 17 | n/a |
| | | | | |
| **Total** | | **2,665** | **100** | **100** |

*Source: HESA Destinations of Leavers Survey 2014/15*

There could be an argument made that if only a quarter of those who studied Journalism at university are working as a journalist, this indicates an element of over-supply of journalism courses. We are not convinced by this: if this was the case, it would be expected that nearly all people who having left HE who are working as a journalist would have studied Journalism. This is not the case: research for the NCTJ on the HESA database suggests that of the individuals who left Higher Education in 2012/13 and were working as a journalist, two-thirds (65 per cent) did not study journalism. Just over a third (35 per cent) had studied Journalism. Significant proportions of these 'new entrant' journalists have studied subject areas outside the 'media' areas: nearly a fifth (18 per cent) studied Languages (which includes English studies, Classical Studies and American Studies, as well as Foreign Language Studies), a tenth (10 per cent) studied Creative Arts and Design (which includes Imaginative Writing, Fine Art, Design Studies, etc) and 7 per cent Historical and Philosophical Studies (including History, Archaeology, Philosophy and Theology).

## Discussion and conclusion

This chapter set out to investigate two questions: what kind of people study journalism at university and why do they do it? Data from HESA suggests that:

- Journalism students look very much like other students:
  - in terms of *personal characteristics*, females are in a majority (57 per cent of Journalism students), the majority (82 per cent) of them are from white ethnic groups and the majority do not have a known disability. These traits are much in line with the general student body. Where Journalism students do vary slightly is in their age: 73 per cent of Journalism students were 20 and under, 22 per cent aged 21-24, with small proportions in older age groups. This is a different pattern to those studying all other subjects – where a much lower 52 per cent are aged 20 and under and higher proportions are at older age levels;
  - in terms of *socio-economic background*, Journalism students are less, not more, likely to have been through private education than their colleagues at university and are from similar socio-economic backgrounds as the wider student body

- Journalism students will typically go to university for the same reasons as other students – to get a job, a graduate level job and a job that they have some affinity with. In this, they are successful and journalism 'works for them':
  - 82 per cent of those who have studied Journalism at a HE institution are in work six months after;
  - just over a quarter (26 per cent) are working as a journalist, with a further 6 per cent working in PR; 73 per cent are working in a 'graduate level' job.

This data shows that, despite much concern about over-supply of journalism courses and the disruption to 'traditional' patterns of journalism employment caused by the introductions of digital technologies, Journalism students are very employable. Not all work as journalists (though if you study a postgraduate Journalism degree the chance is higher), but this reflects the spread of journalists across different sectors of the economy. It should be no surprise that in a workplace where the ability to communicate is valued, those who have been trained to tell stories find themselves in demand.

This data also sheds some light on the concerns about diversity, particularly the impact on social class on the likelihood of becoming a journalist. At this level of analysis, there is no indication recruiters to Journalism courses are disproportionately selecting those from higher socio-economic groups or with a private school background. To the extent this is an issue within journalism, the discrimination appears to be taking place further down the pipeline, when individuals are selected for their first jobs or in the early part of their careers.

## Notes

[1] Journalism at Work, 2012, NCTJ, available at:
http://www.nctj.com/downloadlibrary/jaw_final_higher_2.pdf

[2] See Sutton Trust at http://www.suttontrust.com/researcharchive/leading-people-2016/

## Note on the contributor

Mark Spilsbury is a freelance economic researcher who works frequently in the creative industries. He was responsible for the underpinning work on defining the creative industries on behalf of the Department for Culture, Media and Sport, Creative Skillset. Mark has studied the changing employment patterns of journalists over a number of years in a series of research projects for the NCTJ, including Journalists at Work, 2012, the developing skills journalists will require in the future (NCTJ, Emerging Skills for Journalists, 2014) and the emerging freelance journalism market (forthcoming).

# Pop-up publishing: a new approach for print

**The New European isn't just the story of the fastest national newspaper launch in UK history, though that's a story worth hearing in itself. The New European is a story about how print still has the power to capture the imagination and trigger the kind of emotional engagement we are all striving for as an industry. And it's a story about teamwork, about how setting the right organisational structure and management ethos empowers a business to achieve what others would have seen as impossible, says Archant CEO Jeff Henry**

New national newspaper launches don't appear out of thin air. Even if they only take nine days, which was the case with The New European - a 'pop-up publication' launched by my company, Archant, in the aftermath of the UK's Brexit vote.

June 24 was a shocking day, whichever way you voted in the referendum on Britain's future in the European Union. Many people had gone to bed the night of the vote believing the Remain campaign were on track to victory. UKIP leader Nigel Farage had even conceded defeat. So when the vote went the other way, and by a relatively tight margin, millions of people were left feeling stunned that such an historic decision had gone against them. The sense of dismay in many parts of the country - those parts marked out in vivid yellow on the graphics plastered across all of our TV news channels - was palpable.

That Sunday, I received an email from Matt Kelly, the chief content officer I'd recruited to Archant the previous November. The email read:

"Jeff, I realise this will sound a little crazy but if ever there was a perfect time to launch a new national newspaper, this is it. There are 16.5m people out there feeling really hacked off and I can't think of any newspaper that properly represents that sense of anger many of them are feeling. A pro-European newspaper for the 48%. Wdyt?"

What did I think?

I thought he was right; it did sound a little crazy. Launching newspapers is usually a long, expensive and very challenging process. In very recent history, there were at least two other brave efforts that had bitten the dust prematurely; Trinity Mirror's The New Day and Cumberland News' 24. It was the kind of environment that would make any chief executive think very carefully. But he was also right about the opportunity. The 48 per cent was both a clearly identifiable and very passionate audience. We even knew exactly where they were to be found; the referendum data gave us the perfect distribution map. Plus, it was true there had been newspaper launches in the recent years which had managed to carve a new space in what might have seemed to be an impossibly crowded market, The i in particular.

Of course there were dozens of outstanding questions but I was keen to hear more and perhaps use this idea as a counterbalance to what promised to be a rather sober senior executive meeting that Tuesday as we discussed the potential downsides of Brexit for the media industry.

"Not crazy," I replied. "Bring it up at the exec and let's discuss."

Another reason, particular to Archant, I felt the idea was not entirely crazy is I was confident we could deliver. The company structure I'd inherited when I joined as CEO in 2014 was effectively around 30 different business units, operating more or less in isolation. Since Archant had grown rapidly in size from its roots in East Anglia, spreading across much of the country, and largely through the acquisition of other businesses, this was understandable. But it made for an incoherent - and sometimes inefficient - business, in parts, making strategy on the fly that often contradicted similar work being done elsewhere in the very same business.

A process of centralisation was long overdue and I, together with my executive colleagues, began the process we called One Archant - a profound transition away from localised business management to a central executive team who would co-ordinate and then execute a single strategy throughout the business.

No small challenge in an organisation with more than 1,500 employees spread across vast swathes of England. But, as testing as any significant restructure inevitably is, by late 2015 the benefits had already begun to show through. I look back now and realise, had this work not been done, any talk of galvanising all of the functions within Archant into producing something like The New European would have been fanciful. Matt's addition to the executive team in November was the last piece of a management jigsaw I am confident is as strong as any in the industry. And when I say team, I mean exactly that. We all work with a fierce focus towards a common goal - making Archant the best local media company in the UK.

As it happened, Matt almost forgot to bring the idea up on the Tuesday executive meeting. I think we were all wallowing in a morbid expectation Brexit was going to make a tough industry even tougher. Finally, after a couple of hours of prudent consideration and planning for potential downsides, I looked around the table and asked if anyone had any positive thoughts. This was Matt's cue, and his idea had evolved since the weekend. It would be a paper with a very limited shelf-life, published into the zeitgeist of interest Brexit had stirred up. We described this new formula for print launches as 'pop-up publishing', turning the traditional recipe of high-cost research and development followed by a massive launch advertising campaign entirely on its head. This, instead, would be agile, low-cost, and with an elegant exit baked into the plan.

It would not be a website. Instead, and totally counter to the perceived wisdom of digital-first, we'd focus on establishing it in print. After all, who would care or even notice if we launched a website? And who would pay for it? It would be a blend of serious Brexit debate and news and also the lighter, more fun cultural side of Europe. Every word in it would be original and focussed on the great things that bring us together as European. One thing it would not be, Matt was keen to point out, was party political.

"The whole point is the 48 per cent isn't aligned to any one party. That's why there's no newspaper there for them today," he argued.

This was an important consideration since Archant has a long and proud history of not taking political sides editorially. We like to give our community of readers the facts and assume they are smart enough to make decisions themselves. Framed that way, as transcending party politics, this new newspaper fitted that mandate perfectly. The business case would be centred around cover price. Given we had very recently seen the public's unwillingness to fork out 50p for a new newspaper, the proposed cover price of £2 seemed bold. But both Will Hattam, our chief marketing officer, and Matt seemed sold on the idea this would be a high quality product people would want to carry around like a badge of honour. Cover price was not going to be the thing which made or broke The New European. How close we could get to articulating the emotions of the Remain camp would be the deciding factor.

If Matt or I were expecting the room to push back against this prospect of launching a national newspaper (unknown territory for us as a leading local newspaper and magazine business), we had no reason to worry. Everyone instantly got the idea and saw the potential. Enthusiasm for the project grew quickly as we talked through how we would overcome what might seem, traditionally, to be significant barriers. At Archant we have a very talented team of in-house designers and Matt leads a team of 500 or so journalists. He also had a fantastic contacts book with some of the best writers and thinkers in the UK, having spent 20 years in national newspapers. So we had enough content resource to make it happen. But what about distribution? What about marketing? What about selling advertising?

All these important and challenging questions were compounded by a single, looming reality; if we were going to do this, we had to be quick. The point about zeitgeists is they disappear as quickly as they surface. Today's zeitgeist is tomorrow's fish and chip paper (or was, at least, until the EU outlawed wrapping chips in newsprint for health reasons). We agreed, given the clear impossibility of launching a new newspaper in three days flat, we would still have to aim for a launch the following Friday if we were to have maximum impact. This was late Tuesday afternoon. We were talking about a launch date nine days away. Was that even possible? Even with a fair wind and the necessary expertise and infrastructure, the idea of designing and filling a new newspaper with terrific original content, then getting it printed, then distributing it and marketing it nationwide was daunting to say the least. But as I looked around the table I did some mental maths. The seven senior executives who comprise One Archant's management team had close to 150 years of industry experience between us. If anyone could do it, this team could.

Will was confident in his team's ability to deliver, which was good enough for me. His head of circulation, Darron McCloughlin, was sure he could arrange a national distribution network in time. Nick Schiller, our group operations director, arranged a quickfire deal with the Guardian to use their Berliner-format presses and publish The New European in that most continental of formats. But perhaps it was Craig Nayman, our chief commercial officer, who had the tallest order, selling advertising into a newspaper nobody had ever seen, with a circulation nobody could know and with a polarised audience which might deter some brands. In the event, it was job he managed to carry off and The New European had paid-for advertisers from day one and continues to attract premium rates in the market.

What's the difference, at moments like this, between action and inaction? Between decision and dither? I believe it's an attitude. You just have to be bold enough to open your mind and see the opportunity in any given situation. This was a great case in point. We agreed to reconvene 24 hours later to run through the numbers and give ourselves time to sanity check the proposition. If things stacked up, we would push the button and go for it.

The next day we talked through a business case put together quickly by the finance team. Even without advertising, the commercial proposition seemed strong. Given we weren't going to have an advertising campaign, instead using our marketing team and to generate PR opportunities and spread the word, the project had a remarkably low circulation target to achieve break-even. Not only did it feel like an exciting new newspaper. It felt like an exciting new publishing model.

I decided on the spot to greenlight it. It was definitely worth a punt. Even if the paper did not sell, I was happy the process would be great for us as a team. We would learn new things and take confidence from our ability to innovate and challenge the perceived wisdoms. The fact it was a print project and not digital, which, like all legacy media businesses is a platform we are constantly developing, only seemed to add value to it. It was, in many ways, completely counterintuitive. This was a project very few businesses in the country could undertake. And even fewer, perhaps only one, actually would.

After a last minute wobble on price - we debated the benefits of a cheaper £1 - we resolved on a £2 price, and a large initial run to be printed by the Guardian presses in London and Manchester. We also decided we would only commit to an initial four issues, in keeping with the idea of pop-up publishing. In hindsight, this was the best decision we made in the entire project. Knowing this 'pop-up publication' was only designed for a very short life liberated us from all the typical attendant anxieties and risks associated with a venture of this size.

There was only one thing left. The name. It's called 'The New European', Matt said.

It may have sounded like the title of an Ultravox album from the 1980s but seemed to fit perfectly the spirit of adventure and optimism we had in mind. And it demonstrated yet another great benefit of pop-up publishing; no time to dilly-dally about with dozens of alternatives and weeks or months of market research. No time to let yourself be talked out of the first idea, the idea that got the project started in the first place.

So that was it. The New European and pop-up publishing were born. Then the work really began. Our first issue featured articles from Jonathan Freedland, Miranda Sawyer, James Brown plus Tanit Koch, the editor-in-chief of Europe's biggest selling newspaper, Germany's Bild, Wolfgang Blau, the Conde Nast digital boss, and Peter Bale, CEO of the Centre for Public Integrity.

On its very distinctive front page, there was a large cartoon from Private Eye cartoonists Kerber and Black in which a dog's owners idly wondered aloud if their pet could think.

The thought-bubble above the dopey-looking dog's head read: "These idiots... voting to leave the EU, creating a future of uncertainty and instability that will have a knock-on effect for generations to come... leading to isolation and beleaguerment for this once great nation!!!"

It seemed to capture very well the blend of seriousness and irreverent humour that has since characterised the paper.

The paper's launch attracted considerable interest from other media, even within the crammed news agenda of post-Brexit. The Archant team were interviewed dozens of times, and had appearances on Sky's Ian King Live and the BBC's Daily Politics show with Andrew Neil, besides plenty of radio and press appearances. The striking design of the paper was deliberately bold and the front pages had the feel of great posters. There's really nothing quite like it in the UK market and it really stands out on the newsstand.

Another satisfying aspect of The New European is, although plenty of people disagree with what it stands for, hardly anyone has criticised it as a product. In fact quite the reverse - critics from media as varied as Mashable, Business Insider, The New York Times and The Guardian have showered it with praise. Mario Garcia, the world's leading newspaper designer, dedicated an entire blog post to it. If people knew the entire design was conceived in a single afternoon, and the masthead itself in less than 20 minutes, it could seriously undermine the business of every media design agency in the western hemisphere!

But aside from the quality of the paper itself, it's perhaps the miracle of distribution that was the deciding factor in The New European's success. No point having the greatest new newspaper in recent years if you can't get it to the shelves. That first week, Archant's circulation team managed to have copies on sale in more than 20,000 shops, supermarkets and garages. As I'm writing this, on the eve of Issue 12 (who'da thought it!) that figure is now more than 40,000 retailers in the UK plus outlets throughout the Republic of Ireland, France, Germany, Switzerland, Belgium and Luxembourg. For me, this was the most satisfying aspect of The New European story; the strategy of One Archant had created an environment in which this was achievable. Previously it would have been unthinkable, and actually laughable, to think we could have pulled this off.

That first week, we sold more than 40,000 copies. And although sales dipped in the dog days of August, in September we have seen three consecutive weeks of circulation rises. Every single issue has been profitable. That in itself is an almost absurd achievement. The quality of the paper seems to have got better and better. Contributors to date include Sir Richard Branson, who interrupted his birthday holiday in Necker to write a lead piece for us and then widely praised Archant for the way we'd seized the opportunity, Alastair Campbell, the leading philosopher AC Grayling, Dylan Jones, Hardeep Singh-Kholi, Parmy Olson, Patience Wheatcroft, Bonnie Greer, Nick Clegg, Chuka Umunna, Simon Barnes, Will Self, Howard Jacobson, to name just a few.

Paul Morley's three-week-long articles on David Bowie's European years made for some fabulously striking covers and Issue 11's five-page investigation into how mainstream press had covered the issue of migration before the Referendum won the paper a hugely positive response on social media, and quite a few hardcore Brexit haters as well.

One observation levelled at The New European, though, is it's a one-off, the product of a near-perfect alignment of events which opened up the space for such a new product. And so, the argument goes, while Archant deserves great credit for spotting and seizing the moment, it's not necessarily a repeatable trick. I disagree. I think pop-up publishing, as a model for launching new print products, is a sensible response to a world hungry for in-depth coverage on certain topics but for only a limited period of time. As a content proposition it's well-suited to our fast-moving world. As a business model it's a low-cost, low-risk model which allows for experimentation and dramatically caps the exposure for the business should it turn out we'd got the idea hopelessly wrong. One thing is certain. We were not hopelessly wrong with The New European.

I believe The New European will continue to evolve in shape and form. We will need to think hard about what is the right digital presence for the brand since there is clearly an affection and demand for it. But we should also think beyond that - events, magazines, merchandising. We now print on a rolling four-week basis, but should demand for the newspaper fall away there's no reason why the brand won't carry through to another platform.

Ultimately, that's the beauty of pop-up publishing. You never quite know where you're going to pop-up next. For instance, we've already designed and sold hundreds of mugs and t-shirts bearing the image of that cartoon dog from the very first issue, which has appeared each week in the Kerber and Black cartoon. We've even given him a name. Rexit. Turns out he's not so dopey after all.

## Note on the contributor

Jeff Henry is CEO of Archant, publisher of the New European. Jeff joined Archant as chief executive in September 2014. He has a long and successful background in the media business. He has held senior management positions at a number of companies including Scottish TV, NYNEX, Hallmark and ITV. He was most recently CEO of Filmflex Movies, a joint venture between Sony Pictures Television and the Walt Disney Company, which he developed into one of the largest white label, video on demand (VOD) businesses in Europe. He steered its successful development over three years and oversaw its sale to Vubiquity in May 2014.

CPSIA information can be obtained
at www.ICGtesting.com
Printed in the USA
LVOW13s1731090817

544393LV00005B/181/P

9 781845 496968